TRANSLATING
THE WORD
OF GOD

James T. Jensen

TRANSLATING THE WORD OF GOD

with Scripture and Topical Indexes

JOHN BEEKMAN and JOHN CALLOW

ZONDERVAN PUBLISHING HOUSE OF THE ZONDERVAN CORPORATION GRAND RAPIDS, MICHIGAN 49506

TRANSLATING THE WORD OF GOD
Copyright © 1974 by The Zondervan Corporation

Sixth printing   1980

Library of Congress Catalog Card Number 74-4950
ISBN 0-310-20771-1

Printed in the United States of America

To

TRANSLATORS OF THE WORD OF GOD

CONTENTS

FOREWORD

Translating the Word of God is a book for Christians with a vision — who believe that the Bible is indeed God's word to man, and that every man ought to have the Bible in the language "which speaks to his heart." Christians can therefore be happy for the publication of a book whose primary aim is to help those who are translating the Bible into the languages of hundreds of tribes and peoples around the world whose language, in many cases, had never before even existed in written form.

At the same time, this book of translation principles is not merely a technical handbook for professional translators. It is that, and it will surely help many a translator find his way through problems which would otherwise be time-consuming and frustrating. But it will also provide some fascinating insights into some of these problems for the multitude of Christians who support and pray for these translators. It will show them what is involved in putting the Scriptures into these languages which are so remote in style and structure from English.

Moreover, this book is relevant for the student of the Bible in English as well, and for the student of the original languages of the Bible — Greek and Hebrew. If there is essentially only one form of the original Biblical text (even allowing for the textual variants which are found in the ancient manuscripts) how can there be so many different English translations as are actually found in print? Should the New Testament in English simply render the original language word for word, or should it read as if the New Testament writers had written in English today? Then there are important questions of Biblical meaning which most people overlook; for example, what does "of" mean?

Many of the metaphors and other figures of speech which occur in the original languages of the Bible are carried directly over into English, and we have come to accept them even when they are not a part of our culture. The reader of the present book may find himself better understanding some of these figures of speech which he has taken for granted. He will also be fascinated by the adaptations and changes which must be made in order to make them comprehensible in many tribal languages.

All in all, this book will be of profit for anyone who seriously wants to know what problems are encountered in translating the Bible from the original languages into another language, what the principles are for resolving these problems, and what are some of the rewards which accompany this task. Whether they be translators, teachers, students, or interested lay people, all will want to keep this book handy for use in their own study of the Scriptures.

Few people have had the practical experience in solving New Testament translation problems (as they relate to tribal languages) that John Beekman has. With linguist John Callow as collaborator, he provides a book that is both practical and authoritative.

J. Harold Greenlee

PREFACE

The chapters of this book represent the contents of lectures given by John Beekman in twelve different countries. The subjects treated arise from his translation experience among the Chol Indians of Chiapas, Mexico, and from his experience as a consultant reviewing the translation work of others. As a translator he personally faced the problems which are typical in rendering the message of Scripture into a minority language. As a consultant, he has been exposed to a wide range of language situations presenting him with various exegetical and translation problems.

John Callow has worked in Ghana, West Africa for the past eleven years where he has initiated translation work in the Kasem language and has served as a linguistic and translation consultant. He received his Ph.D. in linguistics from London University in 1962. He has been primarily responsible for recasting the original lecture notes in their present form. The authors are grateful for the theological training without which any translator is at a serious disadvantage, and to which they owe their interest in exegetical matters. John Beekman is an alumnus of Moody Bible Institute, Chicago; John Callow studied at London Bible College, England.

The authors want to express their sincere gratitude to Mrs. Elaine Beekman who prepared the indexes; to Miss Edna Jane Travis for her work on the bibliography; to Miss Eleanor McAlpine for typing the manuscript; and to Dr. Margaret Wasson (Ph.D. in Education) and Miss Betty Huizenga (A.B. in English, M.A. in Latin) who checked punctuation and stylistic features of the book. Translators, translation consultants, professors, Greek scholars, and friends, too many to list, who commented on the first draft of this book, have made a positive contribution to its final form. Special mention is due, however, to Richard Blight and Don Stewart for their detailed suggestions and to Bruce Moore (M.A. in Linguistics) who, during the time that John Beekman was recuperating from open-heart surgery, evaluated and incorporated revisions arising from the many suggestions received. Many improvements in the content and presentation of this book are due to all those who helped with their observations and suggested changes.

JOHN BEEKMAN AND JOHN CALLOW

Dallas 1974

INTRODUCTION

Translating the Word of God reflects the experience accumulated over a period of twenty years by the authors as they have translated and checked New Testaments for minority groups in different parts of the world. It has been written out of the conviction that an accurate and intelligible version of the Scriptures is essential both to the evangelization of the lost, and to the building up of strong communities of believers.

This conviction is borne out by the experience, not of the authors alone, but of many translators throughout the world. In scores of languages, many of the first converts made their decision to follow Christ as they worked at the translation desk. Many of these same converts were instrumental in gaining additional believers and in establishing a local church. The Word of God in the languages of the people has proved to be an effective tool for evangelism, and an indispensable factor in the teaching and encouraging of the young Christian community. The purpose of this book, then, is to provide needed help for the Bible translator, and thus to contribute to the extension of Christ's Church worldwide.

The problems most commonly faced by translators have been extensively studied prior to, and during, the writing of this book. Often a translator spends many hours either in trying to ascertain the exact meaning of the original or in trying to express that meaning in a language which is very different from his own and from those in which the Scriptures were originally written. But many other translators have grappled with these problems before him, and have often found solutions. Over recent years consultation work by a corps of consultants in Wycliffe Bible Translators has made available a listing of such problems and of suggested solutions, and this has been frequently consulted in preparing these pages. Since languages differ so widely, a verse-by-verse approach to specific difficulties has not been attempted; rather, similar problems have been grouped together, and guidelines and principles outlined which should enable the translator to tackle his particular difficulty more quickly and directly, and with understanding.

The translator is not alone in his need to understand the original, however, and to express it accurately and intelligibly. Many of the issues raised and problems studied in these pages will be found to be relevant also to pastors, Bible teachers, Bible students, and indeed to all whose aim is that of "rightly dividing the word of truth" (2 Tim. 2:15). Such persons are concerned to discover the exact meaning of the original text, and to do this they must ask, and answer, the same questions the translator frequently faces. What does this word mean in this particular context? What is the significance of this figure of speech? Is this a real question, or one used for rhetorical effect? The pastor who wants to recast the Biblical message in lively contemporary terms, while remaining true to the original, will find useful guidelines in the chapters on lexical equivalence. Perhaps the most significant chapters for Bible students are those on propositions; those who are prepared for the mental application involved in its mastery should find that it provides an unusually precise approach to exegesis, enabling the student to tackle methodically the untangling of some of the more difficult passages of the New Testament.

Because of the variety of modern translations now available in English, there is widespread interest these days in the whole question of translation. The principles outlined in this book are, of course, applicable to English as to any other language, and as such should be of interest to the evangelical community in general. It should be understood, however, that the background of the authors and their colleagues is that of translating the Word of God into minority languages and that no attempt is made in these pages to go beyond the problems arising in such translations. Translations into major languages such as English do in fact raise a number of additional issues. In such languages there is a written literature already in existence; there is a highly literate community which is organized into complex social subgroups often speaking subvarieties of the same language. The prior existence of ecclesiastical terminology adds further complications. Few or none of these factors are relevant in translating into minority languages; they therefore fall outside the scope of this book. However, there are many issues common to all translations. The study of the issues raised in these pages should make clear to the interested reader why several translations are possible from one original, and should also provide him with criteria for systematically assessing the differences between them.

The fundamental principles of translation are presented in the first three chapters. The rest of the book draws upon these principles in discussing the problems arising from the vocabulary, from certain grammatical constructions, and from the goal of stating the meaning of the original text in a straightforward and direct form. This goal is discussed in the last four chapters, which present an approach to exegesis which requires answers to questions often overlooked in commentaries. The contents of these pages have answered questions raised by advanced translators and have given guidance to others as they embarked on the great task of giving God's Word to a people who have never before had it in their own language. It is hoped that in its present form it will continue to provide guidance to translators and a fuller understanding by others of the principles involved in a faithful translation.

This volume does not deal with all the issues that arise in connection with translation. A companion volume takes up the further question of discourse structure and translation. In addition, a volume of drill material based on the contents of each chapter has been prepared.

A pedagogical style of presentation has been deliberately adopted. Repetition is regularly used; frequent use is made of examples; an attempt is made to keep technical terms to a minimum. This has been done so that the book can be used by any translator, even though his exposure to linguistic and translation theory has been minimal. Undoubtedly, some of the theory presented is complex, and no attempt is made to oversimplify it. But the authors have sought to avoid a technical, academic style of presentation which would undoubtedly deter many translators who might otherwise have been helped by reading it.

The orientation of this book toward the needs of translators for minority languages that have no portion of the Scripture accounts for the fact that most of the illustrations are taken from the New Testament. This must not be taken as in any sense minimizing the importance of the Old Testament. It simply reflects the present situation; most minority languages have very little, if any, of the Old Testament available to them as yet. It follows that the experience of the authors and the needs of their fellow-translators are found predominantly in the area of the New Testament. The same principles of translation will, however, be found to apply to both Testaments.

Quotations throughout the book are normally taken from the King James Version, as being still the most widely known English translation. Where it seemed advisable, however, the authors have not hesitated to quote from other versions, or to provide their own.

TRANSLATING
THE WORD
OF GOD

CHAPTER 1

Literal and Idiomatic Translations

Two Approaches to Translation

All messages between people, regardless of the means used to communicate them, are based upon some system of signs or symbols. While speech is the primary system of symbolizing ideas and thought, a message may be communicated not only orally but also in writing, or by signs, or by codes. To repeat a message using a different system of symbolization within the same language does not constitute translation. If, for example, the message is changed from shorthand to longhand, we call this transcription. If the message is changed from written to oral form, we call this reading.

When, however, a message in one language is communicated in a different language, then translation is involved. It is not necessary that the means used to communicate the original message be the same as that in the translation. Thus, an oral message may be translated into another language using semaphore or morse code, or a written message may be translated orally. The means used to symbolize the message is not an essential component of translation. For example, the words that Jesus spoke in Aramaic were translated by the gospel authors into Greek, and at the same time the form was changed from speech to writing. In other words, the oral presentation of the message was committed to a written form along with the translation process.

It can be seen from the above that the translation process involves (1) at least two languages and (2) a message. These two essential components of a translation may be called, respectively, (1) *form* and

19

(2) *meaning*. The form of an apple may be described in terms of its color, shape, constituent parts, etc. A language may also be described in terms of its sounds (the phonological system), its grammar, and its words (the lexical system). These formal linguistic elements of a language are what is meant by *form*. The *meaning* is the message which is communicated by these features of *form*.

One of these two components of translation, that of *form*, is basic to two different approaches to translation. All translators are agreed that their task is to communicate the meaning of the original.[1] There is no discussion on this point. There is discussion, however, concerning the linguistic form to be used. Some believe that the meaning of the original is best communicated by translating into a linguistic form which closely parallels that of the original language. Others believe that by translating into the natural form of the receptor language,[2] whether this parallels the form of the original or not, the meaning of the original is best communicated.

The choice which the translator makes between these two approaches will determine whether his translation will be classed as literal[3] or idiomatic. These two terms classify a translation in regard to its linguistic

[1] Throughout this book the term "original" will be used to refer to the text of Scripture in the original languages of Hebrew and Greek.

[2] Since the expression "receptor language" i.e., the language into which a translation is made, is used so frequently in this book, it will be abbreviated to "RL" for convenience.

[3] The terms "literal" and "idiomatic" are those proposed by Beekman in his article "Idiomatic Versus Literal Translations" (1965e) and reprinted in an abbreviated form in *The Bible Translator* (1966, pp. 178-89) under the title " 'Literalism' a Hindrance to Understanding." In *Toward a Science of Translating* (p. 159) Nida uses the expressions "formal equivalence" and "dynamic equivalence" in broadly comparable senses. In a later work, *The Theory and Practice of Translation*, Nida and Taber use "formal correspondence" rather than "formal equivalence" as they reserve "equivalence" for "a very close similarity in meaning, as opposed to similarity in form" (p. 202). It should be noted, though, that they define "dynamic equivalence" in terms of the response of the receptor. Their own words (p. 202) are: "quality of a translation in which the message of the original text has been so transported into the receptor language that the RESPONSE of the RECEPTOR is essentially that of the original receptors."

It should be noted that the use of "literal" in this chapter refers to the transference of linguistic form from one language to another in the context of the translation process, and is not to be confused with its use in the context of interpretation. For its use in this latter context, see, for instance, the discussion in Ramm *Protestant Biblical Interpretation* (pp. 89-96) where he says, "The literal meaning of the word is the *basic, customary, social designation of that word*" (p. 90) and hence "to interpret literally (in this sense) is nothing more or less than interpreting words and sentences in their *normal, usual, customary, proper designation*" (p. 91).

A literal interpretation of Scripture, as defined above, contrasts with a typological or allegorical interpretation of Scripture. In this chapter, however, the word "literal" is used in contrast with the term "idiomatic" to distinguish one type of translation approach from another. It is worth noting that an idiomatic translation is conducive to the literal method of interpreting the meaning of Scripture; a literal translation, on the other hand, is not, and may even lead to an allegorical method of interpretation.

form; it does not classify a translation on the basis of the meaning that it communicates which, of course, in a faithful translation should always represent the literal meaning of the original text. If its form corresponds more to the form of the original text, it is classed as *literal*; if its form corresponds more to the form of the receptor language (RL) then it is classed as *idiomatic*. Even though there are few, if any, translations that are completely literal or completely idiomatic, each has been produced with one or the other approach in mind.

FOUR TYPES OF TRANSLATIONS

Although there are these two basic approaches to translation, they give rise to four main types of translations: (1) highly literal, (2) modified literal, (3) idiomatic, (4) unduly free. These four[4] represent a continuum from one extreme to another. Chart 1 shows that the acceptable types of translation intended for general use lie between two extremes.

CHART 1

unacceptable types			
	acceptable types		
highly literal	modified literal	idiomatic	unduly free

The highly literal translation

The highly literal translation reproduces the linguistic features of the original language with high consistency. The result is a translation which does not adequately communicate the message to a reader who does not know the original language or who does not have access to commentaries or other reference works to explain it to him.

One type of highly literal translation is an interlinear translation. This is presumably the closest that one can stay to the linguistic form of the original and still call it a translation. The obligatory grammatical rules of the RL are set aside and the translation follows the order of the original word for word. This type of translation serves best to show the

[4] It will be noted that the word "paraphrase" is not used to designate any of the types of translation. When used to characterize a translation, it is generally with a pejorative sense meaning that an attempt has been made to render the text in a form that is clearer to us than it was to the original readers with the result that extraneous information and unnecessary interpretations are found. Following this sense of the word, Tancock (*Aspects of Translation*, 1958, p. 29) says that a translation which deviates from the meaning is not a translation but a paraphrase.

The usage of the word "paraphrase" in linguistic circles is not applied to translation but rather to two different statements in a single language which have the same meaning. One statement is called the paraphrase of the other. The counterpart of paraphrase within a language is translation between languages. That is, when we find two different statements with the same meaning and each is in a different language, one statement is a translation of the other.

structure of the original but has the lowest communication value to those readers who do not know the original language. It is unacceptable as a translation for general use.

Other highly literal translations adapt to the obligatory grammatical features of the RL, features which may include such things as word order, tense markers, and number markers. For instance, a translation into English from Hebrew changes the common Hebrew order of verb-subject-object to the obligatory English order of subject-verb-object. However, whenever there is a choice of grammatical features in the RL, then, in a highly literal translation, the RL form is chosen which matches the form of the original even though it may sound awkward or occur infrequently. Tojolabal of Mexico has both active and passive verbs. However, the passive is the more common, with the active used only rarely. A translator who observes in Tojolabal that both the active and passive are possible, without also noticing that the active is very rare, will translate all active forms of the original by active forms of the RL. This will result in a highly literal and unnatural translation.

Furthermore, in highly literal translations, not only are many grammatical features transferred literally, but there is also an attempt to match a single word in the original with a single word in the RL, and to use the RL word in every context in which the original word is used. The result of this procedure is that words which never go together in the RL are often put together giving rise to either nonsense or wrong sense. For instance, one translator, taking a highly literal approach, translated Mark 3:26 as follows: "If Satan has risen (in the morning from sleep) and is divided (like an orange is cut in half), he is not able to endure, but is coming to an end." The material in parentheses shows the sense in which the preceding word is normally used in that language.

Ambiguity is also a frequent result of a highly literal translation. Judges 3:6 reads in the RSV, "and they took their daughters to themselves for wives, and their own daughters they gave to their sons; and they served their gods." A native English speaker has to think about this verse very carefully before he can disentangle all the ambiguous "they's" and "their's" — and even then he might arrive at the wrong conclusion.

A particularly difficult area for translators is that of idioms and figures of speech. In a number of languages of northern Ghana, an expression is commonly used which, literally translated, is "he ate a woman." In English this can only mean that he was a cannibal; but in fact, it means "he got married." The literal translation of this idiom gives a totally false impression of the character and practices of northern Ghanaians. In one language of West Africa, a highly literal translation was made of a figure of speech in Mark 10:38, in which Jesus asks James and John, "Are you able to drink the cup that I drink?" When a speaker of this language was asked whether this expression was ever used by his people, he replied, "Yes, it is. It is what a drunkard would say to challenge his fellows as to whether they could drink as much drink, or as strong a drink, as he himself could." To the readers of this translation, then,

Jesus was challenging James and John to a drinking bout. In highly literal translations, where idioms and figures of speech are preserved intact, the resultant meaning is often as misleading as the examples above.

The unduly free translation

The other unacceptable type is the unduly free translation. Translations may vary widely in style and still be accurate in content. Thus, when a translation is classified as too free, this is not a judgment concerning its style but rather concerning the information it communicates.

In this kind of translation there is no intention to reproduce the linguistic form of the language from which the translation is made. The purpose is to make the message as relevant and clear as possible. There are, therefore, no distortions of the message arising from literalisms, but there are, nevertheless, distortions of content, with the translation clearly saying what the original neither says nor implies. Thus, although the highly literal and the unduly free translations are at opposite extremes, they share the same unacceptable characteristic of failing to communicate what the original communicated.

An unduly free translation may substitute historical facts. Whether these involve the names of people, places, things, or customs, undue liberty is taken with the historical context. Furthermore, such a translation may say more than was communicated to the readers of the original text, and, as a result, contain extraneous information. While it is granted that interpretation of the text is an inevitable part of the process of translation, it cannot be overemphasized that every interpretation should be based upon sound exegetical conclusions which have adequate support from the context. Otherwise, the translator will introduce questionable information into the translation. When the above faults are present, the translation will misrepresent the original message and include extraneous, unnecessary information which the author did not intend in his writings.

The modified literal translation

It frequently happens that the translator who takes a highly literal approach to his task hears sermons or explanations of his translation which misrepresent the sense of the original text. As he comes to appreciate the need to correct his translation at those points where it communicates error, he is prepared to allow for more departures from the form of the original than just those necessitated by the obligatory categories of the RL. Whenever he becomes aware that the meaning diverges from the original, then he makes some lexical or grammatical adjustment to correct the error. These further departures from the form of the original result in a *modified literal* translation.

This type of translation represents a considerable improvement over the highly literal translation. Even so, the same grammatical forms as those that are found in the original are generally used, many occurrences of a given word are translated consistently without adequate regard to the context, many word combinations found in the original are awkwardly retained in the RL, and the original message is only partially communicated especially when relevant implicit information is lost. The resultant translation contains unnecessary ambiguities and obscurities and will be unnatural in style and difficult to comprehend. In spite of these disadvantages, the modified literal translation is acceptable in some situations. For a group of believers who have access to reference works, and whose motivation to read and study is high, a modified literal translation is usable. However, for groups just emerging from illiteracy, the disadvantages listed above cannot be overlooked; for these groups, an *idiomatic* translation is much to be preferred.

The idiomatic translation

In an idiomatic translation, the translator seeks to convey to the RL readers the meaning of the original by using the natural grammatical and lexical forms of the RL. His focus is on the meaning, and he is aware that the grammatical constructions and lexical choices and combinations used in the original are no more suitable for the communication of that message in the RL than are, say, the orthographic symbols of the original. The RL message must be conveyed using the linguistic form of the RL.

Jerome, the translator of the Latin version known as the Vulgate, wrote, "I could translate only what I had understood before" (cited in Schwarz, 1955, p. 32). He was aware that he had to grasp the meaning to translate meaningfully. Luther, too, was conscious of this. Schwarz (*ibid.*, pp. 205, 206) summarizes Luther's views as follows: "Luther was aware that a word-for-word translation could not reproduce the literary form and atmosphere of the original. Hebrew, Greek, Latin, and German all had peculiarities which obliged the translator to refashion many of the idioms and even rhetorical devices." He further (p. 207) quotes Luther as saying, "If the angel had spoken to Mary in German, he would have used the appropriate form of address; this, and no other word, is the best translation whatever the phrase in the original may be."

Hollander, in the work *On Translation* (1959, p. 207), says: ". . . statements of all kinds have meaning. To translate a sentence from one language to another is somehow to discover its meaning and then to construct a sentence in the new or target language that possesses the same meaning." In a similar vein, Oettinger states (1959, p. 248): "Corresponding patterns, therefore must be defined as conveyors of equivalent meanings since, whatever meaning is or means, it is generally agreed that it must be preserved in translation."

A comparison can be made between the linguistic form of a language, as a means of carrying the meaning, and a "conveyor" or vehicle. Suppose a road is used to represent one language and a canal a different one. A car is needed to convey passengers by road; to convey the same passengers by water a different vehicle is needed, namely, a boat of some sort. The same is true with conveying meaning. One language will use a certain form to carry the meaning; a different language will use a different form, even though it is the same meaning that is being transmitted. Further, just as you would not attempt to transfer parts of the car to the boat when changing vehicles, so you should not attempt to transfer the grammatical and lexical forms of the original to the RL when translating. The forms are simply a "vehicle" with which to get the message across to the recipients. If the correct meaning is not conveyed to the hearers, it may well be that the translator is not sufficiently familiar with the linguistic form of the RL, or he has an erroneous concept of what translation is. It is like trying to run a boat as if it were a car.

The foregoing quotations and examples all refer to the primary importance of preserving the meaning in the translation process. Form is seen to be important only as it serves to convey the correct meaning. Thus, the approach to translation which is to be preferred is the one which most accurately and naturally transfers the meaning from the original to the RL. The idiomatic approach to translation does this best. It implies that a particular word in the original text may be translated in various ways in the RL version so as to give the most accurate sense and the most natural word combination in each context. The natural order of words, phrases, and clauses is used to convey clearly the meaning of the original text. It is this approach to translation that reduces ambiguity and obscurity to a minimum, that makes use of the discourse and stylistic features of the RL in a natural way, and that results in a translation that is clear and understandable so that even someone who has had little or no contact with Christianity is able to understand the essentials of the message. The authors of this book advocate the idiomatic approach for translations which are intended for general use.

TYPES OF LINGUISTIC FORM OFTEN TRANSFERRED LITERALLY

It has been emphasized in the previous section that one of the characteristic features of a literal translation is that it transfers the linguistic form of the original to the RL, whether or not this is the natural and most clearly understood form. Even translators who want to be idiomatic in their approach to translation may overlook a natural and meaningful form in the RL and unintentionally retain the form of the original. It is useful, therefore, for the translator to be fully aware of some of the linguistic features which are often rendered literally. The following examples are selected to show how wide a range of grammatical and lexical features can be transferred literally and also to show some of the consequences of doing so.

Grammatical features

All languages have *parts of speech*. An attempt may be made to match corresponding parts of speech between languages. Thus, nouns are translated by nouns, verbs by verbs, pronouns by pronouns, prepositions by prepositions, etc. But while it is true that all languages have parts of speech, it by no means follows that they are always used in parallel ways in different languages. For instance, Koiné Greek (in common with other Indo-European languages) could readily nominalize verbs to give corresponding nouns, such as *salvation, forgiveness, faith,* and *justification.* These nouns could then be combined with verbs in ways which cannot be reproduced naturally in many other languages. The following is a partial list of verbs with which *salvation* is associated in the Greek.

"This day *is* salvation *come*" (Luke 19:9)

"*work out* your own salvation" (Phil. 2:12)

"that they also *may obtain* . . . salvation" (2 Tim. 2:10; cf. 1 Thess. 5:9)

"if we *neglect* so great salvation" (Heb. 2:3)

"things that *accompany* salvation" (Heb. 6:9)

Some languages do not have an abstract noun equivalent to *salvation* but only a verb equivalent to *to save.* Even if there is an abstract noun for *salvation* in the RL, it cannot be assumed that it can be used in all of the above contexts. It is necessary to see how it is used in the RL and what combinations it enters into, otherwise a literal translation of these expressions will simply baffle the reader or make him feel that it is a foreign book and therefore of no relevance to him.

1 John 4:8 ends with "God is love." The word *love* is an abstract noun like *salvation.* In many languages abstract nouns representing activities can be expressed only by means of verbs. The natural way of expressing the truth of this part of the verse is to say, "God loves."

Not only must the translator be aware of the danger of "matching" abstract nouns between the original and the RL, but he must also be aware of the danger of "coining" new abstract nouns in the RL. They may not be accepted, or they may already mean something else. For example, in Mazahua (Mexico) abstract nouns can be formed by the addition of the prefix *t'-.* Thus, there is *eñe,* "to play" and *t'eñe,* "game, plaything"; *oxii,* "to sleep, to stay overnight" and *t'oxii,* "nest." There is also the verb *ejme,* "to believe," and the translator may be tempted to nominalize it to get "faith," but, in fact, *t'ejme* already exists in Mazahua and refers to a well-known corn drink.

The attempt to match parts of speech has equally undesirable results no matter what two languages are involved. Tancock in an article, "Some Problems of Style in Translation from French" (p. 32), points out: "Often a sentence in French is virtually untranslatable if you insist upon rendering the verb by an English verb, an adjective by an adjective, and so on, but if you remodel the sentence so that the function of the verb is performed by, say, an adverb, the whole thing becomes natural and the exact sense of the original is conveyed without any violence having been done."

Therefore, the translator needs to guard against this tendency to match parts of speech. A translator has even been known to borrow the word for *and* from the national language to translate *and* every place it occurred in the original. The translator did this because there was no word for *and* in the RL. What the translator did not realize was that simple juxtaposition of clauses without any connecting word was the natural way in the RL to say what was said in the original with the connective *and*.

Just as parts of speech are often transferred literally, so are other grammatical features of the original. A *passive* is translated with a passive, an *active* with an active, *direct speech* with direct speech, a *plural* with a plural, etc., even when this is unnatural in the RL or results in wrong sense. When faced with a choice of categories in the RL, say active and passive, the literal approach to translation leads the translator to choose the form which corresponds to that used in the original, whereas the use of that category in the RL may be quite different from its use in the original.

In some languages, direct quotations are the only form used in quoting; in others, such as Navajo (U.S.A.) and Sierra Chontal (Mexico), both direct and indirect quotations are used, but the former occurs much more commonly than the latter. Hence, statements made in the form of indirect address are usually rendered as direct quotations. Moreover, in such languages, many words which express inner thoughts or attitudes as well as those which imply speech, such as *confess, rebuke,* and *exhort* have to be translated in the form of direct address, e.g., *confess* may be rendered "said, I did wrong."

All languages arrange their words in *order* — some rigidly, others much more freely. What is often not realized is that word order in itself can convey meaning. This is obvious for English from the two examples, "John hit Bill" and "Bill hit John." A translation, however, which preserves the order of the elements as they occur in the original, whether of words, clauses, or sentences, will often convey wrong meaning. For example, since many languages order the statement of events to match the temporal or experiential order of those events, a literal transfer of the linguistic order may give a false impression as to the order in which the events took place or were experienced. Luke 10:34 says that the good Samaritan "bound up his wounds, pouring in oil and wine." When translated in this order, this could mean in many languages that the Samaritan, having carefully bandaged the wounds, then poured oil and wine onto the bandages. A similar example is found in Mark 1:40, which says, "And there came a leper to him, beseeching him, and kneeling down to him . . . ." Translated literally this would mean that the leper besought Jesus and then knelt down; so the order has to be reversed in the RL to avoid this misunderstanding.

A different type of problem may be illustrated from Sierra Zapotec (Mexico). In this language a vocative form of address always *precedes* the statement. In Matthew 6:30, however, Jesus *concludes* a rebuke with the vocative, "O ye of little faith." The next sentence starts with, "Therefore take no thought. . . ." Consequently, the translation helper attached the vocative to that sentence, and interpreted the sequence as meaning, "You don't have much faith, but don't worry about that." The solution was to place the information in the vocative early in verse 30.

A literal approach to translation often preserves in the RL the same *length* of the sentence as is used in the original. Sentence length in the original, of course, varies considerably from the occasional very brief sentence, such as John 11:35, "Jesus wept" (three words in Greek: *edakrusen ho Iēsous*), to sentences that cover a number of verses, as in Paul's letters. 2 Thessalonians 1:3-10 is an extreme example of this latter case. A literal approach to translation, such as that represented by the ASV, preserves the single sentences. Few languages customarily use such long sentences. The RSV breaks it up into four sentences, the NASV into five, but these are still long and complicated. The TEV has nine sentences. In Chuj of Guatemala, it was necessary to render it with twenty-two sentences.

There are many other similar instances of long sentences in Greek which extend through several verses. For example, John 4:1-3 is a single sentence in the Greek, as also in the KJV and the RSV; in the latter version it reads, "Now when the Lord knew that the Pharisees had heard that Jesus was making and baptizing more disciples than John (although Jesus himself did not baptize, but only his disciples), he left Judea and departed again to Galilee." It is an involved sentence with a parenthesis. In Agta (Philippines) and Popoloca (Mexico), it was necessary both to break it up into smaller units and to reorder the units. Hence, the opening statement, "When therefore the Lord knew . . . ." was changed to "When therefore the Lord knew what the Pharisees had heard" and was placed at the beginning of v. 3, so that v. 1 began "The Pharisees had heard . . . ," and the parenthesis of v. 2 was handled as a separate sentence. With these changes in order, the verses would then be numbered as 1-3 rather than 1, 2, 3.

Lexical features

The examples discussed above all have to do with the literal transfer of *grammatical* features of the original. It is even more common in either highly literal or modified literal translations to transfer the *lexical* features of the original.

Perhaps the most obvious case of literal lexical transfer is *the matching of word to word*. A single lexical item in the original, no matter how semantically complex, is matched, if at all possible, by a single lexical item in the RL. There are many languages, however, which have no single word for *to justify, to sanctify, to discipline*, etc., but handle these concepts by means of an equivalent clause. Because of this tendency to match words, a translator can easily overlook an equivalent expression using several words and conclude that there is no appropriate word in the RL and then resort to an unknown loan-word from the national language. On the other hand, translators have been observed to use one RL word to cover a series of related but different concepts in the original because they happened to have no one-word equivalents in the RL. One translator translated *to perish, to be condemned,* and *to be judged* by "to be lost," since judicial expressions, such as "to condemn" and "to judge" required several words. Another rendered *apostle* with the RL equivalent of "servant," *peace* with "happiness," and *faithful* with "good" even though, in each case, there was a more exact equivalent which he should have used. In some instances this more exact equivalent was an idiomatic expression, in others, a phrase involving several words.

Closely related to the tendency to match words between the original and the RL is the tendency to use the same word in the RL in every context in which a word occurs in the original, that is, to maintain *concordance* between the original and the RL. But even between related languages, like Spanish and Portuguese, this is not completely possible, still less so between languages that are quite unrelated.

The following comparison between Vagla (Ghana) and English will serve to illustrate this point. In all of the following expressions the Vagla verb *diy,* "to eat" is used, but English requires a different word or expression each time.

Vagla:	*English:*
he ate his self	he enjoyed himself
he ate his case	he judged his case
he ate shame	he was ashamed
he ate chieftainship	he became the chief
he ate two goals	he scored two goals
he ate him a friend	he chose him as a friend
he ate him an argument	he argued with him
it is eating	it is sharp
you should eat	it's your turn

The translator, therefore, has to be sensitive to the meaning a particular word has in any given context. Failure to do so often results in nonsense. 1 John 3:14 says, "We know we have passed from death unto life" — but in one language the word used for *passed* meant "passed along a trail" hence giving the impression that death and life were physical places. In Romans 1:15 Paul announced, "I am ready to preach the gospel to you," but the word used by one translator for *ready* referred only to physical readiness. The readers concluded that Paul had packed his bag and was about to start on his journey to Rome.

Idioms and figures of speech present special difficulties to the translator, for they are almost always peculiar to the language using them and can seldom be transferred directly into another. If they are, they are usually misunderstood. In Kasem, a Ghanaian language, the literal translation of one idiom would be "his abdomen is hard" which sounds in English like a medical condition of some sort. However, it means "he is brave." Again "he is a person" sounds trivial in English; how could a person be other than a person? But it actually means "he is a decent person." "He follows paths" sounds as if it were stating the obvious way to go about the countryside; in fact it means "he does what is right."

Literal translations of idioms and figures of speech hardly ever mean the same in another language.

Idioms and figures of speech are used in all languages, but it is very rarely found that the idioms and figures of the original match those of the RL. Hence, if they are transferred literally from the original to the RL, they will almost certainly be misunderstood. This is because the figurative words of the original are understood by the readers of the RL in a nonfigurative way, or because the images employed in the figure in the original (e.g., sheep, vines, armor) are unknown, or because the figure or idiom may already have a meaning in the RL that is different from that of the original. Or possibly, figurative language in the RL is confined to certain discourse types, such as speeches, or riddles, or proverbs, but not to the discourse type being translated.

Examples of idioms such as "taste death" (John 8:52), or "bringest . . . strange things to our ears" (Acts 17:20), or "whose mouth is full of cursing and bitterness" (Rom. 3:14) are almost certainly going to need adjusting if the sense is to be preserved. Thus, the literal transfer of lexical units is no more successful than the literal transfer of grammatical features. Both can lead to wrong meaning, and even if they do not, they often obscure the message of the original or make it seem ridiculous and obviously foreign.

Other features

All languages use constructions which communicate some of the *information in an implicit form*. For instance, in Acts 7:9, Stephen says that the patriarchs "sold Joseph into Egypt." Many languages have to fill this out to "sold Joseph to people who took him to Egypt." Or, in Acts again (24:24), Luke records that Felix "sent for Paul and heard him." But he does not mention that Paul actually *came* when Felix sent for him. A further example is found in Luke 1:9-11. We are told that Zechariah's "lot was to burn incense when he went into the temple of the Lord" (v. 9) and that "there appeared unto him an angel of the Lord standing on the right side of the altar of incense" (v. 11), but it is nowhere stated explicitly that Zechariah actually entered the temple. Some languages require this to be stated; otherwise the readers are left puzzled as to the sequence of events.

1 Timothy 5:3 says, "Honour widows that are widows indeed." The significance of the expression "widows indeed" (RSV, "real widows"), is not made clear until v. 5, where Paul says, "Now she that is a widow indeed, and desolate . . . ." Thus he makes it clear that a genuine widow in this context is a woman who is both a widow and who is also all alone in the world with no one to care for her (cf. v. 4). In Chinantec, a Mexican language, this information from v. 5 had to be transferred to v. 3; otherwise it was understood to mean any woman who has lost her husband by death. The full meaning of "widows indeed" is implicit in v. 3 but explicit in v. 5, and so, in some languages such as Chinantec, it is necessary to make the implicit information explicit at some earlier

point in the discourse to avoid communicating error (cf. Phillips' translation of v. 3: "You should treat with great consideration widows who are really alone in the world").

The question of when such implicit information may legitimately be made explicit is discussed in a later chapter. All that needs to be emphasized at this point is that if such implicit information is left implicit in the RL, it can often lead to wrong meaning or leave the translation obscure or meaningless.

Information may also be given in a general form. But *general terms or statements* are not used in the same ways in different languages — the information they convey can differ considerably. In Acts 16:3 it says that Paul circumcised Timothy "because of the Jews." To the Sierra Otomi, this meant that the Jews had demanded that Paul do this and he had done so because he was afraid of their threats to his life. The expression was too general and was rendered more explicitly as "in order that the hearts of the Jews would not be disturbed." At the end of Acts 3:10 it says that the people were astonished "at that which had happened to him." This expression is used in Mazahua, a Mexican language, but it is used only to refer to something *bad* that has happened.

The general expression may be a single word. For example, in Mark 12:11, Jesus quotes from the Old Testament, "This was the Lord's doing." But to the Huave (Mexico) language helper, it was not at all clear what "this" referred to, so it had to be rendered more explicitly. Acts 14:23 reads as follows: "And when they had ordained them elders in every church, and had prayed with fasting, they commended them to the Lord, on whom they believed." The various "they's" were too far removed from the antecedents, Paul and Barnabas, for the Sierra Otomi of Mexico to know to whom they refer. So "Paul and Barnabas" was substituted for the first "they."

Closely related to general terms or statements are ambiguities. All commentators agree that there are *many ambiguities* of expression in the original. However, commentaries find different possible interpretations, not all of which are to be classed as true ambiguities. In the first chapter of Colossians, which consists of 28 verses, there are at least 71 differences of opinion among the 22 commentaries and reference works consulted. The literal approach to translation attempts to translate in such a form that the same number of possible interpretations will be open to the reader. In taking this approach, the translator not only introduces ambiguities which are not really ambiguities, but also runs the risk of introducing different ambiguities from those of the original text. For example, the text may mean either 1 or 2 but the attempt to retain the ambiguity may result in meaning either 2 or a new ambiguity, 3.

Moreover, new ambiguities are inevitably introduced by the grammar or the vocabulary of the RL. Therefore, as a result of a literal approach to translation, the number of ambiguities in the RL tends to be higher than that in the original.

What, then, does a translator seeking to make an idiomatic translation do with these ambiguities? Those ambiguities that arise as a result of the RL grammar and lexicon are detected by questioning the helpers and then removed where possible and natural. Ambiguities in the original, however, are studied in the light of the immediate and more remote context of the original. Often some grammatical or lexical feature or the thematic purpose of the paragraph or section will show that no real ambiguity exists. When, however, no such evidence is found, or when such evidence does not give a highly probable resolution, then the ambiguity is retained in the translation.

Sometimes, however, the structure of the RL is such that the ambiguity cannot be retained. In these instances, a judgment must be made concerning the relative importance of the ambiguity. Where the evidence is balanced, and the ambiguity is ranked low in importance, and a diglot version is planned, one may choose the view represented in that version. If, as will likely be the case, the version to be used in the diglot is also ambiguous, and the ambiguity is ranked low in importance, one may choose what is considered to be the most probable meaning intended in that context by the author. When the ambiguity is important, which usually means that it has theological overtones, then one interpretation can appear in the text, and the others in a footnote.

The above list of linguistic features of the original that are often transferred literally could easily be extended. In fact, it is safe to say that there is no aspect of the lexical and grammatical structure of the original which may not give rise to wrong, obscure, or zero meaning in some language if transferred literally.

Conclusion

Paul was extremely conscious of how important it was that his message was clearly understood, whether it was in written form or spoken form. In 2 Corinthians 1:13 (RSV) he says, "For we write you nothing but what you can read and understand" and in 1 Corinthians 14:8 (RSV) he says, "And if the bugle gives an indistinct sound, who will get ready for battle?" Who indeed? Who is going to pay any serious attention to a translation of the Word of God that is often unintelligible and sounds foreign in many respects? No, the goal should be a translation that is so rich in vocabulary, so idiomatic in phrase, so correct in construction, so smooth in flow of thought, so clear in meaning, and so elegant in style, that it does not appear to be a translation at all, and yet, at the same time, faithfully transmits the message of the original.

CHAPTER 2

Fidelity in Translation

WHAT IS FIDELITY IN TRANSLATION?

In the previous chapter, two approaches to translation were discussed. Whether the idiomatic or literal approach is preferred, all are agreed that the meaning of the original must be preserved in the translation. It seems axiomatic, therefore, to conclude that a definition of fidelity will focus on the meaning of the original. Further, if it is granted, as was shown in the last chapter, that preserving the linguistic form of the original in a translation often results in wrong or obscure meaning, then it also seems self-evident that a definition will not focus on preserving the linguistic form of the original.

One characteristic of that linguistic form does become important, however, when thinking of fidelity in translation. The linguistic form of the original was natural and meaningful. It did not represent a grammatical or lexical structure that was impossible or discouragingly difficult to understand but one that was already in use by the people in everyday conversation. This feature of the original text gave it a dynamic quality which must also be preserved in a faithful translation.

A definition of fidelity will, therefore, not only focus on meaning but will also focus on this feature of linguistic form. In light of these observations, the following definition of a faithful translation is given: A translation which transfers the meaning and the dynamics of the original text is to be regarded as a faithful translation. The expression, *transfers the meaning*, means that the translation conveys to the reader or hearer the information that the original conveyed to its readers or hearers. The

33

message is not distorted or changed; it has neither unnecessarily gained nor lost information. The expression, *the dynamics*, means that (1) the translation makes a natural use of the linguistic structures of the RL and that (2) the recipients of the translation understand the message with ease. The naturalness of the translation and the ease with which it is understood should be comparable to the naturalness of the original and to the ease with which the recipients of the original documents understood them. Such a comparison of the dynamics of the original with that of a translation must bear in mind that the message may have been easier for the original recipients to understand because Greek was the language of both writers and readers, and they shared the same or similar cultures. Also in some cases they had heard the writer speaking. On the other hand, the message was not dependent upon these local advantages since the writers were not penning abstract theses or obscure philosophies but had a very practical aim in view; they wrote to be understood.

The question of fidelity thus comes down to the two questions: (1) Does the translation communicate the same meaning as the original? (2) Does it communicate it as clearly and as idiomatically as the original did? If the answer to these two questions is "yes," then it has every right to be called a faithful translation.

Although the statement of these two principles is relatively simple, their consistent application by the translator is by no means so straightforward. The goal is clear, but to attain it is difficult and demanding, though, one may add, it is also highly rewarding. The rest of this chapter, then, explains in more detail the implications of this definition of fidelity.

Fidelity to the Meaning of the Original

The first step toward preserving the meaning of the original in a translation is for the translator to know how to exegete the text. Only as the translator correctly understands the message, can he begin to be faithful; only then can he translate clearly and accurately the historical and didactic passages of Scripture; only then can he help himself to avoid the pitfalls of communicating incomplete, extraneous, or different information in his translation. There are, then, positive and negative explanations needed as to what is involved in maintaining the meaning of the original.

Exegeting the text

Translating faithfully involves knowing what Scripture means. This is fundamental to all idiomatic translation, and it is at this point that exegesis comes in. Toussaint, in an article in *Notes on Translation,* defines exegesis as follows: "Exegesis is a critical[1] study of the Bible

---

[1] The use of the term "critical" here by Toussaint should not be confused with its use in such expressions as "higher critical studies" referring to the work of liberal theologians. Here it simply means that the analytical and logical faculties of the mind are employed in studying the Scriptures.

according to hermeneutical principles with the *immediate* purpose of interpreting the text . . ." (1966, p. 2). In other words, its immediate purpose is to ascertain, as accurately as possible, using all the means available, just what the original writer, "moved by the Holy Spirit," meant as he dictated or penned his words, phrases, and sentences. Exegesis thus lies at the heart of all translation work, for if the translator does not know what the original means, then it is impossible for him to translate faithfully.

Fidelity to historical references

Assuming, then, that the translator knows what the original means, he must communicate the same information that the original does. This information may be broadly classed as historical or didactic. The historicity of the message must not be lost or distorted. Likewise, the teachings of Scripture must be kept intact.

The Christian faith is firmly rooted in history. The death and resurrection of the Savior took place at a particular time, in a particular country; and it is not part of the translator's task to change this historical framework or to substitute for it in any way.

A recent example of a translation that very obviously departs from the historical framework of the Scripture is one called the *Koinonia "Cotton Patch" Version* by C. L. Jordan. This translation assumes a setting in the southern United States, and is translated as if it had just been written. Thus 1 Corinthians is given the title "A letter from Paul to the Christians in Atlanta." Chapter 8, v. 1, in the same letter, which begins in the KJV, "Now as touching things offered unto idols . . . ," is translated, "Now about working on Sunday , . . ." Jews are represented by "whites" and gentiles by "Negroes" so that 1 Corinthians 10:32, "Give none offence, neither to the Jews, nor to the Gentiles, nor to the church of God," is translated, "Set a good example for both whites and Negroes — for God's whole church — . . . ." Whatever merits this translation may have, it is clear that it has abandoned the principle of historical fidelity, presumably in the interests of vividness and immediate meaningfulness to a particular group of readers. But objects, places, persons, animals, customs, beliefs, or activities which are part of a historical statement must be translated in such a way that the same information is communicated by the translation as by the original statements. This principle applies to items or activities which are known in the RL culture as well as to those which are unknown.

In the record of Paul's journey to Rome by sea, reference is made to *anchors* on three occasions (Acts 27:29, 30, 40). Many tribal cultures are quite unfamiliar with anchors, and even if they use canoes, they usually draw them up on the bank of the river or fasten them to trees. Even though the speakers of the RL are unfamiliar with anchors, the translator is not permitted to substitute some local equivalent. A way must be found to preserve the historical reference to anchors.

The example of anchors, of course, is just one of many. John the

Baptist ate *locusts* (Matt. 3:4, Mark 1:6), but these insects are not known everywhere. The Gadarene demoniac was bound with *chains* (Mark 5:3, 4; Luke 8:29) and so, on occasion, were Peter (Acts 12:6, 7) and Paul (Acts 21:33). *Wine* and *bread* are referred to quite frequently but are not known in many cultures.

Fidelity to didactic references

Translating faithfully means that the same didactic information is conveyed in the RL version as was conveyed in the original. Scripture is not merely a historical record of events of the past; one of its main purposes is to interpret historical facts relating them to the needs of man and applying them to the kind of conduct and life appropriate to these facts. Scripture is therefore replete with commands, illustrations, parables, and similitudes, all of which have a didactic function which in a faithful translation must be preserved.

Romans 13 is a chapter that is didactic in function, dealing with various aspects of a believer's conduct and way of life. Thus, the statements in the following list, which have been selected at random from this chapter, must be translated accurately so that the identical teaching is communicated as was communicated to the original readers.

13:1 Let every soul be subject unto the higher powers. For there is no power but of God:

3 For rulers are not a terror to good works, but to the evil.

4 For he is the minister of God

7 Render therefore to all their dues

9 Thou shalt not commit adultery, Thou shalt not kill,

Whether the ethnic group for whom a translation is made agrees with the didactic statements of Scripture or not, the translator must be faithful to his task by communicating the same information as the author intended for his immediate audience or readers.

Tensions between historical and didactic fidelity

Didactic fidelity is not quite so simple as the previous paragraphs may suggest since cultural items which are used in extended illustrations, similitudes, etc. have a dual function: (1) they reflect the historical setting of the document and (2) they serve to illustrate some teaching. Often a translator realizes that to attempt to be faithful both to the historical and to the didactic function of a cultural referent will inevitably lose some of the dynamics of the original illustration. He finds himself in a dilemma. To keep the unfamiliar items used by an author in an illustration may obscure the teaching. On the other hand, to substitute known items of the RL culture may misrepresent the cultural setting of the original document. Many translators have been uncertain what to do in the face of such problems. Are there any guidelines to follow when special situations of this type arise?

As has already been stated, historical fidelity requires that no substitutions be made when translating historical events. If substitutions are made for historical information, the historical facts are distorted. But what about parables or illustrations which are clearly didactic? Can substitutions for specific references to the Biblical culture be permitted in these contexts?

The basic principle of the idiomatic approach is that the meaning of the original should be faithfully transmitted in a translation. And it is true that, in some cases, when cultural substitutions are made in didactic material, the teaching is faithfully transmitted. When such substitutions are made, however, the cultural setting which the author reflected in his writing will be misrepresented thus violating the principle of historical fidelity.

Hence, references to items of the original culture, such as wineskins or leaven, which are made in extended illustrations and which reflect the historical setting of the document are to be kept in the translation unless their retention results in a serious breakdown in communication.[2] This is a general guideline to which exceptions may be allowed when wrong or zero meaning is communicated. In other words, when the dynamics of an illustration are poor because of ambiguity or some obscurity, the reduced dynamics can be tolerated. In this case, fidelity to meaning takes precedence over dynamic fidelity. However, if retaining an unknown cultural item results in wrong or zero meaning, then some adjustment is necessary. In such circumstances, didactic fidelity takes precedence over fidelity to the historical nature of the imagery.

The manner in which a breakdown in communication can be avoided without having to make substitutions for the cultural images of the original is discussed in parts of chapters 9, 12, and 13. One method is to use a generic term suitably modified. Occasions do arise, however, when even a generic reference for the image cannot be used successfully and it becomes necessary to consider a substitution. The translator should be reluctant to resort to this solution in extended illustrations, but when he does so, it is because he cannot overlook zero or wrong meaning in his translation when the same passage was clear to the original readers. In most cases, however, he is able to make reference to the items of the original culture without having to sacrifice the teaching contained in the illustration.

Avoiding incomplete, extraneous, or different information

Information theory, the theory of communication, has been developed mainly in the context of the transmission of messages by such physical systems as the telephone, but increasingly its concepts are being applied to spoken and written material — speech communication. As can be imagined, communication engineers are very concerned with distortions of the transmitted message — their characteristics, their source, the types

[2] Other instances where cultural substitutions are permissible are discussed in chapters 9 and 13.

of error they produce, and how such distortions can be counteracted. In other words, they are concerned with fidelity in transmission, ensuring that the message received is the same as that transmitted.

Kirk and Talbot (in Smith, ed., 1966, pp. 309-16) discuss various kinds of distortion, two of which they call "fog distortion" and "mirage distortion." In the former, information is lost — it is "fogged out" by distortions; in the latter, "spurious information is added"; information that was never in the original message at all.

These concepts of "distortion" or, to use a more general term, "lack of fidelity," can be applied very readily to the translation process. Part of the original message may get "lost" in the transference from the original to the RL; this is called *incomplete information*. On the other hand, information may be added to the content of the original message; this is called *extraneous information*. In translation, however, it is useful to add a third possible kind of lack of fidelity, which may be called *different information*. In this case, information is simultaneously subtracted from and added to the original message, with the result that a different message is substituted for that of the original. In producing a faithful translation it is important to avoid incomplete, extraneous, or different information.

Incomplete information is information which is neither implicit nor explicit in the translation but which was part of the original communication. It often arises simply by omission; the translator, who has so much to concentrate on, inadvertently omits a verse or part of a verse. But such omissions are regularly caught in revisions and consultant checks and need not further concern us. Another reason is less obvious. It arises when the meaning of some part of the RL version only *approximates* the meaning of the original; or when it communicates no meaning at all. In the one case some of the content is lost to the reader and in the other all of it is.

Incomplete information also arises when implicit information which is relevant to the message and which was communicated to the reader of the original is lost to the RL reader. For example, unless the reference to wineskins in Mark 2:22 includes the implicit information that the opening was tied securely, the illustration fails to communicate to the Abua people of Nigeria. This example shows how implicit meaning may be lost in the process of translation.

Extraneous information is information which is communicated to the readers of the RL version, but which is neither implicit nor explicit in the original; that is to say, it was *not* communicated to the original recipients.

Extraneous information also arises when obligatory grammatical categories of the original text are automatically kept in explicit form in the RL translation even though such information is not relevant to the verse. For example, always to translate the Greek present tense by a present continuous form in the RL would lead to extraneous information, since the component of continuity is not uniformly relevant in every context. The same may occur when using a descriptive equivalent of a word;

more components of the word may be made explicit than are in focus in the context.

Different information may arise from faulty exegesis. However, with the increased emphasis on the centrality of exegesis and the availability of the "Exegetical Helps," this is decreasingly the case. More often it arises from the fact that the translator is not sufficiently familiar with the RL. For instance, a translator had used an expression for *repent* both in Mark and in Acts which seemed to mean "change one's mind." A further check was made of the expression, and it was found that although it did indeed mean to change one's mind, it was in particular circumstances only. The context was that of a witness called to give evidence before a judge. First he told the truth but later "changed his mind" out of concern for the accused and told lies. So the readers of the RL were getting a different message from that which the readers of the original understood — yet one that made sense to them. Since it was considered good to tell lies to help a friend in trouble, they concluded that God rewarded one's "goodness" by forgiving him his sins!

Therefore, the translator must be constantly on the alert to avoid being unfaithful in these ways to the original meaning. Complete fidelity to the meaning of the original is the goal — but it is a goal that requires careful study and constant vigilance to attain.

FIDELITY TO THE DYNAMICS OF THE ORIGINAL

In the general introduction to this chapter "dynamic fidelity" was described as having reference to the naturalness of the linguistic structures utilized in the RL version and to the ease with which the readers could understand the translated message. Naturalness is a prerequisite to ease of understanding. One follows from the other.

The ease with which a message will be understood depends on the naturalness of structure, and such naturalness of structure is assured by the importance the speaker or writer places upon his message. When a person is deeply concerned to pass on a message which is a matter of life and death, a message which is believed with all the heart, and a message, moreover, which is divinely given, he will certainly choose to state that message clearly. He does not write in such a way that the message will be obscure, difficult, or almost impossible to understand. Rather, he makes every effort to communicate the message clearly to reach both the understanding and the heart. This is what every good preacher and every good writer does. That is why they are considered to be good; they make the message clear to all.

The apostles and others who wrote the New Testament were just such men. They preached to be understood and they wrote to be understood. At least two of the New Testament writers explicitly say so. In 2 Corinthians 1:13, Paul says, "For we write you nothing but what you can read and *understand*" (RSV). He was rejecting the charge of duplicity. Luke also says in the preface to his gospel that "it seemed good to me also , . . . to write an orderly account for you, most excellent Theophilus, that you may *know*[3] the truth concerning the things of which you have been informed" (Luke 1:3, 4 rsv). To assume that the original readers had considerable difficulty understanding what was written is, in effect, to assert that the apostles were clumsy and inept in their God-given task of communicating the truth in their preaching and writing. Paul, Peter, John, James, Luke, and the others wrote clearly and were readily understood. The original writings were both natural in structure and meaningful in content.

These two components of dynamic fidelity will now be discussed more fully. One component states that the form of message should be natural and the other that the message should be meaningful. These two components are interrelated; one looks at dynamic fidelity from the perspective of form, the other from that of meaningfulness. When the translation is natural in form, it will also be meaningful.

The linguistic form should be natural

When we say that the Scriptures are natural in form, we are simply saying that, written as they were by native speakers, they fell within the bounds of natural Hebrew, Aramaic, or Koiné Greek. That there are differences, no one would deny; the polished style of Luke is not the simpler style of John. However, they all fall within the bounds of what seemed natural to the readers, even if they were aware of dialectal and stylistic differences. The length of sentences; the ways in which they were connected; the use of words and their combinations; the syntax; the morphology — all was natural.

This characteristic of the original should also be found in a translation. It has already been stressed in chapter 1 that each language has its own inventory of linguistic forms which serve as a vehicle for any message conveyed in that language. The point being stressed here is that there is a natural use of those forms common to the native speakers of each language which should be used in the translation.

The message should be meaningful

The expression *meaningful* is used to mean that the message was clearly and readily understood by the original readers. A meaningful message is not necessarily one which fully treats every aspect of a topic or which anticipates every question that might be raised about it. A message may be understood easily in terms of what is said even though it may not remove difficulties arising from those aspects of the subject which are not treated. Therefore, the component of meaningfulness should be carefully distinguished from both full and familiar information, for they are easily confused.

The well-known reference in 2 Peter 3:15, 16 to the fact that in what Paul wrote "there are some things . . . hard to understand" might well

---

[3] It is not without interest that Luke and Paul use the same verb in the Greek (*epiginōskō*) even though it is translated differently in English.

be discussed here. In terms of the above, it would seem that Peter is not saying that what Paul wrote was not meaningful but rather that it was not full information. Paul wrote on such topics as election, or the Jews in God's purposes, or the Second Coming, or the resurrection body. Some of these matters are still "hard to understand." Who would claim a full understanding of God's purposes for the Jews or of the nature of the resurrection body? This is because of the profundity of the topic itself — not because Paul (or any other writer) used Greek words in peculiar ways or in unfamiliar combinations.

Thus, a translation which is dynamically faithful will be meaningful even though it may not make explicit all that one might want to know. Moreover, the dynamics of the translation are not dependent on familiar information. New information can be presented in a dynamic form. It is often said that a translation should not sound like a translation at all. This statement applies to the *manner* in which the information is communicated but not to the *matter* which is communicated. Thus, the images used in live figures (parables, allegories, illustrations, and similitudes) need not be replaced by substitutes[4] to attain meaningfulness even though to do so would clothe the message in familiar terms and make it more immediately relevant to some particular segment of society. For example, Captain J. Rogers of the Merchant Marines translated the seaman's version of Psalm 23 as follows:

> The Lord is my Pilot; I shall not drift. He lighteth me across the dark waters; He steereth me in the deep channels; He keepeth my log. He guideth me by the star of holiness for His name's sake.
>
> Yea, though I sail 'mid the thunders and tempests of life, I shall dread no danger; for Thou art near me; Thy love and Thy care, they shelter me.
>
> Thou preparest a harbor before me in the homeland of eternity; Thou anointest the waves with oil; my ship rideth calmly.
>
> Surely, sunlight and starlight shall favor me on the voyage I take and I will rest in the port of my God forever.

Note that from the standpoint of what is taught, essentially the same message is communicated. However, from the standpoint of fidelity to the cultural setting of the original text, the shift from pastoral to maritime imagery is unacceptable. The goal of meaningfulness does not necessitate such a shift. Dynamic fidelity requires that a translation communicate familiar *or* unfamiliar information *meaningfully*; it does not generally require that unfamiliar information be recast by substituting concepts already known nor does dynamic fidelity require an answer to all of the questions which might be raised about a topic under discussion.

[4] See chapter 13 for a discussion as to when cultural substitutes may be necessary. See also the discussion earlier in this chapter on tension between historical and didactic fidelity.

Some factors which contribute to loss of dynamic fidelity

It follows from the above that there is a lack of dynamic fidelity if the translation is not natural in form or if it is not meaningful. A translation lacks in meaningfulness whenever it is unnecessarily ambiguous, or obscure, or communicates nothing at all. Many times such problems arise for the reader because the translator has translated literally, transferring the linguistic forms of the original to the RL. For example, a common construction in Greek is the genitive — two nouns linked by means of the genitive case. Translated literally into English, using "of," this often gives rise to difficult ambiguities.[5]

Long sentences are a common cause of obscurity. Colossians 1:9-20 is one long sentence in Greek, and when it is transferred literally into English as one long sentence (even if broken into smaller parts by colons, semicolons, and commas) it is extremely difficult for an English reader to follow. This is because English lacks the many devices of Greek syntax which made the internal relationships clear to the original readers. It is with this in mind, therefore, that modern translations break up this sentence into a number of shorter ones. The RSV has 7 sentences (and 2 paragraphs), while the TEV has twice this number of sentences, as well as the 2 paragraphs. The problem of obscurity is thus met, at least in part, by using sentence lengths which are natural to modern English rather than those that were natural to first-century Greek.

The whole question of "naturalness in form," and lack of it in translations, has been discussed increasingly over the past decade. For instance, in the 1963-1964 volumes of *The Bible Translator*, no less than three articles by Wycliffe Bible Translators were devoted to the subject of "frequency counts" as a measure of naturalness.[6] But six years before the first of these, Lauriault (now spelled Loriot) had written an article entitled, "Some Problems in Translating Paragraphs Idiomatically." After he had done extensive research on paragraph structure in Shipibo, a Peruvian language, he says, "Then I looked back at how we had translated the Gospel of Mark and was appalled at what I read there. It now looked so stilted and unnatural. In many cases, the wrong conjunctive elements had been used and the train of thought either partially obliterated or completely destroyed. Individual sentences were understandable, but many of them had too much crammed into them . . . . I concluded that the translation would be hard to read and follow. I did not have to wait long for the proof . . ." (1957, p. 168).

Basically, lack of naturalness in form means that the translation does not "flow" in a normal way. It may be stilted and jerky; it may have "too much crammed" into too few sentences; or it may emphasize the wrong things and not emphasize the right ones.

An illustration from Bariba,[7] a language of Dahomey in West Africa,

---

[5] See chapter 16 for a detailed discussion of the genitive.

[6] These were by Grimes (1963), Robinson (1963), and Moore (1964).

[7] In a verbal communication from Kenneth L. Pike.

will show what serious consequences can follow from lack of naturalness in form. In Bariba, there are very strict rules about the use of direct and indirect quotations.[8] The linguists had not yet resolved all of these, and so, when they were quoting John 8:12, they would say, "Jesus said, 'I am the light of the world.'" But in Bariba, because of the rules governing the use of direct and indirect speech, this meant: Jesus said that I — the one who is speaking to you — am the light of the world. So the Bariba who were listening, having already gathered that Jesus was someone important, responded, "Since Jesus says you are the light of the world, we will gladly follow you. What do you want us to do?" The missionaries eventually found that the meaning was clear only if they said, "Jesus said that he is the light of the world."

In Munduruhú of Brazil, there is also a rigid and complicated set of rules for putting sentences together to form a naturally flowing narrative. Sheffler (1969, p. 2) says that "each episode is characterized by a thematic unity centering around one main participant labeled the actor of the episode, who in turn has one over-all objective for the duration of the episode — his target." A particular word, *g̃ebuje*, indicates *target changed*, but originally the translator thought it meant *then*. Hence, when translating Mark 7:31-37, which naturally forms one *episode* with Jesus as the *actor* and the deaf and dumb man as the "target," *g̃ebuje* was used a number of times with the result that while Jesus remained as actor, he had a whole series of different "targets" — spitting, his own hand, the sky, and even "Ephphatha." The result was that the story lost much of its unity and was confusing to the Munduruhú.

It is not the purpose of this section to illustrate all the possible ways in which naturalness in form may be lacking. One other way, however, will be mentioned here. This factor was first studied by information theorists who gave it the label "redundancy." This is how Schramm (1966, p. 523) defines it: "Redundancy is a measure of certainty and predictability" — that is to say, the more redundant the form of the message, the easier it is for the recipient to guess what is coming next. So Schramm goes on to say, "In many cases, increasing the redundancy will make for more efficient communication." Nida and Taber (1969, p. 163) state that "there seems to be a relatively fixed tendency for languages to be approximately 50 percent redundant." If this is so, then the Greek of the New Testament is about 50 percent redundant (in this technical sense — it would be bad Greek if it were not), and the translation into the RL also needs to be about 50 percent redundant. There is no reason, however, to suppose that the Greek and the RL use the same methods for building in redundancy. If it is assumed that they are the same and a literal transfer is made, the result so often is that the RL version does not use its own natural redundancy patterns but only the

---

[8] For a detailed discussion of direct and indirect quotations in Bariba see Kenneth L. Pike (1966, pp. 86-92).

unnatural Greek ones. Consequently, as Lauriault pointed out "many of them [the sentences] had too much crammed into them."[9]

This is more serious than might, at first, appear. At best, such lack of proper redundancy will make the translation obscure and difficult to follow. At worst, however, it greatly increases the possibility of error. Schramm (1966, p. 530) says, "In other words , . . . error can be reduced as much as desired if only the rate of transmission is kept below the total capacity of the channel; *but if we overload the channel, then error increases very swiftly*" (italics by the present authors).

In other words, lack of naturalness in form is not simply a matter of sounding a bit stilted, or heavy, or obscure. It can readily lead to distortions of the message itself, so that lack of dynamic fidelity may pass into lack of fidelity to the meaning.

CONCLUSION

Thus the translator has two guiding principles where the issue of fidelity is concerned — fidelity to the meaning and fidelity to the dynamics of the original. Both are hard to attain; but unless they are attained, the message of the Word of God will be distorted or obscure, and the recipients of the RL version will not be given the opportunity to understand clearly what it is that God is saying to them. When this happens, the translator defeats his own purpose.

---

[9] For an interesting discussion of redundancy in the Miahuatlán dialect of Zapotec of Mexico, see Ruegsegger (1966, pp. 2-4).

CHAPTER 3

Implicit and Explicit Information

THE FACT OF IMPLICIT INFORMATION IN THE ORIGINAL
TYPES OF IMPLICIT INFORMATION IN THE ORIGINAL
    Implicit information derived from the immediate context
    Implicit information derived from the remote context
    Implicit information derived from the cultural context
WHEN MAY IMPLICIT INFORMATION BECOME EXPLICIT?
    Required by the RL grammar
    Required by fidelity to the meaning
    Required by dynamic fidelity
TYPES OF EXPLICIT INFORMATION IN THE ORIGINAL
    Grammatical features
    Discourse features
    Components of meaning in words
WHEN MAY EXPLICIT INFORMATION BECOME IMPLICIT?

THE FACT OF IMPLICIT INFORMATION IN THE ORIGINAL

In the first two chapters, it has been shown that accuracy of meaning and naturalness of form are qualities that are characteristic of an idiomatic translation. Also, it comes closer to communicating what the original did than does a literal translation. Furthermore, the ease with which that content is understood is higher in an idiomatic translation. Various structural features of the RL grammar and vocabulary and the changes in linguistic form which they entail are discussed in this and the following chapters. This chapter takes up the question of the implicit information found in the original and how it is to be handled in an idiomatic translation.

In a number of other chapters of this book, reference is also made to implicit information. Metaphor and simile, for example, are studied with this in mind (chap. 8); the discussion of lexical equivalence (chap. 13) raises such questions as the implicit function of Things and Events; the matter of implicit information arises again in connection with abstract nouns (chap. 14), with genitives (chap. 16), and with relationships between propositions (chap. 18). In these, and in other instances, the translator is faced with the fact that the message of the original is conveyed both explicitly and implicitly. Greek and Hebrew, like every other language, had regular and analyzable ways in the grammar and vocabulary to convey information implicitly. It is important, therefore, that the translator clearly understand how to handle implicit information in his translation.

It has long been recognized in the history of translation work not only that there is implicit information in the original, but also that some of this implicit information has to become explicit if the translation is to be understandable at all. The use of italics in the KJV served just that purpose — to show an English reader what had to be expressed in English that was not overtly expressed in the original. Thus, in Matthew 1:6 we have "her *that had been the wife* of Urias," in Matthew 15:6 "and honour not his father or his mother, *he shall be free,*" in Acts 1:13 "James *the son* of Alphaeus . . . Judas *the brother* of James," in Romans 11:4 "who have not bowed the knee to *the image of* Baal," and in 1 Corinthians 10:27 "If any of them that believe not bid you *to a feast.*" The practice of using italics for this purpose was deliberately abandoned in the (English) Revised Version. The preface to the first edition of the Old Testament (1884, p. x) states, "that all such words, now printed in italics, as are plainly implied in the Hebrew and necessary in the English, be printed in common type." Although the printing of italics was abandoned, the principle was clearly recognized and stated that some of the implicit information in the original has to be expressed explicitly in a translation.

One subject that is regularly discussed in grammars of Greek and Hebrew is types of ellipsis found in these two languages. Ellipsis is one of the most common ways in which information is made implicit. Arndt and Gingrich, when discussing the meaning of *hina* (1957, pp. 378, 79), head their major section III with "*hina* is used elliptically," and go on to say, "1. *all' hina but this has happened that,* where the verb to be supplied must be inferred fr. the context . . . 3. *hina* without a finite verb, which can be supplied fr. the context . . ."[1]

---

[1] It is also of interest that theologians recognize the presence of implicit information and quite consciously use it. Berkhof (1950, pp. 158, 159) says: "In giving man his word, He [i.e., God] was not only perfectly aware of all that was said, but also of all that this implied. He knew the inferences that are deduced from His written Word. Says Bannerman: 'The consequences that are deduced from Scripture by unavoidable inference, and more largely still the consequences that are deduced from a comparison of the various Scripture statements among themselves, were foreseen by infinite wisdom in the very act of supernaturally inspiring the record from which they are inferred: and the Revealer not only knew that men would deduce such consequences, but designed that they should do so' (*Inspiration of the Scriptures,* p. 585). Therefore *not only the express statements of Scripture, but its implications . . . , must be regarded as the Word of God.*

"Jesus himself warrants this position. When the Sadducees came to him with a question which, in their estimation, clearly proved the untenableness of the doctrine of the resurrection, he referred them to the self-designation of Jehovah at the bush: 'I am the God of Abraham, the God of Isaac, and the God of Jacob'; and deduced from it by good and necessary inference, the doctrine which they denied. Moreover, he reproved their failure to see the implication of that self-designation by saying, 'Ye do err, not knowing the Scripture.'"

While translators would not be using this type of implicit information in a translation, it is interesting that it is clearly stated by Berkhof that "its implications as well, must be regarded as the Word of God."

The observations made in the previous two paragraphs lead to a third one — the information which is left implicit differs from one language to another. The patterns of a language allow certain information to be communicated clearly even though left implicit. Hebrew has its own characteristic patterns, as do also both Greek and English. As this is another area in which languages differ in structure, these patterns do not correspond with one another from language to language. That is why English translations have to express in explicit form some of the information that was carried only implicitly in the Greek. The patterns of implicitness differ from that of Greek, and so there is some change of form from implicit to explicit. It is clear, therefore, that the translator needs to take into careful consideration the presence of implicit information in the original, so that it may be used explicitly when it is needed in the RL version.

Experience in translation has confirmed that leaving the implicit information of the original implicit in the RL version can mislead the readers of the RL version and cause them to misunderstand the original message. A few examples will make this clear.

In Romans 14:2, Paul says, "For one believeth that he may eat all things: another, who is weak, eateth herbs." When translated in this form, it gave the readers in a particular language the impression that "weak" meant "physically weak," and that was why he could digest only herbs. But the previous verse speaks of "him who is weak *in faith*," and this qualifying phrase is carried implicitly in v. 2. But in many languages "in faith" must be made explicit in v. 2, as it is in v. 1, if the correct sense is to be communicated. Verse 2 may thus need to be rendered: One believes that he may eat all things. Another, who is weak in faith, believes that he should eat only herbs.

Mark 2:4 says, "And when they could not come nigh unto him for the press, they uncovered the roof where he was . . . ." Since no indication was given of how four men, carrying a paralyzed friend, could get onto a roof (and the language helper tended, naturally enough, to think in terms of his own familiar steep thatched roof), the language helper assumed a miracle, similar to Philip's sudden removal from the presence of the Ethiopian official to Azotus. Here, the Greek narrative left an intervening event implicit — that they climbed the outside stairs onto the roof. It is not always possible to leave this implicit in other languages.

"These men are not drunk, as you suppose . . . ." says Peter in Acts 2:15 (RSV), and to an English reader the meaning is clear. But in Huave and Zapotec de Villa Alta of Mexico, and in Aguacatec and Chuj of Guatemala, the use of "these" excluded Peter himself and implied that Peter was drunk, even though the others were not. The information that Peter himself was not drunk is implicit in the Greek, but has to become explicit in languages like these which have a pronominal and deictic system which excludes[2] the speaker.

[2] See *Notes on Translation* Nos. 16, 20, 26 for fuller treatments of this type of problem with pronouns.

In Acts 4:31 Luke records, "And when they had prayed, the place was shaken where they were assembled together; and they were all filled with the Holy Ghost . . . ." When the Chuj of Guatemala read this, they assumed that the building was shaken by the devil, as this type of phenomenon was already known to them and attributed to his activity. There is no explicit statement in Acts as to who was the agent of this event, but most commentators refer the action to the Holy Spirit, mentioned immediately afterwards, or to God. The agent had to be expressed in the Chuj translation to avoid wrong implicit information being supplied by the readers.

It is clearly necessary, therefore, that the translator (a) be alert to the types of implicit information in the original, so as to be able to draw upon it whenever this should prove necessary; and (b) know when and how it should become explicit in the RL version. The next two sections will take up these two points in turn, and a final section will discuss the related question of explicit information in the original being handled as implicit information in the RL version.

TYPES OF IMPLICIT INFORMATION IN THE ORIGINAL

Most of this implicit information is to be found in the actual linguistic forms of the original language, i.e., in its vocabulary, and in its various grammatical constructions. But not all of it is conveyed in this way. Any author writes with a particular audience in mind and adapts what he says accordingly. He will write for an adult audience in a different way than for an audience of children, and for specialists in a different way than for nonspecialists. The more his audience knows, the more he can assume, and the less he needs to state explicitly. The less his audience knows, the more he has to explain and state explicitly.

This difference of audience may explain why Matthew simply says (26:17), "Now on the first day of Unleavened Bread" (RSV) whereas Mark (14:12) and Luke (22:7) add a further comment about the killing of the passover lamb on that day. It is generally thought that Matthew was writing for a Jewish audience, while Mark and Luke had gentile Christians primarily in mind and hence added an explanation. In other words, they made more information explicit and left less implicit. Similarly, it was sufficient for Paul to say to the Corinthians, "Now concerning the matters about which you wrote" (1 Cor. 7:1, RSV), since the congregation there would already know what had been written to him.

A distinction can therefore be drawn between two major types of implicit information. There is the implicit information conveyed in the written document itself by the vocabulary and grammatical constructions of the language; and there is the implicit information which lies outside the document, in the general situation which gave rise to the document, the circumstances of the writer and readers, their relationship, etc.

Although this is a useful distinction, it is not implied that it is a rigid one. There are usually hints in the document itself as to the situation which gave rise to it, and the use of words like "beloved" or "brothers" gives a good indication of the relationship between writer and readers.

Most of the implicit information that is relevant to understanding the document is contained within the document itself, and it is only rarely necessary for the translator to draw on information from outside of it. In fact, most of the relevant implicit information within the document is drawn from the immediate context, that is to say, from within the particular paragraph being studied or from an adjacent one.

In the light of these statements, the following types of implicit information can be established:

1. Implicit information found within the document
   a. in the same paragraph or an adjacent one, (the immediate context)
   b. elsewhere in the same document, (the remote context)
2. Implicit information found outside the document, (the cultural context)

It only needs to be added that, in the particular situation of Bible translation, the "remote context" is extended to include the other writings of the Bible, not just the rest of the book being studied at the time.

One of the problems that faces a translator whose mother tongue is an Indo-European language is that of recognizing the presence of implicit information in the original. The purpose of the next section is to alert the translator to the many ways that information is carried implicitly in the original. The examples illustrate this in some detail and also indicate the variety of ways in which this was done in Greek. The section is divided into three parts, corresponding to the three types of implicit information described above: that derived from the immediate context, that derived from the remote context, and that derived from the cultural context. It is emphasized strongly, however, that the presentation of this material does *not* imply that the translator, working in a particular language, has to make all this material explicit. A decision on this matter must be reached on the basis of the requirements of the RL itself, for each RL is different in this respect.

Implicit information derived from the immediate context

There is a great deal of material to be presented in this section since the immediate context is the source from which most of the implicit information of the original is drawn. It has therefore been grouped under eight headings for convenience: ellipsis, a clause of a complex sentence, discourse features, some grammatical constructions, literary devices, choice of events, components of meaning in words, and ambiguities.

1. *Ellipsis*

As a discourse unfolds, the information that has already been introduced may be assumed to be known. Once information is in this category, it may become implicit or be represented by various "pro" forms (substitute forms for specific nouns or verbs). Grammars regularly refer to information that has been given and then left implied as *ellipsis*.

Most of the examples in this section relate to the time, location, circumstances, etc., which are first stated and subsequently carried implicitly. (Throughout the rest of this chapter, the implicit information is italicized in each case. Where relevant, a reference is given to the verse or verses from which the implicit information has been obtained.)

Rom. 14:2 ". . . another, who is weak *in faith*, eateth herbs" (cf. v. 1) (type of weakness)

1 Cor. 11:7 "For a man indeed ought not to cover his head *praying or prophesying* , . . ." (cf. vv. 4 and 5) (time)

2 Cor. 3:16 ". . . the veil *upon their heart* shall be taken away" (cf. v. 15) (attributive)

Gal. 2:9 "that we should go to the heathen *to preach the gospel . . . .*" (cf. v. 7) (purpose)

1 Thess. 3:7 "Therefore, brethren, we were comforted . . . by *the good tidings of* your faith" (cf. v. 6) (source of information)

Greek, however, can also leave implicit circumstantial details that have not yet been mentioned. This type of implicit information particularly needs to be noted, as it is rather less common in other languages than making implicit what has already been mentioned. Note the following examples:

John 7:21 "Jesus answered and said . . . , I have done one work *on the sabbath day . . . .*" (cf. v. 23) (time)

1 Cor. 9:4 "Have we not power to eat and to drink *at the expense of our converts?*" (cf. vv. 7, 11, and 14) (manner)

1 Thess. 4:14 ". . . even so them also which sleep in Jesus will God bring with him *when he descends from heaven*" (cf. v. 16) (time)

Implicit information is frequently found in conversational sequences. These sequences may be in the form of direct or indirect speech, or they may be statements or question-answer sequences. Generally the question or statement introduces information which is left implicit in the response. For example:

Matt. 26:4, 5 "And consulted that they might take Jesus by subtilty, and kill him. But they said, *Let us* not *take him* on the feast day, lest . . . ."

Luke 7:42, 43 "Tell me therefore, which of them will love him most? Simon answered and said, I suppose that he *will love him most* to whom he forgave most."

Rom. 3:9 "Are we Jews any better off? No, *we are* not *better off* at all . . . ." (RSV)

Comparisons and contrasts frequently involve implicit information. Some of the information included explicitly in the first part of a comparison or contrast is communicated in implicit form in the second part. The examples of comparison make use of the Greek connective *kathōs*:

> Mark 15:8 "And the multitude . . . began to desire *him to do* as (*kathōs*) he had ever done unto them."
>
> John 15:4 "As (*kathōs*) the branch cannot bear fruit of itself . . . no more can ye *bear fruit* . . . ."
>
> Gal. 2:7 ". . . when they saw that the gospel of the uncircumcision was committed unto me, as (*kathōs*) *the gospel* of the circumcision *was committed* unto Peter . . . ."
>
> Gal. 3:6 "*You heard and believed* as (*kathōs*) Abraham believed God . . . ."

Just as the examples of comparison which carry implicit information make use of the connective *kathōs* to signal the resemblance, so almost all of the following examples of contrast make use of the Greek connective *alla*:

> Mark 14:49 ". . . and ye took me not: but (*alla*) *you have taken me now because* the scriptures must be fulfilled."
>
> John 15:24, 25 ". . . now have they . . . hated both me and my Father. But (*alla*) *they have hated me* that the word might be fulfilled . . . ."
>
> Rom. 9:16 "So then *election is* not of him that willeth, nor of him that runneth, but (*alla*) *election is* of God that sheweth mercy."
>
> Rom. 15:3 "For even Christ pleased not himself; but (*alla*), *he pleased God* . . . ."
>
> 1 Cor. 2:13 "which things also we speak, not in the words which man's wisdom teacheth, but (*alla*) *in the words* which the Holy Spirit teacheth . . . ."
>
> 1 Cor. 7:19 Circumcision is of no importance, and uncircumcision is of no importance, but (*alla*) the keeping of the commandments of God *is very important* (authors' translation).
>
> 2 Tim. 1:7 "For God hath not given us the spirit of fear; but (*alla*) *he hath given us the spirit* of power, and of love, and of a sound mind."

An example of contrast which uses *de*, not *alla*, is found in Luke 4:29, 30: ". . . that they might cast him down headlong. But *they could/did not cast him down and* he passing through the midst of them went his way."

The sequence "not only . . . but also" (in Greek, *ou monon . . . alla kai*) nearly always carries implicit information in the second part:

> Rom. 5:2, 3 ". . . and rejoice in hope of the glory of God. And not only *do we rejoice in hope of the glory of God*, but we glory in tribulations also . . . ."

Rom. 8:22, 23 "For we know that the whole creation groaneth . . . .
And not only *the whole creation groaneth*, but ourselves also , . . .
even we ourselves groan . . . ."

2 Cor. 8:18, 19 ". . . the brother, whose praise is in the gospel throughout all the churches; and not only *is his praise throughout all the
churches*, but he was also chosen of the churches . . . ."

2. *A clause of a complex sentence*

Sometimes in a complex sentence one or more clauses are omitted.
The implicit clauses may function as means, conclusion, or consequence.
For example:

Matt. 2:2 "Where is he that is born King of the Jews? *We know that
he has been born* for we have seen his star in the east . . . ." (conclusion-grounds)

Matt. 8:8, 9 ". . . but speak the word only, and my servant shall
be healed. *I know that you can heal my servant by speaking a
word only*, for I am a man under authority . . . and I say . . . , Go,
and he goeth . . . ." (conclusion-grounds)

Matt. 9:6 "But *I will say, Arise and walk*, that ye may know that the
Son of man hath power on earth to forgive sins . . . ." (means-
purpose)

Luke 9:13 "We have no more but five loaves and two fishes; *we are
not able to feed them* except we should go and buy meat for all
this people." (consequence-condition)

Luke 13:9 "And if it bears fruit next year, *thou shalt not cut it down.*"
(condition-consequence)

Acts 13:35, 36 "Thou shalt not suffer thine Holy One to see corruption.
This does not speak of David, for David . . . saw corruption:"
(conclusion-grounds)

Acts 23:5 "I wist not, brethren, that he was the high priest. *If I had
known, I would not have said it*, for it is written . . . ." (conclusion-grounds)[3]

Rom. 8:15 "*You are the sons of God* for . . . ye have received the
Spirit of adoption . . . ." (conclusion-grounds)

1 Cor. 5:3 "*He should be taken away* for I verily . . . have judged
already . . . ." (conclusion-grounds)

1 Cor. 10:5 "But with many of them God was not well pleased: *we
know this to be so* for they were overthrown in the wilderness."
(conclusion-grounds)

3. *Discourse features*

Sometimes the Greek text does not explicitly mark certain discourse
features which are obligatory in other languages. One of the most
common of these is the fact that Greek has no formal marker for the

---

[3] The conclusion is in the form of a contrary-to-fact condition and its consequence.

end of a quotation, whereas many languages must add "he said" or "thus he said" to close a stretch of speech. Another relates to the introduction of a new character into a narrative. Many languages have specific formal methods for doing this, but Greek apparently does not. Examples could be multiplied such as the use of formal openings and/or endings to a narrative; formal indications of paragraph change, or theme, or the principal actor, etc. These features of discourse are implicit in the Greek,[4] but the structure of the RL may necessitate their explicit use in the translation.[5]

4. *Some grammatical constructions*

This is a rather general term covering a number of features of Greek grammar not readily included under other headings. It refers to such constructions as the passive, when no doer of the action is expressed; to transitive or ditransitive verbs whose objects are left implicit; to the use of dependent phrases as titles; and to abstract nouns.

Matt. 1:1 "*This is* the book of the generation of Jesus Christ . . . ."
Mark 1:1 "*This is* the beginning of the gospel of Jesus Christ . . . ."
Mark 3:2 ". . . that they might accuse him *of breaking the law.*"
Mark 6:14 "John the baptizer has been raised from the dead *by God.*" (RSV)
Mark 8:21 "How is it that ye do not understand *that I was not talking about bread?*"
John 1:15 "John bare witness of him *to people* . . . ."
Acts 17:23 "*This altar is dedicated* TO THE UNKNOWN GOD."
Rom. 9:9 "For this is what *God's* promise *to Abraham said* . . . ." (RSV)
1 Cor. 7:14 "For the unbelieving husband . . . ." = For the husband who does not believe *in the Lord.*

Abstract nouns, such as *salvation* and *faith*, represent events and permit the participants in these events to be carried implicitly. Thus *salvation* may carry implicit reference both to God, who saves, and to those who are saved. Similarly, *faith* may carry implicit information both as to the one who believes, and in whom. In most cases the context will make clear whether it is *we* or *you* or *they*, etc., who believe. The implicit information associated with abstract nouns will be discussed more fully in chapter 16 which deals with genitives, and in chapters 17 and 18 which deal with propositions.

5. *Literary devices*

Certain features of Greek writing, which could be called "rhetorical" or "literary" devices, may carry implicit information. These are rhetorical

---

[4] It may well be found, however, when careful studies of Greek discourse have been made, that there are some formal ways in Greek of indicating at least some of these discourse features.

[5] This whole question of discourse structure is taken up in much more detail in *Discourse Considerations in Translating the Word of God* by Kathleen Callow.

questions and such figures of speech as simile, metaphor, and synecdoche. Chapter 15 discusses rhetorical questions in considerable detail,
and chapter 8 analyzes simile and metaphor carefully. Hence, these
will not be discussed further or exemplified here.

6. *Choice of events*

Any writer selects for specific mention those events which are relevant
to his purpose. However, this appears to be a matter which is not only
dependent on the writer's choice, but also on the particular language.
Some languages are more explicit than others in handling a series of
events, and even if two languages choose the same number of events for
explicit mention, it does not follow that they will select the same ones.
These differences between languages can cause confusion particularly in
narratives, when Greek omits what may have to be explicit in another
language. Hence, the translator needs to be aware of this type of implicit information. For example:

> Mark 1:9 ". . . Jesus came from Nazareth of Galilee, *and arrived
> where John was baptizing people.* And he was baptized of John
> in Jordan."
> Mark 1:36 "And *when it dawned* Simon and they that were with him
> *in the house arose and saw that Jesus was not there. They went
> out and* followed after him . . . ."
> Mark 3:6 "And the Pharisees went forth, and *found* the Herodians
> and straightway took counsel with them . . . ."
> Luke 1:9, 10 ". . . his lot was to burn incense when he went into the
> temple of the Lord. *So he went in,* and the whole multitude of
> the people were praying without . . . ."
> Luke 20:9 ". . . and went into a far country *and stayed there* for a
> long time."
> Acts 14:19, 20 ". . . and, having stoned Paul, drew him out of the city,
> supposing he had been dead, *and left him there.* Howbeit, as the
> disciples *arrived and* stood about him , . . ."

Sometimes the event that is left implicit is the response to a stimulus,
as in the following cases:

> John 11:44, 45 "Jesus saith unto them, Loose him, and let him go. *So
> they did.* Then many of the Jews . . . believed on him."
> Acts 24:24 ". . . [Felix] sent for Paul, and, *when Paul arrived,* heard
> him . . . ."

7. *Components of meaning in words*

Chapter 4 discusses the question of the analysis of words, how to
analyze and define their various senses and components. Each word in
the Greek New Testament can be so analyzed, and, as is the case with
any language, a given word may cover as much information as the
speakers of that language want it to convey. For example, "to watch
sheep at night" requires five words in English, but only one in Quiché of

Guatemala. In practice, the translator finds that he occasionally has to "unpack" the components of Greek words which are not matched by corresponding words in the RL, just as English has to do this with the Quiché word referred to above.

Four groups within this general heading may be distinguished: words whose meaning is complex, functions of objects and actions, class membership, and relationships.

Some of the words in the New Testament whose meaning is complex and which have had to be spelled out in some languages are given below:

> *to discipline*: "to punish in order to improve"
> *Scripture*: "what is written in God's word/book"
> *king*: "a man who rules people"
> *centurion*: "a man who commands 100 soldiers"
> *Pharisees*: "a group of Jews called Pharisees"

The function of objects and actions is discussed in detail in chapter 13, so will not be taken up further here.

Proper names carry with them a class membership, which sometimes needs to be made explicit. Depending on the requirements of the RL and on the acquaintance of the RL readers with the Biblical background, the class membership may need to be stated.[6] For example:

> *animal* called camel
> *city* called Nazareth
> *tree* called sycamore

The fourth group is not to be confused with the relationships between propositions which may have no overt signal. What is referred to here are words which require an explicit statement of such information as the purpose, location, direction, result, in the RL, but not in Greek. In other words, this information is implicit in the original, but has to be explicit in the RL. For example, the word "to choose" in Zapotec always requires the addition of a purpose. It is as though the word means not just "to choose" but "to choose for."

8. *Ambiguities*

When a word or a statement in its original context may be understood in two or more ways, then that word or statement is ambiguous. Ambiguities are usually due to the structure of the grammar or lexicon (such as the variety of meanings carried by the genitive construction, or the different senses of a word). It is relatively rare for the structure of the RL to be such that the ambiguity can be retained. As a result, the translator must often choose one of the possible interpretations. But in doing

---

[6] Although this type of implicit information is included here under the general heading of "Implicit Information from the Immediate Context," the class membership is not always carried in the immediate context, but may have to be derived from the remote or cultural context.

so, he has to bring into explicit status information which is implied in the context and on which the particular interpretation is based. Thus, in a certain context, he may choose to follow an interpretation of "the love of God" as meaning our love to God rather than God's love for us, and so translate "we love God" making explicit "we" as the actor and "God" as the goal of the action. Such choices are often unavoidable, and all the translator can do is to weigh the evidence presented in the various reference works, study the context carefully, and reach a reasonable decision.

Implicit information derived from the remote context

The previous section has shown that most implicit information is drawn from the immediate context, usually from an adjacent verse or two. Occasionally, however, because of obligatory categories in the RL or because of the need to avoid wrong meaning, the translator has to draw upon information derived from the remote context. Generally speaking, this means either from the Old Testament or from other books in the New Testament. The following are some examples drawing on information from the Old Testament.

John 8:17 "It is also written in your law, that the testimony of two men is true, *if they agree with each other.*"

Acts 2:16 "But this is that which was spoken by the prophet Joel *long ago . . . .*"

Implicit information drawn from other books in the New Testament is exemplified in the following verse:

Acts 18:22 "and gone up *to Jerusalem* , . . ." (cf. Mark 10:32, etc.)

It is to be noted that examples of this type of implicit information are much fewer than the type of implicit information discussed in the previous section, and make explicit little more than details of time and place.

Implicit information derived from the cultural context

Just as the translator occasionally needs to draw on the information in the remote context, so he also occasionally has to draw on information from outside the Biblical documents. This is already an established practice in connection with the meanings of the Biblical words since lexicons like that of Arndt and Gingrich (1957) draw on early Christian literature as well as the New Testament, and the various translations of the Old Testament into Greek.

It is in four main areas that the translator needs to draw on such cultural information from time to time: those of material objects, geography, religion, and Roman culture.

A number of material objects are simply mentioned in passing in the New Testament. Things such as flat roofs, camels, olives, cummin, etc., all occur in the New Testament, but details concerning them have to be found in Bible dictionaries, lexicons, commentaries, etc.

Similarly, a considerable amount of geographical detail is employed in the historical books, and occasionally in the Epistles. Jesus' journeys to and from Galilee and the travels of the apostles introduce references to many different towns, several seas, a number of islands and mountains, provinces, etc. Our knowledge of the geography of this area enables us to make explicit the implicit information carried by the names, if this should be necessary in the RL.

One particularly interesting example of a reference to geographical data is found in Luke 12:54, 55, where Jesus says, "When ye see a cloud rise out of the west, straightway ye say, There cometh a shower; and so it is. And when ye see the south wind blow, ye say, There will be heat; and it cometh to pass." But these descriptions of the weather are peculiar to Palestine and would sound strange to speakers of languages where the rain or the heat come from other directions. One scholar has suggested it would be possible to preface Jesus' description of the weather with some such phrase as "Here" or "In this country."

A certain amount of information concerning the religious context is provided in the New Testament. Pharisees, Sadducees, and the Sanhedrin are all explained to some extent. There are, however, some items which are not explained, such as "phylacteries," "temple," and "a sabbath day's journey" (Acts 1:12). Details about these have to be obtained from information provided by extra-Biblical sources.

Finally, there is frequent mention of items which were part of the Roman culture which dominated the area during that period: Caesar, governors, proconsuls, tribunes (KJV: "chief captains"), centurions, the praetorium, etc. Again, few of these items are explained in the context, and though certain deductions could be made about them, much fuller information is found from the historical records of the time.

Occasionally, then, the translator needs to draw on information available in the remote and cultural contexts as well as the information he can find in the immediate context. The next section discusses just when it is legitimate to make this information explicit in the translation.

WHEN MAY IMPLICIT INFORMATION BECOME EXPLICIT?

Translating idiomatically and faithfully is a difficult task because it involves the translator constantly in making decisions, in choosing between alternatives, and in applying many different principles. This difficulty is particularly evident when trying to decide what implicit information may legitimately become explicit in a translation. No simple answers are available, no "three easy steps" to a solution can be provided, but it is possible to provide guidelines so that the translator will avoid the two extremes of making *too little* explicit — thus leaving his readers fumbling in the dark or drawing false inferences — or of making *too much* explicit, so that every verse reads like a commentary and not a translation.

Before discussing these guidelines in more detail, the principle of chapter 2 needs re-emphasizing — any information that becomes explicit must be *faithful,* both exegetically and dynamically. It must be supported by good commentary evidence, and it must be so expressed that it fits the dynamic requirements of the RL. Thus, in Luke 12:13, a man in the crowd says to Jesus, "Master, speak to my brother, that he divide the inheritance with me." The implied information is that the father of the two sons had died. Otherwise, presumably, he would have seen to a proper sharing of his inheritance, as in the parable of the prodigal son. In Kasem, a language of northern Ghana, there is no single word for "inheritance" — the appropriate expression here would be "the things our father left when he died," so the implicit information has to become explicit. But then there is the question of dynamic faithfulness. "Master, tell my brother to take and share with me the things our father left when he died" would be a possible way of saying it, but it would not be very natural for it is too compressed and in the wrong order. It would be much better to say "Master, our father has died and left his things. Tell my brother to take those (previously mentioned) things and share with me." In this way, the implicit information is handled faithfully, both as to the meaning and as to the dynamics of the verse.

All the guidelines that follow can be conveniently summed up in one general principle, namely, that implicit information may be expressed explicitly if, and only if, the RL necessitates it.[7] It is not expressed explicitly merely because the translator thinks it would be helpful, or because of his own doctrinal convictions or denominational views, or because some other translator has done so, or because he thinks this is something the RL readers really need to know. It is made explicit because the grammar, or the meanings, or the dynamics of the RL require it in order that the information conveyed will be the same as that conveyed to the original readers.

The rest of this section will take up this general principle in somewhat more detail discussing it under three main divisions: explicit information required by the grammar, by fidelity to the meaning, or in connection with dynamic faithfulness.

Required by the RL grammar

The first specific guideline as to when to make implicit information explicit is the simplest to apply; implicit information must be made explicit when the grammar of the RL makes it obligatory. In every language there are constructions and categories which are obligatory. The translator has no choice but to use them. For instance, in many languages there are two first person plural pronouns *we,* one indicating that the speakers or writers *include* those whom they are addressing, the other indicating that they *exclude* them. So, with every *we* the translator has to decide which of these pronouns to use. This information is im-

---

[7] A particular exception is discussed later in this chapter in connection with obscure meaning.

plicit, since Greek made no such distinction. Thus in Mark 4:38 the disciples say to Jesus, "Master, carest thou not that *we* perish?" When they said *we*, did they mean only themselves or did they include Jesus as well? Or again, in 1 John 1:3, "That which *we* have seen and heard declare *we* unto you, that ye also may have fellowship with *us*: and truly *our* fellowship is with the Father, and with his Son Jesus Christ"; to whom do the various *we*'s refer? Again, the translator has to decide, making full use of what the commentaries say.

Examples of other obligatory constructions and categories could readily be multiplied. Some languages require a suffix that indicates that the action described was either seen by the writer, reported to the writer, or deduced from evidence by the writer. Some languages use honorific terms so that the relationship between the person spoken to and the speaker has to be determined and the appropriate honorific used. Some languages have an obligatory subject and no passive construction so that every verb has to have someone (or something) as its subject. Some languages have specific paragraph markers so that the translator has to decide where paragraphs begin and end. In some languages verbs must take objects, even when there is none expressed in the Greek.

In all these cases, the implicit information has to be studied to make sure that any decision reached is exegetically correct and that its explicit status is required by the obligatory forms of the language. Again, it can be pointed out that this is exactly what the KJV has done when it uses italics, as in 2 Corinthians 2:10, "To whom ye forgive any thing, I *forgive* also: for if I forgave any thing, to whom I forgave *it*, for your sakes *forgave I it* in the person of Christ." Thus, information that is necessitated by the grammar of the RL has to be expressed, whether it is explicit in the original or not.

Required by fidelity to the meaning

The second particular guideline derives from the principle of fidelity to the meaning of the original. If the implicit information of the original is not made explicit in the RL and wrong meaning arises, then the implicit information should be expressed explicitly.

To correct wrong meaning that distorts the message of Scripture, the use of implicit information is always justified. Examples of how such wrong meaning can arise were given earlier in the chapter (under the heading "The Fact of Implicit Information in the Original"). The reason for such wrong meaning is that the RL readers supplied their own implicit information, but in doing so they drew on their own background and so made false inferences.

Not all wrong meaning needs to be corrected by making implicit information explicit. Some wrong meaning does not distort the message of Scripture. For example, Acts 16:27 does not tell why the Philippian jailer was about to kill himself. In Ifugao of the Philippines, the readers concluded from their own cultural background that he was moved with shame and therefore wanted to take his own life. His motive, however, was not shame but dread of the penalty that was inflicted on jailers when their prisoners escaped. This misunderstanding did not distort the focus of this passage since it does not deal with the penalty inflicted on prison-keepers when their wards escape.

This second guideline highlights a very important question that needs to be asked: How does the translator know that the readers of the trans-lation will supply implicit information which is at variance with the true meaning? The answer is — by *asking* the readers, or hearers, of the RL version suitable questions to find out what it means to them or by *listening* to them teach from preliminary drafts of the translation. We will not here enlarge on the matter of asking questions,[8] but it should be borne constantly in mind as these guidelines are read. The translator will know whether his translation is conveying a wrong meaning only if he asks about it. If he does not ask, he will probably never know. Checking, by means of appropriate questions, is an essential part of the total task of translation. It is the counterpart of exegesis. The latter is, in effect, asking the original what *it* means (with the help of reference works such as lexicons, grammars, and commentaries in lieu of the origi-nal writers and readers). Checking is asking the readers and hearers of the RL version what *it* means. When the meaning communicated by the RL matches the meaning intended by the original author as deter-mined through careful study of the original text, then the translator knows he has translated the meaning faithfully.

Required by dynamic fidelity

The third guideline derives from the principle of dynamic fidelity. If the stylistic and discourse structures of the RL require that implicit infor-mation be made explicit, then this is a legitimate reason for doing so. This may mean resolving ambiguities and obscurities; identifying pro-nouns by nouns; it may mean supplying a link in a chain of events which has been omitted in the original (cf. the previous illustration of the four men and the paralytic); it may mean stating a purpose or result which has been left implicit. In other words, even though one may be able to communicate the correct meaning without making implicit information explicit, fidelity to the dynamics of the original may require it to be made explicit. If, for example, leaving information implicit results in too high a rate of new information and too little redundancy in the RL so that the message is difficult to understand, then there would be a lack of dynamic fidelity. To avoid the resultant clouding of the clarity of the message and the loss of ease in understanding the message, implicit information in such cases should be made explicit. Only then will the dynamics of the original be faithfully reflected in the RL translation.

Since ambiguities and obscurities adversely affect the dynamics of a translation and since questions always arise in the mind of the translator as to how to handle these, the next few paragraphs discuss guidelines

---

[8] See the section of chapter 11 on elicitation techniques.

for the resolution of ambiguities and obscurities. Implicit information when not made explicit may give rise to *ambiguities* in the RL version. That is to say, when he reads it, the reader finds that what he is reading may mean at least two different things. If these meanings — as indicated by the commentaries — are acceptable in the context, then no change is necessary. If one of the meanings is wrong, but the right meaning is more likely to be understood, then, again, there is no real need to make use of implicit information. However, if the wrong meaning is the one likely to be understood by the readers, then implicit information may be made explicit to make sure that the readers understand the correct sense.

Implicit information when not made explicit may also give rise to *obscure* meaning, that is to say, the readers cannot really be sure what the meaning is, even after several rereadings. If the obscurity conceals the focus of the passage so that no sense is seen, implicit information drawn from the immediate context may legitimately be used.

It should be emphasized that the use of implicit information to remove an obscurity is required only if the obscurity veils the focus of the verse, i.e., its central message. Auxiliary concepts which are related to the focus but not essential to it may be obscure, but this type of obscurity does not warrant the use of implicit information. An example of this distinction is provided by Hebrews 9:4: "Which had the golden censer, and the ark of the covenant overlaid round about with gold, wherein was the golden pot that had manna, and Aaron's rod that budded, and the tables of the covenant." The main topic of this passage is the "earthly sanctuary" (v. 1, RSV) and the fact that it contained a second room into which the Jewish high priest could enter only once a year (v. 7). The golden censer and the ark are two main details of this second room, and the contents of the ark are therefore subsidiary. To add explanatory details (interesting though these might be) about manna, and Aaron's rod, and the tables of the covenant, drawing on the remote contextual materials of the Old Testament narratives, would not be justified.

An illustration will show how leaving implicit information implicit can distort the focus. In Muong, a Vietnamese language, the word for the coins that the woman lost (Luke 15:8-10) was translated by the normal word for a coin. But when it was read, the Muong expressed surprise that anyone would go to all that trouble sweeping the house to find a coin of such little value when it would have been found eventually anyway! Clearly, it is implicit in the story that the coin was *worth* looking for, so this implicit information was made explicit in the story.

It may be helpful, by way of conclusion, to summarize the main thrust of the above discussion in a matrix. All implicit information must come from the original document or setting; moreover it must be required in the RL by the grammar, the meaning, or the dynamics. The shaded area indicates those circumstances in which the translator needs to proceed with particular caution when making implicit information explicit.

MATRIX 1

THE SOURCE OF IMPLICIT INFORMATION AND
WHEN IT MAY BECOME EXPLICIT

	taken from the immediate context	taken from the remote context	taken from the cultural context
required by the grammar			
required by fidelity to the meaning			
required by dynamic fidelity		/////	/////

TYPES OF EXPLICIT INFORMATION IN THE ORIGINAL[9]

The purpose of this section is to alert the translator to particular types of explicit information in the original which experience has shown may be suitably handled as implicit information in the RL. The material is presented in three broad groupings as follows: (1) explicit information carried by features of the grammar, other than discourse; (2) features of the discourse; (3) semantic components of words.[10]

1. *Grammatical features*

Every Greek verb carries the categories of tense, mood, person, and number; similarly, every Greek noun carries the categories of number, gender, and case. But in many languages such categories are not obligatory. For instance, in the Gê languages of Brazil nouns do not carry the category of number; in many African languages the verb does not carry the categories of either person or number; and in many languages of the Far East mainland, verbs and nouns, as such, are invariant, carrying no categories at all. Another grammatical feature that could be added is the distinction between masculine and feminine, which is not explicit in the pronouns of many languages, but is in Greek. Many instances will arise, therefore, where Greek makes obligatory use of some grammatical category because the grammatical structure requires it, not

[9] Much of the information in this section is derived from Larson, 1969, pp. 16-20, although the presentation has been altered.

[10] Taber (see Beekman, 1968b, p. 13, footnote) suggests the following threefold division: (1) obligatory categories in the source language; (2) any explicit information that "would insult the readers"; (3) anything that "would divert attention away from the main point of the passage."

because the meaning of that form is in focus. Thus, in languages where these categories are not obligatory, they are not rendered explicitly.

2. *Discourse features*

A number of different aspects of discourse can be considered here. The first is the matter of redundancy. Broadly, one may say that many of the repetitions in the original reflect natural forms of redundancy in Greek, but may not do so in the RL. Note the following examples (repetitions italicized):

Mark 2:11, 12 "I say unto thee, *Arise and take up thy bed*, and go thy way into thine house. And immediately *he arose, took up the bed*, and went forth before them all . . . ."

Luke 1:18 ". . . Whereby shall I know this? for I am an *old* man, and my wife *well stricken in years.*"

Luke 2:41-43 "Now his parents went to *Jerusalem* every year . . . and when he was twelve years old, they went up to *Jerusalem* . . . as they returned, the child Jesus tarried behind in *Jerusalem* . . . ."

Luke 8:35-38 ". . . and found the man, *out of whom the devils were departed*, sitting at the feet of Jesus . . . . They also which saw it told them by what means *he that was possessed of the devils* was healed . . . . Now *the man, out of whom the devils were departed*, besought him that he might be with him . . . ."

John 5:8-12 "Jesus saith unto him, Rise, *take up thy bed, and walk*. And immediately the man was made whole, and *took up his bed, and walked* . . . . The Jews therefore said unto him that was cured, It is the sabbath day: it is not lawful for thee to carry *thy bed*. He answered them, He that made me whole, the same said unto me, *Take up thy bed, and walk*. Then asked they him, What man is that which said unto thee, *Take up thy bed, and walk?*"

Acts 26:1-32 In this passage King Agrippa is referred to *by name* in vv. 1, 2, 7, 19, 27, 28, 32 and as "the king" in 13, 26, 30.

The translator must be alert as to whether or not such repetitions are natural in the RL. It cannot be assumed that because they were acceptable in Greek, they will also be acceptable in the RL. Larson (1969, p. 18) points out that the translator should make use of the forms of ellipsis permitted in the RL. She cites an example from Luke 5:5 which reads, ". . . Master, we have toiled all the night, and have taken nothing: nevertheless at thy word I will let down the net." In the immediately preceding verse, Jesus had said, ". . . let down your nets for a draught." The repetition was unnecessary in Aguaruna, a Peruvian language, so the words "let down the net" were represented by a pro-form, as in, "I will do thus," the exact content being clearly implied from what Jesus had already said. Again, in Aguaruna, Luke 1:18 (see above) may be translated by "We are both old," as the exclusive form of *we* includes Elizabeth, but not the angel, and *old* is equivalent to "well stricken in years." Ellipsis, deictic forms, etc., can be used in such contexts to maintain both exegetical fidelity *and* dynamic fidelity.

A second important feature of discourse is the way in which participants are introduced and then referred to. Languages often have specific ways of introducing new participants and of distinguishing these from references to participants already introduced.

A third feature of discourse is the way events are handled. There may be specific preferences for the *order* in which events are described, and, if not all the events are specified, a preference for events which are to be omitted and which included.

Self-evident information which is explicit in the original may be made implicit in the RL if it will still be clearly and immediately communicated. Such self-evident information should be made implicit especially when it detracts from the focus of the passage or when the readers consider the information so obvious that it appears to have been included only for children. The examples which follow are self-explanatory. The second and last examples more clearly illustrate self-evident information if one is aware that the only kind of honey in that culture is wild honey and that the question was raised as to where else the wheat could have been thrown.

Mark 1:6 "a girdle of a skin *about his loins* . . . ."

Mark 1:6 ". . . locusts and *wild* honey . . . ."

Luke 2:36, 37 ". . . *she was of a great age* . . . . a widow of about fourscore years . . . ."

Luke 5:13 ". . . he *put forth his hand*, and touched him . . . ."

Acts 27:38 ". . . and cast out the wheat *into the sea*."

3. *Components of meaning in words*

The analysis of meaning in terms of components is treated in detail in the next chapter. It is sufficient at this point to draw attention to the fact that components of words which are explicit in the Greek may be carried implicitly by the context in the RL.

A good example of this is given by Larson (1969, pp. 16 and 19). Greek has a considerable variety of words dealing with specific aspects of speaking — command, rebuke, exhort, ask, reply, warn, etc. Many languages do not have so many terms, but rather use the usual verb meaning "to say, speak, tell," with such particular components as "commanding, and rebuking," carried by the context, usually by what is actually said. Thus in Aguaruna, Luke 3:14 (RSV) "Soldiers also asked him, 'And we, what shall we do?'" becomes "The soldiers also *said*, 'What shall we do?'" Again, in Siriono (a Bolivian language), in Acts 27:22, "And now I *exhort* you to be of good cheer," it is sufficient to give the imperative, "Be of good cheer" — the component of "exhortation" is carried implicitly by the imperative.

Such explicit components are not confined to verbs. Just as Greek has a number of different words for speaking, so also in the New Testament there are many types of rulers mentioned — kings, governors, the emperor, proconsuls, etc. Such numerous distinctions are not made in many languages, which may have only one indigenous term, such as "chief." In such languages, the distinctions between kings and governors may be mentioned explicitly the first time and then carried implicitly by the term "chief." Thus, in Mark 6:14-29, where King Herod is referred to frequently, it may be best to put the equivalent for "king" in v. 14, where Herod is introduced into the narrative and then refer to him as "the chief" or "Herod" or "he" thereafter, according to the requirements of the language. The lexical component of "king" is then carried implicitly in the context.

WHEN MAY EXPLICIT INFORMATION BECOME IMPLICIT?

Since languages differ in their patterns of explicitness and implicitness, it is to be expected not only that some of the implicit information of the original would become explicit, but also that the reverse process would take place — some of the explicit information would become implicit.[11] For instance, it was discovered that in certain languages of Peru, if *God* was used in the RL every time it occurred in Genesis 1, the readers could only conclude that a number of different gods had been active in creation. The use of the proper name, rather than the equivalent of "he," indicated the introduction of a new participant into the narrative — in this case, therefore, a further god. So, just as failure to make implicit information explicit can lead to a distortion of the meaning of the Scriptures, so distortion can also arise from failure to make explicit information implicit.

The same question arises in this connection as it did in the discussion as to when implicit information may become explicit: "When can the explicit information of the original legitimately become implicit in the RL?" The answer is basically the same as given there. The general principle still holds that it is only permitted if the RL necessitates it, and if such a change makes implicit what otherwise was explicit without violating the principle of faithfulness to the meaning of the original.

The specific guidelines are quite similar. If the original has obligatory categories which the RL does not share, then it may well be that the meanings associated with those categories will be carried implicitly in the RL. If, for example, the RL nouns and verbs do not carry the category of number, then to insist on marking number in every noun and verb in the RL because Greek did so would be a gross violation of the normal use of the language; such information is carried explicitly in the RL only at certain points in the discourse structure, and implicitly elsewhere.

---

[11] This process is briefly mentioned in Beekman (1968b, p. 5): "Although we are not presenting examples of explicit information becoming implicit, one should not conclude that this change does not occur in the translation process." See also the footnote on p. 13 of the same article. Details are worked out in Larson, 1969. See also Taber (1970, p. 3), where he says, "Theoretically, cases may be found in which the translator . . . may leave implicit information which is explicit or implicit in the source."

Again, if retaining explicit information in the same form gives rise to wrong meaning, then it should be handled implicitly. The example of Genesis has already been given. Another arises from the statement made by the angel to Zacharias in the temple (Luke 1:13): "Fear not, Zacharias: for thy prayer is heard; and thy wife Elizabeth shall bear thee a son . . . ." If the phrase "thy wife Elizabeth" is kept in this form in Aguaruna (a Peruvian language) it is (a) unnatural, because her name has already been stated (vv. 5 and 7): and (b) it is misleading because such an expression implies that Zacharias had another wife whose name was not Elizabeth. Again, therefore, the translator must ask questions constantly to ascertain just what meaning is being conveyed to the RL readers and then make the appropriate adjustments to the RL form until the meaning matches that of the original.

Unnecessary explicit information may also give rise to obscurity, ambiguity, or excessive redundancy. The latter occurs more frequently than sometimes is realized. A glance through the examples and the accompanying comments in Larson (1969) will quickly show this. Some typical comments are: "putting *twelve* in v. 20 (i.e., Mark 14:20) would divert attention from the focus"; "to repeat it again . . . makes the passage heavy"; "to include more would detract from the flow of the message and make it unnatural." Every language has its own discourse patterns for ensuring a sufficiently redundant message; but, equally, it also has means available in its structure to avoid excessive redundancy. When the redundancy of the original is transferred to the RL, then it often gives rise to unnaturalness in this area.

In conclusion, it seems clear that translators will increasingly find that if dynamic faithfulness is to be achieved in a translation, one of the ways to do this is to make full use of the patterns of implicit information available in the RL. When explicit information is made implicit, there is no loss in content but there is an appreciable gain in communication, as the translation is not cluttered up with what is, from the RL standpoint, unnecessary explicit information.

CHAPTER 4

Analyzing the Components of Meaning of a Word

A word is a symbol which represents an area of experience or a part of one's environment. That which a word represents, that is to say, its meaning, can be divided into components. In the previous chapter, this fact was mentioned briefly in the context of implicit information. *Centurion*, for example, was spelled out as "a man who commands 100 soldiers." In this chapter, attention is focused on certain features of words which make it possible to discover the components of meaning associated with them. The procedure suggested for determining the components of meaning enables the translator to reach a more precise understanding or definition of the meaning of a word than would result from elicitation procedures alone. Further, in chapters 12 and 13, the subject of lexical equivalence is discussed, and the discussion there presupposes the theory and procedures discussed in this chapter.

SOME UNIVERSAL CHARACTERISTICS OF WORDS

Before the procedure for analyzing the components of meaning can be described, it is necessary to bring into focus certain universal features of vocabularies. An understanding of these features is important to the translator as he looks for ways of expressing accurately the concepts of the original which he is translating into the RL.

The components of meaning of a word

The experience or environment which a word symbolizes, regardless of how little or how much that experience or environment includes, is treated as a unit of meaning. These units are divisible into parts called *semantic components*. Semantic components are the building blocks that are joined together to give the meaning of a word; and they, as well as the words themselves, can be divided into four different classes. These are conveniently labeled Thing, Event, Abstraction, and Relation, abbreviated as T, E, A, R.[1]

Things are inanimate entities and animate beings (including supernatural beings) such as stone, tree, dog, man, ghost, devil. Events are actions and processes such as run, think, die, blacken. Abstractions include qualities and quantities, such as soft, red, round, many, quickly, unexpectedly. Relations are the relationships between any pair of T, E, or A, such as coordinate, simultaneous, sequential, attributive, agentive, part-whole, cause-effect.

To illustrate how words are made up of components of meaning, consider the word *island*, which may be defined as "land surrounded by water." There are three components of meaning in this definition. These three components may be listed and classed as: "land," a Thing; "water," another Thing; and "surrounded by," a Relation. Note, however, that two of these three are not simple components. "Land" and "water" are themselves made up of components. To define "land" and "water," would require the listing of such components of meaning. For example, form distinguishes land from water; the form of land is that of a solid while that of water is a liquid. Other significant components could be listed, but these are not analyzed here since our purpose is to show that an apparently simple word like *island* is semantically complex, that is to say, it consists of various components.

---

1 Probably the earliest analysis in terms of such classes is found in George Campbell's *The Philosophy of Rhetoric*, first published in 1776. A recent edition (1963) has been edited by Lloyd Bitzer and published by the Southern Illinois University Press. On page 385, Campbell labels the four semantic classes as (1) things, (2) operations, (3) attributes, and (4) connectives.

Gustaf Stern, in his *Meaning and Change of Meaning* (1931, p. 19), says, "Words are signs which name that for which they are signs: *table* is the name of an object, *red* of a quality, *run* of an activity, *over* of a relation."

Wilbur Urban, Susanne K. Langer, and Edward Sapir in 1939, 1942, and 1944 respectively, each proposed a set of labels to represent these basic classes of semantic elements.

More recently, E. A. Nida, in *Toward a Science of Translating* (1964, p. 62) speaks of four principal functional classes of lexical symbols, which he labels as object words, event words, abstracts and relationals.

The classification presented in this book is based upon the various authors mentioned above. "Thing" is used by Campbell and Langer; "Object" is used by Stern and Nida. Since "Object" is often confused with the grammatical use of the term "object," the term "Thing" has been chosen as preferable. "Event" is taken from Nida. For the third class, "Abstraction" is used rather than "Abstract" in order to avoid confusion with "abstract nouns," discussed in chapter 14. As used here, "Relation" refers to a semantic relationship between two items and "relational" refers to a word, case ending, or other device which signals a relation.

It should be noted that when a word is being classed as a member of one of the semantic classes, initial capitals will be used for the class label.

Even though the meanings of words are combinations of components, both words and their components may be classified as members of one of the four semantic classes. Referring again to the example of *island*, this word is classed as a Thing. Such a classification is justified by two observations. First, even though words are semantically complex, one of the components is nuclear. The nuclear component may be expressed by a generic term .which includes the meaning of the word. In this case "land" is nuclear. "Land" does not precisely mean *island*, but it is a generic term which includes the meaning of *island*. Land is land whether it takes the form of an island, a plain, or a desert. This generic term, however, lacks some specifications which distinguish island, plain, and desert. But it is this generic term which identifies the nuclear component of meaning in the word *island* and it is the nuclear component which is most important. In *island*, "land" is nuclear and "land" is a Thing.

Secondly, in context, *island* is used to refer to a Thing, in this case, an inanimate entity. Thus, both by identifying the nuclear component and by noting the referential function in context, it is possible to assign words to one of these four semantic classes.[2]

We summarize by repeating that words are generally semantically complex and consist of semantic components. These components are classified as T, E, A, or R, and combine to form the meaning of a word. The nuclear component, that is, the generic component, determines the semantic class to which a word belongs.

The generic-specific relation between words

When a word is compared with some other words in the same language, it can be described as generic or specific. For instance, *chair* may be classed as a specific term along with such words as table, wardrobe, cabinet, and cupboard. All of these words are specific items belonging to the generic class of *furniture*. But when *chair* is compared with such items as armchair, rocking chair, deck chair, and baby chair, it can then be classed as generic since all of these are specific items which belong to the generic class of *chairs*. In this way, *chair* is generic when related to different types of chairs and specific when related to different items of furniture. These two relationships can be diagrammed in the following way, in which the specific-generic relationship is regarded as a "vertical" one, with the more specific items lower down on the diagram and the more generic ones higher up.

2 This chapter focuses on the analysis of the semantic components found in a word. It could just as well speak of words as concepts. Any combination of semantic components with one that is nuclear constitutes a concept. The concept is classed by the class of its nuclear component. The non-nuclear components may also be classified as T, E, A, or R. Thus semantic components are classified as T, E, A, or R; concepts are also classified as T, E, A, or R. A concept is usually represented by a word in the grammar but may also be represented by a phrase.

DIAGRAM 1

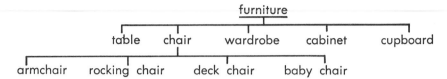

A second example is provided by the Event *to ask*. When *to ask* is grouped with such Events as to command, to reply, to rebuke, and to announce — it can be classed as specific. Each of these Events is included in the generic term *to speak*. But when *to ask* is compared with such Events as to beg, to plead, to implore, and to pray, it stands in a generic relationship to them, as each of these Events is a specific kind of asking. Again, the "vertical" or hierarchical relationships can be shown diagrammatically:

DIAGRAM 2

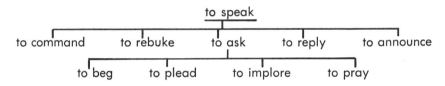

A more extended example of the generic-specific hierarchy begins at the top with the most generic word in one of the semantic classes, i.e., *a thing*, and then moves down through a line of increasingly specific terms to the word *angora*. It will be noted that when moving from the bottom toward the top, each term represents an increasingly more generic term which includes the meaning of the preceding term.

DIAGRAM 3

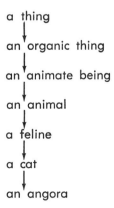

Notice also that, in these examples, all the words or phrases in a generic-specific list remain in the same semantic class. In other words, if the nuclear component is classed as an Event, the word itself will always be classed as an Event regardless of how many words may appear in the generic-specific hierarchy; if an Abstraction, always an Abstraction; if a Thing, always a Thing. While the meaning of a word may consist of various combinations of T, E, A, or R, the generic term covering that word will never have a nuclear component belonging to a different class.

Generic terms and expressions

We have illustrated a well-known relationship that exists in the vocabulary of all languages. Words may be specific or generic in relation to others. When a word is generic in relation to another, that word is not a synonym having the same meaning; however, since it does have a generic relationship, it represents part of the meaning of the more specific word. Since there is this overlap in meaning, the generic includes the meaning of the specific.

To find a generic term which includes the meaning of a specific word, one looks for a word or phrase in the same semantic class whose meaning is somewhat more general. Thus, a generic term for *chair* is "an item of furniture"; for *a rocker* is "a chair." Similarly for Events, a generic term to cover *to ask* is "to speak." A generic term that covers *to pray* is "to ask." The generic term lacks at least one specific component which is found in the more specific term. In these examples, the number of components of meaning that makes the specific term different in meaning from the generic are few in number. The equivalence in meaning, while not exact, is still close.

Sometimes, however, the difference is more than a question of one or two components of meaning. This is because languages do not always have one-word generic terms to represent every small set of words which are closely related semantically. This is not only true of aboriginal languages but also of languages with a long written tradition. For example, the verbs *to run, to jump, to walk, to swim* are obviously related semantically. However, the nearest generic term available in English to cover the verb *to run* is "to move." But *to move* is so generic that the difference in meaning between *to run* and *to move* is such that one can hardly be considered a close generic term covering the other. However, a generic term may be modified to draw its meaning closer to that of the specific term under consideration. Thus, *to move* may be modified as to its source of power, namely, by oneself; and then further as to its nature, that is, not rotating on an axis or moving back and forth, but moving from one place to another. The generic term for *to run* would then be modified into the expression "to move oneself from one place to another."

Notice further, that the English verb *to throw* does not seem, at first, to have a close generic term to cover it. However, the generic term *to propel* can be considered and when modified so as to read "to propel an object through space," gives a close generic expression.

Class labels and semantic sets

Up to this point we have not used the expression "semantic sets." However, the concept of semantic sets has already been introduced. Table, chair, wardrobe, cabinet, and cupboard is an example of a semantic set. The generic term *furniture* may be converted into a class label by adding the phrase "different items of" to give "different items of furniture." If one begins with a specific word, such as *chair* and then moves to the class label, "different kinds of chairs," a semantic set can then be produced such as the one containing *chair* listed above.

The function of class labels can also be illustrated with an example which makes use of an Event: *to speak* is a generic term which includes the Event *to ask*. The class label derived from *to speak* would be "different kinds of speaking (with focus on purpose)."[3] However, when *to ask* is considered as a generic term, then the corresponding class label "different kinds of asking" can be formed. Each class label can be used to produce a semantic set as diagramed earlier. The expression *semantic set* is used, therefore, to describe a group of words which are specific relative to one another, and to which a "class label" may be attached to identify them as a group. A generic term is utilized to make a class label such as "different types of (generic term)." Such a label facilitates the listing of members of a semantic set. Thus, if the word *to beg* were being analyzed, the generic class label, "different kinds of asking," may be used to produce a semantic set of at least to beg, to plead, to implore, and to pray.

Since the vocabulary of all languages is structured with generic and specific terms, one may expect to find generic terms or expressions for the specific terms of a language. While it is true that languages will differ as to the number of one-word generic terms used and will also differ as to what specific concepts are included under each generic term, yet, since the generic terms available can be modified (as was done for the English verbs *to move* and *to propel*), one may expect, as stated above, to be able to construct generic expressions which include the more specific terms of a language.

This characteristic of the vocabulary of all languages, i.e., that words are in a generic-specific relationship, makes it possible to state class labels which can be used to list words that are related semantically. This in turn makes it possible to determine the components of meaning of a particular word. For example, the translator who works with the Manobo language in the Philippines was searching for a term to translate the concept of "to blaspheme." He started with the generic term *to criticize*, modified this with a manner component, and arrived at the generic

---

[3] This generic class is labeled in this way to distinguish it from the generic class which may be labeled "different kinds of speaking (with focus on manner)" which would have such members as murmur, shout, stammer, etc.

expression, "to criticize by speech." With this generic expression he asked his language helper for different kinds of verbal activity whereby one could criticize another. This produced a semantic set of eight words some of which had not before been encountered. Comparing and contrasting the meaning of each of these words revealed significant components which were essential in choosing an accurate equivalent for the biblical term "to blaspheme."[4] The generic-specific character of the vocabulary of each language may be utilized to advantage by the translator to arrive at a more explicit and thus a more accurate understanding of important terms used in his translation.

It may be objected that the construction of generic expressions is a purely arbitrary exercise on the part of the investigator. For example, it could be pointed out that a language may have a generic term which covers fish, turtles, and crocodiles, while another generic term covers birds, insects, lizards, and cattle. Hence, it could be argued that if a class label were set up which corresponded to the English label, "different kinds of insects," it would be an arbitrary one and in conflict with the way the speakers of this particular language already classify their environment.

In answer to this objection, it must be pointed out that the translator is expected to work with a native speaker when analyzing his language. He will not arrive at generic expressions without the corrective interaction of a mature speaker of the language. However, suppose that in the above language the generic term for birds, insects, lizards, and cattle was modified into an expression which produced a semantic set consisting only of different insects. Such a step would be taken for the purpose of learning more about insects or about a particular insect such as the locust. Contrasting the names in the set would show likenesses and differences which would accomplish the purpose intended by the class label and the semantic set it produced. The desired information about a particular insect as well as about similar insects would have been gained.

It is not surprising that the above results would be achieved. The class label for *insects*, although not a single generic term, would not be purely arbitrary. Even though all animate beings that live on the land (with man excepted) may be grouped together under one generic label, this does not obscure the distinction between different species of animate beings. The speakers of such a language clearly distinguish between birds, insects, lizards, and cattle. They may not have a term to distinguish these groups, but their language is such that they can classify with an expression any real-world distinction which they observe and want to make. Therefore, it is not impossible for a native speaker to classify, or to accept an expression which classifies, a segment of his experience or environment which he conceptualizes as a legitimate grouping. That kind of innovative classification would supplement the existing classifications without introducing a conflict. When implied classifications with-

4 See Elkins (1971b, pp. 10-15) for a fuller treatment of his procedures and results.

in the structure of a language are made explicit, the native speakers accept these with interest and even delight.

In summary, then, it can be seen that a word which is specific in its "upward" relationships may also be generic in its "downward" relationships. On the basis of these structural features of the lexicon, it is possible to analyze a word[5] by postulating a class label for a semantic set to which it belongs, finding out other members of the same set, and then contrasting and comparing those members to arrive at the components of meaning of the word being investigated.

Meaning, sense, and collocates

In introducing this chapter, we mentioned that the area of experience or the segment of one's environment symbolized by a word may be divided into components of meaning. This is a statement which needs to be modified inasmuch as a single word may symbolize more than one area of experience or different segments of one's environment, whether large or small. Each such distinct area of reference symbolized by a word is called a *sense* of that word. For example, the word *dress* in "they dress themselves quickly" means "put clothes on," but in "she will dress the chickens for dinner" it means "pluck and clean in readiness for cooking." These two different areas of experience are symbolized by the same word, so that it is said that *dress* has (at least) two senses.[6]

This example illustrates the fact that one cannot speak of analyzing the components of meaning of the word *dress* since different areas of experience are involved. One of the areas of experience symbolized by *dress* must be chosen before the components of meaning which combine to give that sense can be analyzed. Hence, before the components of meaning of a word may be studied, it must first be determined whether the word has only one sense, or several.

Any word will occur in a variety of contexts in the language. It may have the same sense in all of these contexts, or a number of different senses. *Bungalow* is an example of a word with one sense only. Even though it is used in a variety of contexts, such as "He has just bought a new bungalow," "Yes, I pass that bungalow every day," "The police searched the bungalow for clues to the murder," "That bungalow has stood vacant for a long time," no new senses are introduced; it has the same sense in each context.

The verb *to dress* has already been shown to have two senses. Now consider some further contexts in which *to dress* is found:

[5] Or an expression, if it functions semantically as a unit. For example, in the statement, "he paid through the nose for that plot of land," the expression "through the nose" is functioning as an abstraction, qualifying "paid" (more or less equivalent to "exorbitantly").

[6] As used here, different *senses* are confined to usages of a word which are in the same semantic class. In the example cited, for example, both senses of *dress* are Events. The word *dress* in "she wore her new dress," however, is a different type of additional sense because it is a Thing. Different usages which fall into different semantic classes are considered in the next chapter.

to dress timber	to dress the hair
to dress a wound	to dress ranks
to dress a salad	to dress a shop window

Note that in each of the above contexts *to dress* is associated with a different sense. For this particular verb, the significant context for its different senses is that of its grammatical object. If the object is "a wound," then the sense is "clean and bandage" that wound; if it is "a shop window," then the sense is "to arrange in an attractive manner." The significant words associated with *to dress* in these contexts ("timber," "wound," "salad," etc.) are referred to as its *collocates*, so we can say that each sense is associated with a particular collocate, such as "ranks," or a set of collocates, such as "himself," "herself," "oneself," "the child," "the doll," etc.

The meaning of the Event *to dress* consists of all its different senses. A particular sense of *to dress* is that area of experience referred to when it occurs with one particular set of collocates (a set may have only one member). It becomes quite evident that *context* — more specifically, the collocates of the word under analysis — is basic in determining whether a word has a meaning consisting of several senses or of only one. When the senses have been worked out, then the generic term or expression which includes that sense may be determined.

Before leaving this example, which shows the significance of context in making sense distinctions, it is important to note that all of the collocates in this list were quite distinct. When collocates in a list belong to the same semantic set, then those collocates indicate only one sense distinction. Thus, as will be seen later in this chapter, the word *run* collocates with stream, water, faucet, eye, etc. Since all of these, in the context of *run*, refer to liquids, only one sense is posited for these different collocates.

THREE KINDS OF COMPONENTS OF MEANING[7]

The sense of a word consists of a number of meaning components, and the study of the members in a semantic set is a convenient way to arrive at a knowledge of these components. The components of meaning are analyzed as consisting of three different types. There is a generic component, specifying components, and incidental components.[8]

---

[7] The three kinds of components of meaning discussed in the following paragraphs refer to the referential meanings of words. Connotational meanings are not analyzed in this chapter and although not part of the referential meaning of a word are an important aspect of any communication.

[8] Cf. the definition of "definition" in Rubinstein and Weaver (1966, p. 6): "Definition is the process of placing a word (or *term*) into a family (or *genus*) and then separating the word from the other members of the family by showing the difference (or *differentia*). Example: A catalytic agent (*Term*) is a chemical (*Genus*) which quickens the reaction of other chemicals, but is itself unchanged (*Differentia*)."

The generic component

The generic component is the component of meaning *shared by each member of the semantic set*.[9] Thus, every member of the semantic set consisting of chair, table, cupboard, etc. has, as one component, "item of furniture." Naturally, since this component is shared by *all* members of the set, it does not distinguish one member from another, but only from members of other sets, such as "types of buildings in which people live," which has members such as house, bungalow, cottage, etc. Similarly, all the members of the semantic set with the label "different kinds of asking" have the common generic component "to ask." For example, "to pray" is "to ask God."

In discussing the generic-specific relationships that exist in every language, consideration was given to generic terms or expressions. Since a generic term or expression is the same as the generic component, it will not be amiss, even at the risk of repetition, to give examples.

Suppose the investigator has run across the event, "to tell lies," and wishes to analyze its components of meaning. He thinks of a more generic way of stating the meaning, a way that would include "to tell lies," but could also include other similar words. A generic term might be "to deceive." This generic term becomes the generic component for the event "to lie" as well as for other ways one may deceive.[10] Similarly, to analyze "to steal," a generic expression might be "to obtain possession of something." Note that even though one is aware that stealing is socially unacceptable or morally bad, this feature has not been included. This is because, in stating the generic expression, an attempt is made to find one which will be true of several other words as well. If it is too narrow, it will not generate a useful list; if, on the other hand, it is too generic and thus too inclusive, it will generate too large a group of words for easy analysis. In stating the generic term or expression, one attempts to find the next higher useful rank of generic expression. If the only generic term available is remote from the specific, as, for example, *thing* for *eel*, then the term must be made more specific by modification. The purpose of such modifications is to narrow the range of the generic term so that it will focus only on other eel-like creatures. *Thing* could be modified as "things which live in the water" or "long stick-like things that live in the water." Such modifications will lead to a semantic set with members which are useful in coming to know more precisely just what an eel is.

A word has only one generic component but usually several specifying and incidental components. The generic component is basic to the statement of any generic class label.

---

[9] Cf. Rubinstein and Weaver (1966, p. 24): "Classification applies a single, defined consistent factor to all members of a group in order to assign the members to smaller groups. The factor is called *the basis of classification.*"

[10] Some words enter into more than one significant hierarchical structure. *To tell lies*, for example, can be classified under the generic label "ways of deceiving" and also under "ways of speaking."

Specifying components

Associated with each member of a semantic set there are "specifying" (or "contrastive" or "distinctive") components. However, before these specifying components may be fully determined, use must be made of the generic class label to generate a closed set of related words — the generic class or semantic set. For example, the generic class label, "different kinds of bodies of water," will generate a list including such words as harbor, bay, cove, sea, fjord, estuary, etc. The generic class label, "different ways to obtain possession of something," would generate a class with such members as to earn, to inherit, to find, to be given, etc.

The specifying components are those components which give each member of the semantic set its distinctiveness, as contrasted with each of the other members of that set. For example, in the generic class labeled "different types of furniture," the item *chair* differs from *table* or *cupboard* in its purpose — a chair is for sitting on, tables and cupboards are not. Under the generic class label, "different kinds of bodies of water," the item *lake* differs from *sea* in that a lake is fresh water, the sea is salt. It differs from *harbor* in purpose — a harbor is a place where ships may load and unload, but a lake is not. The specifying components of words both of the original and of the RL, are very important for the translator as it is these components he is expected to match when translating.[11]

Incidental components

Incidental (or supplementary) components are those which are present in some contextual usages but not in all. They are not needed to define a member of a semantic set since they are neither part of the generic component nor of the specifying components. Thus, to use the example of *chair* again, as a member of the class of "furniture," the material of which it is made is incidental, as also is its color. The presence or absence of arms is likewise incidental. None of these features is necessary to distinguish *chair* from the other members of the class of "furniture," such as *table*, etc.

Relativity in classifying components

What constitutes a generic, a specifying, or an incidental component is relative to the level being focused on within the generic-specific hierarchy. As one moves down the hierarchy, incidental components become specifying components. For example, such components as the presence or absence of arms are incidental components when *chair* is being classified as a specific item under the generic term *furniture*; but these same components become specifying components when *chair* is taken as the generic term and different kinds of chairs are being classified. Conversely, as one moves up the generic-specific hierarchy, specifying com-

---

[11] For a detailed discussion of this point see chapters 12 and 13 (on lexical equivalence).

ponents become incidental components. Thus, when classifying *chair* under the generic term furniture, the component "to sit on" is a specifying component; but if *furniture* is taken as a specific term and is classified under the generic term *human artifacts*, then the component "to sit on" becomes an incidental component.

CONCLUSION

The procedure suggested in this chapter is based on certain universal linguistic features. All languages have generic and specific words. All languages have words which are semantically related by sharing a generic component of meaning. With the help of a speaker of the language, it is therefore possible to begin with a specific word, find a generic word or expression with which a set of other related specific words may be elicited, and then compare and contrast the words in such a set to specify the differences in meaning between each word. Or one can begin with a generic term of a known semantic set to accomplish the same purpose. It is hoped that the reader will not have lost sight of the fact that the relationship between generic and specific terms, as a means of analyzing in depth the meaning of words, may be utilized whether one begins with a specific term, a generic term, or a set of related terms.

As the previous chapters have emphasized and this chapter has assumed, the translator is constantly concerned with *meaning*, both that of the original and that of the RL. In the context of the RL, he is concerned with every item in the RL vocabulary. To talk the language, he should, ideally, be able to use each item in the range of contexts that the native speakers use it. If he is concerned with the publication of a dictionary of the RL, again, ideally, he should know the components of each sense of each word. But his primary task is translation, and here it is essential that he should have a detailed and thorough knowledge of the RL vocabulary.

Such is the ideal, but it is tempered by the fact that the translation is to be completed within a reasonable time, which makes it difficult to achieve the ideal. Further, the translation of the New Testament will make use of only a portion of the total vocabulary of the RL so that the translator is especially concerned with less than the whole of the vocabulary.

In the process of translation, the translator finds that he is particularly interested in *contrasts* in meaning. He is constantly making choices between lexical alternatives so as to match the original meaning,[12] which

---

[12] This statement carries the implication with it that the translator knows the components of meaning of the words used in the original. In the context of translating the NT, it implies that he knows the components of meaning of the Greek words used there. He especially needs to know what the contrasts are between related words, and whether they are significant in a particular context. Do *ginōskō* and *oidamai* differ — if so, how? Is there a contrast between *agapaō* and *phileō*? Are *allos* and *heteros* different or not? Arndt and Gingrich (1957) have rendered the translator an inestimable service with their Greek-English lexicon, but even they do not tackle the question of differences and contrasts between the lexical items. The basic approach

means that he is interested in the components of the alternatives, and where they differ from each other. It is just at this point that the method of using generic classes, discussed in this chapter, yields results. It is essentially a methodology of *contrast*. Hence, it is invaluable to the translator as he makes his lexical choices.

The translator is often alerted to semantic sets to be investigated when native speakers suggest alternatives to a word or expression he has used in a draft of his translation. Clearly, then, these related terms are well worth investigating, so that his choices will not be based on an incomplete knowledge of the components.

Quite apart from alternatives that arise in the course of checking, or in translation itself, the translator knows he is going to have to make choices between terms in such classes as "different kinds of emotions," "different sins," "different virtues," "different ways of thinking," etc. So, while it is probably impracticable to expect to make a thorough study of the whole of the RL vocabulary in this way, it is by no means impracticable for a translator to investigate all of the important terms of the translation. By so doing, he is much more likely to avoid the common error of "collocational clashes" (see chapter 11) and will also be in an excellent position to represent correctly key terms of Scripture by providing good lexical equivalences" (see chapters 12 and 13).

---

presented in this chapter may also be applied to a study of the words of the Greek N.T. The number of contexts showing the various senses may not be as numerous as one might wish and the impossibility of receiving reactions and information from a live speaker of the language will result in conclusions which are less certain than desired. Nevertheless, such studies would be a valuable area for research and publication which would greatly help the translator.

CHAPTER 5

An Analysis of RUN and BUNGALOW

An Analysis of the Components of Meaning in Run
  Listing the word in all of its contexts
  Finding the generic class of the collocates
  Regrouping the contexts according to the collocates which belong
    to the same generic class
  Stating the generic class of each sense
  Stating the generic component by combining the generic term or
    expression of each sense with its collocational restriction
  Stating the generic class label for each sense
  Generating a semantic set for each sense
  Establishing the specifying components
  Checking to see that no extraneous members are included in the
    semantic set
An Analysis of the Components of Meaning in Bungalow
Diagrams of the Analysis of Run and Bungalow

The translator needs to be fully aware of the components of meaning associated with each word he uses, otherwise he is likely to place it in contexts where the components "clash" with those of other words in the same context, or in contexts where the components do not match the components in the original. In either case the message is affected adversely. The following detailed example is given, therefore, to illustrate the application of the foregoing chapter.

An Analysis of the Components of Meaning in Run

The first word to be considered is *run(s)*, a member of the Event class. Other forms of this verb, such as *ran* and *running*, are not being considered in this example for two reasons. One is to keep the example within reasonable bounds and relatively uncomplicated; the other is because, in principle, each distinctive form of a verb, or noun, or whatever word class is being investigated, should be treated separately, as differences in form may correlate with differences in meaning. Similarly, transitive and intransitive uses of a verb, or the active and passive uses of a verb, should be kept separate until investigation has shown whether they have the same components or not. Further, so far as this English example is concerned, prepositional constructions with *run(s)* will not be considered, e.g., such combinations as "*run for* office," "*run up* a bill," "*run into* difficulties," "*run away from* reality," "*run across* a friend," etc. These would need to be studied separately in an analysis of English. Finally, what might be termed "technical" uses of *run(s)* are omitted, i.e., uses basically confined to a specialist community. Thus, "fish run" is omitted, as it is considered part of the specialized language of fishermen.

In the example, the steps are numbered and labeled for clarity, so that an investigator may work through them methodically when studying the lexicon of another language. Also, for orthographic convenience, *run* will be used to represent the two present tense forms "run" and "runs."

Step 1. *Listing the word in all of its contexts*

Having narrowed the investigation down to *run*, the first step is to list all the contexts in which this form has been found.[1] Since *run* is being studied in some of its intransitive uses, the context will focus on the grammatical subject of the verb, as in the following list.

The bird runs	The paint runs
The boy runs	The solder runs
The car runs	The sore runs
The dog runs	The stocking runs
The eye runs	The stream runs
The faucet (or tap) runs	The ivy runs
The horse runs	The watch runs
The jelly runs	The woman runs
The nose runs	The bean plant runs

Step 2. *Finding the generic class of the collocates*

The second step is to study the collocates of *run*. In particular, do they appear to belong to a number of different generic classes? If the collocates belong to different generic classes, this often signals a shift in sense. Different senses of a word will collocate with words belonging to different generic classes. With the above contexts, the following generic classes are initially postulated:

1. Animals (bird, dog, horse)
2. Humans (boy, woman)
3. Parts of the body (eye, nose, sore[2])
4. Solids (jelly, solder)
5. Liquids (faucet[3], paint, stream)
6. Vines (ivy, bean plant)
7. Knitted clothing (stocking)
8. Mechanical objects (car, watch)

[1] A field methodology, by which such contexts can be obtained, is outlined in chapter 11.

[2] One could also class "sore" separately under "injuries to the body."

[3] "Faucet" is included under "liquids," as it is used, by metonymy, for the liquid passing through it, just as "kettle" is for the water in it, in the expression, "The kettle is boiling."

As these generic classes are studied, it might well be felt that there was no essential difference between humans running and animals running, so these could be combined. Again, when we speak in English of eyes, or noses, or sores running, the reference is to some type of liquid issuing from these as source, so that "parts of the body" and "liquids" could be combined. The same is true of the solids mentioned — the term *run* only collocates with them when they are in a liquid state, i.e., it is presupposed that they have melted. If these various decisions are taken, we find *run* collocated with the following generic classes:

1. Animals and humans, i.e., animate beings with legs (birds, dogs, horses, boys, women)
2. Liquids (stream, paint, faucet, eye, nose, sore, jelly, solder)
3. Vines (ivy, bean plant)
4. Knitted clothing (stocking)
5. Mechanical objects (car, watch)

At this point, take each generic class that has been postulated, and examine either all the words which belong to the same generic class or a fully representative sampling if it is large. Check that each of these words can be used as the subject of *run*, and that the sense of *run* in this context is in fact the same as for the words first examined. If a new sense is discovered, those words which have a different generic class should be separated from the others. If some of the words do not collocate properly with *run*, then attempt to modify the generic class so that these words will be eliminated, i.e., they will no longer share the same generic component. This proviso applies to the last class listed above, "mechanical objects." A bicycle is a mechanical object, but it does not collocate with *run*. Hence, the class "mechanical objects" needs to be stated more specifically, that is, with more restrictions on it. This can be done by expressing the generic class as "mechanical objects which are self-powered." Practical considerations will determine the degree of exactness in stating the generic class of a set of collocates. Sometimes the analyst may wisely choose to exercise flexibility in the degree of detail to be considered in noting collocational limitations since many generalizations are likely to have some exceptions. For example, caterpillars are animate beings with legs, and yet they do not run. When the exceptions are few, the practical value of such generic classes is not affected.

Step 3. Regrouping the contexts according to the collocates which belong to the same generic class

These divisions suggest the number of different senses which the word *run* carries in these contexts, that is to say, to each of the five generic classes suggested above, there corresponds a different sense.

Animate beings with legs:
    The bird runs.
    The boy runs.

The dog runs.
The horse runs.
The woman runs.

Liquids:
The nose runs.
The faucet runs.
The stream runs.
The sore runs.
The eye runs.
The paint runs.
The solder runs.
The jelly runs.

Vines:
The ivy runs.
The bean plant runs.

Knitted Clothing:
The stocking runs.

Self-powered mechanical objects:
The watch runs.
The car runs.

Step 4. Stating the generic class of each sense

Having sorted out the collocates of *run* according to those which belonged to the same generic classes of nouns, the fourth step is to state the generic class of verbs to which each sense of *run* belongs. We will not expect to find a single generic term to express the generic class for every sense that this or any other word represents. Of course, if one is available, it will be used, but we will often need to make use of generic expressions. No language has a generic term to cover every small set of related words. Nevertheless, the language may describe by means of phrases how certain words are related even though a single generic term is not available. As mentioned previously, it is this feature of language which makes it possible to state the generic class both of the word under study and the words with which it may collocate.

Run, in its first set of contexts, is a specific kind of movement. The generic component of *run* will refer not only to the word *run* but also to related words which speak of movement. The generic expression which covers those words with which *run* collocates in the first set of contexts is "animate beings with legs." We note, therefore, that this movement is not in one location as would be true of a branch moving in the wind, nor is it movement in a conveyance. A generic label for the sense of run in this context would therefore be "self-locomotion." In the second context (liquids), there is only the general sense of "movement"; in the third context (vines), it refers to a particular form of "growing"; in the fourth context (knitted clothing), it refers to a type of "damage"; and in the fifth context (self-powered mechanical objects), it signifies that the object concerned "is working."

Thus, a listing of the generic terms or expressions covering each sense of *to run* would be:

1. to move oneself from one place to another
2. to move
3. to grow
4. to become damaged
5. to work (function)

Step 5. Stating the generic component by combining the generic term or expression of each sense with its collocational restriction

The next step is to combine the generic term or expression of each sense with its collocates so that a closer generic component may be reached. The generic term of each sense in its present form is not yet useful to state a class label. The generic terms of the collocates need to be added. These represent a distributional characteristic of the word *run* in each of its senses. This distributional restriction represents part of the meaning of each sense and suggests the kind of modification needed to give the generic component of each sense. Combining the generic term of each sense with the generic term of the collocate gives the generic component for each sense as follows:

1. to move oneself from one place to another (of animate beings with legs)
2. to move (of liquids)
3. to grow (of vines)
4. to become damaged (of knitted clothing)
5. to work (of self-powered mechanical objects)

Step 6. Stating the generic class label for each sense

To convert a generic component into a class label, expressions such as "kinds of," "items of," or "ways of" may be added to it. Sometimes the use of synonyms or paraphrases helps to express the class label clearly. The class labels for each sense of *run* may thus be stated as follows:

1. kinds of self-locomotion of animate beings with legs
2. kinds of movement of liquids
3. ways in which vines grow
4. ways in which damage occurs in knitted clothing
5. ways in which self-powered mechanical objects work

Step 7. Generating a semantic set for each sense

The generic components do not specify the different components of meaning which are essential to a proper understanding of the word *run* in its various contexts. However, they do prepare us to elicit additional words which share the same generic components. Beginning with the generic component of the first sense of *run*, i.e., "self-locomotion of animate beings with legs," we ask for different ways other than *run* by which animate beings with legs may move themselves from one place to another. Such words as walk, swim, jump, etc. will be received. In asking for the movement of liquids we will receive such words as drips, leaks, sprays, splashes, pours, flows, squirts, etc. For the growth of vines we may ask how vines grow and receive such answers as straight down (as a hanging vine), climbing, etc. In asking what may happen to knitted clothing to damage or make it defective, we may receive such answers as tears, rips, is cut, wears, etc. However, when we come to the fifth generic component, no suitable members may be generated. All that can be found are synonyms for *run* such as *work* or *function*. For the contexts given, the sense of *run* is only found by synonyms or by being paraphrased. The generic component with which this sense of *run* is associated does not generate additional class members. This one-member class may be analyzed further, however, in terms of its synonyms to determine the range of acceptable collocations for each. If this is done, it will be found that *function* and *work* collocate more freely than *run*.

Step 8. Establishing the specifying components

Now that these semantic sets have been obtained by elicitation, the eighth step is to study the members of each set to deduce the specifying components of each member, and, in particular, of the word under investigation, *run*. This will now be done for each of the different senses of *run*.

(a) *Generic component*: to move oneself from one place to another (of animate beings with legs)

   Class members: run, walk, swim, jump, climb, etc.

As members are contrasted in pairs, the specifying components become clear. Thus *run* contrasts with *walk* in that it is more rapid, and when running, both feet leave the surface for a part of each cycle of movement, whereas in walking this is not so. *Run* contrasts with *swim* in that it is on a solid surface, whereas swimming presupposes a liquid medium. *Run* differs from *jump* in having a repeated alternate leg movement, whereas in jumping there is a single, quick motion in which both legs leave the surface, usually at the same time. Also *run* presupposes a forward movement, *jump* an upward movement.[4]

Further contrasts produce no new components for this sense of *run*, so the specifying components may now be listed as:

[4] It is interesting to note at this point that, in a particular collocation, one or more components may be canceled. Thus you can "run in place" and the forward movement component of *run* is canceled. The translator should be alert to contexts in which components may be canceled in the RL, and where they may not. For example, Romans 12:1 speaks of a "living sacrifice," where the component of "putting to death" in sacrifice is canceled by the collocation with "living." In Chol, however, this particular component of sacrifice cannot be thus canceled since the word for "sacrifice" in Chol explicitly includes death. Therefore, the expression had to be handled as a simile. In this way, the component of actual death was metaphorized.

1. repeated alternate use of both legs
2. both feet leave the ground during the cycle
3. progress is forward (unless specified differently)
4. rate is rapid
5. motion is on a solid surface

At this point, it is often useful to generalize these components, so that the other members of the class may also be stated in terms of them. For example, *run* and *jump* were contrasted in that *run* involves repeated alternate leg movements, whereas *jump* involves a single, quick leg movement, usually simultaneous. *Walk* is like *run* in that both presuppose alternate leg movements. The first specifying component listed for *run* may be generalized to "motion of legs relative to each other." Reasoning similarly, the second specifying component may be stated generally as "motion of legs relative to the surface." When this is done for the five specifying components of *run*, it gives:

1. Motion of legs relative to each other
2. Motion of legs relative to the surface
3. Direction of movement
4. Intensity of movement
5. Location of movement

One use to which these five generalized forms of the specifying components may be put is in charting the specifying components for each member sharing the generic component. This is done in one of the charts at the end of the chapter.

Another use is to combine these more generalized forms of the specifying components with the actual specifying components to give an accurate statement of meaning. The specifying components of this first sense of *run* may now be stated as follows:

1. Motion of legs relative to each other: alternate
2. Motion of legs relative to the surface: off for part of cycle
3. Direction of movement: forward
4. Intensity of movement: rapid
5. Location of movement: on a solid surface

(b) *Generic component*: to move (of liquids)
   Class members: run, drip, leak, spray, splash, pour, flow, squirt, etc.

Contrasting *run* with the other members of this class, we see that *run* implies an unbroken stream of liquid, as compared with *drip*. When *run* is compared with *splash* and *spray*, it is seen that the latter two imply movement through space in any upward or outward direction but *run* implies following a path usually downward but always that affording the least resistance. *Squirt* presupposes some sort of orifice through which the liquid is forced for a short time or intermittently through space under pressure. *Leak* may be a connected or a broken stream. It contrasts with *run* in that a leak represents a malfunction permitting liquid to go through where it is intended to be completely obstructed, whereas *run* is neutral, applying to the movement of liquid both where it may or may not be desired. Thus the components of run in this sense are:

1. Form of the liquid: an unbroken stream
2. Direction of movement: follows course of least resistance, usually down
3. Location of movement: where intended or not and along a surface (unless falling down through space as off a roof or through a faucet)

In this class, *run* and *flow* are synonymous since they give no contrast, and can be substituted for one another in many contexts where movement of liquids is referred to.[5]

(c) *Generic component*: to grow (of vines)
    Class members: run, climb, grow straight down

Here the contrasts are much fewer, so that the components of *run* are simply:

1. Location relative to surface: in contact (contrast "straight down")
2. Direction of movement: relatively horizontal (contrast "climb")

(d) *Generic component*: to become damaged (of knitted clothing)
    Class members: run, tear, rip, be cut, wear, etc.

The contrasts are again more complex as was the case with the members of the class "kinds of movement of liquids." Each of the defects is related to the threads from which the material is made, but, apart from *run*, the other terms presuppose a fairly large number of adjacent threads which are damaged, whereas *run* assumes one or only a few. Again, they contrast as to how the threads were damaged: *run* implies a snapping due to tension, as also do *tear* and *rip*, whereas *cut* implies a sharp instrument, and *wear* assumes a process of friction. *Run* also has the further implication of raveling along the length of the garment, which is absent from the others. Thus, the components of *run* in this sense are:

1. Number of threads damaged: usually one, seldom more than a few threads
2. Cause of defect: thread(s) broken due to tension
3. Kind of defect: a broken thread and stitches come undone along the length of the garment

[5] It is likely that in any case in which two words are synonymous within a given context, it is because the meaning components which would differentiate between them are incidental components within that context. Given a different context, the differentiating components would again become significant and the two words would no longer be synonymous.

Note that, in this context, *tear* and *rip* are synonymous since each of the three components is the same in each word, i.e., many adjacent threads break due to tension.

(e) *Generic component*: to work (of self-powered mechanical objects)
   Class members: run

There are no contrasts to make. The word *run* in this sense has synonyms "to work," "to function," and antonyms, but no useful semantic set may be established.

Step 9. Checking to see that no extraneous members are included in the semantic set

The final step is to check that there are no members of the semantic set which should have been excluded. Thus, the first semantic set had the class label, "kinds of self-locomotion of animate beings with legs," so that terms like "slither" were excluded, as this is a motion without using legs.

Further words, which can be described in terms of one another, should be excluded, for this implies that one of the terms is a generic term for another more specific class. Thus, *stroll* may be described as "walking slowly and aimlessly," *limp* as "walking, depending primarily on one leg," *march* as "walking with regular or rhythmic steps," *tiptoe* as "walking quietly on one's toes," etc. Hence, terms such as stroll, limp, march, tiptoe, etc., should not be included in the same semantic set as *walk*, since they can be described in terms of *walk*. They belong rather to the more specific class label "ways in which humans walk." On the other hand, *run* cannot be described in terms of *walk*, nor vice versa, thus, they can belong to the same semantic set.

By the method of trial and error, the investigator has therefore to try to ensure that the class label (a) is not so general that the set becomes unwieldy; (b) is not so small as to yield no useful contrasts; (c) does not include terms which are really more specific varieties of another term already in the class.

One of the best ways to check whether the number of senses assigned to a word is correct is to ask a native speaker to replace the word being studied by a synonym or paraphrase. Using the example of *run* again, the following substitutions would confirm the analysis into different senses.

The boy runs	The boy goes faster than fast walking
The eye runs	A pus-like liquid is coming out of the eye
The solder runs	The solder has melted and is flowing
The stocking runs	A thread has broken and the stitches have raveled
The ivy runs	The shoots of the ivy are growing along a surface
The motor runs	The motor works

Then, to check whether an adequate analysis has been made of the specifying components of a sense carried by the word, list the components and ask a native speaker to give the corresponding term. If a mature native speaker cannot supply the term, or, alternatively, can suggest several nonsynonymous alternatives, then this is an indication to the analyst that components have been wrongly analyzed, or, more likely, that some specifying component has been overlooked.

AN ANALYSIS OF THE COMPONENTS OF MEANING IN BUNGALOW

The previous example, *run*, illustrated the analysis of a term from the Event class, with a number of distinct senses, and this may have given the impression that this type of analysis into components is only useful for words of this type. But the method may equally well be applied to members of the Thing class, and also where the term under consideration has only one sense. The word *bungalow* has both of these characteristics.

For a word known to have only one sense, steps 1 through 5 do not apply, as they are procedures for discovering and analyzing multiple senses. The first step, then, for the word *bungalow* is to state a suitable generic class label by means of which we can obtain a semantic set and then the specifying components. The first generic class label that tends to come to mind is "types of buildings," but this is very generic and would include too many items such as airplane hangars and tool sheds. So it is better to find a generic class label closer to the word under study. In this example, the scope may be narrowed by adding further components to give "types of buildings in which humans live" or "types of houses in which people live." This generic class will give, in addition to *bungalow*, cottage, cabin, apartment house, mansion, palace, manse, etc. In addition, *house* itself is a member of the class — that is to say, *house* is both part of the class label and a particular member of the class.[6]

When these items are contrasted with one another, certain specifying components come into focus. *Mansion* and *palace* are large buildings; *bungalow, cottage* and *cabin* are small; with the others size is not in focus. An *apartment house* is a multiple-residence building, but none of the others are. *Manse* and *palace* are basically residences associated with an official position — that of the minister of a church for *manse*, that of a king, or president, or governor in the case of *palace*. A *palace*, however, is always large and elaborate, whereas a *manse* may be any type of dwelling — even an apartment — depending on such circum-

---

[6] This type of double role is not uncommon and occurs in other languages also. Another example in English is the word *man*. In its generic sense *man* refers to all mankind including men, women, boys, and girls; in its specific sense, *man* refers to a part of mankind, i.e., an adult male. The same term represents the generic class as well as one of its members. This semantic feature can cause the analyst considerable initial difficulties, as the language helper appears to be self-contradictory; sometimes he is focusing on the term in its generic use, sometimes on the term in its specific use.

stances as its location (city or country), the wealth of the congregation, whether it is a new or old building, etc.

Up to this point, the analysis leaves *bungalow, cottage,* and *cabin* sharing the same specific components, viz., small, separate, nonofficial buildings. How, then, are they distinguished? At this point, it is necessary to recognize (1) there is a difference between the popular use of these terms and the technical use of architects and builders; and (2) even in popular usage there are differences so that some speakers would use bungalow and cottage interchangeably[7], and others would contrast them. The following distinctions seem to be generally agreed, however. A *cabin* assumes a rough or plain type of construction; a *bungalow* is characterized by "low sweeping lines and wide veranda[8]," and a *cottage* is not rough, or low and sweeping, and may be with or without a veranda.

A further factor to be considered is height (in stories). A cabin, bungalow, and cottage are one story; a house, manse, or apartment may be one or more; and a mansion or palace two or more stories. An apartment building is usually but not always more than one story.

With these assumptions, this would give *bungalow* the following specifying components:

1. Size: small
2. Separate or not: separate
3. Always associated with an official position: no
4. Design: low and sweeping with a porch
5. Height (in stories): one

Terms which refer to the semantic class of Things may also be studied with respect to their constituent parts so that many Things have associated with them one or more other generic classes of Things. Thus, *bungalow* has associated with it the class "parts of a building lived in by humans," with members such as door, roof, wall, floor, etc. Each of these also carries a further class of parts, such as "parts of a door," "parts of a wall," etc. In a culture where many of the members of the Thing class refer to items not in the translator's own culture, the study of the parts is useful to gain a knowledge of all the components that can be associated with a given Thing.

DIAGRAMS OF THE ANALYSIS OF RUN AND BUNGALOW

The following diagrams of the components of *run* and *bungalow* present an overview which, it is hoped, will help the translator see the "wood" as well as the "trees."

It is not expected that a translator will prepare charts of this type for each word he analyzes in depth. The charts are presented here only to show in a concise form what has been discussed in the previous pages.

---

[7] Under *bungalow,* Webster (1966) lists one meaning as "a cottage intended chiefly for summer occupancy."
[8] Webster (1966).

DIAGRAM 1

A SINGLE WORD WITH VARIOUS SENSES

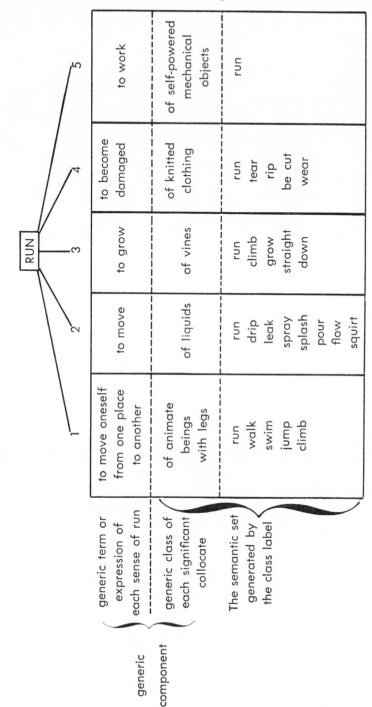

	RUN				
	1	2	3	4	5
generic term or expression of each sense of run	to move oneself from one place to another	to move	to grow	to become damaged	to work
generic class of each significant collocate	of animate beings with legs	of liquids	of vines	of knitted clothing	of self-powered mechanical objects
The semantic set generated by the class label	run walk swim jump climb	run drip leak spray splash pour flow squirt	run climb grow straight down	run tear rip be cut wear	run

generic component

DIAGRAM 2

GENERIC COMPONENT OF SENSE 1 OF **RUN**

to move oneself from one place to another (of animate beings with legs)

SPECIFYING   COMPONENTS   OF   SENSE   1   OF   **RUN**

	Motion of legs relative to each other	Motion of legs relative to surface	Direction of movement	Intensity of movement	Location of movement
RUN	alternate	both off for part of cycle	forward	rapid	on solid surface
swim	—⁹	—	forward	—	in liquid
jump	simultaneous	both off for cycle	upward	—	on solid surface
walk	alternate	contact through cycle	forward	—	on solid surface
climb	alternate	contact through cycle	upward	—	on solid surface

⁹ A dash signifies that this component is irrelevant for the particular term under consideration.

DIAGRAM 3

A SINGLE WORD WITHOUT VARIOUS SENSES

Word	BUNGALOW	Specifying Components				
Generic component	building lived in by humans	size	multiple units in one building	always associated with an official position	general design	height (in stories)
Semantic set generated by the class label	apartment house	—	yes	no	—	one or more
	manse	—	—	yes	—	one or more
	palace	large	no	yes	very elaborate	two or more
	mansion	large	no	no	very elaborate	two or more
	cabin	small	no	no	simple / no porch	one
	bungalow	small	no	no	simple / with porch	one
	cottage	small	no	no	simple / porch optional	one
	house	—	—	no	not very elaborate	one or more

CHAPTER 6

The Nature of Multiple Senses

In chapter 4 we made it clear that before the components of meaning of a word may be analyzed, that word must first of all be studied from the standpoint of whether it has one sense or several. It was also made clear that when a word occurs in a wide variety of contexts, this may indicate the word has various senses. The more different the contexts are in terms of their generic classes, the more likely it is that different senses are involved. In this chapter further characteristics of multiple senses and how they may affect a translation will be discussed.

Types of Senses

A single word may have various senses. These senses may be classified as primary, secondary, and figurative.[1] The primary sense is the first meaning or usage which a word apart from context will suggest to most people. Secondary senses are those which the same word carries and which are related to one another and to the primary sense by sharing some thread of meaning.[2] Figurative senses are based on associative relations with the primary sense.

[1] There is a fourth sense, not the interest of this chapter, which may be called "across-class senses." This type of sense occurs when two senses of a word are related semantically by association and the senses cross both semantic and grammatical classes. For example, "a hammer" and "to hammer" are related semantically; one is a tool and the other what is done with that tool. The two senses cross both semantic and grammatical classes. Semantically, one is a Thing, the other an Event; grammatically, one is a noun and the other a verb. There are many words with such across-class senses in English, e.g., load, walk, feather, wet, heat, tree, drum, etc. In contrast to across-class senses, figurative senses may shift semantic class, but never shift grammatical class. In "He is a fox," there is a shift in semantic class from *fox* a Thing to *fox* an Abstraction (meaning slyness); but there has been no shift in grammatical class. *Fox* is a noun in the above sentence as much as in: "The fox ate the grapes." Secondary senses never shift either semantic or grammatical classes. Since across-class senses have caused no special problems to the translator, they are not given further consideration.

[2] If a form is found which is connected with two unrelated senses, it represents two distinct words, usually referred to as "homonyms." Such a form would be *seal* (the animal and the object used for certifying letters) or *file* (a place for papers and the tool). As it happens, in English there are many such words which are pronounced the same and have two or more unrelated meanings, but they are usually spelled differently, e.g., *tail* and *tale*, *rest* and *wrest*, *pear* and *pair*.

In the preceding chapter a study of the various senses of the word *run* was made. When a native speaker of English is asked to use *run* in a sentence, he will most often produce a sentence such as: "The boy runs." This usage represents the primary sense. Other usages, such as were studied in the last chapter, are secondary senses of *run*.

Primary and secondary senses of a single word are illustrated further in the following two sentences:

1. The old horse *drew* the cart slowly into town.
2. The famous horse *drew* a big crowd to the meeting.

In these two sentences, *drew* is functioning as a member of the Event semantic class in both sentences. The senses in the two sentences are different, but related. Consequently, *drew* is treated here as having two senses; the first example illustrates the primary sense, the second example illustrates its secondary sense.

The distinguishing feature of figurative senses is the type of relation they sustain to the primary sense of the word. There is no meaning shared between the senses but rather a part-whole or contiguous relationship. For example, in the sentence, "The kettle is boiling," the word *kettle* is used in a figurative sense meaning *water* based on the spatial contiguity of the water in the kettle.

The sentences above which make use of the word *drew*, serve to re-emphasize the relation between context and multiple senses. In these sentences two important words in the immediate context are "crowd" and "cart." One is animate and the other inanimate. Since the words belong to two different generic classes, we would suspect (supposing this to be a new language under study) that *drew* is used in two different senses. In this example, the use of the word *drew* did not shift from one semantic class to another, but its context did shift from one generic class to another.

In establishing the senses of words, the investigator is not entirely dependent upon context. He may simply ask a language helper to paraphrase each sentence and conclude immediately that *drew* is used differently in sentences 1 and 2. In the first "pulled" would probably be used; in the second "attracted." Thus, the content of paraphrases is likely to indicate each sense. If not, questions may be used to elicit further the what, when, where, how, and why of each usage. By combining the information received from paraphrases and elicitation, a fairly adequate understanding of the words under study may be gained.

THE SEMANTIC BASES FOR MULTIPLE SENSES

As stated above, the various senses carried by a single word are related one to the other semantically. The relation between the senses of a word is determined by comparing the usage of each sense of the word. Following this course of analysis, there are two semantic bases for multiple senses. They are: (1) a thread of meaning shared by all the senses of the word under study, or (2) an associative relation between the senses.

The first gives rise to secondary senses; the second is the basis for figurative senses.

In the statement of the first semantic base for multiple senses, the word "shared" is significant. It tells us that when a word has four or five different senses, the same thread of meaning will be found in *each* sense of that word. This shared thread of meaning has sometimes been referred to as the common denominator of meaning among the senses. It does not tell us the sense of any usage; it does, however, serve to show one way in which multiple senses arise and how they may be classified. In the statement of the second semantic base for multiple senses, the words "associative relation" are important. There is no common thread of meaning shared as the basis for this type of multiple sense. Rather, it is based on some *relation* between the senses that *associates* one sense with the other. In the first type of multiple sense, a referential thread of meaning relates the senses; in the second, a relationship relates the senses. The multiple senses of the first type are nonfigurative, while those of the second type are figurative.

A thread of meaning shared by the senses—the basis for secondary senses

In chapter 4 we spoke of three different kinds of meaning components, i.e., generic, specifying, and incidental. These are the components of meaning that apply to any given sense. We analyzed five senses of the word *run* indicating the generic components and the specifying components of each. In analyzing the meaning of each sense of *run* we did not discuss the semantic relation between the senses. Each sense was analyzed independently since the relation between the senses merely indicates how a single word may serve to communicate more than one sense. This relation between the senses does not help us to understand the significance of any particular sense. It usually represents a generalization of some specifying component found in at least one of the senses which in its generalized form applies to all the senses. To help distinguish between the generic component, specifying components, and the thread of meaning shared by the senses, see diagram 1.

DIAGRAM 1

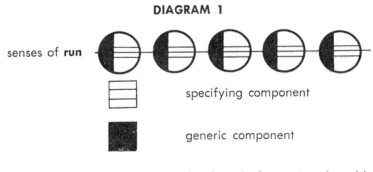

senses of **run**

specifying component

generic component

the thread of meaning shared by all the senses

The thread of meaning shared by all the senses of *run* may be stated as "a movement along a course." While this is a meaning component that applies to each sense, it is neither a specifying nor a generic component of any particular sense of the word *run*. Therefore, its only value is to show that a word has multiple senses based on this shared thread of meaning.

Another illustration follows. The verb "to dress" has several senses which may be seen in the following abbreviated contexts:

> to dress timber
> to dress ranks
> to dress poultry
> to dress a wound
> to dress a salad
> to dress a shop window
> to dress oneself

The shared idea of "making or preparing something in a presentable form" ties all of these senses together. It is the common thread of meaning showing we are dealing with a single word rather than with two or more separate words.

Associative relations between the senses — the basis for figurative senses

Not all multiple senses are related with a shared thread of meaning; many are related through some type of association. For example, the word *heaven* in the New Testament refers either to God or to heaven depending on the context in which it is used. The basis for the dual sense of this one word stems from an associative relation, i.e., heaven is a place and God is one who lives in that place. This relation between the two senses is different from the shared thread of meaning. Different senses based on associative relations are common in Scripture, and account for various figurative senses. It will be seen as the chapter progresses that a discussion of these associative relations leads quite naturally to a discussion of particular figures of speech, such as metonymy.

The different types of associative relations may be classified into two main groups — the *contiguous* and the *part-whole*.

1. *Relations based on contiguity*

There are three contiguous relations — temporal, spatial, and logical. In the *temporal* relation, a time word is put for an event taking place at that time, or vice versa, an event word is put for the time of the event. One of the most frequent examples of the former is the use of "day" by itself, or in such phrases as "day of the Lord," "day of God," etc., for events which will take place on that day. Thus, in 1 Corinthians 3:13 Paul says, "the day shall declare it, because it shall be revealed by fire; and the fire shall try every man's work of what sort it is." Here "the day" refers to the "testing by fire" (to occur at a particular time) that will reveal the quality of the work done. Again, Peter says believers should be "Looking for and hasting unto . . . the day of God" (2 Peter 3:12) where the whole context is that of "the day of judgment of ungodly men" (v. 7). The "day of God," in this context, is the time when God will judge the wicked, parallel with his former judgment of the wicked at the time of the Flood. Jesus also speaks of "my day" when he says "Abraham rejoiced to see my day" (John 8:56). "Day" refers to the event of his incarnation.

Another example occurs in Mark 4:29. Jesus says, "the harvest is come," i.e., the time to harvest the grain has come; so in this case the Event, the ripening of the grain, is used with the meaning of the time when it is ripe.

The *spatial* relationship occurs when the semantic connection is basically one of locality. For instance, as already noted, although "heaven" is commonly used in the sense of the place where God lives, yet sometimes it is actually used for God himself. When Jesus asked the Jewish leaders, "The baptism of John, was it from heaven, or of men?" (Matt. 21:25, Mark 11:30, Luke 20:4), he was clearly saying to them, "Did John get his authority from God or from men?" And many commentators take "the kingdom of heaven," the expression used by Matthew, as equivalent to "the kingdom of God."

Another common example in Scripture is the use of "world" to mean not only the literal physical world, but also the people who live in that world. John 3:16 is probably the best known verse where this is the case, but there are many other such verses, e.g., "that every mouth may be stopped and all the world may become guilty before God" (Rom. 3:19).

The third subsection under contiguous relationships is a *logical* one, and is labeled *cause-effect*, i.e., it is a relationship in which a cause is put for its effect, or vice versa. The label "cause-effect" is used of associative relations to cover various finer distinctions which may be made, such as that between primary, secondary, agentive, material, and instrumental causes. Thus, in the story of the beheading of John the Baptist, Herod would be the primary cause, the soldier who actually executed John the mediate or secondary cause, and the sword he used the instrumental cause. These distinctions will not be used in the analysis of further examples; their relationship is simply labeled "cause-effect."

When the apostles and elders met (Acts 15) to discuss the views of the circumcision party, and James made his speech and suggested that the Gentiles abstain from certain activities particularly offensive to Jews, he supported his recommendation with the statement, "For Moses of old time hath in every city them that preach him, being read in the synagogues every sabbath day," (v. 21). The term *Moses*, of course, usually refers to the man himself, but in this statement by James, it also refers to his writings, read and preached every sabbath. So the word *Moses* refers both to the man and to his writings — a relationship that can be labeled cause-effect.

A number of anthropomorphisms found in the Old Testament fall within this category, where *hand* is used for what God does, *ear* for his act of listening, etc. Occasional examples are found in the New Testament, such as *hand* in Acts 13:11, where Paul pronounces judgment on Elymas, saying "the hand of the Lord is upon thee, and thou shalt be blind"; and *ears* in 1 Peter 3:12 (a quote from a Psalm), "his ears are open unto their prayers."

There are many other examples of the cause-effect relation; notice how *sword* is used in the three following references:

"I came not to send peace, but a sword" (Matt. 10:34)

"Who shall separate us from the love of Christ? Shall . . . sword?" (Rom. 8:35)

"for he beareth not the sword in vain" (Rom. 13:4)

In the first reference *sword* symbolizes "dissension, quarreling, fighting"; in the second "death (by execution with a sword or other means)"; in the third "authority to use a sword for punishment."[3] Again, *lips* is used to refer to what people say with their lips (e.g., Matt. 15:8, Mark 7:6), *bonds* is used for imprisonment (Acts 20:23).

2. *Relations based on part-whole associations*

Three types of relations based upon the general concept of part-whole associations are distinguished: a member-class relation, a constituent-whole relation, and an attribute-whole relation.

It is not uncommon in the Scriptures to find that a *specific member of a generic class* is used to represent that class. When Jesus taught his disciples to pray "Give us this day our daily bread" (Matt. 6:11; cf. Luke 11:3), he did not mean the disciples were to live simply on bread, to the exclusion of all other types of food. He was teaching them to pray for their daily *food*, whatever form it would take. Again, when Jesus repudiated Satan with the words, "Man shall not live by bread alone," he was clearly referring to physical food; there is more to man's life than eating food.

You may have noticed in the examples cited so far that the words involved have been members of the Thing class, and it is true that T-words enter into associative relations readily. However, two E-words also serve to illustrate the member-class relationship. In the fourth Beatitude, Jesus says, "Blessed are they which do hunger and thirst after righteousness" (Matt. 5:6). Here, *to hunger* and *to thirst* are specific members of the general class of "strong desires" and represent that class in this saying. Jesus is not saying the blessed are those whose stomachs ache with hunger and whose mouths are parched with thirst because they want righteousness, but those whose spiritual desire for righteousness is as strong as their natural desires are for food and drink.

---

[3] These examples do raise a theoretical question: If *sword* is used in this way in a number of related senses, is it not better analyzed as having a series of related senses as was discussed for *run* in the previous chapter? The answer is no, as each use is based on an associative relationship, and not a shared thread of meaning. The analysis taken here is to say that *sword* enters into several separate associative relations, rather than sharing a common thread of meaning.

It will be observed that included in the member-class relation is the generic-specific relation in which the generic represents the whole of a concept and the specific a part. Part of Matthew 5:45 says: "he maketh his sun to rise on the evil and the good . . . ." This specific statement followed by another concerning rain refers to the generic concept of God's impartial love. The specific examples illustrate that love.

In 1 Thessalonians 5:19 there is a warning not to "quench the Spirit." *Quench* is a specific term referring primarily to the action of putting out a fire; but when used with the Spirit it takes on the generic sense to suppress or stop his ministry.

In the componential analysis of a Thing word presented in the previous chapter, it was pointed out that a T-word may also be analyzed in terms of its constituent parts, and this relation of *constituent-whole* derives from this. In Matthew 8:8 and Luke 7:6 the use of *roof* for "house" is an example; other examples are *souls* for people as in Acts 2:41, where "there were added unto them about three thousand souls"; *flesh and blood* for people in Matthew 16:17 where Jesus says "for flesh and blood hath not revealed it unto thee, but my Father which is in heaven"; and *necks* for lives in Romans 16:4 where Paul says that Priscilla and Aquila "risked their necks for my life" (RSV).

The reverse relationship, whole-constituent, is also found occasionally as in the command in Mark 16:15, "Go ye into all the world, and preach the gospel to every creature." This is not a command to preach to the animals, but to people, for the whole class of created beings has been put for a particular section of that class, viz., human beings.

At first glance, the relationship of *attribute-whole* may seem simply another way of referring to the previous type. What is in focus here, however, are not the parts of a particular T-word, but the traits of character, or appearance, or purposes associated with a T-word. This is particularly true of the use of animals with whom a particular culture or language associates certain traits and then uses the name of the animal to refer to that trait. Thus the English-speaking world thinks of foxes as sly and crafty, donkeys as stupid and stubborn, goats as stubborn also, pigs as greedy and dirty, etc. The use of animals in this way is common in the Scriptures — sheep, goats, camels, wolves, lions, and snakes are some that can be mentioned. These words for animals usually symbolize the whole animal but in certain contexts they refer only to an attribute of that animal. Thus, in Matthew 23:33 Jesus addresses the scribes and Pharisees as "Ye serpents, ye generation of vipers."

The previous examples show how the whole may be used to refer only to an attribute. The converse is shown in the following examples. God is sometimes referred to by his attributes; in Mark 14:61, Jesus is asked if he is the "Son of the Blessed"; in Luke 1:35, Mary is told that "the power of the Highest shall overshadow thee"; and in Acts 7:48 Stephen testifies that "the most High dwelleth not in temples made with hands."

Nor is this relation confined to animate beings. A characteristic of a stone is applied to Jesus in 1 Peter 2:7, 8; so also to believers in v. 5 of the same chapter. An attribute of grass is applied to mankind by the same apostle (1 Pet. 1:24), and a characteristic of fire applied to the tongue by James (3:6).

It is interesting to note that there are some instances in the New Testament in which the connection between the two senses of a term appears to be based on two relations. For instance, in Revelation 3:7, Jesus tells John to write to the angel of the church in Philadelphia, "These things saith he that is holy, he that is true, he that hath the key of David . . . ." Here, it is generally agreed by commentators, "key" represents "authority." The connection would seem to be that "key" stands in a spatial relationship to the person who carries it, and that person, by virtue of possessing the key(s), has an attribute of "authority." So by a double relationship "key" is used in the sense of "authority."

Though there is some exegetical difference of opinion over the use of "name" in Scripture, it seems reasonable to assume that in such verses as "In the name of Jesus Christ of Nazareth rise up and walk " (Acts 3:6), with such subsequent statements as "And his name . . . hath made this man strong" (v. 16) and "Be it known unto you all . . . that by the name of Jesus Christ of Nazareth . . . even by him doth this man stand here before you whole" (4:10), there is either a single or double associative relationship. "Name" is linked to the person bearing that name by an attribute-whole relation and refers to the person, or in addition to the attribute-whole relation the person is associated with a particular attribute that he has — "power (to heal)."

THE LANGUAGE-SPECIFIC CHARACTER OF MULTIPLE SENSES

Although multiple senses derive either from a shared thread of meaning or from associative relations between the senses, this universal characteristic of all languages does not determine which senses will be symbolized by a given word in a particular language. Languages develop their idioms and multiple senses quite independently of each other. Thus, equivalent words in two different languages may be equivalent as to their primary sense but completely different as to their secondary and figurative senses.

The verb *to dress* has a number of senses, which are illustrated in the following contexts. In the list of Spanish equivalents, note that only the equivalent of the primary meaning makes use of the verb *vestirse*. The rest of the equivalents in the Spanish list make use of some other specific word or of a description.

to dress oneself	vestirse uno mismo
	to dress oneself
to dress lumber	labrar madera
	to work lumber
to dress a chicken	pelar y destripar la gallina
	to pluck and clean the hen

to dress a wound	vendar la herida to bandage the wound
to dress a show window	hacer atractivo al escaparate to make attractive the show window
to dress ranks	alinearse to line up

In the following two sentences Spanish makes use of *vestirse* in a sense that is not used in English for the word *dress*. Note that the second example may be used in English but would communicate a different sense.

El cielo se vistió de nubes.

The sky was dressed with clouds. The heavens were full of clouds.

Tal sastre me viste.

That tailor dresses me. That is my tailor, or that tailor makes my clothes.

In the following comparison of the word *run* we have four different situations which are typical of cross-language lexical studies.

1. Equivalent usages of the word *run* in English and *corre* in Spanish.

The boy runs	El muchacho corre
The river runs	El río corre
The horse runs	El caballo corre

2. Uses of the word *run* not found in Spanish.

The clock runs	El reloj anda	The clock walks
The vine runs	La guía va	The shoot goes
The nose runs	La nariz gotea	The nose drips
The faucet runs	El agua sale de la llave	The water comes out of the faucet

3. Uses found in Spanish but not in English.

| El tiempo corre | (The) time runs | Time flies |
| Corre peligro | Danger runs | There is danger |

4. Uses which appear to be identical but have a different sense.

| The car runs | El carro corre | The car goes fast |

5. Equivalent usages which are similar but not identical in form.

| The stocking runs | Se corre un hilo | A thread runs |

If we were now to consider Chol, a language of Mexico, we would find similar areas of overlap in the usage of the word *run*. The Chol words for boy, river, horse, and car may be collocated with the word "ajñel" with the same sense as in English. Other usages found either in English or Spanish would not be acceptable.

The above examples show that multiple senses based upon a shared thread of meaning develop differently in different languages. The same is true of multiple senses based on associative relations. None of the following usages found in Scripture may be intelligently used in translating into Chol.

Matt. 8:8 "come under my *roof*"; the Chols could only assume that his house was still being built.

Matt. 15:8 "honoreth me with their *lips*"; in Chol "lips" is "the skin of their mouth" and does not have the sense of what they say with their lips.

Mark 3:25 "if a *house* be divided against itself"; "house" only refers to the building, not to the occupants.

Luke 1:69 "raised up an *horn* of salvation"; not understood at all.

Luke 15:18 "I have sinned against *heaven*"; for Chol speakers, the "sky" is the location of God, but cannot be used to refer to God himself.

Titus 2:10 "*adorn* the doctrine of God"; simply provoked surprise — how can we decorate God's teaching? Surely we are not supposed to put the Bible on a decorated table?

Examples could be multiplied to show the unlikelihood that those senses which are based on associative relations will be found symbolized in another language by a literal equivalent. A different word will generally be required to communicate clearly each sense. Whether multiple senses of a word arise from a shared thread of meaning or from relations which associate the senses, the cluster of senses symbolized by a single word is always specific to the language under study.

CHAPTER 7

Translating Multiple Senses

GENERAL GUIDELINES

When a single word has multiple senses based on a shared thread of meaning, those senses will most frequently be translated into another language using a different word or expression for each sense. The example given earlier of the word *dress* showed that a literal translation into Spanish of the primary sense was possible. Additional senses carried by the English word *to dress* could not be translated by using the literal equivalent *vestirse*.

The situation is not appreciably different for multiple senses based on associative relations. The literal sense of the word may often be rendered with a literal equivalent, but the figurative sense of that word almost invariably must be translated using some other word or phrase. This leads us to conclude that the senses carried by a single word in one language are likely to be translated into another language using almost as many different renditions as there are senses.

Basically there are three ways to translate figurative senses, i.e., those that are based on associative relations:

(1) the sense of the word may be translated directly

(2) the word used in the original can be retained along with a direct translation of its sense

(3) the original figure can be replaced by a figure of the RL with the same meaning.

Translating the sense of the word directly is illustrated in the following examples:

Matt. 10:34 "I came . . . to send . . . a sword"; "I came to cause dissension, strife, etc."

1 Cor. 14:21 "With men of other tongues and other lips will I speak"; "I will speak, making use of men who speak foreign languages"

Matt. 27:24 "I am innocent of the blood of this just person"; "I am innocent of the death (or, of causing the death) of this just person"

Matt. 16:17 "flesh and blood hath not revealed it unto thee"; "no human being/person has revealed it to you"

Sometimes, however, the word itself is retained, and implicit information is provided to make the meaning clear: (This type of figure could be also classed as an ellipsis.)

Luke 16:31 "If they hear not Moses and the prophets"; "If they will not hear what Moses and the prophets wrote" (Note that in many languages leaving "wrote" out would tend to imply that Moses and the prophets were contemporaries who could still be heard as they spoke.)

Mark 3:25 "and if a house be divided"; "if the people in a house (family) do not agree with one another"

Matt. 26:45 "the hour is at hand"; "the time (hour, a specific unit of time for time in general) when I must die is approaching"

The third alternative is to replace the original figure by an equivalent one in the RL. The figure of euphemism serves as an illustration of this third alternative. The Scriptures use euphemistic expressions for death, sex, God, and the Gentiles. Many languages have their own euphemistic expressions for death and sex, even if not for God and the Gentiles. Where appropriate, the scriptural euphemism may be replaced by one in the RL. For example, in Villa Alta Zapotec of Mexico the euphemism "he knew her not" was replaced by an equivalent euphemism, "Joseph respected her."

Often, too, it will be necessary to replace statements which are not expressed euphemistically in the New Testament, by euphemistic expressions in the RL. Adultery is referred to directly rather than euphemistically in the New Testament, but many languages refer to this sin with euphemistic expressions. In Chinantec, Otomi, Trique, Mixtec, and Chol of Mexico, adultery is referred to as "to talk to another woman or to another man." In Zoque of Mexico it is "to deceive her husband or his wife." In Ecuador, the Colorado speak of "walking with others," and the Tagabili of the Philippines of "stepping on his or her partner."

The opposite process, i.e., of rendering a euphemistic statement with one that is not euphemistic, is often necessary. For example, the euphemism in Acts 1:25; "he went to his own place," needs to be made specific in most translations or it is understood to mean he went to his home or farm.

EXAMPLES OF TRANSLATING SECONDARY SENSES

The principle to be followed in translating secondary senses is clear. Nevertheless, there are some problems which merit special consideration. One of these is the translation of secondary senses arising from the shared component of number or of person. This arises especially in connection with pronouns, and is now discussed.

What do the italicized pronouns in the following brief quotes from English conversation mean?

(a) "In this paper, *we* have tried to show . . ."
(b) "Let's be quiet, shall *we?*"
(c) "*We* couldn't find mother, so *we* cried. But *we* are all right now."
(d) "*You* can't do that."
(e) "If *I* don't pay my taxes, *I* am not a good citizen."

If the following contexts are now added, does it affect your understanding of what the pronominal forms refer to?

(a) "Dr. X closed his lecture by saying , . . ."
(b) "As the noise got louder and louder, she said to the children , . . ."
(c) "Mrs. A. brought three-year-old Jane back to her home. When her mother opened the door, Mrs. A said to her , . . ."
(d) "As they discussed the arrangements for the party that evening, she asked her sister, 'Do you think it would be all right if we sat all the men at one table, and the women at another?' 'Oh no,' her sister replied , . . ."
(e) "Congressman Z spoke very strongly at the meeting last night about the duty of every citizen to pay his taxes. At the climax of his speech, he thumped the table, and said , . . ."

These examples from English[1] illustrate a special case of a shared thread of meaning being the basis for specialized uses. Each pronoun in English carries, in general, two categories of meaning, those of number and person,[2] and most of the pronouns can carry two or more senses, based on sharing either number or person. Thus "we" in example (a) actually means "I" as only one person was giving the lecture, so the component of first person is retained, but the plural number is used for the singular. But in example (b), the "we" refers to "you (pl.)," i.e., the noisy children, and in (c) "we" refers to the child being returned to its mother. In (d), "you" really makes a general statement, equivalent to "one" or the passive, "that can't be done," and in (e), when the politician uses "I," he includes his audience and really means "we," that is to say, "all of us."

---

[1] Drawn largely from Eunice V. Pike (1966, pp. 17, 18).

[2] Third person singular, of course, also carries gender, and the same form serves for second person singular and second person plural in all conversational English, but these details do not affect the argument.

This special use of number and person is not confined to pronouns, though it is most obvious there. Nouns, too, may be used in this way (nouns being third person, and singular or plural). Note the following examples:

> "Mommy doesn't like you to do that." (Mommy speaking)
> "I would like all the parents of the children . . . ." (parents being addressed)
> "Missionaries are an independent lot." (one missionary to another)

In these examples, a third person form, i.e., a noun, is used for first person singular, second person plural, and first person plural respectively.

These examples from English, then, alert us to the fact that forms carrying the categories of number and/or person may either convey the literal sense of their categories or a secondary sense, given an appropriate context.

When we turn to the Greek of the New Testament, the same type of phenomenon is encountered. In forms which carry categories which refer to persons — nouns, pronouns, participles, verbs — the person reference may be primary or secondary. These special uses of the categories of number and person will be discussed in that order.

Before the details are discussed, however, it is emphasized that the translator must decide how best to translate every form with this type of secondary sense. It is only too easy to assume that a literal rendition will be understood correctly in the RL version. Often it is not, and the readers conclude that Paul was not a Jew, that Jesus was not the Son of man, etc. English is obviously similar to Greek in its flexible use of pronouns. It must not be assumed that other languages are also.

Special uses of the category of number

The nonliteral ways in which number is used are basically two — the singular form is used for the plural, or vice versa.

1. The singular used for the plural

In the New Testament documents, the singular form is used with plural reference with all three persons, and in each case it has the general effect of making what is said more vivid and forceful. It is a rhetorical device used with the intention of catching or holding the hearers' or readers' attention. But this very fact is a warning to translators: what is a vivid rhetorical device in Greek may only prove, on checking with the readers of the RL version, to be misleading. For them, the shift from singular to plural does not signal a rhetorical device but only the normal, nonspecial meaning. Hence, the use of "I" for "we," or "you (sg.)" for "you (pl.)," or "he" for "they," needs to be carefully checked to ensure that (a) it does not convey a wrong sense, and (b) that, even if it does not convey a wrong sense, it is the most natural way available in the RL to hold the attention of the readers or hearers. It may be more natural to substitute the form which corresponds to the referential sense of the pronoun, and use an appropriate rhetorical device of the language — emphatic forms, order shifts, etc.

(a) *The use of the first person singular for the corresponding plural* is almost entirely confined to Paul's letters in the New Testament, and its effect is to make Paul himself a vivid and typical example[3] of what is true of all believers, or, alternatively, what should not be true of any believer. A well-known example is Philippians 4:13, "I can do all things through Christ which strengtheneth me," which is spoken in the middle of a passage dealing with his personal experience. In some languages, the pronominal system is such that when a statement is made, for example, in first person, it is implied and understood that the statement *cannot* be true of anyone else. In such a language, the translation of "I" by "I" in Philippians 4:13 would mean that Paul, being a great apostle, *could* do everything, but that the humble reader was excluded from that possibility. In contexts like these, the translator should see whether the use of the first person singular forms precludes their being appropriated by other believers, or not. If so, then "we" will probably have to be used.

More commonly, however, Paul is making general statements, some of which are connotatively good, others bad. Examples of the former are found in Galatians 2:19-21, which begins, "For I through the law am dead to the law, that I might live unto God. I am crucified with Christ . . . ." Examples of the latter are found in such passages as Romans 3:7, "For if the truth of God hath more abounded through my lie unto his glory; why yet am I also judged as a sinner?"; 1 Corinthians 10:29, 30, "for why is my liberty judged of another man's conscience? For if I by grace be a partaker, why am I evil spoken of for that for which I give thanks?"; 1 Corinthians 13:1-3 "Though I speak with the tongues of men and of angels , . . ."; Galatians 2:18 "For if I build again the things which I destroyed, I make myself a transgressor."[4]

The translator needs to be particularly careful with this last group, to make sure the impression is not being conveyed that Paul told lies, or that he lacked love, or built what he had destroyed. If such passages convey a wrong meaning in the RL version, then examples such as 1 Corinthians 13:1-3 can be handled by some such expression as "If I, or any other person, . . ." In other cases, "we" can be used.

(b) *The use of the second person singular for the plural* is found throughout the New Testament, and two distinct uses may be discerned. In some cases, the "you (singular)" refers to the whole group being addressed, but in other cases it refers only to parts of the group or to some special group different from those being addressed.

[3] Terms used by exegetes and grammarians are "representative" singular (Robertson, 1934, p. 678), "supra-individual first person" (Ridderbos, 1953, p. 102), "typical" (Lofthouse, 1955, p. 73), "exemplary" (Stauffer, 1964, p. 357).

[4] Some commentators, e.g., Burton (1956), interpret this statement as a reference to what Peter had done, but tactfully stated by using "I." If this view is followed, then "I" is used meaning "you (singular)" and it is a case of a secondary sense based on the category of *person* (see section 2) not number. On either view, the sense is a secondary one.

The former type occurs commonly in commands, such as the Ten Commandments, where the singular injunction, "Thou shalt not kill," is addressed to all. In many languages, the plural is more natural for general commands such as these. And in some contexts, the use of the singular may be confusing for the RL reader. For instance, in Matthew 4:7, Jesus quotes the Scripture, "Thou shalt not tempt the Lord thy God" and again in v. 10 he says, "Thou shalt worship the Lord thy God, and him only shalt thou serve." In some languages (such as Sierra Juárez Zapotec of Mexico) these are simply understood as commands addressed to the devil, but not to anyone else.

This use of the singular "you" for the plural is also found in didactic passages. For instance, chapter 6 of Matthew, part of the Sermon on the Mount, alternates between the singular and plural a number of times. Thus, v. 1 is plural, but 2-4 are singular; 5 is plural, but 6 is singular; 7-16 are plural, but 17 is singular again. Such variation just is not permissible in all languages, and the plural has to be used throughout, since the disciples are the ones addressed (cf. 5:1, 2). Other instances where the singular is used in a similar way are: Matthew 7:3-5 (and the parallel passage in Luke 6:41, 42); Romans 12:20, 21 and 13:3, 4; 1 Corinthians 4:7; Galatians 4:7, 6:1. Note, too, that in all these passages the verses in the singular are embedded in larger sections using the plural, indicating that the switch to the singular is for rhetorical effect, and not because only one person is now being addressed.

The second use occurs when "you (singular)" represents only a special group and not all of those addressed. This use poses more problems as chapter 2 of Romans illustrates. The singular is used in vv. 1-5, and again in 17-27, but the whole context makes it clear that Paul is not addressing a particular individual. On the other hand, if "you (plural)" is substituted, this gives the impression that Paul is addressing the believers at Rome, whereas it is generally agreed that chapter 2 is particularly directed to Jews. Therefore, to avoid confusing and misleading the readers of the RL version, it may be necessary to use the term "Jew," found in v. 17, in v. 1 also to make the reference clear.

In chapter 14 of Romans, two subgroups of the Christian community are under discussion — "the weak in faith" (v. 1) and the others. In vv. 4, 10, 15 and 20-22, those who are not "weak" are addressed directly in the singular, apart from 10a which is addressed to the weak brother. Here again, to make the reference clear, it may prove necessary to insert "you who are weak" or "you who are strong" as appropriate.

Yet another example in Romans is found in 9:19, 20, where Paul puts an argument into the mouth of an objector: "Thou wilt say then unto me, Why doth he yet find fault? For who hath resisted his will? Nay but, O man, who art thou that repliest against God? Shall the thing formed say to him that formed it, Why hast thou made me thus?" If this device is misunderstood, and Paul is thought to be addressing one of the Christians at Rome, then a shift to expressions such as "Some of you (plural) will say to me" or "If one of you should say . . . ." may make the meaning clear.

Some further examples are found in 1 Corinthians 7:21 (slaves addressed), 27 (husbands and wives), 28 (an unmarried person), and in Romans 10:6, 8 and 9. Note, too, the direct address to husbands and wives in 1 Corinthians 7:16 by means of the vocative, an implicit second person form.

(c) *The occurrence of the third person singular with a plural sense* is less obvious than with the first and second persons. A specific example is 1 Timothy 2:15, "Notwithstanding, she shall be saved in childbearing, if they continue in faith and charity and holiness with sobriety." Here "she" and "they" equally refer to "women."

The third person singular is often used to refer to all those who fulfill some particular condition or to whom some qualifying statement applies, as in:

John 5:24 "Verily, verily, I say unto you, He that heareth my word, and believeth on him that sent me, hath everlasting life, and shall not come into condemnation; but is passed from death unto life."

Romans 4:8 "Blessed is the man to whom the Lord will not impute sin."

James 1:12 "Blessed is the man that endureth temptation: for when he is tried, he shall receive the crown of life, which the Lord hath promised to them that love him."

1 John 2:4 "He that saith, I know him, and keepeth not his commandments, is a liar, and the truth is not in him."

In cases such as these, the translator needs to know whether the singular or the plural form is the more natural for this type of statement. Even more significant are those languages in which the singular form when used in John 5:24 would lead the reader to conclude that only one individual will be saved.

2. *The plural used for the singular*

(a) The predominant instance in the New Testament of the plural number being used with a singular sense is with *the first person*, i.e., "we" for "I," and has given rise to much discussion, especially in the Pauline epistles. When Paul uses "we," as he does frequently, does he just mean himself, or himself and his associates, or the apostolic band, or Christians in general? Lofthouse (1955, p. 73) says quite clearly, "When Paul wrote 'we,' he was thinking of himself as one of a number, either the little band of his companions, or his readers, or the whole company of believers always in the background of his mind." But this view is by no means undisputed. Stauffer (1964, p. 356) says, "The plural *hēmeis* [we] in Paul's letters is essentially stylistic." Milligan (1953, pp. 131, 2), at the end of his commentary on the Thessalonian Epistles, has a note entitled "Did St. Paul use the Epistolary Plural?", in which he summarizes the conclusions to be drawn from an "elaborate monograph" by Karl Dick in 1900: "And the general conclusion at which Dick arrives after a complete survey of the evidence is that St. Paul uses the first person plural with such a wide variety of *nuances* and shades of meaning, that the *pluralis auctoris* may well have a place amongst them, wherever it is found to be most in keeping with the context, and the circumstances of writing at the time."

This final proviso of Milligan's is particularly important — the commentaries must be carefully consulted on all occurrences of "we" to try to ascertain just who Paul had in mind when he used this plural form. Beekman (1965f, p. 2) suggests three "exegetical factors" that the translator should take into account when trying to decide this question:

"1) How do commentaries and versions interpret the form under consideration?

2) Is the nature of the action which is related to the first person plural form such that the author could have felt a desire to avoid the imputation to him of one of the negative attitudes listed above?[5]

3) Is the action which is related to the plural form only true of the author and not of the persons who supposedly are included?"

In connection with point 3), it is particularly emphasized that in many languages "we write" tends to raise such questions as "What parts did Paul write and what parts did the others write?" The expression "we write" can only be understood by the readers of the RL version as meaning plural authorship in the sense that each wrote part of it, not as referring to the fact that those associated with Paul were in agreement with what he wrote.

Even when the translator is satisfied as to the import of the "we" in the original, the final decision on how to render it in the RL must still take into account the reactions or problems of the readers of the RL. Two points have been noted in this area, particularly if the exclusive form of the plural is used in the RL. First, a plural form is often confusing to the readers if there is no obvious antecedent. In many languages, even those associated with Paul in the initial greetings are too remote for a "we" to be understood as referring back to them. In such cases, the translator may find it best to use the singular, or the singular plus a generic reference to the others, such as "I and my fellow workers," unless it is clear from the context that Paul had some particular fellow worker(s) in mind, in which case they may be named explicitly.[6]

---

[5] These are: "the appearance of bragging, or conceit of office, or arrogance, or egotism, or oversensitivity of feelings, or exaggerated superiority, or exclusive or overbearing authority."

[6] A possible example would be Gal. 2:5 "to them *we* did not yield submission even for a moment," where "we" probably refers to Paul, Barnabas, and Titus (cf. v. 1). Thus Ridderbos (1953, p. 85) says "the apostle describes his attitude and that of his fellows as adamant" and Burton (1956, p. 84) speaks of "Paul and those with him." Some translators have taken the view that Paul's use of "we" always refers back to those associated with him in the salutation, but with verses like 1 Cor. 11:16, "But if any man seem to be contentious, *we* have no such custom, neither the churches of God," it seems unlikely that "we" refers solely to Paul and Sosthenes.

The second objection to the use of the exclusive form of "we" is that it precludes the possibility of the readers' applying the truth to themselves. In other words, where the "we" is used in connection with statements which are generally true of all believers, then the readers of the RL version prefer the "we inclusive" form to be used. Where it refers only to the apostles, or Paul and his fellow workers, then "we exclusive" is quite satisfactory.

It should not be thought, however, that Paul is the only writer to use "we" in an extended sense, though he is the one who uses it the most. In the gospels, Jesus is recorded as saying, "Whereunto shall *we* liken the kingdom of God? or with what comparison shall *we* compare it?" (Mark 4:30), and in the Epistles of John, "we" is used frequently, and with a variety of different senses. See, for instance, the discussion in Stott (1964, pp. 26-34) under the heading, "The author as an eyewitness."

(b) There do not appear to be any clear cases of the use of the *second person* plural for the singular, and instances of the *third person* plural with a singular sense are relatively rare. An example of this latter case is found in Matthew 2:20 where an angel says to Joseph, "Arise, and take the young child and his mother, and go to the land of Israel, for *they* are dead who sought the young child's life." "They are dead" might be thought to refer to the soldiers, but the opening words of v. 19 "But when Herod was dead" makes it clear that it is Herod himself who is referred to.

In Turner (1963, pp. 25-28) and Blass-Debrunner (1961, pp. 77, 78) there are discussions of the use of plural nouns with singular reference. For instance, Matthew 27:44 says, "The thieves also, which were crucified with him, cast the same in his teeth," whereas Luke 23:39-43 says that one did and the other did not. One interpretation would then be that in Matthew 27:44 the plural is used with a singular sense. Other similar examples cited by Turner are Matthew 14:9 and Mark 6:26 ("oaths" in the Greek; translated by the singular in the KJV), and Matthew 21:7 ("he sat on *them*" in the Greek). In addition, these writers discuss such Greek words as *aiōnes* "ages," *ouranoi* "heavens," (*apo*) *anatolōn* "(from the) east," etc., where the form is plural, but the sense is singular. The word for "sabbath" also occurs in the plural form in Matthew 12:1 and Mark 1:21, even though it is an incident that took place on a particular sabbath day being described.

Special uses of the category of person

Just as the category of number is used with a nonliteral sense, so also is the category of person, the number being kept constant.[7] In particular, the third person is used when referring to the first and second persons, a

---

[7] A possible exception to this statement may be found in 2 Corinthians 7:2 where Paul says, "we have wronged no man, we have corrupted no man, we have defrauded no man." The third person form "no man" may be literal referring to anyone he had been in contact with, or it may have a second person plural reference meaning "any of you Corinthians."

semantic device which does not seem to be widely used in languages, and which, therefore, if translated literally in such languages, can only be understood by the readers as intending a third person reference, not a first or second person one. Often these third person forms are nouns, and in many cases titles or personal names, applied to some second or first person referent.

1. *Third person used with a second person meaning*

Most of the occurrences of a third person form being used to refer to the second person, i.e. the person addressed, are found in the New Testament letters. Thus, each of these letters is addressed to some individual person, such as Timothy, Titus, Philemon, etc. or to some group, such as "the church of God which is at Corinth, to them that are sanctified in Christ Jesus" (1 Cor. 1:2), "to the strangers scattered throughout Pontus . . . ." (1 Pet. 1:1), etc. In all of these cases, the persons are referred to by third person forms — "*them* that are sanctified," etc. — even though they are being directly addressed. This is normal letter-writing style for the Greek of the time, and is quite acceptable and intelligible in some languages, but not all, where the addition or substitution of "you" is necessary to identify the recipients. This means that "you that are sanctified" is needed in 1 Corinthians 1:2, and in similar contexts. Occasionally, in the body of a letter, individuals are addressed in the third person. Note, for instance, Philippians 4:2, "I beseech Euodias, and beseech Syntyche, that *they* be of the same mind in the Lord." In many languages, a straight vocative, followed by "that, *you* . . ." would be much clearer; otherwise, the implication may be that Euodias and Syntyche were not members of the church at Philippi.

Examples of this usage outside the Epistles are not common. In Luke 1:43 and 45, Elizabeth speaks of Mary in the third person as "the mother of my Lord" and "she that believed," but in v. 42 the second person is used, "thy salutation." "You" would be needed in all three of these verses in many languages; otherwise it would be implied that two different people were being spoken of by Elizabeth. Similar problems arise in Mark 15:9, 12 where Jesus is described as "the King of the Jews" when Pilate is addressing a Jewish audience.

2. *Third person used with a first person meaning*

The use of a third person form by the speaker to refer to himself seems to be a fairly common device in the New Testament, the best known example being Jesus' own use of the title, "Son of man," to refer to himself.[8] Often, this device is not found in the RL, so that a first

---

[8] For a detailed discussion, see Beekman (1965c, pp. 177-93). The points he makes may be summarized as follows: (i) Jesus was not attempting to hide the fact that he was referring to himself, because the title "Son of man" is used, in the same context, interchangeably with first person forms. Examples of this are found in Matt. 8:19, 20, 9:3-8, 19:28, 26:21-24, 45, 46; John 6:53-56; (ii) those who heard him use this title knew that he was referring to himself, see Matt. 17:22, 23, 26:64, 65; John 6:27-30; (iii) detailed discussion is given to those passages which would seem to present evidence in contradiction to the two points made above.

person singular form has to be added to the third person title. However, this practice is often objected to on the grounds that the speakers who used a third person form to refer to themselves did so because, for different reasons, they were hesitant about referring to themselves openly and directly in the first person, and that therefore the third person form should be retained in the RL.

In considering this objection, several points may be made. (1) It is true that third person forms are used in the New Testament somewhat in this way. Jesus used the "Son of man" as a "veiled title to avoid an open claim that he was the promised Messiah" (Beekman, 1965f, p. 5); Paul speaks of "a man in Christ" in 2 Corinthians 12:2-5, yet many commentators hold that he is referring to himself, but does not wish to boast. (2) It is usually assumed by those presenting this view that the use of the first person form in the RL will be interpreted in an egotistic manner, and the substitution of a third person form will obviate this problem. But this is rarely, if ever the case; the use of "I" simply means that the speaker is referring to himself, and the third person means that he is referring to *someone else*, thus conveying a totally wrong meaning. (3) Even where the translator knows that third person forms are used in the RL with a first person reference, careful inquiry needs to be made as to what the switch in person means to them. For instance, in the Mixe language of Mexico, a speaker will use a third person form for himself if he is ashamed of what he has done and wishes to hide it. To use a third person form in Mixe would grossly distort the meaning, and ascribe bad actions and motives to Jesus, Paul, and others who use this device. It cannot be emphasized too often that if the translation means something other than it should, then it is an unfaithful translation, and must be adjusted to convey the correct meaning.

A speaker's use of third person forms to refer to himself in the New Testament may be divided into three broad groups: Jesus speaking about himself, authors about themselves, and others about themselves.

Jesus often uses titles when referring to himself — Son of Man, Son of God, the Son, the Christ, the First and Last, the Amen. Beekman's discussion referred to above shows clearly that "I" can be added to the title "Son of Man" (as well as substituted for "he" in subsequent statements referring to the Son of Man), except in John 9:35 where Jesus asks the blind man, whom he had healed, "Do you believe in the Son of man?" (RSV),[9] and he answers, "Who is he, Lord, that I might believe in him?" The same use of "I" may well be needed in most translations where the title "Son of God" is used in John 5:25 and 11:4 by Jesus. Similarly, Jesus speaks of "the Son," in reference to himself,[10] in Matthew 11:27, 28:19; Mark 13:32; Luke 10:22; John 5:19-23, 6:40, 8:35, 36,

---

[9] The KJV has the "Son of God" at this point, but "Son of man" is used in other texts. See, for instance, Nestlé's Greek text, and the Bible societies' Greek New Testament, both of which have "Son of man" in the text.

[10] References to "the Son" and to the 'Son of God' in John 3:16-18 have not been included, as exegetical opinion is divided as to whether these are Jesus' own words, or those of John.

14:13, 17:1. With one exception,[11] Matthew 28:19, "I" may be used in these passages. In the introductions to the seven letters in Revelation, chapters 2 and 3, Jesus refers to himself on each occasion with one or more third person titles, and these may well need the introduction of a first person reference if Jesus is to be identified as the speaker. However, the use of "Christ" by Jesus needs handling with care. In such passages as Matthew 23:10, Mark 9:41 and John 17:3, a first person form may be needed. But in such passages as Matthew 22:42, Mark 12:35, Luke 20:41, 24:26, 46, Jesus is arguing about "the Christ" as to his person and sufferings, and there is only an indirect reference to himself. In these cases, no first person form is necessary.

Not only does Jesus refer to himself by means of third person forms,[12] but so do almost all the writers of the letters in the New Testament (only Hebrews and 1 John lack such a reference). In these letters, the writer's name is the third person form used — "Paul," "James," "Peter," etc. The translator may well find it necessary to translate with an additional first person form, such as "I, Paul, . . ." etc. In 2 and 3 John, the appropriate expression would be "I, the elder, . . ."

There are also one or two occasions in the epistles when the third person is used to refer to the author. One of the most difficult of these is in 2 Corinthians 12:2-5, which starts, "I knew a man in Christ . . ." and which concludes "Of such an one will I glory: yet of myself I will not glory . . . ." In spite of this final statement, many commentators take the view that, although Paul puts these statements into the third person, he is in fact referring to his own experiences, but wishing to avoid any impression of boasting (cf. v. 1), he does not use "I." But to simply substitute "I" makes nonsense of v. 5 which could then read "Of myself will I glory: yet of myself I will not glory." One way of meeting the problem of reference in this passage is to retain the third person forms in vv. 2-5, but to add "to me" to the statement in v. 1, so that it then reads, "I will come to visions and revelations of the Lord to me"; and possibly in v. 7 add some term referring back to the previous verses, such as "through the abundance of *such* revelations" (as in the NEB).[13]

The apostle John prefers not to name himself explicitly in his gospel, but to refer to himself as "the disciple whom Jesus loved" (13:23, 19:26, 20:2, 21:7, 20), and then, in subsequent references in the same passage he continues to use third person forms, usually deictics (for example "that") together with "disciple" (see 13:24, 25; 19:27; 20:3-10; 21:21-24).

---

11 In this case, Jesus is giving the trinitarian baptismal formula, and since the formula would be used in the third person, it is probably better to leave "the Son" unless the RL readers can only conclude that Jesus (the speaker) and "the Son" are different people.

12 Other references in the gospels where Jesus uses the third person of himself are Matthew 10:25, 12:41, 23:10; John 4:10, 6:58, 9:37, 10:36.

13 It should be noted, however, that an alternative interpretation is that "such an one" in v. 5 refers to the experience, not to the person who had it. Hence, it would be possible to say "I will boast of such an experience; but I will not boast about myself."

In languages such as Ojitlán Chinantec, and Otomí of the State of Mexico, although the readers of the RL version could deduce from a comparison of 21:20 and 24 that "the beloved disciple" wrote the book, they could not understand in view of the title of the book why he wrote as if it were someone else. So first person forms had to be used, and the RL users did not indicate that it was improper for John to refer to himself as the one "whom Jesus loved." In fact, the use of first person forms removed the conflicts between the title and the text and the misconception that it was someone else who wrote the gospel.

There are other occasional uses of third person forms to refer to the speaker(s) in the New Testament, such as in John 7:48 where the Pharisees say, "Have any of the rulers or of the Pharisees believed on him?" In many languages, this would require the use of "we" to identify the persons referred to as belonging to the same group as the speakers. Some similar instances are found in Acts 2:9-11, 27; 4:29; and in Romans 9:4, 5.

3. *First person plural used with a second plural meaning*

There is one further example of the use of the category of person with a nonliteral sense to be considered, and that is Paul's use of "we" for "you (plural)" in exhortations, where he addresses the exhortation to himself as well as to those to whom he is writing. He identifies himself with them as a fellow-believer, standing in as much need of exhortation as they themselves. Normally, this does not cause any problem for the RL readers, but occasionally, when the injunction carries negative implications as to past conduct, or possible future conduct, it does cause difficulty. For instance, the Sierra Juárez Zapotec language helper was unhappy with the use of "us" in "Neither let us commit fornication . . . ." (1 Cor. 10:8), as he felt that in this dialect of Zapotec it implied that Paul had committed fornication, or was in imminent danger of doing so. In this type of situation, "you (plural)" can be substituted or an indefinite construction such as "none of us."

EXAMPLES OF TRANSLATING FIGURATIVE SENSES

It is of considerable interest that many of the figures of speech classified by Aristotle, and which are still referred to by their classical names in dictionaries and books on rhetoric, are the very ones which are based on associative relations of the type described in this chapter. The particular figures of speech referred to are Metonymy, Synecdoche, Hyperbole, Euphemism, Metaphor, and Simile. In addition, some idioms are included in this discussion.

The figure of metonymy[14] is based on any of the associative relations listed under the general heading of "contiguity," i.e., temporal, spatial, and logical relationships. *Synecdoche*, however, with which metonymy is often associated, is based on any of the "part-whole" relations — member-class, constituent-whole, attribute-whole. Note, however, that the

---

[14] A detailed analysis of metonymy and synecdoche, with extensive exemplification, and a partial listing of these figures in the New Testament will be found in NOT 23, pp. 12-25 (Beekman, 1967b).

term synecdoche covers the relation in either direction: part for the whole, or whole for the part. This latter relation was only briefly illustrated earlier in the chapter, so some examples are given at this point.

There are two main types of whole-part relations in the New Testament. In the first, the whole of a group of persons is put for part of that group; in the second an absolute negative is used when it is a partial negative that is intended. The first type is seen in John 1:19 where it is said that "the Jews sent priests and Levites from Jerusalem." Here "the Jews" does not mean the whole Jewish race, but the leaders of the Jews in Jerusalem, men who were particularly concerned about the implications of Jesus' teaching. Again, in Galatians 2:13 "the other Jews" does not mean the rest of the Jewish race other than those just mentioned, but the other Christian Jews present in Antioch at the time of this incident.[15]

Another example is the use of "all" in the Scriptures when it means "the great majority" or "very many." In Matthew 10:22, Jesus warns his disciples, "ye shall be hated of all men for my name's sake," where he clearly means that the majority of men, or all sorts of men, would hate them. Again, in John 8:2, it says, "And early in the morning he came again into the temple, and all the people came unto him," but the writer does not intend us to understand that the whole Jewish nation crowded into the temple to hear Jesus. It may mean "all the people who had heard him previously" (note the use of "again"), or simply "a great crowd of people." A further example occurs in John's gospel, when Jesus says, "All that ever came before me are thieves and robbers" (John 10:8). Who did he refer to when he said, "All that ever came before me"? Does he refer to *all* the men from Adam to his own time? Clearly not. Does he refer to *all* those who spoke to Israel in God's name, as he himself was doing? Clearly not, as that would include Moses and the prophets as "thieves and robbers." Views differ between false messiahs, false leaders (like the Pharisees, to whom he was speaking), etc., but all commentators consulted agree that the "all" is to be understood in some nonabsolute sense.

Exegetically, therefore, "all" presents its problems. The translator should bear in mind that various theological differences hinge on the interpretation of certain of the "all's" in Scripture. Where a study of the commentaries reveals this to be the case, the translator should retain the "all."[16]

The second type, in which an absolute negative is used with the sense of a partial negative, is seen in such statements as "and he that hath not, from him shall be taken even that which he hath" (Mark 4:25); "and he could do there no mighty work, save that he laid his hands upon a few sick folk, and healed them" (Mark 6:5); "drink no longer water, but use a little wine for thy stomach's sake and thine often infirmities" (I Tim.

---

[15] This illustration also highlights the fact that a given term, "Jews" in this case, may have several associative senses, depending on the context.

[16] Some verses where the "all" is interpreted differently by different theological schools are Rom. 11:26, 32; 2 Cor. 5:14, 15; 1 Tim. 2:4, 6.

5:23). "He that hath not" in this context is equivalent to "he that hath only a little"; "no mighty work" means "only a few mighty works"; "drink no longer water" means "drink no longer only water." The use of such strong negatives adds force and vividness to the statements, but they are not to be literally understood; they are figurative in use.

Hyperbole is metonymy or synechdoche with more said than the writer intends the reader to understand. The "exaggeration" is deliberately used for effect, and is not to be understood as if it were a literal description. As might be expected, therefore, hyperbole is often based on the group of part-whole relations, but in the reverse order, i.e., the whole is used for the part.[17] An example of hyperbole based on the whole-attributive relation is found in Matthew 23:24, where Jesus says to the scribes and Pharisees, "Ye blind guides, which strain at a gnat, and swallow a camel." Here *gnat* is used for its attribute of smallness, *camel* for the opposite attribute of largeness. But *camel* is also used hyperbolically, as there is no thought of being able to swallow a camel. This is often misunderstood even after explaining what a camel is like. Here the sense of *camel* does not refer literally to the animal. A component of meaning true of a camel, namely, its size, is in focus. To render this verse without retaining the hyperbole, a rendition focusing on size would have to be used. Rather than substitute an animal or insect that is relatively large yet can still be swallowed, it is preferable to introduce a generic rendition such as "strain out a gnat and swallow something big." This cares for the hyperbole but, of course, leaves the metaphor yet to be cared for. As will be seen in chapter 9, a possible rendition might be: What you do, is like one who strains out a gnat from his drink and then he overlooks/swallows something much bigger.

A whole-part example is the statement in John 12:19, where the Pharisees said to each other, "Perceive ye how ye prevail nothing? behold, the world is gone after him." Here, the "world" refers to a large crowd of people, not the whole world.

Contiguity in logic is another way to express the relation utilized in these hyperboles. For example, in Mark 9:43, "cut off your hand," there is a means-result relation on which the hyperbole is based. This metonymy-based hyperbole is analyzed more fully since when it is completely misunderstood it may need to be recast to state what the author intended to communicate. The statement, "If thy hand offend thee, cut it off," is, of course hyperbolic. In this statement *hand* is used in a figurative sense based on an associative relation. The *hand* is represented as the efficient cause of sin, when in actuality it is the instrumental cause. Our first step in adjusting this figurative statement involves adopting a usage of *hand* in relation to offend (sin) which can be understood literally. For example: If you sin by what you do with your hand, cut it off. This

---

[17] This is why, of course, there is liable to be confusion between hyperbole and synecdoche, as both are based on the same relationship. It is difficult to make any rigid distinction; all one can say is that where there is an element of "overstatement" for vivid effect, the figure is hyperbole.

cares for the figurative sense of hand, but still does not face the problems which may arise in understanding the hyperbole. A means is stated when the result is really intended. Thus, this statement has been rendered in some translations as: "If you sin by what you do with your hand, stop it as though you had cut off your hand." The same analysis and adjustments would apply to the adjacent statements concerning the foot and eye. The rest of the related statements present no special problem and need no adjustments of this type.

Hyperbole may use the associative relation between antonyms as its basis. For instance, in the parable of the Prodigal Son, the father says to the older son "for this thy brother was dead, and is alive again" (Luke 15:32; cf. also v. 24). "Dead" and "alive" are antonyms, opposites in meaning. The son was not actually physically dead, but, compared to his life back with the father, it was as if he had been dead. A further example using antonyms is in the contrast between "love" and "hate" in such statements as "If any man come to me, and hate not his father, and mother , . . ." (Luke 14:26), or "Jacob have I loved, but Esau have I hated" (Rom. 9:13). Here, the antonym is used where what is actually meant is "love less" not actually "hate." This meaning is confirmed by the comparison of Luke 14:26 with Matthew 10:37, "He who loves father or mother more than me is not worthy of me."

The opposite of hyperbole is not common in the New Testament.[18] Like hyperbole it is basically metonymy or synecdoche but with less said than is intended to be understood. In Mark 14:27, Jesus quotes the Old Testament prophecy, "I will smite the shepherd, and the sheep shall be scattered"; and Stephen says that Moses "smote the Egyptian" (Acts 7:24). In both cases, the person "smitten" was actually killed, not simply struck. The associative relationship involved is logical, i.e., cause-effect — the cause of death, understood in this figure, is for the death itself. A similar example is found in Hebrews 11:28 where it is said that, by faith, Moses "kept the passover . . . lest he that destroyed the firstborn should touch them," where "touch" is an understatement for "kill" or "destroy." Again, in Acts 16:28, Paul calls, "Do thyself no harm," although it is stated quite explicitly in the previous verse that the jailer planned to kill himself.

Euphemism is generally based on metonymy but may be based on metaphor. It may be further defined as to its purpose as the substitution of an acceptable, inoffensive expression for one that is socially unacceptable, offensive, or which may suggest something unpleasant. In the New Testament, euphemistic expressions are mostly used to refer to God, death, the Gentiles, and sex.

It is well known that the Jews used many substitutions for God so as

---

[18] No specific name is given to this figure, as (a) it is rare in the New Testament, and (b) there is no commonly agreed term. "Hypobole" is used in SIL (Summer Institute of Linguistics) circles, but is not in the standard dictionaries; "meiosis" is used with this sense, but is also often used to refer to litotes as well, which is treated separately in chapter 14.

to avoid using his name. Some of these substitutes, such as the use of the passive with no indication of the actor, do not fall within the study of figures of speech, but others do. Mention has already been made of the use of attributes such as "Blessed" and "most High," and of the use of "heaven." A further, somewhat similar example, is John 19:11 where Jesus tells Pilate that he would have had no power over him "except it were given thee from above," where "from above" is euphemistic for God.

A number of expressions are used euphemistically for "death" in the New Testament.[19] Jesus tells his disciples in Matthew 26:24 that "the Son of man goeth as it is written of him," where "goeth" means "will die" or "will be killed." Paul says, in a somewhat similar way, "For I am in a strait betwixt two, having a desire to depart, and to be with Christ." In these cases, "going" or "departing" is a result arising out of a cause, i.e., death, so the relationship falls within the general heading of cause-effect. Other expressions used for violent death are found in Mark 9:13 "they did to him whatsoever they listed"; and in Acts 22:22 "Away with such a fellow from the earth." In the first, the means is stated; in the second, the effect.

The Gentiles are referred to several times by the euphemistic expression, "those that are afar off" (cf. Acts 2:39; Eph. 2:13, 17), where the associative relationship is spatial — where the people live is put for the people themselves. Also, Jesus refers to the Gentiles in Luke 13:29 as those that "shall come from the east, and from the west, and from the north, and from the south." That such euphemisms were necessary is apparent from Acts 22:21, 22 where Paul's use of the word "Gentile" in the mention of his divine mission to the Gentiles provoked the listening crowd to wild demonstrations of anger.

Sex, as in many languages, is referred to euphemistically. The Hebrew euphemism of "to know" for sexual intercourse is found in Matthew 1:25, and a Greek one is found in 1 Corinthians 7:1 where Paul says "It is good for a man not to touch a woman." Later in the same chapter Paul uses "and come together again" (v. 5) as a euphemism for resuming normal marital relations. These are all based on a means-result relation.

Metaphor and *simile* are two further figures based upon associative relations. They involve more than this relation however, as they always involve an implicit or explicit comparison with something else in the context. Since this pair of figures poses a variety of problems for the translator, they are discussed in much more detail in the next two chapters. At this point, we are only interested in the relation between the

19 "To sleep" or "to fall asleep" is used a number of times in the New Testament for dying or death, as in John 11:11; Acts 7:60, 13:36; 1 Cor. 7:39 (translated with "be dead" in KJV), 11:30, 15:6, 18, 20, 51; 1 Thess. 4:13-15; 2 Pet. 3:4. This is a euphemism used in Greek going as far back as Homer, and is based upon a metaphor that assumes a point of similarity between these two senses of "to sleep." Sleep and death share several outward physical features and this may be the point of similarity. Some other metaphors may be found which are exceptions in that they are based on a shared meaning rather than an associative relation.

sense which is carried by the word when used in the figure as compared to its sense when used nonfiguratively.

In Acts 2:20, Peter quotes Joel's prophecy "and the moon [shall be turned] into blood," where "blood" is not to be understood literally, but has the sense of "red." In this case, the relation between the senses of blood is one of attribute-whole. When Paul instructs Titus to exhort slaves to certain patterns of good behavior "that they may adorn the doctrine of God our Saviour in all things" (Titus 2:10), he is using a metaphor based on a logical, i,e., a cause-effect relation, where "adorning" is the means to the end of making attractive or producing a favorable impression on others. Again, when Paul warns the Ephesian elders that "grievous wolves shall enter in" (Acts 20:29), he refers, not to actual wolves, but to an attribute of wolves, i.e., they attack and harm sheep. The attribute-whole relation is the basis for the two senses of wolves.[20]

Finally, a number of *idioms* are based on some type of associative relationship. An idiom may be defined as an expression of at least two words which cannot be understood literally and which functions as a unit semantically. An example is "step on the gas." This expression is used in its primary sense if you are giving instructions to someone driving a car, but it is also used figuratively to mean "hurry." In this usage, neither "step on" nor "gas" are intended literally, and the underlying associative relationship is a cause-effect one — the effect of greater speed is produced by depressing the gas pedal. However, it is not now possible to state the associative relationship underlying many idioms. "Through the nose" is used literally in "the farmer put a ring through the nose of the bull," but it is no longer apparent how "through the nose" came to be collocated with "pay" to mean "exorbitantly." Guidelines numbers one and three which were stated earlier in this chapter apply to the translation of idioms; that is to say, the sense may be translated straightforwardly or an RL idiom, with the same sense, may be used.

It is likewise impossible to state the associative relation underlying most gestures and other symbolic actions. These, however, are similar to figures of speech and idioms in that the primary sense is not the intended sense. Because of this similarity between symbolic actions, idioms, and figures of speech, the meaning intended by symbolic actions may properly be classed as a figurative sense. These are explained more fully in the following paragraphs.

The first-century cultures reflected in the Scriptures had their own *symbolic gestures* — actions and movements that had a figurative sense in that culture. In translating these, we should refer to the actual form of the gesture, since most of these represent historical references. As it happens, however, one or more of these significant actions is often known

---

[20] This note is intended to re-emphasize that in this discussion we are restricting our study to the metaphoric word in its context and showing how this word has a relation to the literal sense of that word. While it is true that context will guide to the specific metaphoric sense intended, we are here showing the basis upon which a word may be used in a new context with a sense other than its literal sense.

in the receptor culture, and has a *different* meaning associated with it than that of the original.

In Matthew 19:13, children were brought to Jesus so that he would "put his hands on them." But in some cultures, putting your hand or hands on someone is associated only with the curses of shamans. Luke described how the tax collector "smote upon his breast" in remorse and repentance before God (Luke 18:13). In Mezquital Otomi (Mexico) this same action accompanies anger, and in Teutila Cuicatec (Mexico) an Indian was observed walking out of a saloon doing this and shouting the equivalent of "I am a he-man." When Jesus condemned Chorazin and Bethsaida for not repenting, he contrasted them with Tyre and Sidon who would have repented "sitting in sackcloth and ashes" (Luke 10:13). Among the Cuicatecos, someone who is lazy and spends his day sitting by the fire instead of working is spoken of as "sitting in ashes." Those who were passing by Jesus on the cross "reviled him, wagging their heads" (Matt. 27:39). In Chol (Mexico) wagging your head from side to side indicates an emphatic "no," and wagging it up and down signifies joy.

These examples highlight the fact that a literal transfer of the form of an action may prove to be quite misleading in the RL. What is important, in such instances as the above, is the significance of the action.

If the form of the action is already associated with a different function in the RL, how are such symbolic actions to be translated? Should the intended meaning be added and the form of the action be retained literally in the RL? If the symbolic action already has another symbolic meaning in the RL, this will probably produce a semantic clash. It would be like attempting to change the gesture of shaking one's fist at another by saying, "He shook his fist in his face in a friendly manner." The implicit meaning of the gesture is not erased by the addition of "in a friendly manner." The combination just does not make sense and confuses the reader.

In such cases, the translator needs to drop specific reference to the symbolic action and keep explicit the particular meaning of the action. The symbolic action may be referred to generically by something like "they showed," or "they did that which showed," or "they expressed," using an RL term that covers actions of the sort discussed. Hence, it could be said of the tax collector, "he showed that he was repentant." Of Tyre and Sidon it could be said, "they would have shown that they repented a great while ago." Similarly, the passers-by could be said to have "reviled him, expressing their contempt." Such a generic term still leaves it possible for teachers and preachers to explain the different customs prevailing elsewhere without introducing a semantic clash into the translation itself. Another possibility is to translate the action literally and explain in a footnote that the Jews used this gesture with a different significance.

However, when the particular action described is unknown in the receptor culture or is known but has no symbolic significance, then a literal reference to the form of the action should be retained. At this point the translator will not expect the readers to understand the symbolic significance of the particular action. Although in some cases it will be clear from the context, so that the form alone is sufficient, yet in many cases a wrong meaning will be communicated. When the Chols (Mexico) read that the high priest "rent his clothes" (Mark 14:63), they could only guess at why he did so. Perhaps he had gone temporarily insane, for if he was angry with someone, he would have torn their clothes, not his own. Or perhaps he had become too warm in the course of the trial, and was trying to cool himself off. If the translator hears this type of discussion, it is an indication to him that it is necessary to state explicitly just what the action means. The original readers knew, of course, and the author did not need to give the meaning explicitly.

Thus, when an action is understood in its literal sense and that action does not already have a symbolic sense, then one may add to the action its extended or symbolic sense without introducing a semantic clash. The disciples are spoken of as shaking the dust off their feet (see Matt. 10:14; Mark 6:11; Luke 9:5; Acts 13:51). This suggests to the reader that they wanted to get rid of the dust. This primary meaning, however, does not preclude the addition of its symbolic meaning, which will probably need to be added either in the text or in a footnote. Otherwise it may be quite obscure as to *why* they wanted to get rid of the dust of their feet.

Skirtaō in Greek means simply "leap," but it is used symbolically as an expression of joy. Therefore, the KJV translators, translating that word into English, rendered it "leap for joy" (Luke 6:23), carrying over the form of the action and adding a phrase to show what its function was. Similar solutions have been used in the following examples; the form of the action has been translated literally and the meaning has been made explicit by the addition of the material following the dash.

Matt. 26:65 "rent his clothes" — in anger   Lalana Chinantec (Mex.)

Mark 7:4 "washing" — so that, according to their belief, God would consider them good   Cuicatec (Mex.)

Mark 12:38 "in long clothing" — to show their importance   Lalana Chinantec (Mex.)

Acts 13:51 "they shook off the dust of their feet against them" — to show that the people of the city would be responsible for their own actions   North Puebla Totonac (Mex.)

Acts 14:14 "they rent their clothes" — because they wanted the people to know that they did not see well what they were doing   Sierra Otomi (Mex.)

— to show that they were not to do this   Teutila Cuicatec (Mex.)
— because they were distressed   Lalana Chinantec (Mex.)

CHAPTER 8

The Nature of Metaphor and Simile [1]

In the previous chapters, it was shown that multiple senses, when based on an associative relation, give rise to various figures of speech, metaphor and simile among them. In these two figures, a word or expression is used in a figurative sense, and that sense provides a point of comparison with the topic which the writer is discussing. Consequently, in these figures, there is not only the use of a figurative sense of a word, but also the comparison of this sense with some other term.

COMPARISONS, FULL AND ABBREVIATED

Comparisons are widely used as an effective way to make information more vivid and meaningful, and such comparisons occur in a number of literary forms. In the Bible, comparisons underlie not only metaphor and simile, but also parables, allegories, and some proverbs and symbols. Jesus made extensive use of these various forms in his public teaching, and Paul and the other New Testament writers used them frequently in their letters.

Full comparisons

Comparisons may be either full, or abbreviated in some way. A *full comparison* states both items of the comparison along with the similarity between the two items. A full comparison may be a contrast or a resemblance. There are two types of contrast, by opposition and by degree.

> By opposition: I am tall, (but) he is not.
>   I am tall, he is short.

---

[1] This chapter and the following are based on the article with the same title, NOT 31, 1-22 (Beekman, 1969).

By degree: I am taller than he (is).
I am the tallest of all.
I am not as tall as he (is).

There are also two types of resemblances, relative and absolute.

Relative: I am tall (and) he is tall.
I am tall, like he is tall.

Absolute: I am just as tall as he (is).

Resemblances which compare two items by the use of a word such as "like" or "as" are known as *similes*. When similes are full comparisons, they explicitly compare the two items and also give the point of similarity. For example:

> "the heavens shall vanish away like smoke, and the earth shall wax old like a garment" (Isa. 51:6)

> "All we like sheep have gone astray" (Isa. 53:6)

In the first example, the heavens are compared to smoke and the earth to a piece of clothing. The heavens resemble smoke in that the latter disappears fairly quickly; the earth resembles a piece of clothing in that the latter gets old. Thus, the points of similarity are the relatively rapid disappearance and the getting old, respectively. In the second example "we," that is, the Israelites of Isaiah's time and Isaiah himself, resemble sheep in that these have a tendency to wander off from the flock and so get lost. This proneness to wander away from where they should be, then, is the point of the comparison.

A *metaphor*, when it is in the form of a full comparison, compares two items and gives the point of similarity, but differs from a simile in that the comparison is not made explicit by the use of such words as "like" or "as." Rather, it is left implicit. The two items being compared are apparently equated. For example:

> "His watchmen . . . are all dumb dogs, they cannot bark" (Isa. 56:10)

> "My people hath been lost sheep" (Jer. 50:6)

> "Go rather to the lost sheep of the house of Israel" (Matt. 10:6)

Such full comparisons do not usually cause serious difficulty to the readers, as all the essential parts of the comparison are explicitly stated. Sometimes, however, as in the three examples cited above, the points of similarity ("dumb . . . cannot bark," "lost," "lost") are themselves presented in figurative form, and this may cause misunderstanding that will need to be removed.

Abbreviated comparisons

Many of the comparisons in the Scriptures are not stated in a full form; they are abbreviated to some extent. In most abbreviated comparisons the point of similarity is left implicit, with the result that the reader has to supply them himself. Some examples of simile and metaphor without the point of similarity follow:

Simile	"his eyes were as a flame of fire . . . and his voice as the sound of many waters" (Rev. 1:14, 15) "and it [the sea] became as the blood of a dead man" (Rev. 16:3) "I saw three unclean spirits like frogs" (Rev. 16:13)
Metaphor	"Ye are the salt of the earth" (Matt. 5:13) "he is a chosen vessel" (Acts 9:15) "the tongue is a fire" (James 3:6)

In these two figures of simile and metaphor, the word which is being used to illustrate the topic under discussion is referred to as the *image*. Thus, in the three examples of metaphor immediately above, the three images used are "salt of the earth," "chosen vessel," and "fire" respectively. These are used by the different writers to illustrate the topic of "ye," that is, Christians; "he," that is, Paul; and "the tongue." Sometimes, however, not only is the point of similarity omitted, but also the topic being illustrated, so that only the image itself is explicitly stated. This is the case in the following examples, in which the images are italicized.

"I am come to send *fire* on the earth" (Luke 12:49)
"*Feed* my *sheep*" (John 21:17)
"he shall receive the *crown* of life" (James 1:12)

In a few instances, the point of similarity is stated explicitly but the topic being illustrated is left implicit. An example of this is "the sheep shall be scattered" in Mark 14:27. In this example, "sheep" is the image and "shall be scattered" is the point of similarity, but just who it is that will be scattered like sheep is left implicit.

Before leaving this general introduction to comparisons, it is important to notice that metaphor appears in the form of a collocational clash.[2] This is not the case with a simile, as it explicitly compares the two items, thus alerting the reader to the fact that he is dealing with a figure. But the comparison is implicit in a metaphor, and the two items are apparently equated. Thus, in the examples of metaphor above, the tongue is said to be a fire; and Paul is said to be a household utensil.

A distinction can be drawn between "overt" and "covert" collocational clashes. The examples just cited are all "overt" — people are not utensils; a human organ is not a fire. Other examples are "having the understanding darkened" (Eph. 4:18), where a term that applies to the sense of sight is used to describe the mind; "nailing it [the law] to his cross" (Col. 2:14) applies an act done to people to an abstract entity; and "soweth the word" (Mark 4:14) combines an action done by hand with an activity of the speech organs.

The presence of a "covert" clash is only realized when the sentence containing the metaphor is compared with the larger context. In fact, the figure may be understood literally to start with. Thus when Jesus warned his disciples to "beware of the leaven of the Pharisees" (Matt.

---

[2] A collocational clash is the juxtaposition of two or more words which are incompatible semantically. See chapter 11 for a detailed discussion of collocational clashes.

16:6, 11; Mark 8:15; Luke 12:1), the disciples understood it literally until Jesus went on to explain to them its figurative sense. The illustration drawn from the new and old wineskins and new and old cloth (Mark 2:21, 22) is a covert clash also. Within the illustrations themselves there is no clash (wine is put in wineskins, patches are put on garments, etc.), and the covert clash becomes evident only when it is seen that the larger context is not that of preserving wine or patching clothes, but of the contrast between the new and old teaching (cf. Mark 2:18). Similarly, in Matthew 9:37, 38, Jesus speaks about the harvest and the laborers, but the context is not that of farming, but Jesus' compassion on the people, who lacked true spiritual leaders.

There are, undoubtedly, several hundred examples of simile and metaphor in the New Testament alone, and any one of these, being language-specific in meaning, may convey zero or wrong meaning in the RL if rendered literally. It is important, therefore, that the translator clearly understand the pitfalls associated with these figures, and know how to handle them so that the meaning they conveyed to the original readers is faithfullly transmitted to the RL readers. Consequently, the rest of this chapter discusses the structure of metaphor and simile, and the differences between dead and live metaphor, and the following chapter takes up reasons why metaphor and simile are misunderstood by speakers of the RL, and how they can be accurately and faithfully translated.

THE STRUCTURE OF METAPHOR AND SIMILE

Definition of metaphor and simile

Bearing in mind, then, that there are full and abbreviated forms of simile and metaphor, we can define simile as follows:

> A *simile* is an explicit comparison in which one item of the comparison (the "image") carries a number of components of meaning of which usually only one is contextually relevant to and shared by the second item (the "topic").

Similarly, a metaphor can be defined as follows:

> A *metaphor* is an implicit comparison in which one item of the comparison (the "image") carries a number of components of meaning of which usually only one is contextually relevant to and shared by the second item (the "topic").

The three parts of metaphor and simile

As has been stated above, metaphor and simile are similar, except that the comparison is made explicit in the case of a simile by the use of a word such as "like" or "as." There are three parts to these figures, which are as follows:

(1) the *topic*, that is, the item which is illustrated by the image;
(2) the *image*, that is, the "metaphoric" part of the figure;
(3) the *point of similarity*, which explains in what particular aspect the image and topic are similar.

In the following examples, each part that is present is identified by the appropriate number preceding it.[3]

"(1) the heavens shall (3) vanish away like (2) smoke" (Isa. 51:6)

"Go rather to the (3) lost (2) sheep of (1) the house of Israel (Matt. 10:6)

"I saw three (1) unclean spirits like (2) frogs" (Rev. 16:13)

"(1) ye are (2) the salt of the earth (Matt. 5:13)

"he shall receive (2) the crown of (1) life" (James 1:12)

The *topic* is the particular item or event under discussion or, it may be, the people being addressed. In the five examples cited above, the topics are respectively the heavens, the Jews, demons, the disciples, and a reward. Metaphor or simile is used to impart information about a particular topic in a vivid and memorable way.

The term image may be briefly defined as "that part of the comparison which is intended to illustrate the subject under discussion." It follows that there can be no metaphor or simile without an expressed image. The points of similarity are often omitted; the topic which the image illustrates may be left implicit in metaphor; but the image in explicit form is essential in both simile and metaphor.

The *point of similarity* states what the comparison or resemblance between the topic and the image is. Like the topic, the point of similarity may or may not be stated explicitly. If it is not stated explicitly, it has to be inferred from the context. This requires a careful study of the context since the same image may be used with different points of similarity in different contexts. Any image carries a number of components of meaning, and, in different contexts, different components of the image may be relevant. For example, "sheep" is a frequently used image in the Scriptures, but it has associated with it a number of different points for comparison. Note the following examples, in which the points of similarity are italicized:

"All we like sheep *have gone astray*" (Isa. 53:6)

"As a sheep before his shearers *is dumb*, so he . . ." (Isa. 53:7; cf. Acts 8:32)

"pull them out like sheep *for the slaughter*" (Jer. 12:3)

"and the sheep *will be scattered*" (Zech. 13:7)

"as sheep in the midst of wolves" (point of similarity: *defenseless*) (Matt. 10:16)

In Luke 13:32, Jesus says, "Go ye, and tell that fox, . . ." Chart 1 illustrates the structure of a metaphor, using "fox" as the particular

---

[3] On the surface, the two expressions, "x is like y" and "y is like x" appear equivalent. Both expressions compare x and y, stating that they are similar at some point. In a context, however, x is the topic and y the image in the first expression, and vice versa in the second. This has caused problems in translation. In analyzing simile, therefore, it is important to choose the topic correctly.

example. (It is assumed here that the point of similarity is "slyness." This is not overtly stated in the metaphor.)

CHART 1

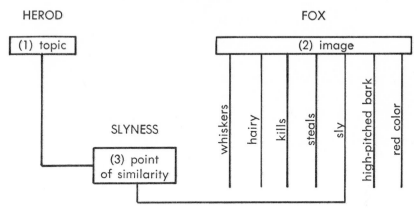

Four types of abbreviated metaphor or simile

Four abbreviated types of these figures are found as follows:

Type (1) *The point of similarity is not stated.* This may occur with either metaphor or simile.

Type (2) *The topic is not stated.* This can only happen in the case of a metaphor, since in a simile both the image and the topic always occur.

Type (3) *Neither the point of similarity nor the topic is stated.* Naturally, from what has been said above, this form is found only with metaphor.

Type (4) *The point of similarity and part of the image are implicit.* These appear to be a combination of metaphor and metonymy inasmuch as the image, and the point of similarity, are in an associative relation such as specific-generic or means-result.

Some further examples are now analyzed to illustrate these four types.

Type (1) "And he is the head of the body, the church" (Col. 1:18). There are two metaphors combined here, which can be separated out as "He is the head (of the body)" and "the church is the body." The topics are "Christ" and "the church" and the images are "head" and "body," respectively. The points of similarity are omitted, but it is clear that the point is that just as the head directs or rules, so Christ rules; and just as the body is directed or ruled, so the church is ruled. Stated nonmetaphorically, it says that Christ rules the church.

Type (2) "The sheep will be scattered" (Mark 14:27; cf. Matt. 26:31). In this metaphor "sheep" is the image, "will be scattered" is the point of similarity, and "disciples" is the implied topic. As sheep would be scattered if the shepherd were killed, so the disciples will be scattered.

Type (3) "Beware of the leaven of the Pharisees" (Matt. 16:6, 11; Mark 8:15; Luke 12:1). In this statement by Jesus to his disciples, only "leaven," the image, is explicit. Leaven is compared to teaching, the topic (Matt. 16:12), since each in its own way has a permeating effect. Both the topic, i.e., teaching,[4] and the point of similarity, i.e., the permeating effect, are implicit.

Type (4) Because the analysis of this type of metaphor is not as straightforward as the previous types, more than one example is given. It will be noted that whereas a Thing was central to metaphors and similes of types (1), (2), and (3), in this type an Event is central; and also the image needs to be filled out with the appropriate Thing which underlies the comparison.

"It is hard for thee to kick against the pricks" (Acts 9:5 and 26:14). The explicit part of the image consists of an Event "kick against the pricks." An agent, i.e., ox, is implied by the Event. Paul's actions, then, are compared with those of an ox. We may restate the comparison in the following form.

It is hard for an ox to kick against the pricks.

It is hard for thee to _____.

In this comparison between Paul and an ox, we are not left without a clue as to what is similar between the two since a specific action of an ox is stated, i.e., "kicking against the pricks." This action helps us to fill in the blank with the Event "to rebel" by noting that this specific action of an ox is one way in which rebellion may manifest itself among animate creatures. The relationship between the image and the point of similarity is that the former is specific and the later generic. Perhaps what is really intended from the context are the specific acts of rebellion of which Paul was guilty, but since these cannot be listed in a translation, the general point of similarity between the actions of Paul and an ox is used to fill in the blank. Thus, in the form of a full comparison, one would translate: It is unpleasant for you when you rebel just like it is unpleasant for an ox when he kicks against the pricks.

"Blessed are they which do hunger and thirst after righteousness" (Matt. 5:6). The figurative part of this beatitude is the coordinated verbs "hunger and thirst," which imply the objects "food" and "drink" respectively. A full statement of the image would then be: those who hunger and thirst for food and drink. This is compared to: they which _____ righteousness. The choice of an Event word to fill this blank is limited on the one hand by its collocation with "righteousness," and on the other hand by its comparison with "hunger and thirst." These

---

[4] This is an example in which the unity of Scripture is recognized in the process of translation. When implicit information must be made explicit, one should avoid introducing a conflict with another verse in some other context where that same information is stated explicitly.

considerations lead to some such choice as "intensely desire," "long for," etc.

"Quench not the Spirit" (1 Thess. 5:19). This is a further example of a metaphor where the image centers on an Event word, in this case, "quench." The full form of the image would be "people quench fires," and the topic may be put in the comparable form, "people (are not to) _____ the Spirit." The point of similarity between a fire and the Spirit is that a person may put an end to or diminish the activities of each.

"That they may adorn the doctrine of God" (Titus 2:10). The full image is "people adorn themselves" (or houses, rooms, etc.). The topic is "people (ought to) _____ the doctrine of God." The point of similarity between doctrine and other things as suggested by the word "adorn" is that each may be made attractive. Perhaps a specific way to make doctrine attractive to others is in Paul's mind when he uses the word "adorn." Perhaps he was thinking of "obedience." There can be little doubt, however, that his use of "adorn" was intended to focus on the purpose of adorning anything, namely, to make it pleasing to others. It is in the purpose of adornment that we find the point of similarity. Here it means that slaves were to conduct themselves in such a way that they made the Christian faith attractive to their masters.[5]

While the basic structure of a metaphor or simile is essentially simple, the fact that one or more parts of the figure may be omitted and that an image may be associated with several different points of similarity make the interpretation and translation of these figures quite different at times. However, before the question of translating these figures is discussed, it is necessary to make a distinction between "live" and "dead" metaphor and simile.

LIVE AND DEAD METAPHOR AND SIMILE

The distinction between live and dead metaphor

The distinction between "live" and "dead" metaphor is basically a question of the role of the image — how focal, how central, is it? The difference may be put this way. A *live metaphor* is understood by a native speaker only after some attention has been given to the primary meaning of the words being used metaphorically. On the other hand, a *dead metaphor* (like an idiom or any dead figure) is understood directly without such attention being given to the primary meaning of the words.

The distinction may be diagrammed using an adaptation of the triangle

---

[5] An alternative view would be to consider "hunger and thirst," "kick against the pricks," and "adorn," not as part of the image, but as the point of similarity between the topic and the implied image. Since the point of similarity should apply to both the topic and the image, and since these terms do not equally collocate with both, it is deemed best to consider such terms as part of the image. Also, such an interpretation would introduce an element not found in other metaphors and similes, an *implied image*.

found in Ogden and Richards (1952). First there is the "symbol," i.e., the spoken or written word. Second, there is the concept called up to the listener's mind when he hears or reads the word. This is termed by these authors "thought" or "reference." Finally, there is the thing itself to which reference is made, the "referent." A single triangle represents the process involved in understanding a dead metaphor, an idiom, or any word not used as a live figure.[6]

CHART 2

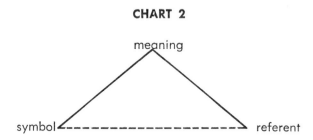

The process involved in understanding a live metaphor is more complicated and may be represented by two contiguous triangles.

CHART 3

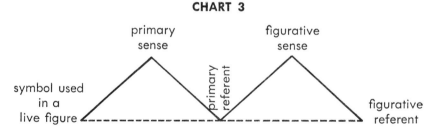

Thus a live metaphor does not lead directly to the intended meaning but is interrupted, however momentarily, by some attention that is diverted to the primary meaning. A dead metaphor, on the other hand, leads directly to the sense intended, without the primary referent coming to mind.

In an earlier chapter, we mentioned three different kinds of senses that words may carry: a primary sense, secondary senses, and figurative senses. In daily usage, all three of these types of senses may be communicated directly by words used in their appropriate contexts. However, there are some figurative senses which are not communicated directly to the reader or hearer without his first thinking of the primary sense. These figurative senses which are dependent upon the primary sense of a word are the basis for classifying metaphor and simile as

[6] Note that the relationship between the symbol and the referent is reciprocal as indicated by the dotted line. Not only does the symbol call to mind the referent but the referent can also call to mind the symbol.

"live." On the other hand, figurative senses which are not dependent upon the primary sense of a word are the basis for classifying all such figures as "dead." Thus, when Jesus said, "I am the true vine" (John 15:1), he was deliberately calling to his disciples' minds the activities associated with grapevines in their own culture; caring for them, pruning them, collecting fruit from them, etc. They had to think of a vine in its primary sense before arriving at its figurative sense. A *live metaphor* is understood by a native speaker only after some attention has been given to the primary sense of the words being used metaphorically.

On the other hand, a *dead metaphor* (like an idiom or any dead figure) is understood directly without such attention being given to the primary sense of the word. For example, *pin* is used in a dead figure when we speak of "*pinning* someone down" to an agreement, a particular time, etc. The original reference was, presumably, to pinning down pieces of paper. Likewise, when we use the dead metaphor, "leg" of a chair, we do not normally first think of its primary sense, that is, of a person's leg. We understand the proper sense directly. The same is true of such dead metaphors as "a bottleneck," or "cultivating" friends, or "golden" hair, or "winding up" an argument. The primary senses of these metaphoric images are not called to mind when such expressions are used.

Criteria for recognizing live metaphors

Although a native speaker of a living language can generally tell which are live and which are dead metaphors, it is another matter when it comes to deciding about the various examples of metaphor and simile occurring in a document almost 2000 years old. Since no native speakers are available, what may have been a dead metaphor for an author will strike us as a live one if it is not current in our own language.

The following contextual factors are therefore proposed as a means by which it may be decided with reasonable certainty whether a metaphor in the Scriptures is dead or alive.

(1) the number of figurative items, or images, used in the metaphor;

(2) the order of the figurative items;

(3) the nonfigurative items in the context which are closely related to the metaphorical images.

(1) The number of figurative items

When a metaphor consists of several interrelated images, this is a clear indication that the author is using these images to convey his message in the form of a live figure. Mark 2:21, 22 speaks of sewing a piece of new cloth, an old garment, a new piece tearing away from the old, a worse tear; it also speaks of new wine, old wineskins, the skins bursting, the wine being spilled, the skins spoiled. Such an interrelated series of images indicates a live figure.

The same is true of Matthew 9:37, 38, where Jesus speaks of the harvest, the laborers, their scarcity, the owner of the harvest, and the request for laborers. Other obvious examples come to mind such as the parables Jesus told, Paul's discussion of the church under the image of a body in 1 Corinthians 12:12-27, and his allegory of Sarah and Hagar in Galatians 4:21-31.

(2) *The order of the images*

If the order of the images is clearly chronological or logical, then this indicates it is a live figure. Archibald Hill in his article, "Principles Covering Semantic Parallels," illustrates this point with four lines from Frost's poem, "Bereft."

> "Where had I heard this wind before
> Change like this to a deeper roar?
> Leaves got up in a coil and hissed,
> Blindly struck at my knee and missed."

First of all, he points out there are four metaphorical items: "coil," "hissed," "struck," and "missed." Second, these four items, all appropriate to snakes, are applied to leaves in the poem. And third, the sequence of these words follows the sequence of what a snake would do. He concludes, therefore, that the author has intentionally used these terms in a metaphorical sense to call to the reader's mind the image of a snake. In fact, he suggests there is only one chance in ninety-six that the reference to a snake is not deliberate. If this poem were to be translated into another language, these images would be handled as *live* images, and translated accordingly. Two obvious examples of ordered images in the New Testament are the Parable of the Tares (Matt. 13:24-30) and the Parable of the Dragnet (Matt. 13:47, 48).

(3) *Related nonfigurative items in the context*

If, in a particular context, there are nonfigurative items which stand in a close semantic relationship to the metaphorical image(s) being used, then this also indicates that the figure is a live one. The speaker or writer deliberately calls to the listener's or reader's mind images chosen from that setting. For example, in Mark 1:17, Jesus says, "I will make you to become fishers of men." The immediate context refers to the Sea of Galilee, fishermen, nets, a ship, and hired servants. The whole setting is appropriate to fishing and so we conclude that this metaphor is a live one.

Similarly, when Jesus warns his disciples with the words, "Take heed, beware of the leaven of the Pharisees . . ." (Mark 8:15), the immediate context is that of how little bread the disciples had brought with them. This being the situation, they understood Jesus' words literally. We conclude, therefore, that "leaven" is used here in a live figure.

Whenever one or more of these three criteria apply, the figure may definitely be analyzed as live. In the absence of all three of these criteria, it is best to regard the figure as dead. There is also a fourth criterion which can help to confirm the conclusion that a figure is dead. If the figure is used a number of times in the New Testament by several different authors and if none of these principal criteria apply to the occurrences, then this strengthens the analysis as a dead figure.

For example, "flesh (Gk. *sarx*) is used in a figurative sense quite frequently in the New Testament. It is used by Paul, Peter, John, and Jude in their writings, and the three criteria discussed above do not apply. The conclusion, then, is that "flesh" is a dead metaphor.[7] A further example is found in the expression "open a door." This is found (in slightly different forms) in Paul's writings (1 Cor. 16:9; 2 Cor. 2:12; Col. 4:3) and in Acts (14:27). A similar expression, "I have set before thee *an open door*" is found in Revelation 3:8. None of the three criteria apply, so this data would indicate this expression is a dead figure.

However, the criterion of frequency is subordinate to the three main criteria. A good example is the term "fruit," often used metaphorically. One might conclude that it is always used as a dead metaphor. However, in some contexts the principal three criteria would indicate otherwise. For example, in Matthew 7:16-20, "fruit" or "fruits" is clearly used metaphorically, the opening comment being, "Ye shall know them by their fruits." In the following verses, however, Jesus goes on to speak of "grapes," "figs," a "good tree," a "corrupt tree," cutting trees down and burning them. This series of interrelated images indicates that "fruit" is being used as a live metaphor in this context. Also, in Matthew 12:33, a similar but briefer passage, "fruit" is part of a series of related images; likewise in Luke 6:43, 44; John 15:2-8.

Proverbs, thematic images, and symbols

Proverbs are often used in a metaphorical manner. If the proverb itself is in the form of a metaphor or simile, then it is analyzable as outlined above. Proverbs not in the form of a metaphor may nevertheless be used metaphorically in a suitable context. All such examples of the metaphoric use of a proverb are considered dead. What the author intended his reader to understand was not the literal sense of the proverb, but rather its application in the particular context in which the author used it.

When Jesus urged the women following him to weep for themselves and their children and not for him, he used the proverb, "For if they do these things in a green tree, what shall be done in the dry?" (Luke 23:31). Although the images used are green and dry trees, there is nothing in the context to indicate that Jesus is speaking about trees — rather, he is saying, "If this is what they do to someone who is innocent,

---

[7] In connection with this conclusion, it is interesting to note that Arndt and Gingrich (1957), when discussing the figurative use of *sarx*, especially in Paul's writings (Section 7, p. 751), make the following statement: "But for Epicurus the *sarx* is the bearer of sinful feelings and desires as well as the means of sensual enjoyment . . . ." On p. xxxi of the introductory material, Epicurus is dated as "c. 300 BC." This statement would appear to imply that this figurative use of *sarx* had been current in the language for a considerable time and represents a dead figure.

what will they do to the guilty?" The proverb is used as a dead metaphor to convey this meaning.

Another proverb is used in Luke 4:23, "Physician, heal thyself." This is often understood literally by the readers of the RL version, who take it to mean that Jesus was ill and needed healing, but it is really being used metaphorically. On the face of it, it would mean, "What you have done for others, do for yourself," but the rest of the verse, which reads, "Whatsoever we have heard done in Capernaum, do also here in thy country" would indicate that the proverb means, "What you have done elsewhere, do here." It is thus dead, so that when translated, (1) the words following the proverb could be introduced as the meaning of the proverb; or (2) it can be replaced with an equivalent local proverb; or (3) its nonfigurative meaning could be stated straightforwardly.

There are certain metaphors, however, where other considerations are more important for the translator than a decision as to whether a given figure is live or dead. These metaphors may be considered as representing a *thematic image*, that is to say, one that is quite widely used in the Bible by a number of authors, and which has become part of general Christian vocabulary. Examples are the images of "light" and "the body of Christ." In the case of such thematic images, the image is to be retained in the translation.

Closely connected with thematic images are *symbols*.[8] A symbol of the New Testament is a word which in isolation called to the mind of the original readers the figurative sense as strongly or more strongly than the literal sense, and both the literal and figurative senses apply to the context. "The cross," "the blood," are two such symbols, and like thematic images, they should, if at all possible, be retained.

The preceding discussion indicates that the number and order of images contained in a figure help to determine whether or not that figure is live or dead. The dead figure, as we have noted, need not be retained. On the other hand, a live figure should be retained if possible. This means that an attempt is made to retain reference to the image of live figures rather than to move directly to a nonfigurative expression. Likewise, if a substitute image is considered, it will only be used keeping in mind the principles of fidelity explained in chapter 2 and of cultural substitutes in chapter 13.

---

[8] "Symbol" is used here in a specialized sense, not in the more general linguistic sense in which words are spoken of as symbols. Nor, in following this definition, are the symbols found in apocalyptic literature, such as the book of Revelation, included. They are considered to be live metaphors or simile, not symbols. What is meant here is an image used in a figure which has become firmly entrenched in Christian vocabulary, and which has some important theological significance, and often carries with it strong emotional overtones. In many contexts, the term refers to both the literal object and its figurative sense.

These symbols may be retained in the translation without sacrificing meaningfulness by giving a slight clue to the sense intended or by accompanying the imagery with its nonfigurative sense. See the suggestion on "blood" given in the chapter on Concordance.

CHAPTER 9

Translating Metaphor and Simile

Why the Metaphors of Scripture Are Often Misunderstood
>   The image may be unknown
>   The topic is implicit
>   The point of similarity is implicit
>   The items compared have no plausible resemblance in the RL
>   The metaphorical meaning is excluded in the RL
>   New metaphors are no longer being formed in the RL

Choices in Translating Metaphor and Simile
>   Some preliminary considerations
>   Retaining the metaphorical form
>   Using the form of a simile
>   Using a nonfigurative form
>   Combining the different forms

Before taking up the question of how metaphor and simile should be translated, it is useful to discuss some of the reasons why literal translations of metaphors and similes found in the Scriptures are often misunderstood in the RL version. This discussion will serve to show the translator that this is an area where careful checking is essential. The meaning conveyed to the readers of the RL version needs to be ascertained from a cross section of those readers so that the translator can find out whether the figure is properly understood; if it is not, he can discern what is causing the trouble by the same procedure.

Why the Metaphors of Scripture Are Often Misunderstood

The misunderstandings that arise can be related to the three parts of the figure — the image, the topic, and the point of similarity. Further factors derive from the RL itself, such as whether new examples of metaphor and simile are resisted or welcomed in the present state of the language, or whether the items compared bear any plausible resemblance.

The image may be unknown

Naturally, the original writers drew on their own culture for the images they used; and for any given receptor culture, it is likely that some of these images will be unknown. Such images as "wineskins," "whitewashed sepulchres," "anchor," "shipwreck," "sword," and "crown" are familiar in relatively few of the cultures for which new translations are currently being made. Hence, the meaning of the figure breaks down at its very center — the image itself, since the image conveys no meaning at all to the readers of the RL.

The topic is implicit

In the discussion of the structure of metaphor and simile, in the preceding chapter, it was pointed out that the topic is sometimes implicit. Some examples were given there, but some more examples are given here to illustrate this point further. John 12:24 says, "Except a corn of wheat fall into the ground and die, it abideth alone: but if it die, it bringeth forth much fruit." No direct statement is made as to what the corn of wheat illustrates, though the following verses give some clues. Matthew 7:6 says, "Give not that which is holy unto the dogs, neither cast ye your pearls before swine, lest they trample them under their feet, and turn again and rend you." Again, no statement is made as to what is illustrated by the words, "that which is holy," "pearls," "dogs," and "swine." A third example is found in 2 Timothy 2:3: "Thou therefore endure hardness, as a good soldier of Jesus Christ." This is a straightforward simile comparing Timothy to a good soldier, with the grounds of comparison being the hardships endured by soldiers as an integral part of their work. However, this is followed by the metaphorical statement, "No man that warreth entangleth himself with the affairs of this life; that he may please him who hath chosen him to be a soldier." This is a straightforward statement of the conditions under which a soldier operates, but in this context it is not referring to actual soldiers, but Christians. This is only implied, however, by deduction from the previous statement. Two further statements follow, neither with an explicit topic: "An athlete is not crowned unless he competes according to the rules" (RSV), and "The husbandman that laboureth must be first partaker of the fruits."

It is not uncommon for the readers of the RL version to fail to recognize that these are metaphorical statements, and so to interpret them literally, that is to say, as laying down principles for soldiers, athletes, and farmers. The absence of an explicit statement of the topic that is illustrated by these images is interpreted to mean that there is none, and so the images are not recognized to be images at all.

The point of similarity is implicit

The first kind of misunderstanding due to the implicit status of the point of similarity arises because the image is already being used metaphorically in the RL. When this is the case, its Scriptural usage is almost certain to be interpreted in the sense it has in the RL. For example, Jesus calls Herod a "fox" in Luke 13:32. To the Zapotecs of Villa Alta this means someone who cries a lot; for the Otomi of the State of Mexico it is someone who steals; for the Cuicatecs of Teutila it refers to a good hunter; and to the Pame it indicates the heartless killing of domesticated animals.

"Sheep" is used figuratively in a number of Mexican languages. For the Pame it is someone who does not understand; for the Teutila Cuicatecs it refers to a man with long hair; for the Tepeuxila Cuicatecs it means a drunkard who does not yell when he is hit; to the Otomi of the State of Mexico it is a person who does not answer; and to the Villa Alta Zapotecs it refers to a young fellow who is often seen waiting for his girl friend or following her.

In Mark 4:17, the statement, "and have no root in themselves," was translated retaining the image "root." The helper responded to this translation with laughter and then explained that "root" is used of a person when "he takes root in a place" or "takes root in his work." In the former case, he overstays his welcome; the owner of the house wants him to leave but he still stays on. In the latter case, it refers to someone sent on an errand such as fetching firewood, and who takes a long time to return. The New Testament term "root" therefore suggested an RL idiom and so was misleading to the readers.

A similar thing occurred in connection with Luke 23:31, which refers to a green tree and a dry tree. To the Otomi helper this suggested an RL idiom in which these particular images refer to a person who speaks half Spanish and half Otomi.

If the image is not used metaphorically in the RL, misunderstanding can still arise because any of the components of meaning of the image may serve as the point of similarity. For instance, if "stone" is used as the image, it may suggest permanency, a dumb person, something or someone who destroys, weight, strength, usefulness in grinding, something over which one stumbles, hardness, something that sinks easily. Until the reader knows the point of similarity, the message is incomplete, and so the reader seeks to complete it by choosing some suitable point of similarity. Naturally enough, he will choose something that makes good sense to him, in harmony with his own religious and cultural background. Even if he is a believer, and even if there are some clues to the meaning in the context, he is still likely to choose a similarity which seems plausible in the light of his own culture.

Consider the example of "stone" as the image when the topic is a person. For the Zapotecs of Villa Alta it means "one who refuses to move from a job or location"; for the Chichimeca Pame it means "to live to be old"; for the Mixtecs of San Esteban it means "a selfish person who hangs around and is useless"; for the Cuicatecs of Tepeuxila it means "someone who cannot talk or walk." These are the points of similarity given when speakers of these Mexican languages were tested as to what they thought "stone" would mean. Hence, when they come to interpret statements such as "a living stone" used to refer to Jesus by Peter in 1 Peter 2:4, they will have difficulties, since no point of similarity is clearly stated by Peter.

A further occasion for misunderstanding arises when the image used occurs in the Scriptures with several different senses. For example, the term "baptism" is used literally to refer to water baptism and figuratively to refer to Spirit baptism and suffering. John the Baptist also says of Jesus, "he shall baptize you . . . with fire" (Luke 3:16).[1] Other examples are "salt," "light," and "lion." If no grounds of comparison are stated, then the RL reader is baffled to know which of the possible ones to select.

The items compared have no plausible resemblance in the RL

This problem can arise if the image is not used metaphorically in the RL. For example, Matthew 3:3 says, "Prepare ye the way of the Lord, make his paths straight." Paths and tracks are familiar to all cultures, but in this metaphor the image is that of working on roads to prepare them for the arrival of some dignitary. This may be quite a unfamiliar idea in some cultures. The topic illustrated by this image is preparation of heart needed for the coming of Jesus. To make such a metaphor plausible, it is usually necessary to find some word or expression which collocates properly with both the image and the topic. In this particular case, such a word might be "prepare" or an expression like "make straight." This "pivot" word or expression then links the image and topic in a way which gives plausibility to the underlying comparison.

One such metaphor has caused many translators difficulties. It is the one Jesus uses in Mark 1:17, where he tells his disciples he will make them into "fishers of men." One solution is to find some suitable pivot term for "men" and "fish." Sometimes "gather" may be used of both, but it is more common to find that the word that collocates with fish does not do so with men. And even if it does, it may have vulgar or other wrong connotations. One approach is to note that "work" is a term that can be used to link the two parts as in "you have been working catching fish, now I will give you a new work making disciples for me." However, in some languages, even this will not meet the problem, as "work" refers only to manual work — not to preaching or teaching.

Even when a correct pivot word has been found, the way in which the figure is expressed needs to be carefully checked. In Amuzgo, the "crown of life" (James 1:12) was translated as a simile: "receive life like a crown." The language helpers would not accept this, as it seemed

---

[1] William Barclay (1968, p. 321) makes the following comments on the Greek word *baptizein* "to baptize": "In secular Greek the word *baptizein* has many metaphorical meanings. It was not originally a religious or liturgical word. It simply meant to dip something below the surface of a liquid. It is, for instance, used of dipping a garment in dye. It thus acquired most of the meanings which the English word 'submerge' possesses. It can be used of a ship being sunk at sea. To be 'baptized' in wine is to be dead drunk. To be 'baptized' in debts is to be head over ears in debt. A boy, defeated by a cross-examiner's questionings, is said to be 'baptized' — in the English colloquial idiom, sunk. The word therefore means in its metaphorical use to be submerged in any experience, usually a bitter experience." These comments would certainly indicate that 'baptize" and "baptism" are a dead metaphor in such passages as Mark 10:38, 39 and Luke 12:50. One could only wish that more such studies of the figurative use of Greek terms were available.

quite implausible to them. Further questioning revealed that since "receive" was the pivot word, it was automatically transferred to the other side semantically to give the absurd comparison: "receive life like a crown receives life." The simile was then recast in the form "receive life as people receive a crown." This made good sense, as it was then interpreted in terms of an honor or reward.

In many of the Mayan languages of Mexico and Guatemala, there is a choice of link words for the two items compared in a simile. One word indicates that the resemblance may be perceived by the eye; another that it may be perceived by one of the senses of hearing, smell, or touch; and a third that the likeness is to be found in some verbal action. If an inappropriate link word is used, it will lead the reader to expect the grounds of comparison in an area of experience which the original author did not intend and so lead to a false interpretation or the reaction that the comparison is absurd.

The metaphorical meaning is excluded in the RL

Even if a language uses metaphors, and has no resistance to new ones, certain types of metaphor may fail to communicate a metaphorical sense. For example, in Isthmus Zapotec, Bachajón Tzeltal, and other Mexican languages, animal names may only refer to the extra spirit of a person. In Mayo, animal names simply refer to the last name of the individual. He is a "fox" since he belongs to the family called "fox."

New metaphors are no longer being formed in the RL

One of the aspects of the receptor culture that the translator needs to be alert to and to study is whether new metaphors are being created and deciphered. Most translators come from an urban-type culture, where new metaphors are constantly being created and deciphered, so there is a high degree of tolerance for unusual and unfamiliar collocations. Metaphors are also frequently used by authors, and the high degree of literacy means that most speakers are being constantly exposed to new collocations and metaphors. This is so much a part of the background of most translators that they tend to assume it is also true of the people for whom they are translating.

However, experience has shown that this can by no means be assumed. Cultures vary considerably in this matter. Many of the cultures of Mesoamerica are intolerant of new and unfamiliar collocations; others welcome them and take a real delight in deciphering them. Of course, it should be clear that this has nothing to do with intelligence at all; it is simply a matter of the current practice in a given culture.

It is easy for the translator to jump to false conclusions in this matter, as all languages have their stock of dead metaphors. The translator finds himself continually running across these, and so he tends to assume that the people for whom he is translating use new metaphors and readily decipher them. But that does not follow. All it shows is that the metaphoric use of terms has been current in the RL; it proves nothing either way as to whether the process is still current or not.

Another factor can give the translator the impression that meta-phor is still current in the RL. It is that of comparative magic. When metaphor was being studied among the Chols, it was noted that com-parative magic occurred quite frequently. For example, when a baby is born with two or three kinks in the cord, this is understood to mean the baby will become very wealthy. Underlying this belief is an old worn-out comparison. In former generations, the men used a red cloth belt in which they tied their money. Those with more money had several knots whereas a poor person only needed the knot that kept his trousers in place. Also, during the rainy season when the river is high, those who are suffering from tuberculosis go to the riverside to scoop up the white foam, as this is regarded as the cure for the "white cough." There is also a tree with a red bark which, when boiled down, is said to be a cure for bloody diarrhea. However, when these comparisons were investigated, it was found that no new ones were being produced — they were dead comparisons.

To assess objectively some of the factors that influence the deciphering of metaphor, a test was run with ten translators and their helpers. A number of examples of metaphor were prepared using images based upon items known to the culture and central to their needs. Others were prepared based upon items that were known but were peripheral to the culture. Of the first group, about one in five of the examples was accept-ably deciphered (there was no expectation that all the examples would be deciphered as the author intended). Of the second group, about one in twenty of the examples was deciphered acceptably, thus suggesting that culturally relevant items lend themselves to metaphorical usage more readily than items peripheral to the culture.

A second test was more significant. Metaphor, simile, and other fig-ures of speech were placed in the context of a story. All of the images used were well known, and an effort was made to use images highlight-ing a feature likely to be important in their own thinking. Under these circumstances the number of examples correctly deciphered doubled to about two in every five.

A study was then made of the figures which had not been understood, and it was observed that there were fewer contextual clues in these cases. This appeared to show a correlation with the metaphors which are most frequently misunderstood in the Scriptures. Where there is a full context for a figure, there is less likelihood of misunderstanding. On the other hand, when the contextual clues are few and the topic is left implicit, then it becomes extremely difficult for the user of the RL version to decipher the figure.

After several years of exposure to the language, the translator should be able to say whether new examples of metaphor are being regularly produced by the people. He should be constantly on the alert for them. For example, when a major road was constructed in the area inhabited by the Tzotzil Indians of Mexico, one of the Indians referred to the first car passing through as the "metal pig." This was because the horn was sounded at every curve and went "oink-oink." Such an example, although it did not become general, indicated that new metaphors were being produced.

Around 1950, when translators went to the Huichol Indians (Mexico), they introduced lettuce. Years later, other workers in this same area heard a love song of which one line was, "You are my lettuce." Here was obviously a new metaphor. Another translator was having difficulty with a certain verse, so his helper commented, "We're in a big gully and can't get out." An Aztec preacher spoke of a broken-down car and portrayed Christ as the mechanic who restored the car to life. In another Aztec message the statement was made: "Christ is our gasoline. He is the source of our power."

When the Gospel of Mark had been finished, the Cayapa translation helper prayed, "May Thy Word spread like gasoline." The Cayapa are fishermen in Ecuador and use Coleman lamps at night. They filter the gasoline with an old cloth and had noted how rapidly it spread by the process of osmosis.

These are all examples of the creation of new metaphor or simile in the language. If new metaphors are regularly being coined, then the translator may reasonably expect that no resistance will be offered to the metaphors of Scripture. On the other hand, if new metaphors are not being created, the metaphors of Scripture are likely to prove a real hindrance to understanding if retained in the form of a metaphor. And even if the people are receptive to metaphor in Scripture, this does not guarantee they will decipher the metaphors of Scripture in the right way — that they will be able to ascertain the right points of similarity or the right topic. That would have to be checked in each case. But if there is definite resistance to figurative language, it is virtually certain that the correct meaning will have to be conveyed by means of non-figurative language in many cases. To fail to do so would be a failure in the area of exegetical accuracy, as zero or wrong meaning would be conveyed rather than the correct meaning of the original.

CHOICES IN TRANSLATING METAPHOR AND SIMILE

Some preliminary considerations

The previous section has shown that misunderstandings of simile and metaphor are common and arise from a number of different reasons. This being the case, the question naturally arises — when is it appropriate to translate one of these figures in other than its literal form? The answer is — whenever such a literal transfer communicates wrong meaning, and usually when it communicates ambiguous meanings (one of which is wrong), obscure, or zero meaning. When careful questioning of the RL readers reveals that a particular metaphor or simile is failing to communicate the meaning of the original, then the translator needs to find out what is causing the problem — the image, the topic, the point of similarity — and to correct the translation so that the problem is resolved.

However, care should be taken with metaphors which were misunderstood by the original hearers. When Jesus warns his disciples to "beware of the leaven of the Pharisees," (Mark 8:15), the whole thrust of the passage hinges on the fact that they misunderstood him and took him literally; and if a translator renders this as a simile, with topic and point of similarity explicit, the readers will wonder how the disciples could possibly have misunderstood. Hence, it is not possible to drop the reference to leaven nor to make the topic explicit at this point, as then the disciples would have no reason for misunderstanding. Yet, without making the topic explicit, the passage means little or nothing to many RL readers. At the beginning of v. 17, however, it says, "And when Jesus knew it, he saith unto them , . . ." The Greek just says, "And when Jesus knew," not specifying what it was he knew, but the following verses (18-21) make it clear that he was quite aware they had misunderstood his metaphorical statement. To make the topic clear, what Jesus knew can be stated explicitly: When Jesus knew they were thinking of bread rather than the teaching of the Pharisees, he said to them . . . . The Gospel of John contains several such figurative expressions not understood by the original hearers, as for instance, when he referred to his body under the image of a "temple" (John 2:19-21).

The choice as to how to translate depends first on whether the figure is live or dead and whether it is considered to be a thematic image or a symbol. If the figure is dead, the image is not the focus of attention, so it can be dropped, and only the topic and the point of similarity expressed explicitly in the RL. But if the figure is live, or if it is a thematic image or a symbol, the image should be retained if at all possible.

If the translation of a live metaphor or simile does need to be corrected to assure understanding on the part of the readers, what types of modification of form are permitted? What are the criteria that the translator may appeal to as guidelines in reaching a decision?

There are two principal modifications of the form which are permissible for the translator. One is adjustment of the actual literary form of the metaphor or simile. (A metaphor may be translated as a simile, a simile as a nonfigurative comparison.) The other is making explicit some part of the implicit information which is carried by the figure.[2]

Chart 1 displays the range of possibilities open to the translator for handling any metaphor or simile in the original. In the left-hand half of the chart it is shown that there are four forms of explicitness that the translation may take in the RL — the topic and the point of similarity implicit, the point of similarity implicit, all parts explicit, the image dropped. In the right-hand half of the chart, the literary form that the figure may take in the RL is indicated. The numbers show that there are seven choices of form, and these numbers will be referred to in the examples that follow.

---

[2] See chapter 3 on Implicit and Explicit Information for a fuller discussion as to when implicit information may be made explicit.

CHART 1

FORMS THAT METAPHOR AND SIMILE OF THE ORIGINAL
MAY TAKE IN THE RL

Degree of Explicitness in the RL		Literary Form in the RL		
Type of Comparison	Parts of the Comparison Expressed Explicitly	Metaphor	Simile	Neither
Abbreviated	Image	1		
	Image, Topic	2	4	
Full	Image, Topic, Point of Similarity	3	5	6
None	Topic, Point of Similarity			7

The following discussion and examples are presented in four groups, reflecting the possible shifts in form from a metaphor in the original; (a) the metaphorical form may be retained in the RL; (b) the metaphor may be shifted to a simile; (c) the metaphor may be handled in a non-figurative way; (d) or combinations of these three possibilities may be used. It is worth pointing out that the first three possibilities can be regarded as "progressive" in the sense that the translator is encouraged to try them in the above order for live figures, until the RL form communicates the meaning of the original. In other words, the first approach is to retain the form of a metaphor (possibly with expansions of the parts — see below). If this is inadequate, then the form of a simile is tried. If this still fails to communicate the right meaning, then a nonfigurative form is used.[3] Of course, this suggestion assumes that the literary form used will be natural as well as meaningful.

Retaining the metaphorical form (types 1, 2, and 3)

In some cases, a metaphor in the original in which only the image is explicit may be rendered in the RL in the same way, without the addition of either topic or point of similarity. For example, "way" in the parable of the wide and narrow way may be translated directly into Colorado of Ecuador because "way" in that language is already used in the same metaphorical sense. This corresponds to type 1 on the chart.

[3] From the general theoretical standpoint, this discussion is a further illustration of the principle that while in an idiomatic translation meaning always takes precedence over form, this does not mean that the form of the original is completely ignored. There are circumstances, as in the present discussion on translating metaphor and simile, when the special literary form of the original is taken into consideration when deciding on the RL form.

A metaphor may also be rendered, retaining the metaphorical form, by filling out in more detail one or more of the parts of the metaphor, so as to make the meaning of the figure clear in the RL. Mark 4:17 says, "and (they) have no root in themselves." Throughout the parable of which this verse is part, the "seed" is the image and the "Word" the corresponding topic (see 4:14). In San Esteban Mixtec (Mexico), the topic was filled out to make the meaning of the metaphor clear by adding *the Word* so that it was rendered, "and the Word did not take root in them." This form made the metaphor clear, and was collocationally acceptable to the language helper.[4] This way of handling a metaphor, by filling out the stated topic in more detail, comes under type 2 in the chart.

It is more common, however, to have to make explicit the topic of a metaphor which has been left completely implicit in the original. In Luke 5:34 Jesus answers a question with the metaphor, "Can ye make the children of the bridechamber (RSV: wedding guests) fast, while the bridegroom is with them?" Here the images are drawn from a Jewish wedding; the "wedding guests" are one image, the topic being the disciples; the "bridegroom" is the other image, the topic being Jesus himself. But no reference is made in the original to either of these topics. Hence, some languages have found it necessary to make at least part of the topic clear by adding "about himself" to the introductory words, so that they read, "And he said unto them *about himself* . . . ."

Matthew 3:10 has been handled in this way also. It reads, "And now also the axe is laid unto the root of the trees: therefore every tree which bringeth not forth good fruit is hewn down, and cast into the fire." Here the principal image is "trees," but no topic is explicitly given. However, the context makes it clear that it was John's audience. Hence, the topic has been supplied in some such form as "You are trees that do not bear fruit."

A similar example is found in Mark 2:21, 22 where Jesus speaks of mending an old garment with a new patch and putting new wine into old wineskins. Again, the topic is not given, so it may be supplied initially with some such words as "He told them another parable concerning his teaching" or "Jesus spoke to them about his teaching."

Each of these last three examples exemplify type 2 — the form of the translation in the RL is a metaphor, with both the image and the topic expressed explicitly.

It is often necessary, however, to make the point of similarity as well as the topic explicit, for the point of similarity provides the basic key to understanding the metaphor. For example, Jesus addresses the scribes and Pharisees as "Ye blind guides" (Matt. 23:24). In the Greek, it is just "blind guides," so only the image is formally expressed, though the vocative form of address identifies the topic as "you (plural)." But what

---

[4] The translation follows the interpretation which relates the "root" to the seed or the Word; the other interpretation relates it to the hearer's character, or state of heart. For the former view note the NEB translation "but it [the word] strikes no root in them," and the TEV "But it [the message] does not sink deep into them."

is the point of similarity? It is not stated but can be deduced to be "because you yourselves are in error and you lead people into error." This can then be translated explicitly in the RL. It should be noted, however, that only for equational or vocative metaphors (which are implied equations) has the metaphorical form been retained *and* the point of similarity made explicit. This, then, illustrates type 3 on the chart, where all three parts of the metaphor are explicit in the RL.

The metaphorical form when it does not represent a live metaphor can also be retained by substituting a metaphor from the RL which has the same meaning as the original metaphor. For example, Paul says in 1 Corinthians 14:9, "ye shall speak into the air." In Sierra Juarez Zapotec (Mexico) this was expressed metaphorically as "you will just be speaking into your own mouth." When it says in Luke that "the babe leaped in her womb" (Luke 1:41), it was translated by "the baby played" in Carib (Guatemala). The expression "your hearts are hard" (or equivalent ones; see, for example, Matthew 19:8; Mark 3:5; 6:52; 8:17; 10:5; 16:14; Heb. 3:8, 15; 4:7) is used quite often in the Scriptures, and is frequently replaced by an equivalent metaphorical expression in the RL, such as "your ears are hard" or "your stomach is hard" (both used in African languages). In these cases a dead metaphor in the RL is substituted for a dead metaphor in the original.

Using the form of a simile (types 4 and 5)

One of the simplest adjustments that can be made to the form of a metaphor is to translate it as a simile, thus making it explicit that a comparison is intended. For example, 2 Peter 2:17 says of false teachers, "these are wells without water." This can be expressed in the form of a simile: "these are like wells without water." However, while this does make it unambiguously clear that a comparison is being made, it says nothing about the point of similarity and so even the simile form may leave the reader puzzled as to why false prophets resemble dry wells. If the point of similarity is not included, type 4 on the chart is exemplified; if it is included, then it is type 5. In this particular case, type 5 would apply to a rendition such as "these (false teachers) are as useless as wells without water."

As was mentioned earlier, James 1:12, which reads "he shall receive the crown of life," was translated as a simile but without the point of similarity; "he will receive life as people receive a crown." Another language found it necessary to translate the metaphor "the moon [shall be turned] into blood" (Acts 2:20) as a simile, and also to make the point of similarity clear, giving a final form "the moon will become red like blood."

Matthew 23:24 combines several metaphors and a hyperbole: "You blind guides, straining out a gnat and swallowing a camel" (RSV). One of the metaphors is "straining out a gnat and swallowing a camel," and is explained by the previous verse, where Jesus points out that whereas the scribes and Pharisees were so scrupulous as to tithe their garden herbs, they neglected such vital principles of the law as "justice, mercy, and faith." Clearly, the point of similarity is the foolishness of paying such attention to insignificant matters while ignoring fundamental moral principles. This metaphor may then be translated as a full simile, with all three parts as follows: "What you do is just as foolish as a person who strains out a gnat and swallows a camel."[5]

Using a nonfigurative form (types 6 and 7)

The third possibility open to the translator is to give the meaning of the original figure in a nonfigurative form. Within this possibility, the translator may choose to retain the image used in the original, or he may not. Retention of the image corresponds to type 6 on the chart; non-retention to type 7.

In Mark 1:17, "I will make you to become fishers of men," the image is that of catching fish. This should be retained, since this is a live metaphor (see the discussion in the previous chapter). However, the whole may be cast in a nonfigurative form. It would then read, "You have been working catching fish, now I will give you a new work making disciples for me." (Note the problems that may arise using "work" that were discussed earlier in the chapter.)

When preaching to the crowds, John the Baptist said: "Prepare ye the way of the Lord, make his paths straight" (Mark 1:3). The image is "prepare . . . the way" and "make the paths straight," and it is one's heart or life that is compared to a way or path. The point of the similarity lies in the fact that it was customary to prepare for the arrival of an important person by improving the condition of the roads over which he would travel. So John's hearers were to prepare their hearts for the arrival of Jesus. In some languages this metaphor has been rendered with two nonfigurative statements, retaining the image. This gives a translation such as: "When an authority is coming we prepare the paths and straighten them out. The Lord is coming, so get your hearts right."

The above examples have retained reference to the image of the original form but cast the whole nonfiguratively. In the following examples — type 7 on the chart — the image, which is considered to be dead, is not retained. The figure is again rendered in a nonfigurative form but this time without reference to the image.

Acts 15:10 reads as follows: "Now therefore why tempt ye God, to put a yoke upon the neck of the disciples . . . ?" Here the image is the action of putting a yoke on the neck of an ox, and the event compared to this is that of requesting the disciples to comply with various regulations. The point of similarity is seen in the fact that a burdensome obligation is placed on the ox, on the one hand, and on the disciples on the other. A translation without the image being expressed gives: "Therefore, why do you tempt God by asking the disciples to do something very difficult?"

---

[5] The question of how to handle the hyperbole of "swallowing a camel" is discussed in chapter 7.

Paul uses the metaphor, "adorn the doctrine of God," in Titus 2:10. Here the image is "people adorn themselves, or buildings." The topic is what is done to "the doctrine of God," and the point of similarity is the purpose of the action of adorning — to make more attractive or pleasing to others. (This metaphor is analyzed in the previous chapter.) A translation without the image gives "so live that people will speak well of the teaching that comes from God."

Similarly, "tell that fox" (Luke 13:32) may be translated as "tell that sly man," dropping the image, but retaining the topic (Herod) and the point of similarity (sly).

Combining the different forms

The fourth alternative is to combine any two of the three literary types — metaphor, simile, nonfigurative. Thus, a metaphor may be combined with a metaphor, simile, or a nonfigurative form; a simile may be combined with a nonfigurative form, or an abbreviated simile may be combined with a full simile.

In Matthew 3:10, John the Baptist warns his hearers of impending judgment, the statement being metaphorical in terms of an ax being laid at the root of the trees, ready to cut down the fruitless ones. This is all metaphoric image; so, the topic may be introduced in the form of a metaphor, "you are trees which do not bear fruit," or in the form of a simile, "you are like trees which do not bear fruit." Then the metaphor as it appears in the original will follow. This illustrates combining a metaphor with a metaphor and also a simile with a metaphor.

The same approach was taken with Matthew 9:37 in Trique (Mexico). The metaphoric part of this verse reads, "The harvest truly is plenteous, but the labourers are few." A simile was used to make explicit the topic: "Like ripe wheat awaits the harvesters, so the people are waiting to hear my word. There is much wheat already ripe, but there are not many harvesters." Here again a simile is followed by a metaphor.

John 12:46 uses both "light" and "darkness" figuratively: "I am come a light into the world, that whosoever believeth on me should not abide in darkness." "In a dark place" was already in use in Mixe (Mexico) referring to a condition of sin and perhaps also ignorance, but "light" was not used metaphorically in the language. The first attempt used "light" in collocation with "come," and the helper interpreted this to mean that Jesus came to earth just as light comes through space. This problem was met by using the metaphorical idiom first and then a simile using the unfamiliar figure of light. "I have come into the world so that whoever believes in me should never be in a dark place. I am like a light that shines so people can see." Presented in this way, the metaphorical use of "light" was understood.

A metaphor may also be combined with a nonfigurative statement. For example, James 3:6 says that "the tongue is a fire." This metaphor may be retained and the nonfigurative statement added: "A fire ruins things; what we say also ruins things." The content of this nonfigurative statement could follow the metaphor in the form of a simile: "Like a fire destroys things so what we say destroys people." A variation on this last possibility is to reverse the order, so that the topic is presented before the image: "What we say ruins people like a fire ruins things." Yet another possible combination is to make the opening statement a simile, "the tongue is like a fire," and then follow it with the nonfigurative statement above.

An example of combining a simile without the point of similarity with a simile including the point of similarity is provided by the Chol translation of Proverbs 26:11. This verse reads: "As a dog returneth to his vomit, so a fool returneth to his folly." The Chol translation reads: "A fool is like a dog. Like a dog goes back to his vomit so a fool goes again to his foolishness."

Flexibility and sensitivity are thus needed by the translator in handling the many cases of metaphor and simile in the New Testament. In each case, there are a number of possible alternatives open to him, so he needs to be sensitive to the reactions and difficulties of the RL readers on the one hand and flexible in his approach to translating these figures on the other. Only in this way may he be assured that the RL readers are receiving the same message as did the original readers.

CHAPTER 10

Concordance

CONCORDANCE DEFINED
PSEUDO CONCORDANCE WITHIN A TEXT
REAL CONCORDANCE WITHIN A TEXT
PROBLEMS IN MAINTAINING REAL CONCORDANCE IN TRANSLATION

The translators of the KJV state quite openly in their preface, "We have not tied ourselves to a uniformity of phrasing or to an identity of words"; that is to say, they did not feel that they had to translate the different occurrences of a word or phrase uniformly. The question of whether they should have been more uniform has been vigorously debated since. At the time of the preparation of the (English) Revised Version (ERV), published in 1881, the revisers discussed this question at length. Three leading scholars — Lightfoot, Trench, and Ellicott — published a book entitled *The Revision of the English Version of the New Testament* in 1873, and in pp. 46-79, Lightfoot accuses the KJV of two groups of errors arising from the principle quoted above. The first group he describes as "various renderings of the same word or words, by which artificial distinctions are introduced in the translation which have no place in the original" (p. 46); the second group he refers to as "the obliteration of real distinctions by the same rendering of different words" (p. 65). He cites examples of these "errors" for both groups.

For those who are engaged in the task of translation, the question naturally arises — who is right? Are Lightfoot's criticisms justified? Or did the translators of the KJV really have a good translation principle at this point? After all, there is no denying that the KJV has always been much more popular than the ERV, which has tended to become a "student" Bible only.

CONCORDANCE DEFINED

As is often the case, a problem such as this may not be discussed profitably until there are clear definitions to work from. Two definitions are given here, one relating to concordance in an original document and the other to concordance between an original document and its translation. The type of concordance which has been in focus so far in this chapter, relates to the "consistent matching" of the Greek or Hebrew terms by corresponding English ones (or RL ones). This, however, omits an important consideration so that this type of concordance is more precisely defined as follows:

> Concordance between an original document and its translation occurs when a word or expression in the source document is translated in each of its occurrences with the same word or expression wherever contextual usage warrants.

The other type of concordance refers to a phenomenon within a single language, a formal feature of the lexical structure that at times is used as a stylistic device with an important semantic function. This type of "concordance" may be defined as follows:

> Concordance within a document occurs when the same word or expression is used repeatedly to refer to the same specific concept.

The crucial part of the first definition — the one that has most relevance to translators — is the final condition: "Wherever contextual usage warrants."[1] This gives a "happy medium" between variations *not* necessitated by contextual considerations (as sometimes practiced in the KJV), and forced concordance (as sometimes found in the ERV), where this condition is ignored, giving the translation a "wooden" and "unnatural" sound because normal usage is violated.

In spite of a long history of discussion, the issue is still a live one. Questions such as the following are still being raised: Why is it that the internal concordance of the Greek and Hebrew originals cannot be carried over, by means of cross-language concordance, into the RL? Why cannot the same word in Greek or Hebrew be matched with 100 percent consistency in English or some other RL? Is there not an inevitable *loss* if there is not such consistency? Will not the message of the original be distorted to some extent?

To discuss these questions, it is necessary to distinguish between two types of concordance within a document: one type may be termed "pseudo" and the other "real."

PSEUDO CONCORDANCE WITHIN A TEXT

Pseudo concordance is the reoccurrence of the same word in a text but with different senses. Several occurrences of the same word in its different senses gives the appearance of real concordance within a document while in fact there is only pseudo concordance. One language assigns senses A, B, and C to a single word, and all three may occur in the same paragraph or in adjacent paragraphs. When that word is rendered by three distinct words into a language that assigns senses A, D, and E to a single word, and B and C to two other words, it might be argued that concordance has been lost. However, the use of three distinct words for one word with three senses is not a violation of concordance between

---

[1] Cf. Longacre (1958, p. 487): "It follows that a conscientious translator avoids irresponsible and random variations in translating an SL [source language] lexical item, but chooses equivalents with due consideration of the requirements of each context." It is worth noting that he goes on to say, "On the other hand, he of course recognizes the impossibility of preserving intact the concordance of the SL text — unless he wants his 'translation' to be a grotesque caricature."

documents, and all that is lost is the pseudo concordance of the source document.

True concordance within a document occurs when the word is used several times representing only one of its senses. Lexicons of the Greek, such as the one prepared by Arndt and Gingrich, list various senses of single words. It is not likely that all of these various senses will be symbolized by a single word when translating into another language. To attempt to do so would overlook normal contextual usage and preserve what is here termed pseudo concordance.

An example may help at this point. The following is a paragraph in Chol, a Mexican language:

> Jini año' b⌃ ti yotot Lopez pejtel ora mi cha'len e'tel. Che' tsa' k'otiyon lojon to jula', jini i tat woli *juc'* te', jini i ña' woli *juc'* pisil, jini askunil woli *juc'* i machit, jini chich⌃ 1 woli *juc'* ti jabon i ts'i'.

In this paragraph, the Chol word *juc'* occurs four times, but in the following English translation there is no corresponding English term occurring four times.

> The Lopez family is always working. When we visited them, the father was *planing* a board, the mother was *ironing* clothes, the oldest boy was *filing* (sharpening) his machete, and the oldest daughter was *rubbing* soap *on* her dog.

The italicized terms in the translation show that the Chol verb *juc'* corresponds to four different verbs in English — "to plane," "to iron," "to file," and "to rub (soap) on." In other words, *juc'* is a Chol lexical item with four different senses, the senses occurring with particular collocations — "a board," "clothes," "a machete," and "soap." Further, there is a shared thread of meaning, namely, a "back and forward action," which further confirms that we are dealing not with a single concept but with four different senses carried by a single word.

In the English translation, four verbs had to be used to replace the one Chol verb. Has there been any *loss* in the translation process? If so, what *sort* of loss?

First, note there is *no loss in meaning* — the information conveyed to a Chol speaker and the information conveyed to an English speaker is the same; the message has not been distorted. Second, note that there is no alternative in English — there just is no single English word that corresponds to the Chol *juc'*.

What has been lost then? The "loss," if it may be called such, is in terms of the structure of the Chol lexicon. In Chol, one term represents these four senses, and this is a language-specific, arbitrary feature of Chol lexical structure. It is, in that sense, "pseudo concordance" within the Chol language. There might just as easily have been four terms in Chol, or three, or two. It "just happens" that there is only one in Chol, and four in English. The number and type of senses which may be carried by one word in a language is unpredictable and arbitrary, and can only be discovered by investigating that language. All that is lost, then, is a particular language-specific characteristic of Chol; an aspect of Chol linguistic "form" which is not only unnecessary but impossible to reproduce in English. The translator should not attempt to reproduce, by means of concordance, features of pseudo concordance in the original lexicon.

What has been said above about pseudo concordance is based on the principle brought out in chapter 5, that different senses of a word may be related by sharing a thread of meaning. The same chapter also mentions that an associative relation may relate the senses of a word; and this also may result in pseudo concordance. Thus, the Greek term *glōssa* has a primary sense of "tongue" as in Mark 7:33, 35: "[Jesus] touched his [the deaf and dumb man's] tongue . . . and the string of his tongue was loosed." However, *glōssa* has two other senses by associative relationship with the primary sense. One is "a language" as in Acts 2:4, 11 and also a number of times in Revelation in such combinations as "of all nations, and kindreds, and people, and tongues" (7:9), "all kindreds, and tongues, and nations" (13:7), etc. The other is "what is said, the content of one's speech" as in 1 Peter 3:10, 1 John 3:18 ("let us not love in word, neither in tongue; but in deed and in truth"). Such associated senses are just as arbitrary and language-specific as those sharing a thread of meaning, and no attempt should be made to maintain in a translation the pseudo concordance resulting from these different senses. Multiple senses, whether arising from a shared thread of meaning or from associative relations,[2] should not be rendered with a single form under the assumption that one is thereby mirroring the real concordance of the original.

REAL CONCORDANCE WITHIN A TEXT

Not all concordance is pseudo; there is real concordance as well. *Real concordance* within the text of a document is the deliberate reoccurrence of the same word with the same sense. Pseudo concordance is both arbitrary and inevitable, but real concordance is just the opposite — it is deliberate, a specifically chosen feature of discourse, intentionally used by the writer. Real concordance is used by the author to keep a certain topic, or theme, clearly in focus, so that the maximum impact is made upon the recipient. Thus, in 1 Corinthians 13, Paul uses the Greek word *agapē*, "love," no less than eight times, including the opening and closing

---

[2] Related to the question of concordance is the translation of parallel passages in the gospels and of Old Testament quotations which occur more than once in the same form. These should generally be rendered in each of their occurrences in the same form. However, the principle of contextual usage should not be overlooked. The saying: "with what measure ye mete, it shall be measured to you" occurs in Matt. 7:2, Mark 4:24, and Luke 6:38, each of which has a somewhat different context. It is unlikely that the word used to translate "measure" will be generic enough to apply correctly to each of these three contexts. The saying will then be rendered in an appropriate manner for each context even though it will then appear in more than one form.

verses. The theme is "love" and the key term, *agapē*, is repeated as one means of emphasizing and reinforcing the theme. This is designed concordance, a linguistic feature of form that the translator should, if at all possible, carry over into the RL version.

Real concordance, however, is not confined to a theme that is developed within a particular passage. There is a (divinely) designed concordance throughout Scripture, so that, although a particular theme is not dealt with at length in a particular passage, it is developed in the Scriptures as a whole. Such themes are repentance, redemption, forgiveness, etc. For instance, in the case of repentance, the two Greek words translated in English by "to repent" and "repentance" (*metanoeō* and *metanoia*) occur 58 times in the New Testament, and are spread over ten different books. This is real concordance also, and the translator should aim at consistency in translating "to repent" and "repentance" throughout the New Testament, otherwise the users of the RL version will be unnecessarily hindered in their study of the full Scriptural use of this expression.

Problems in Maintaining Real Concordance in Translation

There is no question, therefore, that the retention of designed concordance is the ideal for the translator. Differences in the lexical structure of languages, however, pose problems which result in either a reduction or gain in the internal concordance of the translation as compared to that of the original document. In Ephesians 4:32, Paul says, "forgiving one another, even as God for Christ's sake hath forgiven you." Here the obvious parallel drawn between divine and human forgiveness is reflected in the use of the same term for "forgive" in each case (*charizomai*), and this concordance the translator wishes to retain. However, in one of the Otomi languages of Mexico, there are two different words for "forgive" neither of which may be used on both sides of this comparison. One is used of a "deity" forgiving; the other is used of a human forgiving. Misuse of these terms only results in laughter, and ignoring the difference just is not possible. Hence, the first use of "forgive" must be translated by the "human" term, the second used by the "divine" one.

The author of the original had a choice of terms to express the idea of forgiveness. He chose to use the same term in each part of this comparison. There is a sense in which the meaning is more apparent when both words are the same. However, when, as in Otomi a different word must be used, the meaning itself remains unchanged, and in that sense nothing essential has been lost. When the total theme of forgiveness as found in the Bible is studied, then we find that forgiveness will be considered under two divisions, i.e., God's forgiveness of us and our forgiveness of one another. The reduced concordance arises since one word refers to forgiveness in the original but two different words refer to the two different aspects of forgiveness in Otomi. The meaning is unchanged even though the parallelism in the comparison is not as forceful.

A more extensive problem of this type occurs in Amuzgo, another Mexican language. One of the major themes of 1 John is "love." *Agapaō, agapē*, and *agapētos* ("to love," "love," "beloved") are used no fewer than 51 times in 1 John, that is to say, about once in every other verse (105 verses). Here is designed concordance right through a whole book of the New Testament. However, Amuzgo has one term for love toward God and others and a separate term for God's love for us. So, concordance is not strictly possible in a way that will match the Greek; for if the wrong term for man loving is used, it makes him equal to God.

In such cases as these, there is undoubtedly a reduction in concordance. But how serious is it? Nothing of the message has been lost; the meaning of 1 John (for instance) has been by no means distorted. What has happened is that a single original concordance has been replaced by a double concordance in the RL version. Instead of "love" being handled completely by one original root, it is now handled by two RL roots, so that there is concordance on the divine love for man, and a separate concordance on the human love for God and others. The change is, therefore, not so serious as might at first be thought.[3]

Concordance applies not only to a book of Scripture, or to the New Testament, but to the whole Bible as well. The Old Testament employs the word "blood" a little over a hundred times referring to the blood of sacrifices. When the death of Christ is referred to by the New Testament writers with the use of the word "blood" there is an allusion back to the Old Testament sacrificial system. This deliberate use of the word "blood" establishes a concordance which has often been referred to as the "red thread" found running throughout the Scriptures. To translate this symbol "blood" simply as "death" loses or at least obscures this designed concordance.[4]

Concordance also applies to the translation of Old Testament quotations. One would normally expect that the translation of Old Testament quotations used in the New Testament which are parallel to the Old Testament form, would be parallel in their Old and New Testament contexts. The assumption that such Old Testament quotations can always be translated concordantly, i.e., that both the Old and New Testament materials will be translated the same, fails to give due regard to the differences in the lexical structure of the languages involved. It assigns higher importance to the linguistic form of the quotations than to the purpose and meaning which such quotations are intended to communicate in their contexts. It is often impossible to avoid some reduction in concordance.

Generally speaking, the same translation of the Old and New Testament materials will adequately serve both contexts. There are exceptions,

[3] For a more detailed and technical discussion of reduction of concordance, see Longacre (1958, pp. 486-89).

[4] It will be granted immediately that a literal rendition of "blood" is often misunderstood. However, one can render a metonymy, such as this one, by using both the word "blood" and "to die" in a clause. See chapter 7 which deals with the translation of various figures of speech.

however. One occurs in Ephesians 4:8 where, as the *International Critical Commentary* notes, "the Psalm [68:18] speaks of . . . (material) gifts; the apostle, of . . . (spiritual)gifts." The Hebrew word *mattānāh*, whose plural is used in this Psalm, is used in the Old Testament only of material gifts. Paul quotes the Septuagint translation which uses the Greek word *domata*, and extends the sense of gifts so that it includes both material and spiritual gifts. In some languages, the word for "gifts" is only used in a material sense. To use such a word in both the Old and New Testament contexts would not do justice to the intended purpose of the quotation. In all probability, it would obscure rather than support the argument. Thus in Chol, one word meaning "gifts" is used in the Psalm and another word meaning "enablements" is used in Ephesians 4:8. The concordance is reduced, but the contextual sense and intention is kept in each passage.[5] This gives higher importance to meaning than to form and is not only consistent with the principles stated in chapter 1 but also seems consistent with the way New Testament authors quoted from the Old Testament. The New Testament contains 269 direct quotations from the Old, not counting allusions and other references. Of these quotations, 90 are the same in wording as either the LXX or the Masoretic sources. The New Testament writers did not have the same rules for quotations as are nowadays enforced. They were interested in the divine authority of the quotation and its application to the context in which they used it.[6]

A similar situation, resulting in reduced concordance between the material of the Old Testament and its quotation in the New, arises when part of the quoted material is generic and has a different but linguistically acceptable application in the two different contexts of the Old and New Testaments. When translating, the generic material may not give the correct sense in both of these contexts. For example, Matthew 2:18 quotes Jeremiah 31:15 using it in the context of the slaughter of children by Herod.

> "A voice was heard in Ramah,
> wailing and loud lamentation,
> Rachel weeping for her children;
> she refused to be consoled,
> because they were no more." (RSV)

[5] This approach may be applied to the case of the quotation of Isa. 7:14 in Matt. 1:23. If *'almāh* has the two senses "young woman" and "virgin" then Matthew chose the sense of "virgin" which is the sense particularly relevant to his own context. If *'almāh* means only "young woman" then Matthew extended the sense to "virgin." In either case, the context of Matthew definitely focuses on the absence of sexual relations and the translation of *parthenos* by "virgin" seems the only choice in English faithful to the author's purpose in making the quotation.

[6] Hughes (1962, p. 253) says: "Paul confirms what he has just been saying with a chain of quotations (2 Cor. 6:16-18) from the Old Testament Scriptures . . . . Yet a comparison of texts reveals that he did not feel himself bound to quote slavishly word for word, but rather according to the sense and with the purpose of applying and showing the relevance of the revelation to the circumstances of his readers."

In Jeremiah the context concerns the exiles from Jerusalem being led past Rachel's tomb on their way to captivity. The last clause then, means they had gone into captivity, while in Matthew's use of it, it means they are dead. In some languages, the generic clause cannot have either of these meanings. Context certainly affects the meanings words carry, but only within certain restrictions established by convention. Thus, it may happen that in some languages these two passages cannot be translated concordantly without distorting the meaning in one or the other context.

Another factor which can create reduction in concordance is stylistic variation. In some languages (for instance, German and some in India), it is considered poor style to constantly refer to the same theme in the same words — variation must be used if it is not to sound clumsy and inept. In such languages, there will also be a reduction of concordance, though not in content, nor in vigor or forcefulness of style.[7]

A third, though less significant factor, can temporarily affect concordance. This is uncertainty about which terms or expressions to use for such key terms as baptize, repent, forgive, and Holy Spirit. If a translator appears to have several equally good alternative terms for a key Biblical term, then it is quite permissible to use all of them in early editions of books, until it becomes apparent that the Christian community has come to prefer and use one of the alternatives. When this has happened, the preferred term may then be used concordantly in subsequent editions.

When using figures of speech, an author may treat as real concordance that which, under other circumstances, would clearly be classified as pseudo concordance. For example, when James says "as the body without the spirit is dead, so faith without works is dead also" (James 2:26), he is using "dead" in two distinct senses. However, the unity of the verse and the point of the comparison hinges on the concordance in this case, so that the translator should treat it as real concordance and maintain it in the RL if at all possible. If the same direct concordance is not possible, a change in the form of the figure of speech will sometimes make it possible to maintain the unity of the passage. In Colorado (Ecuador) this verse was rendered "as a dead body with the spirit gone is useless, in the same way faith without works is useless," so that the concordance of "useless" replaced the concordance of "dead."

Before closing this discussion of problems in maintaining real concordance, it is worth noting briefly that sometimes "there is some gain of concordance in the [RL] version relative to the [original] text.[8] Where

---

[7] It may be unwise to assume a stylistic uniformity in the New Testament itself. See, for instance, the interesting discussion by Morris in *Studies in the Fourth Gospel*, pp. 293-320, where he concludes that variation is a conscious feature of John's style. The variations noted (which are numerous) extend to both grammar (e.g., such features as word order) and lexicon (use of synonyms, etc.). His own words are, "John makes it a habit to repeat his sayings usually with a slight variation . . . . It is fair to say that he rarely alters the sense materially in such variation . . . . But the variation is there" (p. 317).

[8] Longacre, (1958, p. 489). See his section 3 (pp. 489, 90).

Greek has several terms for one concept such as *hamartia, hamartēma, paraptōma,* and *opheilēma* for "sin/s," or *apoluō, aphiēmi,* and *charizomai* for "to forgive," the RL often has only one term, so that there is a gain in concordance, although in some contexts, there may be a slight loss in fine lexical distinctions.[9] In the above instance, the gain in concordance arose because there were no other synonyms for the word sin.

CONCLUSION

The translator will expect some gain and some reduction of concordance in the process of translation. This is inevitable, since the lexical structure of each language is different. However, every effort should be made to retain concordance for those words which represent the different themes of a section, a book, or all of Scripture. In order to assure this result, the translator is encouraged to keep a file of different ways in which he translates key terms of Scripture. If variations from the original are justified by reasons already noted, then any reduction or gain in concordance need not disturb the translator; if, on the other hand, there is no justifying reason for the variety of renditions, then the preferred choice can be used throughout in order to restore concordance. The final form of the translation should contain the same coherence, unity, and focus of theme as is found in the original.

---

[9] If the lexical distinction is crucial to the proper understanding of the context, the RL term for "sin" may be modified by a phrase or in some other way. In many contexts, however, commentators, lexicographers, etc., are by no means agreed on whether there is any real difference between comparable terms, such as the above. Even the loss of fine lexical distinctions, therefore, is by no means certain.

CHAPTER 11

Collocational Clashes

COLLOCATIONAL CLASHES DEFINED

The word *collocate* means to place side by side. When people compose a sentence, they make use of a very complex set of habits in selecting certain words and in placing them side by side. When this is done correctly, one's experience or interpretation of experience is clearly communicated. If the sentence introduces a combination of words which does not sound correct to the hearer or reader, this may be due to collocational clash; but it also may be caused by other factors, such as an ungrammatical combination or something which contradicts the cultural viewpoint held by the people. Thus, a collocational clash is first described negatively — explaining what it is not.

What a collocational clash is not

A collocational clash is not to be confused with clashes with the cultural viewpoint. A statement made in the translation — even if grammatically and lexically correct — may still clash with the belief system or the cultural viewpoint of the readers. This type of clash is between the meaning communicated by a text and what the reader holds to be true. There is not a conflict of meaning components in what the text itself says. If, for instance, a given culture holds that God punishes people but does not *love* them, then objections will be raised to verses such as John 3:16, or passages such as 1 John 4:8-12. In a language of Vietnam, when John 13:5 was read to the translation helper, he laughed and explained that "hands" had been translated in error as "feet." After a meal, he continued, Jesus would wash the disciples' hands, not their feet. When the translation of Acts 8:20 into Ifugao of the Philippines was being drafted, the helper asked, "Why couldn't Simon buy the power of the Holy Ghost with money? We buy power from the witch doctor. Can't we buy power from God?" In Matthew 9:9 it is stated that there was "a man, named Matthew, sitting at the receipt of custom." In one of the Australian aborigine languages, this was translated as "a man named Matthew sitting where he collected money for the government." But the helper objected to the translation, with the comment, "No, he was giving people money from the government." The Australian aborigines have been receiving money from the government for so long the helper could not conceive that Matthew was collecting money for the government.

When faced with this type of objection to the translation, what is the translator to do? Generally, such culturally-based objections have to be disregarded, especially for those truths and morals of Scripture which transcend culture and have a universal validity.

However, not all cultural clashes need to be left unresolved. An example is found in Mark 13:15, where Jesus says to the disciples, "And let him that is on the housetop not go down into the house, neither enter therein, to take anything out of his house." The "housetop" referred to here is a flat one, typical of houses in Palestine in Jesus' time. However, in many cultures, especially in jungle areas, "housetop" refers to the ridge of a steeply sloping roof and gives the impression the owner of the house was repairing the roof in some way. The translator has two alternatives in handling this kind of cultural clash. He can use the RL word or expression for "housetop," and put a picture of people on a flat Palestinian housetop at this point in the text. The less preferable alternative is to use a generic locational term rather than a specific one. It could thus be translated, "Let him who is *not in his house/outside his house* . . . ." This is meaningful in the RL, and it does not preclude reference to "housetop" by someone explaining the meaning of the passage.

In all the passages which use some form of *anakeimai, anaklinō,* or *katakeimai* ("to recline") the KJV uses "to sit" except in John 13:23 where it is rendered "leaning." In all probability, the KJV translators saw a cultural problem here, since reclining is not the position in the English speaking world for eating. However, reclining is a historical reference to the cultural practice of that day, and substituting sitting for reclining misrepresents this practice. Some cultural clashes of this type may be rendered in a generic form which harmonizes with both the original and the RL cultures. For instance, Matthew 9:10, "as Jesus was reclining in the house," may be rendered, "as Jesus was at the table in the house" or more specifically, "as Jesus was eating in the house." This solution, like the previous one, chooses a rendition which does not misrepresent the historical facts of the text and yet permits the readers to understand the text according to their own cultural viewpoint until such a time that a fuller knowledge of the Biblical culture extends their viewpoint. Generally, however, cultural differences between the RL and the original need not be resolved. It is only reasonable to expect to be able to teach people an appreciation for new ideas — a different view of God, his activities, what he expects of us — whether they come to accept that different view or not. The original cultural viewpoint must be maintained either specifically or generically.

Further, a collocational clash is not to be confused with a grammatical clash. In a grammatical clash there is a conflict of meaning components within the text, not between the text and one's cultural beliefs as in a cultural clash. Even though a translator may have a good knowledge of the grammar of the RL, the particular difficulties of a verse or passage may temporarily obscure that knowledge so that statements like "me want soup" or "the boys is in school" may be used inadvertently. Such errors, of course, may also arise through inadequate control of the grammar. These "grammatical clashes" are not permissible. The constraints of the RL grammar must always be followed and such "clashes" must be replaced by the correct grammatical forms.

What a collocational clash is

In a collocational clash there is a conflict of meaning components within the text carried not by the grammar but by the lexical choices made. In the expression, "the silent paint," there is a collocational clash between the components of meaning carried by the words "silent" and "paint." Part of the meaning of "paint" excludes the notion of it making a noise. Paint may be loud in a metaphorical sense but is not attributed with silence either metaphorically or literally. The word "silent" presupposes the possibility of its opposite, i.e., making a noise. Herein lies the conflict between the components of meaning carried by the combination of these two words. Joos (1958, p. 58) makes the interesting observation that the statement, "I never have heard a green horse smoke a dozen oranges," is gramatically correct. Nonetheless, it contains four collocational clashes, four lexical combinations with components of meaning that are not compatible.

Languages may accept collocational clashes when the context makes it clear the situation is not normal, that is, when the context is fantasy, miracles, etc. Green horse, hearing smoke, horses smoking, smoking oranges, and even noisy paint are perfectly acceptable to the English speaker, given the right context. Biblical miracles will fall into this category. Since one of the components of meaning carried by the word "water" is that it is not a solid, walking on top of water presents a collocational clash, but this should present no difficulties once the context is clear.

CHARACTERISTICS OF COLLOCATIONAL RANGE

Another way of looking at collocation is by means of the concept of range. Each word and idiom in a language is selective with respect to the company it keeps, and the list of permissible company defines its *collocational range.* As soon as the collocational range of a word is violated, then some new component of meaning is introduced into the context and a collocational clash results. Of course, for a given word, there may be several sets of collocational ranges. For instance, a transitive verb will collocate with a selection of subjects and a selection of objects, and the translator must be sensitive to these ranges and must keep within them.

A collocational clash arises from an overextension of the collocational range of a term. For instance, when a foreign speaker of English says, "What delicious singing!", he is extending the range of the adjective "delicious" beyond its normal collocation with food and drink and applying it to auditory experience as well. The concept of collocational range, therefore, is a useful way of approaching the question of correct and incorrect collocations, and is developed in the rest of this section.

Each word in a language has a unique collocational range, both qualitatively, in its selections, and quantitatively, in the number of possible collocations. Some words can collocate with only one generic class, or even only certain members of it; others can collocate widely. For instance, the verb "to run" collocates with several generic classes — humans, animals (with legs), liquids, garments, for example — as subject, whereas the verb "to mew" only collocates with cats and certain birds, such as gulls and hawks, which have a cry like the mewing of a cat. "To run" also has a wide range of "prepositional" collocations, such as "run out of the house," "run for office," "run into trouble," "run over a child," "run below average." No other word has this particular collocational range in English.

Nonequivalence of collocational ranges between languages

What is true within one language is also true for equivalent words across languages. The collocational range is different for equivalent words across languages. *Run*, in its usual sense of people or animals running, has a corresponding term in Chol. However, many of the collocations permissible for *run* in English are not permissible in Chol — Chol noses do not run, nor do their stockings, jellies or motors. They do not run for office, or into debt, or trouble, or out of money or time or patience. None of these are acceptable collocations in Chol, where *run* has a much narrower collocational range than in English.

It works the other way around, too — other languages use the equivalent of *run* in collocations impossible in English. Kasem of Ghana can say "he ran his pity" meaning "he took pity on him," but "pity" does not collocate with *run* in English. The Greek of 2 Thessalonians 3:1 says (literally), "Finally pray, brethren, for us, that the word of the Lord may run . . . ," where "may run" translates a form of the usual Greek verb for "to run," viz., *trechō*. In spite of the wide range of collocations that *run* has in English, it does not include "word" as subject. Hence, in the KJV it is translated as "have free course," in the RSV as "speed on," and in the TEV as "continue to spread rapidly," each rendition attempting to convey, by a different collocation, what the original Greek collocation meant.

The nonequivalence of collocational ranges between languages may seem obvious enough. Nevertheless, translators often use words outside their normal collocational range because they have, usually quite unconsciously, *assumed* that the particular collocation they are translating — the original collocation — is transferable to the RL. The translator therefore needs to be alert to collocations in the original which are potential trouble spots and to avoid transferring them into the RL.[1]

Factors affecting collocational range

The more generic a term is, the greater will be its collocational range. A generic term such as "animal" will collocate more widely than a specific term such as "dog." Animals, for instance, can swim, fly, and run, but while dogs can swim or run, they cannot fly. Or again, a generic verb like "do" will collocate more widely than a more specific verb, such as "hit." Such specific terms as bevy, flock, herd, and swarm have very restricted collocations.

Terms with multiple senses, such as "to run," also collocate more widely than terms with only a single sense, such as "to stroll." "To run" collocates with humans, with animals (with legs), with liquids, clothing, and plants, but the more specific verb "to stroll" collocates only with humans; animals do not stroll, nor do liquids, clothing, or plants.

Extension of collocational range

You may have gathered from the above discussion that for any given lexical item the collocational range is *fixed*. But this is not so; the collocational range of words is subject to constant change, or drift. New experiences and new ways of looking at experience can all lead to new collocations. McIntosh (1961, p. 336) observes: "The dictates of range are such as to permit the admission of new exponents on the very margin of tolerability without our even feeling that these are in any way dubitable."

An amusing example of the extension of collocational range is found in the following series of statements:

> "A KISS is a NOUN because it is both common and proper.
> A KISS is a PRONOUN because 'she' stands for it.
> A KISS is a VERB; it is either active or passive.
> A KISS is an ADVERB; it modifies the action.
> A KISS is an INTERJECTION; it shows sudden feeling.
> A KISS is a CONJUNCTION because it connects."[2]

Although it is true that collocational range is subject to change, it is rare that a nonnative speaker successfully extends the collocational range to include a new sense. The nonnative speaker lacks the intuitive knowl-

---

[1] This matter is discussed in more detail later in this chapter.
[2] Source unknown.

edge of the lexicon and its components which the native speaker has, and therefore he is not in a good position to judge whether a new collocation involves a collocational clash.

Once the acceptable syntactic patterns of the language have been learned, it is not a difficult matter to generate new utterances following these patterns. Words will be combined which perhaps have never before been combined. As long as the usage of these words does not represent an extended sense never before carried by the word, the new combination should present no communication problem. However, as soon as new collocations are introduced, which involve figurative extensions of meaning, the probability of a collocational clash is high.

Because of the concepts he is seeking to convey in translation, the translator is under constant pressure to generate new collocations and if he is not a native speaker, he may sometimes do this by generalizing from one or two examples. For instance, a translator notes the expression, "sickness grabs people." In English it is animate beings that "grab people," but here an abstract noun is the subject. Further, he interprets the expression as meaning "people are under the control of sickness." He concludes that other abstract nouns can be the subject of "grab" and that "being under the control of" is the sense conveyed. So he begins to use such expressions as "sin grabs people" or "death grabs people," and is surprised to find his helper reacts with "Oh no, we would never say that." In Popoluca, "night grabbed us" means that "night overtook us unexpectedly." But the language helper would not accept "sin grabbed us" as an acceptable Popoluca collocation.

The translator in one of the Aztec dialects was searching for a suitable term for "spirit." He and the language helper began to experiment with a term which had the basic meaning of "evil wind," in which it was felt that the component "evil" was probably no longer active. It was also felt that by collocating this term with "good," any possibility of the component "evil" being present in the collocation would be removed. When, however, the expression was checked with different native speakers, they simply laughed at the collocational clash — "God's good (evil) spirit" because, although only implicit, the component of evil was still a very active part of the word "spirit."

An unacceptable extension of collocational range may arise from ignorance of some component which restricts the range. Stated in other words, an unawareness of some relevant component of meaning which restricts the range of acceptable collocations may result in a collocational clash. This type of error is common in the translation work of those who do not realize that restrictions in collocational range are important and must be taken into consideration. Some examples follow, taken from different languages. In each case, it should be noted that the translator carried the original collocation over into the RL without first finding out if that usage was within the collocational range of the RL word involved; and the result was a collocational clash that had to be corrected.

	Collocation	Reason for Collocational Clash
Mark 14:24	"blood . . . poured out" (RSV)	The verb "pour out" assumes a vessel from which a liquid is being poured; it is not used of bleeding.
Mark 14:31	"deny thee"	A person cannot be denied, as such, but only some statement by or about the person.
Mark 15:1	"bound Jesus"	The term used for "bound" or "tied" collocated only with animals such as pigs or cows which were tied up in preparation for butchering.
John 1:29	"taketh away . . . sin"	Only tangible objects can be taken away.
Acts 7:40	"make . . . gods"	The word for the true God cannot also be used for man-made idols since it has the component of "self-existence."
Acts 27:4	"the winds . . . against us" (RSV)	The term "against" collocates only with an animate being who "is against." The language helper could understand the statement as referring to a spirit called "the wind" but not as referring to the physical wind itself.

How to Avoid Collocational Clashes

Since collocational clashes are a not infrequent translation error, the question must be asked: How, then, can a translator avoid them? There are three ways in which this may be done: (1) by a careful study of the components of meaning of the RL vocabulary; (2) by an extensive and thorough use of elicitation techniques; (3) by being alert to the collocations in the original likely to give trouble in the RL. It is understood that points 1 and 2 will be done with the help of a native speaker, and that they will be done both before and during the translation process.

Study the components of meaning for each word

To really understand a word one must know its various senses and the specifying components of each sense. If these are not understood, error is certain to enter the translation. There are three types of error which can be avoided by a proper analysis of the meaning of the words used. These are wrong meanings, ambiguities, and collocational clashes.

Wrong meanings may arise from a wrong assignment of components to a word or combination of words. The situations under which this happens are numerous, and the results are always unfortunate. For example, what a translator thought meant "repent" turned out to mean "replace the truth as a witness with false testimony in order to help the accused." In another language, "signs" used in Scripture as an indication of something beyond the event itself was rendered "holy illuminating things." Upon fuller investigation, this new construction merely referred to candles lit before the saints.

Wrong meanings may also arise from not knowing all the components in a word. Unfortunately for the translator, often the unknown component introduces wrong meaning. In translating the account of the disciples who untied the donkey so that Jesus could ride it, a translator used a term which he understood to mean "unloose." It was a correct term to use with animals like horses, mules, donkeys, cows, etc. However, this word also carried with it the component of malicious, revengeful action. It would only be done with evil intent.

In Acts 1:8, Jesus tells the apostles that they will be "witnesses" to him throughout the world. In one of the dialects of Aztec, a term for "witnesses" was used which includes the component of "in a court case," but this component was overlooked by the translator. As used by native speakers, the term did not extend beyond the legal context. Further, in this particular dialect, its usual meaning was "witness for the prosecution," and so it tended to imply that Jesus was the accused.

Ambiguities often arise when the translator knows only one sense of a word. As he uses such a word he is unaware whether the context rules out further senses or not. In this way, ambiguities, including vulgarisms, may be innocently communicated by the translation because of a failure to understand the full meaning of a word.

Unawareness of lexical components may thus give rise to wrong meanings or unwanted ambiguities, but even when it does not, it often gives rise to collocational clashes and this may obscure the sense so that the native reader considers it nonsense. Sometimes the meaning is still evident, but the native reader reacts to the combination of words as humorous or peculiar — the sort of combinations children make when learning to talk, saying such things as "sharpen me a carrot," or "my toe has a tummyache."

Use elicitation techniques

If the translator is to become thoroughly familiar with the lexicon of the RL, a systematic method of study is needed. It is all too easy to hear a new word, or find one in a text, check its phonology and morphology, and then, conscious of how much other work there is to do, give it an English gloss as it is placed in the file. But such an approach to the lexicon leads the translator to include in his translation both false equivalences and partial equivalences. Ballard (1968) gives an example from his initial translation work in the Inibaloi language of the Philippines. He had noted *kibot* as "a very common word for 'stealing,'" and so he had used it for "spoil" in a first draft of Mark 3:27, which reads: "no man can enter into a strong man's house, and spoil his goods, except he will first bind the strong man; and then he will spoil his house." (RSV uses "plunder" for "spoil.") But this was unacceptable to his Inibaloi helper. When asked why, he said: "How can anyone *kibot* if the owner of the house has to be first overpowered and tied up?"[3] Ballard had overlooked the component of "stealth" in the term *kibot*.

The systematic method of elicitation to be outlined here makes two basic assumptions. The first is that the mature native speaker of a language can provide, when questioned, the sort of lexical and contextual information the translator needs to know. As it is put in Beekman (1968a, pp. 3, 4): "Any adult representative of the language to be learned has an accumulation of experience and understanding concerning his culture and his environment *which he can convert into speech*. All of this experience and understanding hidden away in his mind can be made available to us in small digestible pieces *through the use of questions*" (italics by present authors). Although it is best to use several helpers and cross-check their responses,[4] the basic principle holds: the native speaker can verbalize the information and will do so in response to questions.

The second assumption is that the lexicon can be divided into four broad semantic groupings, Thing, Event, Abstraction, and Relation, as discussed briefly in chapter 4. The questions asked will differ somewhat according to the semantic classification of the item being investigated. The study of the class of Relations is sufficiently different from the study of the other three classes that it is taken up in a separate chapter.

The use of the question technique — "elicitation procedures" — can start from the point when the translator is not even sure as to what semantic class an item belongs. His initial questions, whether or not he knows to which semantic class the word belongs, are general, such as, "How do you use this word?" or, "What does this word mean?" When the helper has given instances of the word's use, then the translator will have a good idea of its semantic class, and so he can begin to use the sort of questions appropriate to that class.

1. *Event words*

If the word is an Event word, it will be related to Things, Abstractions, and other Events; and each of these areas of relationship may be investigated adequately by means of questions. To discover what Things can collocate with the Event word being studied, the investigator asks for participants involved in the event — subjects, objects, indirect objects, benefactors, etc. Hence, such questions as the following are asked:

> Who/What does it?
> To whom/what is it done?[5]
> For whom/what is it done?
> With what is it done?

---

[3] Ballard (1968, p. 13).

[4] See Ballard (section D, 1968, p. 13).

[5] The form of the questions used here is one that is convenient in English, and it is assumed that the translator will recast them into a suitable form in the RL he is studying.

The investigator should not stop with just one or two answers to the above questions. He should see whether he can exhaust the responses which come readily to the helper's mind. Stopping too soon — an all too common fault — can easily lead to a distorted interpretation of the item under consideration.

It should be borne in mind that references to Things may be carried *implicitly* in an Event word. For instance, in the statement, "he nodded" (in English), there is no need to say what was nodded; it is carried implicitly, as only heads are nodded in English. Again, such verbs as "to kick," "to punch," and "to slap" carry the implicit instruments foot, fist, and open hand respectively.

The members of the Abstraction class that can be associated with an Event word relate to such modifications as time, space, intensity, appraisal, and manner. Temporal modifications include such concepts as duration, frequency, and speed; spatial specifications include the direction of the Thing that is moving, its position, as well as the location of the Event, its distance, etc. Thus, the sort of questions that would be appropriate to use would be:

> How long is it done?/How much time does it take to do it?
> How frequently is it done? (from time to time, weekly, annually, repeatedly, etc.)
> How quickly is it done?
> When is it done?
> In what direction/s does the Thing move?
> What position does the Thing take?
> Where is the Event done?
> How far does the Thing move?
> What do people say about that Event?
> How is the Event done?

Just as Things which are related to an Event may be implicit in the Event word, so also Events may carry implicit Abstractions. Verbs such as "to wink," "to glance," and "to stare" carry an implicit component of duration; speed is implicit in "to sprint" and "to spin"; and verbs such as "to sway," "to climb," "to come," and "to go" have an implicit component of direction. Location, too, may be implicit as in "to swim," or "to skate" or "to dig"; and distance is implied by "to hike."

Event words often stand in relationship to other Event words, and this area should also be investigated by questions. For instance, Events may be temporally related to each other, as antecedent, simultaneous, or subsequent. Further, sequentially related Events may not be purely chronological, but they may stand in a cause-effect relationship such as purpose, motive, intention, reason for, occasion of, grounds, cause, or condition. An Event simultaneous with another one may indicate means or manner or occasion, and a subsequent Event may be related as effect, result, or consequence. The following questions may prove useful in seeking to investigate how Event words are related to other Event words.

What causes this Event to happen?
Why does this Event happen?
Why is this Event done?
When is it done?
How is this Event done?
What is done at the same time?
What happens at the same time?
What will happen if this Event is done?
What will happen after this Event is done?
What is another way of speaking of this Event?[6]
What is the opposite of this Event?[7]

Again, Events may be implicit in an Event word. Thus, the verb "to martyr" has the central Event concept "to kill," but in addition, there is an implicit reason for that Event, i.e., the person was killed because he refused to forsake what he believed, and the statement of that implicit reason involves other events such as "to refuse" and "to forsake." A further example is provided by the verb "to blame" which involves the Events "to say" and also "to do something bad."

2. *Thing words*

Just as Event words are related to Things, Abstractions, and other Events, so also Thing words enter into relationships with Events, Abstractions, and other Things. When investigating a Thing word, even if the investigator has seen the person or thing referred to, it is best to start with a general question, such as, "Tell me about this person/Thing." Then, when the helper has supplied the information that comes to his mind, the translator can narrow down to more specific questions.

The relationships which may exist between Thing words are relationships such as kinship, role, generic classifier, part-whole, spatial, resemblance, opposition, and causal agency. Questions suitable for discovering such relationships are:

[6] This question is to elicit any synonyms for the term under consideration, or any more generic terms that can include this particular Event.

[7] As the translator looks at these questions, especially terms like "the opposite of," he may well wonder how such concepts could possibly be expressed in his own RL. For example, in the Gahuku language of New Guinea there are no words meaning "size," "shape," "position," "age," "color," etc., so that the translator cannot ask, "What color is it?" etc., but must frame his questions as alternatives: Is it green or red? Is it big or little? Is it thin or thick? etc. This problem is briefly discussed in Beekman (1968a), page 3, paragraph 3, where another method, the "pattern" method, is suggested as a way of handling the lack of terms for "shape," etc. A much fuller discussion is found in NOT 36, in an article "More on Elicitation" by Pallesen. He describes in considerable detail how he handled these questions in Samal, a Philippine language, and makes a number of useful suggestions as well as pointing out some potential pitfalls.

Who calls this Thing "son"?
What does a man call this Thing?
Who refers to whom as being this Thing? (e.g., man calls his mate "wife," king calls those he rules "subjects," etc.)
What other Things are this Thing?
What kind of Thing is this?
What are the parts of this Thing?
How is this Thing spatially related to the other Thing?
What does it resemble?
What is its opposite?
Who made it?
What caused it?

Events may be related to the Thing word under consideration, either behaviorally or functionally. The function of a Thing always has reference to its usefulness or value; behavior does not. The function of the Thing covers its purpose, use, role, or duty, while the behavior of the Thing includes what it can do or what can be done to it. Some questions covering this area of relationship are:

What does the Thing do?
How does the Thing act?
What happens to it?
What is its purpose?

Members of the Abstraction class are commonly related to Things. The relationships between them may be spatial (size, shape, position, and location), temporal, tactile, visual, audio, olfactory, gustatory, or relating to quantity, quality, sex, or substance. Appropriate questions are:

What size is the Thing?
What shape is it?
What position is it in?
Where is it?
What age is it?
What does it feel like?
What color is it?
What sound does it make?
What kind of smell does it have?
What taste does it have?
How many are there?
What do people say about it?
What sex is it?
What is it made of?

3. *Abstraction words*

The third semantic class is the class of Abstractions. Again, the investigator starts with a generic request such as, "Use this word in as many different ways as you can think of." Abstractions may co-occur with

Events, Things, and other Abstractions. Some attention has already been given to the former two types of collocation. Abstractions in relationship with other Abstractions have not yet been discussed, however. They may be related to each other in a scaled series of opposites, as antonyms, as synonyms, or as a member of a generic classifier. Questions such as the following may be asked:

> What Things have this abstract quality?
> What Events have this abstract quality?
> What is the opposite of this abstract quality?
> What is another way to say the same thing?
> What kind of abstract quality is this?

The translator may feel that such a prolonged investigation of the lexicon is hardly worth his while, especially when there is a lot of translation waiting to be tackled. But he should bear two things in mind. One is that fluency is the basic requisite for a translator, and that the constant use of such questions, and the listening to and recording of the responses, will give him constant (and purposeful) practice in this area. The other is that if he relies heavily on an inadequate study and knowledge of the lexicon, his translation will certainly be marred by collocational clashes and wrong meanings, making it sound foreign and strange. Hence, neglect of the lexicon is defeating his own ultimate goal of an idiomatic and meaningful translation.

Recognize potential collocational clashes

So far, suggestions for avoiding collocational clashes have focused attention on the RL — analyzing the components of words which have been thoroughly investigated by means of the question technique. However, the examples quoted earlier in the chapter showed that collocational clashes often arise from a literal transfer of a collocation in the original. Doubtless, the original collocation seemed ordinary to the translator because of his Western language background, but it was not so from the standpoint of the RL reader. How, then, can the translator alert himself to those collocations in the original which are likely to produce clashes in the RL?

In answering this question, it is useful to reintroduce the concept of "primary sense." It is not at all easy[8] to define this concept, yet the

[8] Although no attempt is made to define "primary sense" in any formal manner, it seems likely that the following two criteria are helpful for distinguishing primary from secondary and figurative senses:
> (1) that sense which is culturally more relevant to more people, and
> (2) that sense whose collocates either represent a larger class or are more generic.

The first of these is the basic criterion, the second an auxiliary one which is usually a correlate of the first. Thus, the sense "self-locomotion of animate beings with legs" is the primary sense of *run*, for it is culturally more relevant than the other senses and it also collocates with the largest class ("animate beings with legs" as opposed to "liquids," "clothing," "vines," and "self-powered mechanical objects"). The verb *to spit* not only collocates with people, but also with cats, guns ("spitting bullets"), mature native speaker rarely has difficulty in stating the primary sense or recognizing senses of a word which are not primary.[9] Generally speaking, if a native speaker is given a word in isolation, he is likely, nine times out of ten, to give the primary sense of the word. Or, if asked to give it in a context, he will choose a context that corresponds to the primary sense. This also means that, given a larger or smaller context, the native speaker can say whether a word in that context is used in the primary sense, or not. For instance, given the two statements, "The man ran out of the house" and "The man ran out of money," a native English speaker would indicate the former as giving the primary sense of "ran out of."

Words used in their primary sense in the Scriptures present relatively little problem to the translator, as in most languages it is possible to use the literal equivalent. Thus, *run*, discussed earlier, would be readily translated into most languages when used in its primary sense of "self-locomotion of animate beings with legs"; so also would *to dress* in its primary sense of "to put clothes on."

In the following sentences, all the words are used in their primary sense:

> I saw some trees near their house.
> The baby was born yesterday.
> The baby grew rapidly.
> It was very cold yesterday.
> He came to see me at my house.

But in the following sentences, some of those same words are used in a secondary or figurative sense, as indicated by the italics:

> His love *grew cold*.
> Faith was *born*.
> Salvation *came* to his *house*.

The translator's task, then, is to notice which words in the original are *not* being used in their primary sense, as a literal translation of these is likely to produce a collocational clash — to the amusement or bewilderment of the readers. Unfortunately, the translator is so used to the collo-

---

motors, rain, eggs ("spitting in the pan"). Here the primary sense is that which collocates with human beings, since, in each of the other senses, the collocate is very restricted — a particular type of animal, certain manufactured items, a particular type of weather, etc.

An interesting case is provided by *to drive*. Consideration of the various collocates that can occur as the object of this verb gives a list such as car, truck, tractor; nail, stake; cattle; bargain; etc. Using criterion two alone would make it difficult to know whether "motor-powered vehicles" or "cattle" was the collocate of the primary sense. But criterion one settles the question, as the sense which is culturally more relevant to more people in a modern industrialized society is driving a motor-powered vehicle.

[9] See appendix B for a brief discussion of an experiment testing native speakers for recognition of primary sense.

cations of his own language he may unconsciously assume that they will seem equally natural in another language.

Nonprimary senses may be determined by a native speaker by finding the primary sense as discussed earlier in this chapter. Although the translator cannot do this for the language into which he is translating, he can do it for a version in his own language. It thus becomes part of his task to recognize potential collocational clashes and to be suspicious of retaining the same collocations in the translation. He is hindered in this not only because they all seem perfectly natural to him, but also because of a commonly held assumption that primary senses account for the majority of the concepts he is translating, and hence any potential alertness in this area is dulled. But primary senses do not occur with such a high frequency. Sayce, in his *Introduction to the Science of Language* (p. 181), remarks that "three-fourths of our language may be said to consist of worn out metaphors," and Walpole in his volume *Semantics* (p. 145) says: "We use every one of our words metaphorically as well as literally. Our most basic words, leg, foot, give, take, in, are used metaphorically more often than not." As native speakers, we are so adjusted to this phenomenon, that we take figurative expressions quite for granted, and assume that the same figurative expressions are natural to all other languages.

It may be objected, however, that English is unusual in this respect, and that the use of secondary and figurative senses are much less frequent in the Scriptures, and, in particular, in the New Testament. In the article on Metonymy and Synecdoche (Beekman, 1967b), a list is given (no claim is made for completeness) of instances of Metonymy or Synecdoche in the New Testament. There are well over 800 instances cited. A list of Rhetorical Questions has also been prepared for the New Testament, and this gives a count of about 700. Counts are not readily available for other Figures of Speech, but clearly it is no exaggeration to say that some use of a secondary or figurative sense occurs in the New Testament, on the average, every four or five verses. Nonprimary senses are by no means a rare phenomenon in the New Testament.

When preparing a passage for translation, therefore, the translator needs to ask himself, "Are there any instances of secondary or figurative senses here?" and then make a careful note of them. Nor can this type of preparation be left until the epistles are being translated, as may be assumed. The count on Metonymy and Synecdoche showed that a little over half of the instances are found in the gospels. From the very beginning of his translation work, the translator must watch for the pitfalls created by the use of nonprimary senses in the original.

CHAPTER 12

Lexical Equivalence Across Languages —
When Concepts Are Shared

WAYS IN WHICH LANGUAGES DIFFER IN LEXICAL STRUCTURE

LITERAL AND NONLITERAL LEXICAL EQUIVALENCE

TYPES OF NONLITERAL LEXICAL EQUIVALENCE
    Equivalence involving semantically complex words
    Equivalence involving synonyms
    Equivalence involving antonyms
    Equivalence involving a reciprocal
    Equivalence involving generic or specific terms
    Equivalence involving figurative expressions

WAYS IN WHICH LANGUAGES DIFFER IN LEXICAL STRUCTURE

Although it is generally taken for granted that a translator will have to change from the grammatical structures of the original to those of the RL, it is often thought that similar changes will not be necessary when it comes to handling the lexical structure. It is assumed that, apart from one or two possible exceptions, all the translator has to do is to match words with the same meaning as he translates. But languages not only differ in their phonological and grammatical structures, but also in their lexical structures.

One misconception underlying the assumption that lexical structures are practically identical is the idea that all languages, wherever they are spoken, share the same concepts — that the same specific areas of experience are handled by the lexicon of each language. Now, it is true that there is an extensive core of shared concepts between languages, but total matching cannot be assumed. Among tribal groups, in particular, there are concepts which are unknown, or have become lost through changed historical circumstances. Hinterland tribes, far from rivers or sea, do not handle concepts dealing with fishing or boating. Other tribes, such as some of those in Brazil and Colombia, have no words for legal processes. The Aztecs and Mayans obviously had vocabulary to handle the astronomical observations on which their accurate calendars were based, but their descendants have lost most of this vocabulary now. Geographical circumstances differ; historical experience differs; present conditions differ; and all of these factors influence the range of concepts handled by any particular language.

A second misconception is that where languages do share concepts, they will represent those concepts in the lexicon in the same way. This is by no means the case.

An idea may be expressed from different "semantic perspectives," from different points of view. It may be stated figuratively or nonfiguratively, as in "he paid through the nose" and "he paid an exorbitant price." It may be viewed from a reciprocal point of view, so that one can say, "I received it from him" or "he gave it to me." It may be expressed either positively or negatively: "he left" or "he did not stay." It may be expressed synonymously as "he almost failed" and "he nearly failed."

These differences of semantic perspective provide stylistic options in speaking or writing. However, not all concepts may be expressed using all the perspectives. This is especially noticeable when rendering a concept into another language. Where several perspectives are possible in English, there may be only one in another language, and vice versa. In some languages, "it is bad" can only be expressed negatively by "it is not good"; there is no affirmative expression, "it is bad."

Again, there may be no matching in the area of synonyms. While Greek has two adjectives meaning "full," *mestos* and *plērēs*, English has only one. Hebrew has at least three separate terms for a "spring (of water)" — *cayīn* as in Genesis 16:7, 24:29; *gullāh* as in Joshua 15:19 and *mabbûac* as in Isaiah 35:7, 49:10; English has but one. Similarly, the use of antonyms is language-specific. For instance, in English "old" is the antonym of both "young" and "new"; "short" is the antonym of both "tall" and "long." Other languages may not have the antonym "short" at all, or have distinct ones, or have "tall" and "long" represented by the same form, but with distinct antonyms.

A third misconception arises when it is assumed that words from different languages will cover the same range of experience or ideas. Often, however, a particular word represents a "bundle" of components of meaning; that is to say, a number of ideas are represented by a single word. *To dive* is an example of such a componentially complex verb. It may be possible to render this verb into another language only as "to jump into the water head first." How many ideas and what combination of ideas may be packed into one word is a language-specific feature that only occasionally corresponds between unrelated languages. Thus a concept symbolized by a single word in one language may require several words in another — or, alternatively, the word may symbolize only some of the meaning carried by a single word in some other language. For instance, in a Vietnamese language, there is a form *giong* which means, "when someone is going somewhere, and something changes at home that cancels his reason for going, then someone from home goes *giong*, that is, to tell him." The number of ideas packed into the sense carried by a word, or alternatively, the number of words needed to cover a given concept is language-specific, and the translator may make no *a priori* assumptions as to what a particular RL will do; it can be found out only by investigation.

From the foregoing discussion it becomes clear that when speaking of lexical structure we are referring to two general features which are found in every language but are applied to the vocabulary of each language in a different way. These two features which have already been alluded to as "bundles of components of meaning" and as "semantic perspective" may be restated as (1) the number and selection of meaning components combined in a word and (2) the semantic interrelationships that may exist between different words. Languages differ from one another as to how these two features have been utilized in the structure of their vocabulary. Thus, the translator can take nothing for granted, and, in particular, it is unreasonable to expect that, as the many different concepts of the original are translated into another language, these concepts will be represented in the same way in the original and in the RL. Since the lexical structures differ, so will the way in which these concepts are symbolized.

LITERAL AND NONLITERAL LEXICAL EQUIVALENCE

When the differences between the lexical structures of languages are not fully appreciated, then it is naturally assumed that in the process of translation all lexical equivalence should be "literal." By a "literal" lexical equivalence here is meant that the sense is conveyed without any change in the lexical structure — one word for one word, figurative expression for figurative expression, synonym for synonym, antonym for antonym, etc. By a "nonliteral" lexical equivalence is meant that the same sense is conveyed with at least one change in the form of the lexical structure (literal in *meaning*, but not literal in lexical *form*) — several words for one word, a nonfigurative expression for a figurative one, a reciprocal form for a direct one, etc.

Readers who are familiar with several Indo-European languages may well feel that literal lexical equivalence is the norm and that nonliteral equivalence should be resorted to only occasionally. Consequently, nonliteral equivalents are looked at with some degree of suspicion and translators who make use of them may be accused of "paraphrasing" rather than translating. However, the thrust of this chapter is to show that if divinely inspired concepts are to be rendered accurately and faithfully, a direct word-for-word equivalence will be impossible because of the differences between languages. In 1 Peter 1:18, for example, the KJV refers to "your vain conversation *received by tradition from your fathers.*" These last six words are the translation of one Greek word, *patroparadotou.* English has no one-word equivalent for this particular Greek word. This rendering of the KJV is not an unjustifiable paraphrase, nor is it unjustifiable when translators today do the same thing. Nevertheless, when translating between related languages, such as Greek and English, the structural differences are slight, so that relatively few such "nonliteral" equivalents are necessary. When translating into completely unrelated languages, however, the substantially greater structural differences will result in correspondingly greater use of nonliteral equivalents, if the meaning of the original is to be closely and faithfully maintained. A good translation, then, will make extensive use of *both* kinds of equivalence, according to the requirements of the RL. Literal and nonliteral equivalences will be found throughout, since there will be both differences and similarities in the structure of the lexicon.

Chart 1 lists a variety of structural features of the lexicon of the original and indicates how these may be matched in a literal or nonliteral manner in a translation.

CHART 1

LITERAL AND NONLITERAL LEXICAL EQUIVALENCE

STRUCTURAL FEATURE OF THE LEXICON	LEXICAL FORM IN THE ORIGINAL LANGUAGE	LEXICAL FORM IN THE RECEPTOR LANGUAGE	
		Literal Equivalent (Form of original and RL match)	Nonliteral Equivalent (Form of Original and RL do not match)
Componential Complexity	Single word	single word	phrase or clause
	phrase or clause	phrase or clause	single word
Synonymy	several synonyms	same number of equiv. synonyms	fewer, more, or no synonyms
	no synonyms	no synonyms	several synonyms
Antonymy	positive	positive	antonym negated
	negative	negative	antonym stated positively
Generic-Specific	generic	generic	specific
	specific	specific	generic
Reciprocity	nonreciprocal	nonreciprocal	reciprocal
Figurative-Nonfigurative	figurative	figurative	nonfigurative
	nonfigurative	nonfigurative	figurative

This chart does not attempt to show the fact that more than one of the features may converge in either a literal or nonliteral equivalent. It does make clear, however, why a translator feels more "comfortable" when he can use a suitable literal equivalent, for in that case the form of the RL version matches the form of the original as well as its meaning. Such an equivalent presents him with relatively fewer problems, whereas the use of a correct nonliteral equivalent is a recurring problem to most translators. Since nonliteral equivalence is the problem area, the rest of the chapter is devoted to a detailed discussion of types of nonliteral equivalence so as to alert the translator to ways in which to render a word when a literal equivalent is not available or suitable.

TYPES OF NONLITERAL LEXICAL EQUIVALENCE

Before taking up the discussion of the various types of nonliteral equivalence in detail, two assumptions underlying the presentation should be made clear. One is that, in the discussion in this chapter, the original language and the RL *share the same concept,* even though its lexical expression may be quite different.[1] The other is that literal equivalence requires no further comment or illustration; if a literal equivalent is available and gives the right meaning in the context, then there is no particular problem and further discussion would be redundant.

Equivalence involving semantically complex words

We have already laid considerable stress on the semantic complexity of words. In chapter 4, it was shown that a word can have several senses and that any one of these senses can be broken down into a number of components, both shared and contrastive. A word can symbolize a large or a small area of experience. Since words are semantically complex, it is often necessary to "unpack" the bundle of components when translating into another language and to use a phrase or clause as an equivalent. Consider the following examples from English where the equivalent expression uses the generic component and some or all of the specifying components.

> *island*: land entirely surrounded by water
> *intercede*: talk to A on behalf of B
> *glutton*: one who eats too much
> *praise*: A says: B is good
> *confess*: A says: I did something bad

Several of these examples show that many words imply speech, and often this necessitates that this particular component of the word be expressed in the RL in the form of direct speech.

Some terms which are semantically complex are somewhat different from those discussed above in that they can best be described in terms of a different system of units, or by naming an item to which they are related serially.

For example, it is occasionally necessary for the translator to give the equivalent of money terms by using an appropriate number of local monetary units. Just giving the original form — denarii, minas, talents, shekels, etc. — conveys virtually nothing to the RL reader. Giving some modern equivalent is acceptable in some instances, but it has the obvious

---

[1] The following chapter will discuss the situation in which a specific concept of the original is not present in the RL.

drawback that monetary units tend to reduce in value over the years due to inflation. A modern equivalent will usually be acceptable in (1) didactic passages, or (2) passages in which the focus is on the extremely small value of the coin referred to. These two categories would include all occurrences in the New Testament of *talantōn* (talent), *mna* (pound), *assarion* (farthing), *kodrantēs* (farthing), and *lepton* (mite).

In some contexts, even though a specific coin is named, value is not in focus as such. This is the case in Mark 12:15 and Luke 20:24 in which Jesus asks about Caesar's likeness on the *denarion* (denarius).

All other uses of money measurement in the New Testament involve the denarius, which, on the basis of Matthew 20:2, is generally agreed to have been the equivalent of a day's wages in the time of Jesus. This fact is sometimes used as a basis for translating denarius, rendering 200 denarii as 200 days' wages, etc. This may be used in either didactic or historical references.

The serial relation between terms sometimes becomes the basis of a lexical equivalent. Mark 16:9 states that Jesus rose from the dead early "on the first day of the week," but in some languages ordinal numbers are not available, or, alternatively, the expression is already current, but refers to Monday. "The day after the rest day" would also be understood to be Monday. In such cases, "Sunday" is a possible translation. It is worth noting that in one language, the Spanish word for Sunday, i.e. *domingo*, sounded like a vulgar word in the RL, and so could not be used. In this case, "the day after Saturday" was used, i.e., a serial relation was the form of the nonliteral equivalent. Other parts of the lexicon, such as the number system, can also make use of this type of equivalent, as necessary. In Kusal of Ghana, "the third floor" (NEB) of Acts 20:9 was rendered "the room above the second floor."

The process of "unpacking" semantically complex words sometimes works in reverse and several words of a phrase or clause in the original become a single word in the RL. An example has already been given from a Vietnamese language concerning the meaning of *giong*. A further example is provided by Quiché of Guatemala and Otomi of Mexico where the expression used in Luke 2:8 "keeping watch over their flock by night" is rendered by one word in these languages.

Equivalence involving synonyms

It is not uncommon for a translator to find that while the original has several synonyms for a particular concept there is only one term for that concept in the RL. For instance, such terms as *trespass, unrighteousness, lawlessness, bad, evil* and *offend* can, in a particular context, be synonymous with *sin*. If the RL has only one way to express the concept of *sin*, then the translator has no choice but to use it in those contexts where terms such as the above are synonymous with *sin*. Of course, in other contexts where these words are not synonymous with *sin*, they would be rendered in some other way.

The concept which is the opposite of *sin* often poses the same problem for the translator. There are relatively few languages for which translations are being made that have a range of terms like *holiness, goodness, righteousness* and *virtue*. One or two synonyms may exist, but rarely four (or more). Again, of course, it is only in certain contexts that these terms are synonymous; in other contexts *righteousness* will contrast with the other terms in a number of ways.

The two Greek words *naos* and *hieron* are similar in meaning and are always translated by "temple" in the KJV except for Acts 19:24 where "shrine" is used. A third term, *oikos*, the usual word for "house," is also used to refer to the temple,[2] but it is never so translated by the KJV except in Luke 11:51. The problem of synonyms is not confined to unwritten languages, but is a universal cross-language phenomenon.

When faced with several synonyms or near-synonyms in the original, the translator may use reference works, along with the general principles outlined in chapter 4, to isolate and focus on the individual components of meaning of those words in the original. Once these are known, it will be easier to identify those components which are significant within the specific context and in that way determine whether certain words are synonymous in that context or not.

One particular area of the use of synonyms may be of special difficulty to the translator. This is the use of two (or more) synonymous words or expressions together in what may be termed a "doublet," or a "rhetorical parallelism." In the particular context, there is no focal difference in meaning between the terms used; rather, they represent a single concept. However, the doublet form may be used to emphasize the idea, or to modify the area of meaning slightly, or it may be a type of stylistic redundancy.

Broadly speaking, two major types of semantic relationships can exist between the members of a doublet.[3] They may be synonymous, or they can stand in a generic-specific relationship. Examples of the former are:

Matt. 2:10 "rejoiced with . . . joy"
Eph. 2:19 "strangers and foreigners " (RSV: "strangers and sojourners")
Heb. 12:28 "reverence and godly fear" (RSV: "reverence and awe")
2 Pet. 2:13 "spots and blemishes"

Examples of the latter are:

Matt. 3:15 "answering said" ("answering" is specific, "said" is generic)
Matt. 21:5 "sitting upon an ass, and a colt the foal of an ass" ("ass" is generic, "colt" and "foal" are specific)
Mark 2:25 "he was in need, and was hungry" (RSV) ("need" is generic, "hungry" is specific)

[2] Examples are Matt. 21:13; Mark 11:17 and Luke 19:46; John 2:16, 17; Acts 7:47.

[3] The approach used here is based on the study of doublets by Moore (1972) in NOT 43. He distinguishes the following semantic categories of doublets: synonymous, near-synonymous, repetitive, generic-specific, positive-negative, active-passive, figurative. The first two and the last are much the commonest, accounting for 80 percent of the 613 doublets studied and listed.

It should be pointed out that not every pair of words that appears to be synonymous is indeed so. The translator must check carefully with lexicons and commentators to see whether the terms used really are synonymous. An example cited by Moore is "do wrong and defraud" in 1 Corinthians 6:8. The Greek verbs used are *adikeite* and *apostereite*. Arndt and Gingrich (1957) give the meaning of the former in this verse as "do wrong to someone, treat someone unjustly" (p. 17) and of the latter as "steal, rob someone . . . defraud" (p. 98). It could thus be considered a generic-specific doublet, but Moore considers that both terms are in focus separately, i.e. not only were the Corinthians cheating each other, they were also doing other wrongs (of which cheating was a particular example).

How is the translator to handle such doublets? The basic principle to apply is that of chapter 1 — the *meaning* of the doublet is to be preserved faithfully, even if the form cannot be. In fact, the translator should use a doublet *form* only in those ways and contexts in which it is naturally used in the RL. In practice, this means that a synonymous doublet is often handled by one of the equivalent forms; for instance, "rejoiced with . . . joy" becomes "rejoiced" or it is handled as an intensification of the concept as "rejoiced much." In the case of generic-specific doublets there is the choice of using both terms or of using just the term which is in focus in the context which is usually the specific one. For instance, "answering said" in Matthew 3:15 is a generic-specific doublet. The focus is on the *specific* term "answering," as Jesus is replying to John the Baptist's question in the previous verse. Thus, for semantic or stylistic reasons the two terms may be rendered by the one term, "answered."

Finally, there are languages which for stylistic reasons prefer to use synonyms when reference to a single concept is repeated. In these instances, which have been rare, a concept of the original which is not represented with synonyms may have several synonyms to choose from in the RL.

Equivalence involving antonyms

Antonyms are found in all languages, generally in connection with the semantic class of Abstractions. Terms such as big, fat, wet, and hot generally have a corresponding opposite form.

Antonyms, however, are also found in connection with members of the Event and Thing classes, but in the case of these the meaning component which has an opposite is in the class of Abstractions. Thus, *boy* is a member of the Thing class, but its opposite can be *girl* if sex is the Abstraction component under consideration, or *man* if maturity is the component. Similarly, *come* is a member of the Event class, and its opposite is *go*, where the Abstraction component is that of direction. Similarly, *descend* and *ascend* are opposites with respect to direction.

Negating an Abstraction may affect its collocational range. In Colorado of Ecuador, the word "good" is highly generic, and one of its collocates is one's health. When it is negated, it no longer refers to health; the range has been restricted.

Negating an antonym, then, is one way of handling a positive term for which there is no literal counterpart. Yet translators have been observed struggling to find an equivalent for a difficult term and overlooking the possibility of finding the antonym and negating it. In some instances, an RL may already use a construction with two negatives as the normal way of handling certain positive concepts. In Bila'an of the Philippines, the expression, "it is *not* possible we will *not*," is how "we must" is expressed.

Not only is the negation of antonyms used in the RL to render straightforward expressions in the original; this same type of construction is also found in the original itself. Greek, along with some other languages, uses the negation of antonyms to make an emphatic affirmative. This type of rhetorical device, known as litotes,[4] is not uncommon in the New Testament. In these cases, the translator seeks a positive term to render an antonym already negated, unless it so happens that the RL already uses that particular litotes. The following are some examples of litotes from the New Testament, with an equivalent affirmative rendering given for comparison. In each example the negative term and the antonym being negated are both italicized.

Mark 9:41 "shall *not lose* his reward" (RSV: "will by *no means lose* . . .") shall certainly receive his reward

Luke 1:37 "with God *nothing* shall be *impossible*" with God everything will be possible

John 6:37 "I will in *no wise cast out*" I will certainly receive

Acts 20:12 "and were *not* a *little* comforted" and were greatly comforted

Acts 21:39 "a citizen of *no mean* city" a citizen of an important city

Rom. 1:16 "I am *not ashamed* of the gospel" I am proud of the gospel[5]

Rom. 4:19 "*not weak* in faith" strong in faith

Gal. 4:12 "ye have *not injured* me at all" (RSV: "you did me *no wrong*") you treated me very well

The quotation from Isaiah in Matthew 12:20 may also be an example of litotes: "A bruised reed shall he not break, and smoking flax shall he not quench." Some commentators view it as litotes, others do not. But, in any case, where translators have found it necessary to make explicit the comparison between people and the bruised reed and smoking flax,

[4] Webster (1966) defines litotes as an "understatement in which an affirmative is expressed by the negative of the contrary . . . — opposed to hyperbole." As used in Greek, this figure of speech should not be confused with the grammatical construction in which the two negative particles *ou mē* are used together. These do not give an affirmative sense, but simply strengthen the negative.

[5] In his volume, *Romans (3:20-4:25)*, Lloyd-Jones quotes Rom. 1:16 and then adds: "By that he means, of course, that he is very proud of it. He uses litotes, the figure of speech in which, in order to give emphasis to what you are saying, you put it negatively" (p. 4).

it has usually been necessary to render the negated antonyms with some positive affirmation, such as "he helps."

An interesting example of a negated antonym rendered positively is in 1 Timothy 4:12, which begins, "Let no man despise thy youth." In Balangao of the Philippines, this was translated by "All should respect you even though you are young."

Equivalence involving a reciprocal

In the reciprocal equivalent the participant who has been the subject assumes a different role in the sentence, and another participant becomes the subject. The verb also is different, since it is the reciprocal that is now used. It still represents the same event but from a different perspective. For example, the reciprocal equivalent of "John said it to me" is "I heard it from John." "Said" and "heard" represent the same event reciprocally. Thus, when a reciprocal equivalent is used, the event is the same; it is the *participant focus* that has shifted.

This type of equivalence should not be confused with the active-passive equivalence, although they both share this feature of shift of focus. Consider the following examples:

Active: John gave the hat to me.
Passive: The hat was given to me by John.
Reciprocal of the active: I received the hat from John.
Reciprocal of the passive: The hat was received by me from John.

In the active-passive pair there is no shift in *choice* of verb, only in the grammatical *form* of the verb that is used. In the active example, "John" is in focus; in the passive, it is "the hat." In the reciprocal pair, however, there is a different choice of verb: "receive" now replaces "give." Further, there is a shift of focus in the reciprocal to "I," whereas in the reciprocal of the passive it is still "the hat."

The translator should be alert to this inevitable shift of focus when a reciprocal equivalent is used and should check to make sure that such a shift of focus is compatible with the context. However, in practice, it often turns out that the translator has only a reciprocal equivalent available and so has no choice but to find some way to compensate for the shift in focus.

It should not be thought, however, that all shifts of focus are serious: the difference may be relatively slight. Kirk and Talbot, in an article "The Distortion of Information," describe three different kinds of information distortion, one of which they call "stretch distortion" (SD). The example they use is one based on the antonymous relationship *tall-short*:

> In natural language SD exists between such statements as "Tom is taller than Bill" and "Bill is shorter than Tom"; here, the "rule of recoding" is a simple rule of relational logic. Grantedly, the SD here is small. Most of us would say that these statements are two different maps of the same territory and that it is a matter of no consequence which one we use. Since we have "got used to" reading

each kind of map we do not find one a "distortion" of the other. The creative writer may be sensitive to the fact that for some readers, these two maps carry a slightly different emotional freight. If the writer wants Tom to be the target of empathy and admiration, he will use the first statement; the second would appear a slight "distortion" of his intent. If he wants initial sympathy bestowed on Bill, he will choose the second statement; the first would then prove a bit "distortive."

Some examples where reciprocal equivalence has been used in translating passages of the New Testament are found in 1 Corinthians 11:23 and Matthew 1:20. 1 Corinthians 11:23 opens with the words, "For I have received of the Lord that which also I delivered unto you," and this was rendered reciprocally as "What the Lord gave to me is what I also gave to you." Matthew 1:20 says, "the angel (RSV: an angel) of the Lord appeared unto him," and this was translated reciprocally into Huixteco Tzotzil, a Mexican language, as "he saw an angel which came from our Lord God."

Equivalence involving generic or specific terms

In chapter 4, some of the factors relating to generic and specific classifications of vocabulary were discussed. For instance, generic-specific relations are relative. *Chair* is specific when related to other types of furniture, but it is generic when related to various types of chairs. Some specific terms belong to more than one generic classification, as, for example, *to lie*, which can be classified under speech activities and ethically bad activities.

Further, the way in which concepts are grouped together under a generic label is a language-specific phenomenon. In English, we have one term *banana* for all varieties of bananas. The Chols of Mexico have a generic term, and also half a dozen or so specific names. Central American countries where bananas are grown for export have a yet higher number of specific names for bananas.

The Chols have no generic term for "to carry," but they have a number of specific terms indicating whether an item is carried on the back, on the shoulder, in the arms, with the hand, or with the finger. In a Philippine language, ants, crocodiles, foxes and cobras are grouped together under one generic word based on the fact that they bite. The python, therefore, is not included in this classification.

This last example shows that the classification of concepts by people of any particular language is based upon how these people conceive of similarities among objects, or actions, or qualities. Since generic vocabulary is thus conceptually based, there is considerable scope for variety in the ways in which different societies classify their world of experience.

Since languages vary in this way, three kinds of problems arise in connection with the process of translation. The first is that the original uses a generic term, but the RL only has one or more specific terms in that semantic area. The second is the reverse: the original uses a specific term, but the RL has only a generic word available. The third is a special problem which occurs when an RL word intended to be understood in a generic sense is interpreted in a specific sense.

1. A generic term rendered with a specific

An example of a generic term used in the original is *himation*. Meaning (1) given by Arndt and Gingrich (1957, p. 377) is "garment, clothing." Examples of its use in this generic sense are Matthew 9:16 (and its parallels in Mark 2:21 and Luke 5:36) "No man putteth a piece of new cloth into an old garment . . ." Hebrews 1:11, "they all shall wax old as doth a garment." In languages where no such generic term exists, as in some languages of Mexico, "shirt" has been used.

Another generic term of the New Testament is *skeuos*. Arndt and Gingrich (1957, p. 761) give as its first meaning "generally *thing, object* used for any purpose at all." Thus, in Acts 10:11, Peter sees "a certain *skeuos* descending unto him," the thing itself being described as "like a great sheet." Hence, in this context, the translator will need a very generic term. But Luke 8:16 says, "No man, when he hath lighted a candle, covereth it with a *skeuos*." Here there is a general reference to any suitable household vessel. However, if the RL has only specific terms available, then some plausible choice has to be made.[6] The same situation is met in John 19:29, "Now there was set a *skeuos* full of vinegar," and in many languages a suitable specific word would have to be used.

In Mark 11:16, however, a different situation is faced. There it says that Jesus "would not suffer that any man should carry any *skeuos* through the temple." Here *skeuos* is used with reference to the whole class of vessels that were regularly carried through the temple precincts as a shortcut. In this context the translation must be generic in sense, so preferably a generic term should be used. If there is not one available, however, a specific term plus some qualifying phrase such as "and whatever else was used to carry things in" may be used to convey the generic sense of *skeuos*.

"Miracle" is a generic term in the sense that it refers to different types of miraculous deeds — healing, exorcising, calming a storm, etc. In Mazahua and Trique, two languages of Mexico, there were words available only for specific types of deeds. In these circumstances, a specific with a modification was used: "He healed the sick and did other such deeds."

In Romans 6:13, "Neither yield ye your members . . . unto sin," the word "members" is a generic term for the parts of the human body. However, many languages do not have this particular generic term in the lexicon. Mazahua is one such language, and this verse was translated by listing several specific words, "not even your eye, nor your tongue, nor your hands," etc. In the Ömie language of New Guinea, there is no generic expression for "the whole world." When translating Mark 8:36,

---

[6] Another solution would be to leave implied what was used to cover the candle or to use a very generic term for a covering.

"For what shall it profit a man, if he shall gain the whole world . . . ?",
the translator used "cargo, big and small, land, earth, water."

The Greek word *echidna* translated "viper" in Acts 28:3 (". . . a viper
. . . fastened on his hand") is probably a generic term for a poisonous
snake, so if the RL does not have such a generic term, but only specific
terms, then some particular species of snake will have to be named. In
a case like this, an expression such as "something like a _____" may
be helpful in making the reference more generic.

In the above examples, it can be seen that generic terms in the original
are sometimes used to refer generally to a whole class of objects and
sometimes to a specific member of that class, so the translator must make
sure that the corresponding sense is preserved in the RL.

2. *A specific term rendered with a generic*

When the original uses a specific term for which the RL has only a
generic term, it is usually not too difficult to handle the adjustment. The
generic term may be used as it stands if it can represent the specific
sense in that context, or it may be modified so that it takes on a more
specific sense. The latter is especially useful when the specific concept
is unknown, and this is treated in detail in the next chapter.

Matthew 6:28 probably speaks of a specific flower, translated "lilies"
in the KJV and RSV.[7] In many languages this would simply have to be
"flowers." In John 6:33, 35, Jesus speaks of himself as "the bread of
God" and "the bread of life." In many languages, this specific term is
better rendered by the corresponding generic term "food."

Another example is *keration*, which Arndt and Gingrich (1957, p. 430)
define specifically as "carob pods (fruits of the carob tree)." In Luke
15:16 this is translated in the KJV by the more generic term "husks."

Sometimes a generic word or expression is the best way to render a
specific reference to a person's role or work. Matthew 4:18 refers to
Simon and Andrew as fishermen. The Halang of Viet Nam have to use
the expression, "they made their field with fish," i.e., they got their living
by fishing. An alternative way of handling this term would be to note
that the verse has already mentioned they were throwing a net into the
lake. With this context supplied, a generic expression such as "that was
how they made their fields" could well be adequate. Similarly, the Greek
uses a specific term "sower" in Matthew 13:3, but some languages, such
as Otomi and Huixteco Tzotzil of Mexico, use a generic term, "a man"
or "someone," since the specific verb that follows "sower," i.e., "to sow"
defines the activity.

3. *Ambiguously generic or specific*

It is not uncommon to find a specific member of a generic class also
serves as the class label — it has a double function in the language. In

---

[7] The Greek word is *krina*, and Arndt and Gingrich (1957, p. 452) do not definitely commit themselves as to whether a particular flower was referred to (they
give four possible alternatives), or flowers in general. TEV translates "the wild
flowers."

such cases, the translator needs to be certain there is sufficient context (which may include illustrations) to ensure that the sense of the passage is not distorted.

For instance, the Chamulas of Mexico have specific words for various sorts of vegetables — carrots, cabbages, beets, etc. In addition, the word for "cabbage" serves as the generic term for plants of this sort. In Mark 4:32, Jesus states that the mustard seed "when it is sown , . . . becometh greater than all herbs." In this context, "herbs" is clearly generic in meaning. It was translated by "cabbages" in Chamula, as the collocation with "all" makes it clear it is being used in its generic sense, not its specific sense.

In Viet Nam, the phrase, "eat rice," refers to any meal whether it includes rice or not. In other contexts, "rice" refers to the specific grain. However, when pictures of wheat are shown, the word "rice" is applied to the grain. Hence, the word for "rice" can be used to refer to other types of grain mentioned in the Scriptures, but it is helpful to illustrate with a picture the kind of "rice" being referred to.

In the Muyuw language of New Guinea, the word "canoe" is used to refer to boats of any size or description, all land vehicles, and any type of airplane. The generic sense has become the primary sense.

Also in New Guinea, some languages use the word for "pig" in a generic sense to refer to the larger quadrupeds, as well as specifically to pigs. When the context mentions the activities or characteristics of an animal other than a pig, then ambiguity is avoided; it is clear a pig is not being referred to. However, where such contextual clues are lacking, the readers are likely to think a pig is being referred to. Here the specific sense is still the primary sense. This is another case where pictures would be a suitable form of context to remove all possibility of ambiguity.

In some cases the sense of a passage will not be adversely affected even if the readers temporarily misinterpret a generic term as a specific one or vice versa. For example, one language of Ecuador has a generic word for "fish" that is also the name of a particular species of fish. But in most New Testament passages involving fish the meaning will not be distorted if the reader envisions the particular species rather than "fish" in general. In such a case no special explanatory context is needed. In the example above, however, where the use of "pig" in New Guinea was discussed, it could be quite important in certain Jewish cultural settings that it be clear that livestock in general, and not pigs in particular, are being referred to.

Equivalence involving figurative expressions

Of course, the translator does make full use of the idioms and figures already current in the RL, as this makes the translation both natural and vivid. It is when the original makes use of figures, however, that the translator has more of a problem. There is the question of what the original figure actually means, and then there is the further matter of how this meaning is going to be conveyed accurately in the RL.

The particular figures under consideration here are those which are dead, together with various idioms. Such figures and idioms in the original have to be handled nonfiguratively in the RL in many cases. The following examples illustrate different ways in which this has been done. With the exception of the last one, which is from Peru, they are all taken from languages spoken in Mexico.

Matt. 10:34	"a sword"—be against one another — there will be dissension among the people	Huixteco Tzotzil Mazahua
Matt. 20:22	"the cup" — pain	Copainala Zoque
Matt. 23:30	"the blood" — killing	State of Mexico Otomi, Huixteco Tzotzil, and Mazahua
Matt. 28:3	"white as snow" — very white	Huixteco Tzotzil
Acts 13:17	"with an high arm" — he showed he was strong	State of Mexico Otomi and Guerrero Mixtec
Acts 14:27	"he had opened the door (of faith)" — made it possible (to believe) — gave them opportunity (that they might believe) — how God had allowed . . . to go in (so that they had believed)	State of Mexico Otomi Tetelcingo Aztec Lalana Chinantec
Acts 15:10	"a yoke upon the neck" — requiring to do many things — say that it is necessary that it be done	Tetelcingo Aztec Huave
Acts 22:22	"away . . . from the earth" — kill (him)	State of Mexico Otomi
Acts 23:3	"thou whited wall" — you do not speak like one man — hypocrite (lit. "two-faced two-mouthed") — deceiver	Isthmus Mixe Teutila Cuicatec N. Puebla Totonac
James 4:8	"cleanse your hands" — clean up your sin	Aguaruna

When a word of the original can be rendered with a word of the RL which carries the same selection and number of meaning components with no shift in semantic perspective, then the translator has no need to consider using a nonliteral equivalent. If such a word is not available, however, then equivalence in meaning can only be reached by using one or both of the following possibilities:

1. Shift to the number of words which will match the selection and number of components of meaning of the word to be translated.
2. Shift to an appropriate semantic perspective available in the RL which gives equivalence of meaning. These semantic perspectives have been listed as synonymous, antonymous, generic-specific, reciprocal, and figurative-nonfigurative relative to the source perspective.

CHAPTER 13

Lexical Equivalence Across Languages —
When Things or Events Are Unknown in the RL

EQUIVALENCE BY MODIFYING A GENERIC WORD
 Modified with features of form
 Modified with a statement of function
 Modified with both form and function
 Modified with a comparison

EQUIVALENCE USING A LOAN WORD
 Modified with a classifier
 Modified with form or function or both

EQUIVALENCE BY CULTURAL SUBSTITUTION
 Cultural substitutes defined
 Precautions to be observed in the use of cultural substitutes
 Cultural substitutes in relation to anachronisms and dynamic
  fidelity
 Concordance and cultural substitutes
 Cultural substitutes and fidelity to meaning
 Testing reader reaction

The first half of the discussion of lexical equivalence between the original and the RL presupposed that any given concept being translated was found in both the original and the RL. The issue discussed was whether the symbolization of the concept in the RL was the same as its symbolization in the original or whether it took a different form. Sometimes it was one, sometimes it was the other, depending on the lexical structure of the RL.

In this second half, however, the discussion will center on a more difficult question — what sort of lexical equivalence can there be if a specific concept of the original is unknown or lost in the RL? The original refers to such things as snow, rudders, phylacteries, and cummin; there are events such as sowing by scattering, plowing, and fishing with a net; there are particular geographical features referred to such as the River Jordan, the Lake of Galilee, and the town of Jerusalem; there are religious groups such as the Pharisees and Sadducees, the high priests

191

and the scribes. Many of these concepts are simply unknown in the receptor culture and so are not spoken of.

In this type of situation, the translator has three different approaches to lexical equivalence available to him. Each of these three is related to some of the types of nonliteral equivalences discussed in the last chapter. He may choose (1) equivalence by modifying a generic word, (2) equivalence using a loan word, or (3) equivalence by cultural substitution. The first two possibilities generally involve some descriptive modification. When a modification of either a generic term or a loan word is needed, the principles discussed in chapter 4 apply. There it was made clear that any sense of a given word is separable into a number of components of meaning. These components are carried by the word implicitly, as part of its total meaning. In the RL version, therefore, the translator may make explicit the components that are appropriate to a particular context.

In the last chapter it was seen that the same concept may already be expressed and in use by two different language groups, but while one may use a single word, the other may use a phrase or clause. For example, all of the components of the concept *island* are expressed by only one word in English and some other languages, but in Inibaloi, a Philippine language, it is expressed as "small place in the sea," thus spreading the components out over several words. This example involving known concepts, then, gives us the basis for deciding how concepts which are unknown to a people may be rendered into their language, namely, the various components of meaning can be stated explicitly. The components of meaning which are added to a generic term or to a loan word are referred to as a "descriptive modification."

In any one context, however, not every meaning component of a word will be significant. The descriptive modification will not, therefore, make explicit all of the components of meaning a word carries. For example, the word *passover* has quite a few significant components of meaning, including feast, religious, Jewish, the passing over of the angel without hurting them, deliverance from Egypt, and eating sheep. However, a descriptive equivalent including all of these would be cumbersome, and in a case like this, a good equivalent can usually be arrived at which focuses on those components which are most significant to the context, leaving the others to be implied or taught. Some renditions of *passover* have been "the feast at which they ate sheep," "the Jewish feast about God delivering them," and "the feast remembering when God's angel passed by."

A descriptive modification to a generic term or a loan word may take various forms. The modification may be a description of the form of the Thing or Event or of its function, or perhaps both; or it may be a comparison or a classifier. This gives us the combinations shown in matrix 1.

MATRIX 1

TYPES OF DESCRIPTIVE MODIFICATIONS[1]

Base	Descriptive Modifications				
	Form	Function	Both	Comparison	Classifier
A Generic Word	X	X	X	X	
A Loan Word	X	X	X		X

It will be noted that there are five types of modification. Of these, only two, form and function, need to be defined. They account for most of the X's in the chart.

When discussing meaning, it is usual to make a broad distinction between "denotation" and "connotation."[2] For example, the word *apple* denotes the fruit produced by a certain tree. In addition to this denotative meaning, it may have a special connotation. A boy once stole some green apples from a neighbor's orchard. To him, apples connote both a bad conscience and a bad stomach-ache. This, of course, is a personal meaning for him, but there are many words, such as *Christmas*, which have connotational meanings shared by most or all of the speakers of a language. Note, too, it is the same word that has both denotational and connotational meanings.

Within this basic distinction, a further distinction may be made. For many words, the denotational meaning may be divided into "form" and "function." An apple may be described from the standpoint of its *form*: it is round, hard, red. It may also be described from the standpoint of its *function*. Normally, it serves as food. In particular circumstances, however, some function other than this general one may be in focus. At Halloween a boy can throw rotten apples for a quite different purpose than the general one stated above! Note that *form* refers to the real-world form of the apple and is not to be confused with linguistic form, which refers to structural features of a language.

A further example is provided by *dog*. So far as *form* is concerned, a dog may be described with respect to its size, shape, color, and anatomy until the purpose of the description has been met. A description of its *function* would state what the purpose of the dog was — for hunting, or to guard one's property, or as a companion for children.

The examples so far have been drawn from the semantic class of Things, but the concepts of form and function may be applied equally well to members of the class of Events which involve visible action. In this case, *form* would involve a description of the visible action, and *function* would describe its significance. For instance, shaking a fist at

---

[1] The X's indicate the combinations which are known to have been used in actual translations.

[2] Also referred to as "referential" and "emotive" meanings; see, for example, Nida's chapter 5 in *Toward a Science of Translating*.

someone is such a visible action. Form, then, would describe the shape and movement of the hand, and function would indicate, in most cultures, that this gesture was a warning of anger, which threatened to pass into blows. Thus, any visible events — symbolic actions, church services, agricultural activities, religious ceremonies, etc. — may be described from the dual standpoint of form and function.

In summary, then, *form* has to do with (1) any feature or characteristic of a Thing (size, shape, quantity, color, taste, temperature, substance, material, etc.), or (2) a description of any Event involving visible movement. *Function* refers to the significance of, the reason for, the purpose of, the use or uses of a Thing or an Event.

Equivalence by Modifying a Generic Word

The use of a generic word as a starting point in arriving at an adequate equivalent is extremely useful in translating specific concepts not known in the RL. The generic term may be sufficient by itself as illustrated in the last chapter, or it may need to be modified with more specific features of the form, or with a statement of the function, or with both.[3]

Modified with features of form

It is sometimes necessary to provide a brief description of the item, either of its appearance or its activity. The following are some examples of how this has been done. The generic term is italicized.

Matt. 11:21	"sackcloth" — *that* which is scratchy	Mazahua (Mexico)
Matt. 13:31	"mustard" — *plant* whose seed is small	Dibabawon (Philippines)
Matt. 13:44	"treasure" — lots of valuable *things*	Mazahua (Mexico)
Matt. 17:4	"tabernacles" — little *houses* made of branches grass *houses*	State of Mexico Otomi (Mexico) Huixteco Tzotzil (Mexico)
Mark 1:16	"sea" — flat *water*	Wantoat (New Guinea)
Mark 7:4	"bronze" — yellow *metal*	Wantoat (New Guinea)
Mark 8:12	"generation" — *people* of the time which begins now	Samal (Philippines)
Mark 12:42	"two mites, which make a farthing" (RSV: "two copper coins, which make a penny") — 2 pieces of money worth 5 centavos (i.e., the smallest coin minted)	Isthmus Mixe and Michoacan Aztec (Mexico)

[3] In some cases the generic element may not be a separate word, but only an affixial morpheme.

Mark 15:23	"wine" — fermented grape *juice* — strong *drink*	Hopi (U.S.A.) Trique (Mexico)
Luke 1:9	"incense"—*that* which smokes and is fragrant	Ifugao (Philippines)
John 10:12	"wolf" — fierce wild *animal*	Tepehua (Mexico)
Acts 7:44	"tabernacle" — cloth *house*	Chol (Mexico)
Acts 8:28	"chariot"—*box* that is dragged by an animal	Lalana Chinantec (Mexico)
Acts 13:29	"sepulchre" — *hole* in the rock	Lalana Chinantec (Mexico)
Acts 21:28	"Greeks [Gentiles]" — *people* not Jews	Sierra Otomi (Mexico)
Acts 27:40	"main sail" — thick *cloths* that hung from the pole	Teutila Cuicatec (Mexico)
Rev. 18:13	"flour" — dry *seed* ground	Trique (Mexico)

Modified with a statement of function

Describing the form of an unknown object does not always give sufficient information. The purpose or use may still be unknown or misinterpreted from the description given. It often becomes important to specify its function. The following examples illustrate this in different languages. In each case, the generic reference has been italicized.

Matt. 2:19	"an angel" — *one* of God's work*ers*	Mazahua (Mexico)
Matt. 5:23	"altar" — *where* they place God's gifts — sacrifice *place*	Huixteco Tzotzil (Mexico) Chol (Mexico)
Matt. 5:34	"God's throne" — *where* God sits and rules — *where* God reigns	State of Mexico Otomi (Mexico) Mazahua (Mexico)
Matt. 8:5	"centurion" — *man* that commands 100 soldiers	Mazahua (Mexico)
Matt. 9:12	"a physician" — *one* to make them well	Mazahua (Mexico)
Matt. 10:27	"the housetops" — *where* you meet your fellowmen	Mazahua (Mexico)
Matt. 13:33	"leaven" — the *thing* that swells the stomach of bread	Huixteco Tzotzil (Mexico)
Matt. 25:27	"exchangers" (RSV: "bankers") — *those* who make gain with it (money)	Huixteco Tzotzil (Mexico)
Mark 1:21	"synagogue" — *place* to talk God's talk — *house* where they study doctrines of God	Wantoat (New Guinea) Rincon Zapotec (Mexico)

Mark 6:4	"a prophet" — *one* who speaks God's things	Totontepec Mixe (Mexico)
Mark 15:30	"cross" — killing *post*	Samal (Philippines)
John 2:13	"the Jews' passover" — *a time* when they celebrate the day they were brought out of bondage — *a feast* to celebrate the deliverance of Jews from Egypt	Agta (Philippines) Copainala Zoque (Mexico)
Acts 12:3	"unleavened"—no *thing* mixed in for swelling	Ibaloi (Philippines)
Acts 19:29	"theatre" — *place* where they have meetings	Huave (Mexico)
Acts 20:13	"ship" — *that* with which we can walk on water	Chichimeca Pame (Mexico)
Acts 27:29	"anchors"—those *things* which make a boat stay	Chol (Mexico)
Acts 27:40	"the rudder" — *board* to steer	Tetelcingo Aztec (Mexico)
Phil. 1:1	"deacons" — *those* who help in the church	Tabasco Chontal (Mexico)

Modified with both form and function

Often, however, neither a description of appearance and behavior alone nor a statement of purpose alone is sufficient to make clear to the readers of the RL what is being referred to, nor is it clear to them from the context. This means that the translator finds it necessary in these cases not only to provide features of the form, but also to specify the function, thus combining the modifications of the previous two sections.[4]   The following examples illustrate this:

Matt. 21:33	"winepress" — *hole* in a rock where they could take out the juice of the grapes	Huixteco Tzotzil (Mexico)
Mark 8:11	"seeking a sign (from heaven)" — saying '*Do something* marvelous to show your authority is from God'	Colorado (Ecuador)
Acts 1:26	"cast lots" (RSV) — there were little round *things* that they *played* with which made it evident who would be favored	Lalana Chinantec (Mexico)

[4] The reader will notice that some of the examples cited above are connected with the same Things as were exemplified under Function and Form. This shows that the translator of an idiomatic translation makes a suitable choice, in any given context, according to the requirements of the RL readers.

Acts 7:44	"tabernacle of witness"—leather *house* that could be picked up again where they remembered God	Lalana Chinantec (Mexico)
Acts 15:1	"circumcise" — make a *mark* in the body to show that they belong to God	Tetelcingo Aztec (Mexico)
Acts 16:24	"made their feet fast in the stocks" — put the feet where boards have holes in them . . . where feet are tight	Lalana Chinantec (Mexico)
Acts 27:29	"anchors" — irons to which were attached ropes in order that they would get stuck in the dirt	Tetelcingo Aztec (Mexico)
	— iron *hooks* that make the boat stop	Isthmus Mixe (Mexico)
Acts 27:40	"rudder" — flat *board* which steers	Lalana Chinantec (Mexico)
Acts 27:40	"mainsail" (RSV: "foresail") — *cloth* on the pole that was more in front of the boat in order that the wind might push the boat	Tetelcingo Aztec (Mexico)
	— big *cloth* which is stuck to the head of the boat . . . the cloth which takes the wind so that the boat enters trail	Lalana Chinantec (Mexico)

Modified with a comparison

A good principle in teaching what is unknown is to build on the known. This principle underlies this last type of modification, labeled "Comparison." In this case, the generic reference (italicized) is followed, not by a specification of function, or appearance, or behavior, but by a comparison with something already known in the receptor culture which refers to form and function implicitly. A few examples are given below:[5]

Mark 15:17	"crown" — *hat* like that of an important person	Wantoat (New Guinea)
John 19:29	"sponge" — *that* which is like a big piece of cotton	Tepehua (Mexico)
Acts 27:40	"rudder" — *thing* like an oar	Sierra Otomi (Mexico)

[5] For further comments on this type of modification, see the last paragraph under *Cultural Substitutes in Relation to Anachronisms and Dynamic Fidelity* later in this chapter.

Equivalence Using a Loan Word

Before dealing with the use of loan words, it is helpful to distinguish three categories of loan words. In the first two, the speakers of the RL have themselves borrowed words into their language, and these two types are conveniently illustrated from two dialects of Otomi, a Mexican language. One of these dialects, Mezquital Otomi, borrows *concepts* from Spanish rather than actual Spanish words. For instance, the native idiom has a number of separate words expressing the idea of "carrying," but under the influence of Spanish these are now all expressed with one single word, which corresponds to the wider area of meaning of the Spanish word *llevar*. "Translationisms" from Spanish are also used, where the literal Otomi equivalent of a Spanish idiom or expression is used. For example, there is an Otomi verb "to shout," but it is quite common to hear a literal translation of the Spanish expression *lo hizo con voz grande* (literally, "he did it with a big voice") using Otomi words. Because of this mode of borrowing, it is not so obvious that borrowing has taken place.

Otomi of the State of Mexico, however, borrows the actual Spanish *words* either with the same meaning, or with some shift from its use in Spanish. When the words are borrowed, it is more obvious that borrowing has taken place. This second type of borrowing may cause problems because a borrowed term often receives a meaning from the particular situation(s) in which it is used that is quite different from its original meaning. For example, Spanish speakers in the town of Yajalón used to use the word *golosina* (seldom used now) with the Chol Indians. They used it to refer to a gift of a piece of candy that was made with a sale, but the Chols interpreted it as meaning "a strong craving." So it is now used by the Chols to mean "lust" and is written *colosojlel*.

Another example is the use of the word *plaza*, referring to the town square. Since most of the selling of goods takes place in the *plaza* on market days, the Mixes use the word to refer to any group of vendors. In a somewhat similar way, the word *patio* is used by the Chols to refer to any place for drying coffee. The *patio*, or open courtyard, of wealthier Mexican homes was often used for drying coffee, and so this has become the meaning of *patio* for the Chols.

A borrowed term, especially where transistorized radios are becoming more and more widespread, may also be identified with some well-advertised product. Thus, the Spanish word for "crown," *corona*, is also the name of a widely advertised beer. Hence, when the translator tried using *corona* in the translation, it was interpreted as "beer." Similarly, *vino* "wine" is also the name of a tonic quite popular with some Indians of Mexico, so, in these languages, it cannot be used for "wine."

If a borrowing is not too recent, it may no longer be recognized as a loan by the speakers, and this may sometimes be of help to the translator. For instance, in Totonac (Mexico) the Spanish word, *Judio*, meaning "Jew," had undergone various phonological adaptations. This loan word, however, could not be used in the translation to mean "Jew" since it now meant "devil" or "very evil person." But the unmodified form of *Judio* was not recognized as connected with the assimilated form, so the word was reborrowed with its proper sense of "Jew." This sense was further assured by adding "people." Hence, "Jews" are referred to as "people called Judios."

The translator should therefore avoid jumping to conclusions about the meaning of a loan word which he recognizes. It should be checked just as carefully as any indigenous term, for sometimes there are quite unexpected shifts of meaning. In Huave (Mexico), the Spanish expression for "Holy Spirit" refers to one's own spirit, not God's; also, the loan word for "pardon" means "favor" in the noun form, but "to forgive" when a verb. In Cuicateco (Mexico), John the Baptist is simply understood as having a last name, *Bautista*, which indicates nothing about his work although it does distinguish him from John the Apostle. It thus was translated "John Baptist who watered people."

The third category of loan words consists of words newly borrowed into the language by the translator in the process of translation. It is this category of loan word that is referred to in discussing equivalence for unknown concepts using a loan word.

The use of new loan words in the translation is inevitable, since the proper names of the participants in the Biblical materials must be borrowed, even if they are adapted (to a greater or less extent) to the phonological structure of the language. The same is true of the names of places referred to, names of groups, and titles.

However, since new loan words often carry zero meaning to the readers of the RL, how is the problem of "meaninglessness" to be met? One approach is to provide a glossary of terms at the end of the book, and this is helpful for those who are sufficiently well-trained to make proper use of it. For groups just becoming literate, it has been found helpful to add classifiers, or concise descriptions, to the loan word in the actual text.

As in all the other cases, the translator needs to check on the understanding of the RL readers to see when such classifiers or descriptions are needed. For example, they are not needed with the name of Jesus and the names of his disciples, since the context makes it clear that these names refer to persons. This is not as true of places and group names, and the translator may find it necessary to clarify these. Some examples are given below, and the loan word involved is italicized.

Modified with a classifier

One way of handling concepts which are unknown in the RL is to use a generic classifier from the RL together with a specific loan word which serves to indicate that a specific member of the generic class is under consideration.

| Matt. 2:11 | "myrrh" — *myrrh* perfume | Huixteco Tzotzil (Mexico) |
| Matt. 26:2 | "passover"—celebration called *passover* | Sierra Zapotec (Mexico) |

Mark 1:5	"Jerusalem"—city called *Jerusalem*	Cora (Mexico)
Mark 1:6	"camel"—animal called *camel*	Cora (Mexico)
Mark 1:9	"Jordan"— river called *Jordan*	Trique (Mexico)
Mark 1:10	"dove" — bird called *dove*	Wantoat (New Guinea)
Luke 10:32	"Levite" — Jew of the group called *Levites*	various

Modified with a specification of form or function or both

If the description associated with the loan word is rather lengthy, it is probably more natural in most languages to use it once or twice when the item is first referred to in a section, and then later on in the same context to use a suitable back-reference form — perhaps the loan word on its own, or a pronoun, or a deictic form. In some situations it is also possible to use only the loan in the text and to confine the descriptive material to a footnote. It may be that in trial portions the description will be included in the text, but that in the final New Testament, when the loan words have become more familiar, it will be relegated to a footnote or to a glossary.

Mark 1:13	"Satan" — *Satan*, the ruler of demons	Sambal (Philippines)
Luke 1:5	"priest" — *priest*, the person who deals with that given to God	Kalinga (Philippines)
John 3:28	"The Christ" — *Christ* whom God chose for a task	Ojitlan Chinantec (Mexico)
	— *Christ*, the one God chose to be Savior	Tetelcingo Aztec (Mexico)
Acts 27:29	"anchors" — irons called *anchors* with ropes . . . so it could not go any farther	Teutila Cuicatec (Mexico)

A problem may arise with a newly borrowed word. The word may suggest another one which is phonologically similar. As a second language is acquired, unknown words are related to those already known, especially if they are pronounced similarly. For example, the Spanish word for "publicans" can come to mean "people who do evil in public" for the Mazahuas of Mexico. The word *alabar* "to praise" was borrowed in one translation until the translators discovered that it was being interpreted as *a lavar* "to wash." Since their own idol gods needed to be washed, the idea of "washing God" sounded reasonable enough.

The Spanish word *desierto* "desert, wilderness" was understood as *de cierto* "for certain"; *Tiro y Sidón* as *tiro y azadón* "a gun shot and a type of hoe"; *nardo* "nard" as *Leonardo*; *presencia* "presence" as *presidencia* "the presidency"; *la oveja* "the sheep" as *la vieja* "the old woman."

In one case, the demoniac's name "Legion" was translated with *ejército* "army," only to learn that it was understood as *ejercicio* "exercise." The confusion may also arise from phonetic similarities between loan words and words in the RL itself. "Manna" in Spanish is *mana*, but in Colorado of Ecuador *mana* means "deer." In the same language, a loan for "myrrh" (*mirra* in Spanish) was confused with the word *mira*, a medicinal tree sap used by the medicine men.

One further potential problem in connection with loan words is that the translator may hear native preachers freely using such loan words as sanctification, justification, and salvation, and so may conclude that these words are generally known and understood. That may not be the case, however. It is quite possible that the loan words are used for prestige value and actually communicate little more than a religious atmosphere. *All* loans should be carefully checked to see what sense, if any, they convey to the users of the RL. Wrong meanings will then be avoided, and zero meanings may be handled by means of a classifier or modifying phrase as just discussed.

EQUIVALENCE BY CULTURAL SUBSTITUTION

In certain situations the translator may find that equivalence using a generic term or a loan word is impossible or impractical and may need to resort to the use of equivalence by cultural substitution.

Cultural substitutes defined

A cultural substitute is the use of a real-world referent from the receptor culture for an unknown referent of the original, both of the referents having the same *function*. In this respect, it is somewhat similar to synonyms which share the same components of meaning but more similar to the method of comparison discussed earlier in this chapter. In a cultural substitute, however, there is no comparison; the item from the receptor culture is actually substituted for that referred to in the original. To understand what is involved in this procedure, it is necessary to keep in mind the distinction between form and function.

When the form and function of a Thing or an Event match between the original and the receptor culture, the translator is not faced with any problem of equivalence. If *snow* or *bread* or *wheat* occurs with the same function in the receptor culture as it does in the original, then there is no problem of equivalence. The same applies to Event words. Among the Quiché and Uspantecos of Guatemala, and the Huixtecos of Mexico, there is a custom of superiors placing the backs of their hands on the foreheads of those of inferior status. This action is closely parallel in form and function to Jesus' action in placing his hands on little children. The superior (in age and social status) shows his well-wishes by placing his hand on the other.

It is sometimes the case, however, that there are equivalent functions in different cultures but associated with different forms. For example, all cultures have some way in which they dispose of the dead. In some cultures they are buried, in others they are burned; in some they are placed in tombs, and in yet others they are tied to rafts and set adrift. In each case, the form of disposal is different; but the *function* of disposal is basically the same — the body has to be removed in some way.

Another example is provided by agriculture. Many cultures share the common function of getting seed into the ground so that it will germinate and grow. But different methods — or forms — are used to accomplish this end. Some cultures scatter the seed by hand, as in first century Palestine; others scatter more narrowly in the furrows made by a plow; yet others plant in holes. Some cultures may use all three methods, depending on the type of seed being used. But the basic function is the same — getting the seed into the ground.

It is thus a matter of common observation that similar functions are fulfilled in different societies by different forms. It is also a fact that there are places in the Scriptures where form is not in focus, but only the function served by the particular form. It is in these contexts, then, that it is sometimes permissible to substitute a form from the RL culture whose function is identical or nearly so to the function associated with the form used in the original.

In the Sermon on the Mount, Jesus draws an illustration from the birds, and points out that "they sow not" (Matt. 6:26). Here, no particular method of sowing is in focus, simply the fact that they do not sow at all, using any method. The same is true of the saying Jesus quotes in John 4:37, "One soweth, and another reapeth." But in the Parable of the Sower, the particular form of sowing by scattering is in focus — indeed, the whole parable hinges on it. In this context, therefore, reference to the form must be retained in the translation, but in the former two contexts this is not essential to the meaning being conveyed.

The following is a list of examples of cultural substitutes used in passages *where form was not in focus* and where the requirements of the RL led the translator to this particular choice of lexical equivalence.

Matt. 8:20	"foxes" — coyotes	Mazahua (Mexico)
Matt. 10:16	"wolves" — coyotes	Huixteco Tzotzil and Isthmus Mixe (Mexico)
Matt. 18:24	"ten thousand talents"—many millions of pesos	Mazahua (Mexico)
Mark 2:22	"wineskins" (RSV) — skins for *pulque* (i.e., juice of the century plant)[6]	State of Mexico Otomi (Mexico)
Mark 4:21	"on a candlestick" (RSV: "on a stand") — on a grain bin	Korku (India)

[6] The use of the term translated *pulque* here is not ideal, as it introduces an anachronism (for discussion, see later in the chapter). It was chosen, however, as the best alternative available since a descriptive equivalent was very cumbersome in this context.

Mark 6:9	"two coats" (RSV: "two tu-nics") — two shirts[7]	Chol (Mexico)
Luke 9:62	"plough" — hoe	Carib (Central America)
Luke 12:24	"storehouse" — basket (about 3 feet high and wide, used for storing corn and other goods)	Villa Alta Zapotec (Mexico)

Precautions to be observed in the use of cultural substitutes

Although the use of cultural substitutes is sometimes necessary and justified, it should be done with great caution. Following are further discussions of some factors which the translator must keep in mind when he considers using a cultural substitute:

1. Distinguish between historical and didactic references

In chapter 2, the section entitled "Fidelity to the meaning of the original" made it clear that cultural substitutes are not permitted for words making a historical reference. While a broad distinction may be drawn between types of historical discourse, such as historical narrative, miracle, and biography, and types of didactic discourse, such as parables, extended metaphors and similes, moral injunctions, etc., it is probably more useful to the translator to think in terms of historical and didactic references. Passages that are mostly teaching can readily draw on historical facts to illustrate a teaching point; passages that are giving a historical account may use conversation, sermons, etc. containing didactic material.

For historical references, it is inappropriate to make use of cultural substitutes, as this would violate the fundamental principle of historical fidelity. For example, in Mark 2:23 and Luke 6:1, it is recorded that as Jesus' disciples walked through the grain fields, they plucked some heads of grain, rubbed them in their hands, and then ate the grain. This is a particular historical incident, so it is not permissible to replace grain by bananas, and have the disciples pick, peel, and eat bananas instead, even though bananas may be much more familiar to the members of the receptor culture.

In Matthew 21:19-21 and Mark 11:13, 14, Jesus curses a fig tree. This is again a historical incident, so the translation should refer to a fig tree, not an avocado or some other better known, local tree.

The implication of the above discussion is that while cultural substitutes are not permissible in historical references, they are permissible when it comes to didactic references. This is an oversimplification, how-

---

[7] It could be argued that there is a lack of historical fidelity with this rendition and a generic term for clothing together with a modification of some sort, as discussed earlier in the chapter, should have been used. However, the presence of the numeral "two" precluded the use of a generic term. In addition, when shown pictures of the tunics referred to in the original, the native speakers used the term "shirt" to refer to them.

ever. In chapter 9 it was brought out that in translating live figures the image should be retained. It follows from this that when cultural references are focal in illustrations or live figures, especially extended figures, then the original referents should be retained if possible. If the cultural references are part of the background to parables and illustrations, then cultural substitutes are more acceptable. If they are used in dead figures or idioms, then the discussion in chapters 8 and 9 would apply.

2. *Determine which function of the word is in focus*

When the use of a cultural substitute becomes necessary, the translator should first be careful to ascertain whether the word to be replaced was used with its normal, general function in focus, or whether it has a special function in the particular context being considered. For example, as was mentioned earlier, an *apple* serves generally as a food, but in the particular context of Halloween, rotten apples may be thrown for an entirely different purpose.

A *table knife* usually serves as an instrument at the table for cutting food or for spreading butter or jam on a piece of bread. But a table knife has also been used, on occasion, as a screwdriver, or as an instrument to pry the lid off a jar. The handle has also been used as a hammer. These usages represent special situational functions.

In the New Testament, the same type of phenomenon is observed, and the translator needs to study the context carefully to be sure the item to be substituted has the same function within the specific context that the original item did. Three different types of situations may be distinguished with regard to the function of the original:

a) Only the general function is in focus.

b) The general function is relevant, but the context also requires that the particular form of the original referent be preserved.

c) The general function is irrelevant, and some special function is in focus.

a) In the Parable of the Ten Virgins (Matt. 25:1-13), the virgins were using "oil" in their lamps. No special function was in the mind of the speaker — it was being used for fuel in a lamp, which was the normal usage. In Matthew 5:40, when Jesus says, "let him have thy cloak also," only the normal use of the garment is in focus. The same is true of the use of "wolves" in Luke 10:3 where Jesus warns his disciples, "I send you forth as lambs among wolves."

b) As was mentioned earlier, although planting and sowing serve the same general function of getting seed into the ground, it is essential in the Parable of the Sower that the form used be that of scattering, not planting in furrows or holes. Similarly, in many of the didactic passages in which bread is mentioned, the fact that it is made with yeast is completely out of focus; only the nutrient function is significant. But in Mark 8:15 Jesus tells his disciples to "beware of the leaven of the Pharisees, and of the leaven of Herod" and they think he is talking about bread; and in this context the fact that bread is made with leaven is significant. In all such cases, where the form as well as the general function is in focus, the translator needs to preserve the original form as well as its function.

c) There are contexts where the normal purpose for which a thing is used is quite irrelevant, and only some special purpose is contextually relevant. Thus, the normal purpose of a *millstone* is to grind grain. But in Matthew 18:6, Mark 9:42, and Luke 17:2 it is used to drown someone. In this case, certain components of meaning of the form, such as its composition or density, are relevant, since a wooden mortar, while serving the same general purpose as a millstone, would serve the *opposite* purpose in this special context and would help the person to float.

It is therefore essential that the translator make sure that any proposed cultural substitute is appropriate to the context and matches the original as to function and, where necessary, as to form also. To make this point yet clearer, some examples follow of cultural substitutions which were considered, but which were rejected because the function associated with the substitute was inappropriate for the original context.

In Revelation 18:19, those who derived their living from trade by sea "cast dust on their heads" as a sign of their sorrow and distress over the destruction of Babylon. A translator considered rendering this as "they threw sand backwards over their shoulders." At first sight, this appears to be a good substitute, as it indicates bereavement at the side of a grave. The general function of sorrow corresponds with the original, and the form is closely similar. But the particular function in the context of the original event is sorrow and grief at the destruction of a city, and is quite different from sorrow at the death of a friend. The substitute suggests a situation not found in the original context.

A few verses later in the same chapter, it states that "the sound of a millstone shall be heard no more at all in thee" (v. 22). At first it was thought to change this to the noise of a sugar cane press, as in this culture a millstone, i.e., a corn-grinding stone, makes very little noise. But this reflected a misunderstanding of the context. The focus is not on the *intensity* of the sound made by a millstone, but on its *absence* altogether to show how completely desolate the city had become.

3. Avoid clash of functions

After ascertaining whether the word in the original was used with its normal function or some special function, it is also necessary to consider well the normal function of the proposed RL substitute.

Substitutes which suggest the form of the original referent but whose function is quite unrelated to that of the original referent are, by definition, not cultural substitutes; and they should not be used. To take an obvious example, a wooden tub suggests a certain function (even when modified by "big"), which has no relationship at all to the function of a boat. In a case like this, a descriptive equivalent would be called for.

Thus, in Pame (Mexico), *boat* is translated "that with which we can walk on water."

The rudder of a ship provides another example. Rudders are unknown in many of the cultures for which translations are being made. However, the Colorados of Ecuador use cradle boards and also stiff mats, both of which are roughly the size and shape of a rudder. But if the translator were to have substituted "cradle board" or "mat" for "rudder" in James 3:4, it would have been an equivalence of form only, and would have resulted in a clash between the implicit, normal functions of these artifacts and the explicit function required in the context. Instead of understanding the passage, the readers would simply have been baffled as to what these objects had to do with turning a ship.

Cultural substitutes in relation to anachronisms and dynamic fidelity

In using a cultural substitute, the translator makes use of some Thing or Event which was not known in the culture of the Near East during the first century, but has only become known there since, or has not yet become known. In any case, the substitution will introduce at least some degree of anachronism, with a consequent lowering of historical fidelity; but, on the other hand, the absence of cultural substitutes will lower dynamic fidelity, with the result that parts of the original message will probably be misunderstood. This is a tension between principles which every translator faces.

Before going further, consider the following instances of actual or potential substitutes involving anachronisms.

Matt. 25:3ff "They . . . took no oil with them." In Chol (Mexico) the word *cas*, which refers to kerosene, was used for oil here. In the original, the oil used was olive oil, and was used for cooking, for fuel, for medical purposes, and for anointing. In Chol country, the oil which is used for cooking is not the same as that used for fuel. The latter is bought in shops for the purpose of burning in lamps. Nothing is known by them as to its source — it is simply a liquid fuel. In the original, although it is true that the oil burned there came from olives, yet there is no attention paid to its source — only its function is relevant to the context. (In fact, although the Greek word, *elaion*, means specifically "olive oil," most English versions translate it simply "oil.")

Luke 6:44 ". . . of thorns men do not gather figs." If a translator substitutes "peaches" for "figs," this is also anachronistic in that peaches were not introduced to the Near East at the time of the first century.

Mark 2:21 "No man also seweth a piece of new cloth on an old garment." Some of the Australian Aborigine groups are unfamiliar with garments made of cloth. The shrinking action of new cloth as referred to in Jesus' metaphor had no meaning to them. As a last resort the translator introduced a substitute image. The

Aborigines used to make a rug from opossum fur. The old rugs were not mended with new furs since the old would split. The old was discarded instead. With this clue, the verse was rendered: "No one puts new opossum fur onto old opossum fur to mend the fur rug. If one does, the old fur will split and be worse."

Luke 12:3 ". . . shall be proclaimed upon the house tops." In this verse, a conceivable substitution, very definitely anachronistic, would be to say "shall be announced on the radio."

Two principles should be noted here: *First,* there is no sharp division between what is anachronistic and what is not, but rather there is a gradient from less to more anachronistic as shown in the examples just given. There is probably no translation in use today which does not involve some small degree of anachronism, but serious anachronisms may and must be avoided.

To discover the degree of anachronism involved in a proposed substitution, the translator may ask the following questions:

1) How similar are the original and the proposed substitution? The more similar they are, the less anachronistic will be the impact of the substitution. Thus, oil and kerosene are reasonably similar in form and function, and this is also the case with figs and peaches. There is, however, no resemblance at all between a housetop and a radio.

2) Were items similar to the proposed substitution known in the Middle East in the first century? If so, the anachronism will be less. While peaches themselves were not known, fruits and fruit trees were well known.

3) Was the proposed substitution unknown only in the Middle East, or was it unknown everywhere in the world at that time? A closely related question is, Does this substitution presuppose a degree of technological development unknown at that time? A *yes* answer to either of those questions indicates a greater degree of anachronism. This criterion would argue against substitutions involving "kerosene" and "radio."

Second, whether or not a given cultural substitute will be used will depend not only on the degree of anachronism, but on the other factors as well.

To investigate these other factors, the translator should ask such questions as:

1) How great a distortion in dynamic fidelity would result if a descriptive equivalent were used here? If that distortion would be slight, a cultural substitute should not normally be used; but if the only descriptive equivalents available are extremely complex and awkward, then even a more anachronistic substitute may, by comparison, be the better choice. In the Chol example Matthew 25:3, using a description of the oil of the first century instead of using

cas would have resulted in a very awkward construction. This argues in favor of using the substitution. On the other hand, using a descriptive expression such as "a fruit called figs" would not be as awkward.

2) How culturally isolated are the speakers of the RL? More isolated groups will require more substitutions; but it should be kept in mind that today even the most isolated groups are fast losing their isolation. It was only the cultural isolation of the aboriginal group that prompted the translator in Australia to render "garment" as "opposum fur rug."

There is another type of anachronism which the translator needs to beware of, that is, anachronisms which are implied. In one of the Otomi languages the word "wine" in Matthew 9:17 was translated: "a drink like *pulque*." (*Pulque* is the slightly alcoholic juice of the century plant.) Here a generic term was modified with a comparison. However, this equivalent for "wine" implies that both Jesus and Matthew knew what *pulque* was. Although the equivalent does not say the drink was *pulque*, and allows one to explain what the drink really was, it does imply that the author or speaker knew what it was. Because of this, a loan word for *wine* would be preferable.

Another example of implied anachronism is found in the translation of "leprosy" as "a sickness like *pinto*." From one point of view this is a good comparison, since *pinto* is a skin disease involving semi-ostracism; no eating or sleeping together, no bathing or washing clothes in the regular place. But to use this comparison implies that the original writers knew what *pinto* was, and such anachronistic implications should be avoided if possible.

Concordance and cultural substitutes

There are quite a number of cultural references which occur in both historical passages and didactic ones, and in some cases the two are closely intertwined. For example, in Mark 8:14-21, the fact that the disciples had brought only one loaf with them is made the occasion of teaching about "the leaven of the Pharisees," and this teaching also refers back to the two miracles of feeding the four thousand and the five thousand. Should the translator maintain concordance between historical and didactic passages, even if the dynamic fidelity of the didactic passage is adversely affected as a result?

Undoubtedly, the ideal is that he should, and normally this ideal should be met by the time the whole New Testament is ready for publication. However, there is usually quite a period of time between the first trial editions of selected passages, or Bible stories, or the first book, and the whole New Testament. During this period the translator will become more and more skillful in the RL, and his translation helpers will be gaining ever clearer insights into the culture of first century Palestine. Consequently, they will find it possible to express clearly and succinctly many concepts which at first were considered too complex to handle, and this in turn will make concordance less of a problem. Also, one of the aims of the translator during this period will be to introduce the RL readers to the Biblical culture. In this he is helped by the fact that some of the least known items occur quite frequently and in contexts which help to build up an understanding of them. If these are not translated concordantly in both historical and didactic passages, the number of different contextual settings which can serve to provide this understanding will be reduced considerably. The related terms *vine, vineyard, grapes,* and *vinegar* are known in relatively few cultures for which translations are being made, but they occur quite often, and in a variety of contexts, in the New Testament. The same could be said, though to a lesser degree, of *threshing, winnowing, sowing, wheat flour, dough,* and *yeast.* These items have to be referred to in historical contexts, and so there is something to be gained by rendering them concordantly in both historical and didactic contexts as soon as possible.

In early portions, however, the translator may feel that maintaining such concordance in didactic passages mars their dynamic quality and fidelity, and so he may prefer to use cultural substitutes instead. But there should be a gradual switch over to a more complete concordance as further books are published, thus paving the way for virtually full concordance with respect to such cultural items in the final New Testament.

Cultural substitutes and fidelity to meaning

When it proves necessary to use cultural substitutes, there are two ways in which the potential loss of fidelity to meaning can be compensated for. The translator may use footnotes or modify the substituted expression.

1. Footnotes

Cultural substitutes are usually specific rather than generic terms. If there is a generic term available and it is appropriate to use a generic term in the context, then a cultural substitute will not normally be used; the generic term will be used together with a modification of some sort, as described in the first major section of this chapter. It is when such a generic term is not available or is inappropriate that a specific cultural substitute may be used, and it is the fact that substitutes tend to be specific terms that makes it advisable to use footnotes. The substitution will have distorted the historical accuracy to at least some degree. Although the distortion will be slight, the educated reader, through his general knowledge of other cultures or by comparing the RL version with a national language version, will notice it, and it will raise valid questions in his mind. The footnotes, then, will serve to answer those questions and give him a more accurate historical and exegetical perspective. For example, money values may be stated in terms of the local currency, and then a footnote can give the original terms. This is done in the NEB in Mark 6:37: "twenty pounds" is in the text, and a footnote reads, "*Literally* 200 denarii."

2. Modification

A specific substitute may be improved by the addition of a modifying phrase to remove unacceptable aspects of form or to add aspects of the form which may be needed or helpful. A Japanese Christian always thought of the temple in Jerusalem in terms of the form and the ritual of the temples in Japan. It was not until he was studying at a Bible School in the United States that he became aware of the differences. Obviously, if this can happen in a culture where reference books are generally available and where literacy is high, then we may expect the same sort of misunderstanding in groups where there is a relatively low level of literacy.

It is not possible, of course, to modify a cultural substitute so that it completely matches the form and functions of the referent in the original, but it is always possible to provide sufficient modification so that the reader is not likely, for example, to identify the local priest with those of New Testament times.

It should be borne in mind, however, that some specific terms of the receptor culture, even with modification, may not be acceptable as an equivalent for a similar term in the original. The Villa Alta Zapotec (Mexico) language helper objected to the proposed translation of "synagogue," which included the term for "church" plus the modification "of the Israelites." He knew that the services were different, so he preferred to say, "place where the Israelites worship." The translator is liable to find that some of the RL terms are interpreted so specifically and locally that they cannot be used as substitutes for terms in the original. Terms that have been found to be limited in this way are those such as *priest, synagogue, temple,* and *church.*

Testing reader reaction

One of the main reasons for publishing portions and individual books before the full New Testament is printed is to obtain reader reaction to the translation. This is true regardless of the form in which the portion or book is published. The translator should note how the readers react to cultural substitutes. Reactions tend to depend on the degree of sophistication of the readers and on the extent to which the Gospel has spread among them. If there are only scattered believers or a new group of believers who are monolingual, then more substitutions are needed, and are appreciated, than would be the case where there is a well-established church or a fair degree of bilingualism. In either case, initial portions are likely to contain more substitutions than will later ones, as the Christian community grows in knowledge of the Biblical culture and background.

If some of the believers have had reasonable contact with Christians of the national language, they are likely to be influenced by what they have learned through this contact. The reasons for substitutions should be discussed with them; otherwise, they may object to the substitutions because they do not know the reasons for them. Similarly, if there are bilingual leaders associated with the work, their opinions should be sought and the issues discussed with them, both to help the translator get a better feel of what substitutions are necessary, and so that the leaders themselves can appreciate what has been done and why, and be able to explain this to others.

Most people are very interested to learn more about the customs, work, and food of other groups of people. In particular, they are often especially interested in animals. If the animals referred to in the Bible are replaced by local animals as cultural substitutes, especially if this is done without keeping the leaders informed, then later the translator may find himself faced with negative reactions.

On the other hand, retaining reference to the real world form of terms in the original may result in negative reader reaction also. When James 3:12, with its reference to figs, olives, and vines, was first translated into Aguaruna (Peru), no cultural substitutes were used. The translator wrote: "All this verse brought was a great deal of discussion about the characteristics of these fruits. So I have changed and used the names of two native fruits and the native palm tree. I will change back in a later edition when they have had more stories which have reference to fig trees, olive trees, and vines, but since this is one of the earlier books they are receiving, it seemed wiser to focus more on the idea."

Although the final decision on the use of cultural substitutes cannot be based entirely on reader reaction, this can in many cases give valuable information concerning whether certain substitutes are necessary and acceptable.

CHAPTER 14

Multiple Functions of Grammatical Structures

HENDIADYS
SEMITIC PASSIVE
IRONY
TENSE
ABSTRACT NOUNS
ORDER

In chapters 6 and 7, discussion centered on the fact that a word may have a number of different senses. This association of one form with several senses is not confined to words, however; it is observed also with grammatical constructions involving a number of words, such as phrases, clauses, and sentences. Further, just as the senses associated with a given word in a particular language are specific to that language, so also are the various functions associated with a particular grammatical construction.

Because of the language-specific nature of this phenomenon, it is important that the translator be aware of it. If he is not, he is liable to match a structure of the original with a corresponding RL structure, in spite of the fact that the structure of the original may have several functions, one or more of which does not correspond to those carried by the RL structure.

No attempt is made here to discuss all of the grammatical structures in the original which have more than one function. Rather, five have been selected because they have been found to present translators with problems, and because they illustrate the principle of multiple-function structures clearly. These five are Hendiadys, Semitic Passive, Irony, Tense, and Abstract Nouns. In addition to these, two other structures with multiple functions, Rhetorical Questions and the Genitive Construction, will be dealt with in the following two chapters.

HENDIADYS

When two nouns are joined by *kai*, "and," they normally stand in a coordinate relationship of A *and* B. Occasionally, however, they stand in a subordinate relationship of some sort, in which they represent a single modified concept, rather than two concepts as in the coordinate relationship. The general term given to this special use of the coordinate "and" is *hendiadys*, from the three Greek forms, *hen* "one," *dia* "by means of," and *dis* "twice," that is, one concept expressed by means of two nouns. The following is a list of examples which, however, is not intended to be exhaustive.

Matt. 4:16 "the region and shadow of death." This expression does not refer to two places, but one. The TEV renders it with "the dark land of death," and the NEB has "the land of death's dark shadow."

Mark 6:26 "for his oath's sake, and for their sakes which sat with him." Turner (1963, pp. 335, 36) and Blass-Debrunner (1961, p. 229) both suggest "because of the oaths sworn before the guests." In line with this, TEV translates "because of the vows he had made in front of all his guests." Compare also Barclay (1968) "because he had given her his sworn promise in front of his guests."

Luke 2:47 "his understanding and answers." Turner (p. 336), Blass-Debrunner (p. 228), Arndt and Gingrich (1957, p. 392), and TEV all suggest "his intelligent answers."

Luke 21:15 "a mouth and wisdom." Turner (p. 336), Blass-Debrunner (p. 228), Arndt and Gingrich (p. 392), and Bullinger (1898, p. 663) all treat this as hendiadys. Arndt and Gingrich suggest the translation "wise utterance."

Acts 1:25 "this ministry and apostleship." Turner (p. 336), Blass-Debrunner (p. 228), and Bullinger (p. 665) class this as hendiadys. TEV renders it as "service as an apostle."

Acts 14:17 "filling our hearts with food and gladness." Turner (p. 336), Blass-Debrunner (p. 228) and Arndt and Gingrich (p. 392) handle this statement also as hendiadys. Blass-Debrunner give the translation "with joy *for* food," while Arndt and Gingrich have "joy concerning (your) food."

Acts 23:6 "of the hope and resurrection of the dead." Turner (p. 336) lists this as hendiadys and gives the translation "hope of the resurrection"; Arndt and Gingrich (p. 392) suggest "hope of a resurrection"; and NEB and Barclay similarly have "hope of the resurrection of the dead."

Rom. 1:5 "grace and apostleship." Again Turner (p. 336), Blass-Debrunner (p. 228), and Bullinger (p. 666) list this as hendiadys. Note that TEV translates this with "the privilege of being an apostle," and NEB with "the privilege of a commission," both using the link-word "of" between the two nouns. Bruce (1965) has "my apostolic endowment."

Col. 2:8 "philosophy and vain deceit." Bullinger (p. 667) cites this as an example of hendiadys, and proposes the meaning "a vain, deceitful philosophy." TEV renders it "the worthless deceit of human wisdom," and NEB has "hollow and delusive speculations." Vincent (1946) says, " 'and' is explanatory, philosophy 'which is also' vain deceit." A number of other commentators agree with this, such as Hendriksen (1964) and Bruce (1957).

2 Tim. 1:10 "life and immortality." Bullinger (p. 669) suggests, and TEV translates this as "immortal life." Hendriksen (1965) says, "The two concepts 'life and incorruptibility' probably constitute a hendiadys; hence, *incorruptible* (or imperishable) life." Kelly (1963) states "It is a *life* characterized by *immortality* . . ."

SEMITIC PASSIVE

In the gospels, it is not uncommon to find that a passive construction has been used to avoid the necessity of naming God as the subject of the action.[1] It is a type of euphemism, therefore, which the Jews had developed because of a reluctance to pronounce the divine Name. The original readers readily understood from the context when God was the subject of the action expressed in the passive voice, but today, even in those languages where it is possible to use a passive form, it is unlikely that the readers will understand God as the subject. In those languages where there is no passive construction, an active construction needs to be used with God as subject rather than some indefinite form as the subject. The following is a selection of examples (it will be noted that such passives are confined to the gospels, and almost exclusively to Jesus' own teaching):

Matt. 5:4 "they shall be comforted"

Matt. 5:6 "they shall be filled"

Matt. 5:7 "they shall obtain mercy" (literally, "they shall be mercied")

Matt. 5:9 "they shall be called the children of God"

Matt. 6:33 (and Luke 12:31) "All these things shall be added unto you"

Matt. 7:7 (and Luke 11:9) "it shall be given you"
"it shall be opened unto you"

Matt. 7:8 (and Luke 11:10) "it shall be opened"

Matt. 12:31 (and Mark 3:28) "shall be forgiven unto men"
"shall not be forgiven unto men"

Matt. 12:32 (and Luke 12:10) "it shall be forgiven him"
"it shall not be forgiven him"

Matt. 13:12 (and Mark 4:25, Luke 8:18) "to him shall be given"
"from him shall be taken away"

Matt. 21:43 "shall be taken from you"
"(shall be) given to a nation"

---

[1] See Blass-Debrunner (1961, pp. 72, 164, 176); he cites as examples Matt. 7:2; Matt. 7:7; Mark 4:24; Mark 4:25; Luke 6:38.

Matt. 23:12 (and Luke 14:11, 18:14) "shall be abased"
"shall be exalted"

Mark 4:24 "it shall be measured to you"
"shall more be given"

Mark 10:40 "it shall be given to them for whom it is prepared"

Luke 14:14 "thou shalt be blessed"
"thou shalt be recompensed"

The third person plural is occasionally used as the equivalent of a Semitic passive.[2] An example is found in Luke 12:20, where the Greek says, "this night your soul they are demanding from you." The KJV translates this by "this night thy soul shall be required of thee," using a passive construction for the third person plural; cf. Arndt & Gingrich (1957, p. 79) who translate, "your soul will be demanded of you." If this is interpreted as a Semitic passive, then the meaning is, "God will demand your soul tonight."

A further example is found in Luke 16:9. The KJV reads, "that . . . they may receive you into everlasting habitations." This may be interpreted as equivalent to a Semitic passive, and thus as meaning "that God may receive you. . . ." Moule (1960, p. 28) footnotes an alternative interpretation that the unexpressed subject is the friends.

In Luke 6:38, the KJV translates the Greek *dōsousin* "they will give" with "shall men give," and in Luke 12:48 the two third person plural verbs *parethento* and *aitēsousin* are translated with, "and to whom men have committed much, of him they will ask the more." An alternative interpretation, however, is to take these indefinite third person verbs as equivalent to Semitic passives, so that the subject is God (so, for instance, Turner — see list of verses cited, footnote 2 in this chapter).

IRONY

Irony may be briefly described as criticism or ridicule in the form of a compliment. An affirmation is made, but the opposite is meant. Some languages, such as Trique and Otomi of the State of Mexico, add a morpheme at the end of an ironical statement which reverses the meaning. However, if a language uses only intonation to signal irony, the context in a written document may be insufficient to signal the irony to the readers, and so the statement will be misinterpreted. If this is the case, then the irony needs to be rendered in a more straightforward manner, so that the meaning is faithfully preserved. Some examples and suggested renditions follow:

Mark 7:9 "Full well ye reject the commandment of God, that ye may keep your own tradition." (The RSV translates, "You have a fine way of rejecting . . .") "Don't consider yourselves clever because you are rejecting God's commandments, so that you . . ."

[2] For a brief discussion of this phenomenon, see Turner (1963, p. 293) who gives as examples Luke 6:38, 12:20, 48, 16:9.

1 Cor. 4:8 "Now ye are full, now ye are rich, ye have reigned as kings without us." "You think you are full but you are not, you think you are rich but you are not, you have not really reigned as kings without us."

1 Cor. 4:10 "We are fools for Christ's sake, but ye are wise in Christ; we are weak, but ye are strong; ye are honourable, but we are despised." "People say that we are fools for Christ's sake, but you imagine/think you are wise in Christ you imagine/think yourselves strong; you imagine/think yourselves honorable, but we are despised."[3]

TENSE

The present tense is sometimes used for future or past time. In the first instance, reference is made to an event still future as if it were present; in the second, reference is made to an event of the past as if it were present. When the present is used for a past event, the aim of the author is to add vividness; when the present is used for a future event, the purpose is to add a tone of assurance.

Some examples of the present tense referring to the future follow (the second line gives the meaning):

Matt. 21:5 "Behold, thy King cometh unto thee"
            Behold, your king will come to you

Matt. 26:18 I keep the passover (literal rendition)
            "I will keep the passover" (KJV uses the future here)

Mark 9:31 "The Son of man is delivered"
           The Son of man will be delivered

Some examples of the present equivalent to the past follow:

Mark 1:21 They enter into Capernaum (literal rendition)
           "They went into Capernaum" (KJV)

John 18:28 They lead (literal rendition)
            "Then led they" (KJV)

1 Cor. 11:18 "I hear that there be divisions"
              I heard that there are divisions

These uses of the present tense are often referred to as the "prophetic" and "historic" presents. France (1972, p. 5) gives sound advice when he says: "In translation the important point is not to aim at wooden literalness of tense, but to achieve the same degree of vividness as the Greek intends, by whatever idiomatic means the language offers. Beware of making a lively narrative stuffy by being too literal. Translate idiom into idiom."

---

[3] The attempt to catch the irony in these suggested renditions does not fully succeed. There is some loss since the renditions are still quite dependent upon supplying the right intonation.

ABSTRACT NOUNS

At the beginning of chapter 4 the classification of lexical items such as words and idioms into four semantic classes was discussed. These classes were labeled Thing, Event, Abstraction, and Relational. It was pointed out that, in general, Things are symbolized by nouns, Event by verbs, and Abstractions by modifiers, but that there are many exceptions. Abstract nouns are one type of exception. An abstract noun is a noun which symbolizes an Event or an Abstraction, not a Thing.[4] For example, in the statement "love is patient" the word "love" is a noun, but it refers to the Event of loving, not to a Thing. When we say "he killed him by kindness" the word "kindness" is a noun, but it refers to the acts of a kind person, or a person's kind deeds; in either case "kind" is an Abstraction.

Abstract nouns, then, represent a mismatch or skewing between the semantic classification and the grammatical classification,[5] and any such mismatch represents a potential problem area for the translator. In addition, languages differ considerably in the extent to which they use abstract nouns and how and when new ones may be formed. Some languages have current, productive derivational processes for forming certain types of abstract nouns. For example, in English the suffix -*ing* is a productive suffix forming nouns from verbs, and even a foreign speaker can coin a new abstract noun using this construction.[6] In other cases, however, abstract nouns currently in use will have been formed according to patterns which are no longer productive; and foreign speakers of a language should not expect to be able to coin new ones. English examples in this category are *love* and *height*. The implications of this for the translator are clear: The translator should use those abstract nouns that are already current in the language in the ways that the native speakers themselves use them; but he should not attempt to create new ones unless he is sure the pattern he is using is genuinely and currently productive. In most cases, if there is no abstract noun already in use in the RL corresponding to a concept expressed by an abstract noun in the original, it will be better to use a more direct translation in terms of verbs and adjectives or adverbs. The rest of this section will discuss some advantages and disadvantages in the use of abstract nouns and some factors to be taken into consideration in their translation.

Advantages and disadvantages of abstract nouns

There are two main disadvantages associated with the use of abstract nouns. The first is: information that would normally be carried explic-

[4] An abstract noun crosses grammatical classes but not semantic classes. *To save* is a verb, *salvation* is a noun but both are Events.

[5] For brief discussions of this "skewing" see Beekman (1967a, p. 1) and Eunice V. Pike (1967, pp. 1-3).

[6] Once the translator has determined that an abstract noun-forming pattern in the RL is indeed currently productive, he still needs to determine the distribution of nouns formed in that way. They may occur only in certain grammatical slots or with a restricted collocational range. In Colorado of Ecuador, for example, certain abstract nouns may occur as objects of verbs but never as subjects.

itly — such as participants in events and the things modified by attributives — are frequently carried implicitly. This is not always the case. For example, in "The judge's conviction of the robber was upheld," the abstract noun "conviction" expresses the Event "convict"; and the participants "judge" and "robber" are also stated explicitly. Frequently, however, the expression will be in abbreviated form such as "the conviction was upheld," with no explicit reference to participants. The second disadvantage has already been mentioned: the lack of correlation between the grammatical and semantic classes. Both of these features of abstract nouns tend to make the message difficult to follow, so that the information being conveyed is not as clear as it should be and is not really understood.

The first disadvantage will not be discussed in detail in this chapter, as chapter 3 on implicit information takes up the matter of implied information and deals with it extensively. It is shown there that wrong meaning is often communicated in the RL if necessary information (from the standpoint of the RL) is left implicit. The implicit information associated with abstract nouns may cause wrong meaning if not explicitly stated in the translation, but more often it leaves the message obscure; the RL reader has considerable difficulty in understanding what is being said.

An example is provided by 1 Corinthians 13:4 (RSV), "Love is not jealous." *Love* is an abstract noun in this verse, so the one who loves and the object of the love are both unexpressed. If the abstract noun is translated by a verb, with an appropriate subject and object stated, as in "When we love others, we are not jealous of them," the meaning of the expression is less compact, and is therefore more easily understood.

The second disadvantage is that a mismatch between the grammatical and semantic classes imposes a burden on the understanding of the message. This fact has found support in the work of psychologists, who have shown that there is a significant correlation between grammatical and semantic classes. When Things are symbolized by nouns, Events by verbs, and Abstractions by modifiers, then a communication is more readily understood. For example, it has been found that college students scored higher on comprehension of new material when the grammatical and semantic classes were matched. Psychologists have also found that the earliest words acquired by children consist primarily of Thing nouns, and that in children's speech there seems to be a much greater consistency between the grammatical and semantic classes.

This type of evidence would seem to indicate that abstract nouns represent a type of complex communication; the information is being presented in a form which is not the most simple or the most direct. This is confirmed by the evidence produced by Edward Coleman (1961) which shows that complex sentences are understood in terms of their kernel sentence forms, which have just about a total correspondence between the semantic and grammatical classes.

It might be inferred from the above comments that there are no advantages at all to abstract nouns — that their use is attended only by disadvantages. This is not so; they do have a positive value. This can be illustrated from the example given above, "Love is not jealous." In this form, there is an evident focus on the topic of "love." In the fuller form using verbs, "When we love others, we are not jealous of them," the focus could be on "love" or "not jealous," both or neither. Thus, a statement using an abstract noun may have a more clearly defined focus. Hence, if an abstract noun is translated by means of a verb (with any necessary participants, etc.), then the original focus may be adversely affected. When appropriate, therefore, the use of abstract nouns may be preferred in the RL to maintain focus, or to avoid a clumsy or awkward mode of expression.

In spite of this statement, the formation of new abstract nouns by the translator is not encouraged. It is not categorically prohibited, but it is an activity much better left to the translation helper. If, in restating a sentence, he introduces an acceptable abstract noun where there was none before, it will probably indicate this is what seems natural to him as a native speaker. Care must be taken, however, if the translation helper is working from or is familiar with a national language version which uses many abstract nouns; the influence of that version may lead him to introduce abstract nouns which are awkward or unnatural.

Translating abstract nouns

In the following discussion some suggestions are given on different ways in which abstract nouns may be translated into another language if the language has no abstract nouns which are equivalent and natural. These suggestions are presented in a framework to further highlight why abstract nouns are not so directly understood. It has already been mentioned that when participants are left implicit the context must be clear to lead one to the implicit information. It has also been mentioned that the mismatch between semantic and grammatical classes slows down comprehension, especially of new material. The first reason is obvious enough. The second reason will be better appreciated when it is seen how abstract nouns either objectify or personify an Event or Abstraction.

Abstract nouns may cause the Events or Abstractions they symbolize to be either (1) objectivized, or (2) personified. In other words, because a noun is used, with its appropriate collocations, the impression is given that a thing or person is being referred to. These two effects are discussed below.

(1) *Objectivization*

Objectivization of an Abstraction can be illustrated from Luke 1:12, where it says, "fear fell upon Zacharias." Generally speaking, solid objects are collocated with the verb "to fall" — things such as books, trees, stones. Hence, when an abstract noun like *fear* is collocated with "fall," and so occurs in contexts where Things are usually found, it tends to become objectivized, it attracts to itself the idea that it is a Thing. Compare the following sentences with the statement, "fear fell upon Zacharias"; "the book fell on the floor," "the tree fell on the boy," "the stone fell on his head." These are closely parallel statements, and since "Zacharias" is a Thing word comparable to "floor," "boy," and "head," this gives the impression that fear is closely parallel to "book," "tree," and "stone." The semantic distinction between an Abstraction, such as *fear* and Things, such as book, tree, and stone, is blurred. The correlation between the semantic and grammatical classes is preserved if the equivalent statement is made, "Zacharias became afraid," and consequently the statement is clearer and more direct.

In Matthew 26:66, the statement is made, "He is guilty of death." *Death* is an abstract noun, representing an Event semantically. If the semantic and grammatical classes are made to correspond, then some form of the verb "to die" will be used instead of the noun *death*. Hence, the statement could be rendered, "He is guilty and should die."

A frequent abstract noun in the New Testament is "salvation," as in the statement in Acts 4:12, "Neither is there salvation in any other." Like death, *salvation* represents an Event, "to save," and since this is a transitive verb, there is a subject and an object associated with it. When the semantic and grammatical classes are matched, and the verb "to save" is used, then these associated participants have to be stated, in some such form as, "No one else is able to save people."

The Beatitude which states, "Blessed are they which are persecuted for righteousness' sake" (Matt. 5:10), uses the abstract noun *righteousness*, which represents an Abstraction, "(that which is) righteous." Matching classes gives this statement the form, "Blessed are those who are persecuted because they are righteous," or "Blessed are those who are persecuted because they act righteously." Note that in this case, since "righteous" is an Abstraction, it has to modify some Thing or Event — here it is made clear that it is either the people themselves or what they do.

In the following three examples, the abstract nouns used are italicized, and are followed in parentheses by a capital letter indicating whether they represent an E(vent) or an A(bstraction). The statement using the abstract nouns is then recast, replacing the abstract nouns by appropriate verbs or modifiers and indicating necessary participants.

> 1 Cor. 13:6 "[*Charity*] (E) rejoiceth not in *iniquity* (A), but rejoiceth in the *truth* (A)." "The person who loves does not rejoice when someone does what is evil, but he rejoices when someone does what is true/right."

> James 1:20 "For the *wrath* (A) of man worketh not the *righteousness* (A) of God." "When man is angry, he does not do righteously like God wants him to."

> James 5:15 "And the *prayer* (E) of *faith* (E) shall save the *sick* (A)." "And when they pray and believe, the person who is sick will become well."

(2) *Personification*

When abstract nouns are associated with other forms which imply personality, then these nouns tend to *personify* the Events or the Abstractions which they represent. Such personification occurs in two forms. It occurs in the third person, when the abstract noun is being talked about; and it occurs in the second person, when the abstract noun is addressed directly, as if it were a person. In the first case, the attribution of personality derives from the other words used in the context; in the second case, it derives from the use of the vocative construction.

John 1:17 says, "grace and truth came by Jesus Christ." When the corresponding abstract nouns in Trique (Mexico) for "grace and truth" were combined with "came," they were understood to be the names of two angels. They were interpreted as living beings because they were collocated with "came." Similarly, in Luke 19:9 the statement, "This day is salvation come to this house," can give the impression that "salvation" is a person or a spirit. If this is the reaction of those who hear the RL version, then this problem may be avoided by some such translation as "Today, God has saved those who live in this house."

Some further examples of third person personification are given below, the abstract noun being italicized.

Luke 7:35 "*wisdom* is justified of all her children." "When God does what is wise, those who are wise know it is good."[7]

Rom. 5:17 "*death* reigned." "We all have to die."

Rom. 5:21 "*sin* hath reigned unto death." "We all sin and therefore we have to die."

Rom. 6:9 "*death* hath no more dominion over him." "He will never die again."

In I Corinthians 15:55, there is a well-known example of second person personification:

"O *death*, where is thy sting
O *grave*, where is thy victory?"

Here, "death" and "grave" are addressed directly, and consequently, some language helpers have understood these questions to be addressed to spirits. In discussing how these personifications can be translated, however, certain other translation difficulties have to be faced. There is the metaphor of "sting," which suggests the power to cause death based on a comparison with the poisonous sting of a scorpion, or the bite of a poisonous snake. Also, both questions are rhetorical, and are equivalent to negative statements. There are also various textual variants, the most important being the substitution of "death" for "grave."[8] Keeping

---

[7] This rendition reflects one widely-held interpretation; another is exemplified by NEB, which says, "And yet God's wisdom is proved right by all who are her children."

[8] This substitution is in the text in the Bible Societies' *Greek New Testament*, 1966, and it is classified as "B" which "indicates that there is some degree of doubt" (p. xi).

in mind the general context of the resurrection, then, if the figures of speech used in this quotation will communicate wrong meaning a possible translation would be:

> "Nothing will at that time cause people to die.
> People will never die again"

Conclusion

The Greek of the New Testament is a language which uses many abstract nouns, and does so extensively. Much of the teaching of the Scriptures is associated in our minds with these abstract nouns — faith, truth, grace, salvation, redemption, forgiveness, love. But there are few languages that can match Greek in this respect. So the translator finds that, if his translation is to communicate the inspired message accurately, many of these abstract nouns need to be translated by terms corresponding to the semantic class represented.[9]

ORDER

In the chapter on multiple senses of a word, no mention was made of the fact that several different linguistic forms may represent the same sense. Neither was this mentioned in chapter 12 on lexical equivalence where this feature of lexical structure underlies all of the nonliteral equivalences. Repeated reference has been made, however, to the fact that a single word may have several senses. In this chapter we have again been focusing on this same feature as it is found in connection with grammatical structures; that is to say, one structure with two or more possible meanings. The opposite — different structures which have the same essential meaning — is, of course, also frequent. These structural variations on the grammatical level do not generally cause the translator any problems. However, one does, and that is the structural feature of *order*.

The order of words within a phrase, and the order of phrases within a clause, are known to vary from language to language. The translator is

---

[9] Because of the factors set forth in this section, a matching of semantic class and grammatical class is aimed at in examples giving the basic meaning here and in chapters 16, 19, and 20. However, there are some Event and Abstraction concepts which may be expressed in English *only* by means of nouns or expressions which use nouns, and this may possibly be true of all languages.

Some words having to do with the physical senses and speech activity are in this category. *Word*, for example, is an Event; and yet in the clause "he heard the word," that Event cannot be expressed without the use of a noun. In a paraphrase such as "he heard that which was said," "that which" is still a nominal expression. Some other Event words in this class are *noise, sound, taste, message,* and *gospel*.

The word *tradition* is an Abstraction in this class. Any paraphrase, such as "culturally-imposed behavior patterns" or "the way they say you should act" do, in themselves, make use of nouns ("patterns," "way"). *Color* and *fellowship* are other Abstractions in this class.

The implication of this is that although the aim may be a correlation between semantic and grammatical classes in the examples presented, a complete correlation is not possible; some abstract nouns are unavoidable.

aware of this and uses the appropriate RL order for words and phrases. But the same principle is also found to apply to the order of clauses within the sentence, and to the order of sentences within the paragraph. Here, too, the order of the original must not be slavishly followed for it may not convey the original message faithfully in the RL.

Chronological and linguistic order

When the linguistic order corresponds with the chronological order, there is generally little problem in communication. But the order of clauses in the original does not always correspond with the order in experience, and it is at this point that the translator who preserves the original order may well find he is not communicating the original message accurately.

The classic example in the New Testament of noncorrespondence between linguistic and chronological order is found in Mark 6:17, 18. In the KJV, which follows the Greek closely, this reads:

> "For Herod himself had sent forth and laid hold upon John, and bound him in prison for Herodias' sake, his brother Philip's wife: For he had married her. For John had said unto Herod, It is not lawful for thee to have thy brother's wife."

Nida (1964, pp. 138, 39) and Deibler (1968, p. 14) have previously discussed the lack of correspondence between the linguistic order of these events and their historical sequence. The linguistic order may be listed as follows:

1. Herod arrested John and imprisoned him.
2. Herod did this because of Herodias.
3. Herodias was Philip's wife.
4. Herod married Herodias.
5. John rebuked Herod.

If these events are rearranged in their chronological order, it will be seen that the order would be 3, 4, 5, 2, 1; that is to say, the last three events linguistically are the first events chronologically, and are then followed by events (1) and (2), but in the reverse order. If the RL has no clear method of indicating "flashback," that is, where the linguistic order is the reverse of the temporal order, or cannot use flashback in this type of discourse, then the translator must present the material so that the linguistic and temporal orders coincide. If this is not done, it is almost certain some wrong meaning will be communicated. For example, in several languages, when the clauses were kept in the order found in Greek, the translation helpers understood it was John the Baptist who had immoral relations either with Herod's wife or Philip's.

Another chronological inversion is found in Mark 7:17: "And when he was entered into the house from the people. . . ." There are two events described here; (1) he left the people, and (2) he entered the house, and they obviously occurred in this order. Hence, in most languages, it is necessary to translate them in the chronological order.

Acts 8:1, 2 presents this type of problem spread over two verses. They read as follows:

1. "And Saul was consenting unto his death. And at that time there was a great persecution against the church which was at Jerusalem; and they were all scattered abroad throughout the regions of Judaea and Samaria, except the apostles.

2. And devout men carried Stephen to his burial, and made great lamentation over him."

It can be seen that the first sentence of verse 1, and all of verse 2, belong together, and speak about Stephen's martyrdom, while the rest of verse 1 describes a new subject, the persecution of the church in Jerusalem. The Seri (Mexico) language helper indicated these verses would more likely be understood if the first part of verse 1 were followed immediately by verse 2, and then the rest of verse 1. This was done, but it necessitated putting the numbering of verses 1 and 2 together as "1, 2."

One final example may be cited from Revelation 5:2, where an angel asks, "Who is worthy to open the book, and to loose the seals thereof?" In a number of languages, it has proved necessary to put these two questions in the opposite order, so that the opening of the seals precedes the opening of the book.

There are thus a number of reasons why a translator may choose to rearrange the linguistic order of the original so as to make it correspond with the chronological order. The structure of the RL may, of course, make it obligatory, but even when this is not the case, frequency of one order over another may lead the translator to shift order so that the translation will conform to the patterns of naturalness of the RL. It has also been mentioned above that a change in order may be necessary to avoid obscurity, or even wrong meaning, such as the confusion that can arise in connection with Mark 6:17, 18. In some cases, there may be a free choice of order, and the translator chooses that order which is most easily understood.

It is worth mentioning that, just as psychological studies have indicated there is greater ease of comprehension when the semantic and grammatical classes match, so there is a certain amount of evidence confirming this is also the case when the linguistic and temporal orders coincide. Eve Clark (1971, p. 267) has conducted certain investigations with children on their use of conjunctions. She concludes: "In a study of spontaneous use of conjunctions by English-speaking children, [it was] found that young children (aged 3:0-3:6) rely almost exclusively on an order of mention' strategy to describe events in time, i.e. they talked about events in simple sentences in the order in which they occurred." Obviously, what holds for children cannot necessarily be fully applied to adults. However, this study would seem to indicate that when there is correspondence of both linguistic and chronological order, then the message

is more easily understood. Also, it is worth noting that a correct understanding of a reversal of chronological order is dependent, in most languages, on clearly reading or hearing the form(s) which signal the
reversal.

This last factor is especially significant in the case of "flashback" (in
which an event previous to those being mentioned is brought into the
narrative) and "flashforward" (in which an event future to those being
mentioned is brought in). An example of flashback is found in John
19:39, in which Nicodemus is identified as the one "which at first came
to Jesus by night," referring back to the incident in chapter 3. Matthew
10:4 uses flashforward when it identifies Judas Iscariot as the one "who
also betrayed him," referring ahead to what takes place in chapter 26.

With flashback and flashforward it is impossible to rearrange the linguistic order to match chronological order; and this means that careful
attention must be given to the linguistic signals of the RL which show
the relative times involved.

Logical and linguistic order

These observations apply to logical order, as well as to chronological
order. In English, we can say equally well, "I didn't go out today,
because it was raining," "Because it was raining, I didn't go out today,"
and "It was raining today, so I didn't go out." Logically, the fact of the
rain is the reason for my not going out; the rain is logically (as well as
temporally) prior. In the first sentence, however, this order is reversed,
and the rain is referred to last. This shows, therefore, that different linguistic orders can express the same logical order — the forms are different, the meaning is the same.

This phenomenon of the noncorrespondence of the linguistic and
logical order is found in the New Testament. Mark 6:31 states, "And
he said unto them, Come ye yourselves apart into a desert place, and rest
a while: for there were many coming and going, and they had no leisure
so much as to eat." The reason for Jesus' suggestion of a rest is given
after the suggestion in the linguistic order, but logically and temporally
it *preceded* his suggestion. In Tewa (U.S.A.), therefore, where the
reason is always stated first and then the result, the order of the two
halves of the verse was reversed. If the translator had carried the Greek
clause order over into the RL, the message of the original would have
been distorted.

A linguistic reversal of logical order is also found in 1 John 5:2, "By
this we know that we love the children of God, when we love God, and
keep his commandments." Logically, the two halves of this verse stand
in a grounds-conclusion relationship; the conclusion that we love God's
children is based upon the grounds that we love God and obey him. But
the linguistic order reverses the logical order with the conclusion preceding the grounds. In Colorado (Ecuador), however, in order for the
sentence to be understood it was necessary to make the linguistic order
conform to the logical order, so that it was translated, "Loving God, we

obey His commandments. In this way we know that we really love God's children."

Negative-affirmative statements

There are some statements in the New Testament where a negative and a closely related affirmative are joined together. When presented with such pairings, some language helpers have suggested they be translated in the reverse order, i.e. with the affirmative assertion first.[10] Two examples are given below, which needed reversing in different languages of Mexico.

> John 6:38 "For I came down from heaven, not to do mine own will, but the will of him that sent me," became: For I have come down from heaven to do the will of him who sent me and not to do my own will.
>
> 1 John 2:16 "All that is in the world . . . is not of the Father, but is of the world," became: All that is in the world . . . is of the world; it is not of the Father.

Chiasmus

A rhetorical device which is used a number of times in both the Old and New Testaments is that referred to as *chiasmus*. The name comes from the Greek letter *chi*, which resembles a St. Andrew's cross in shape. It describes the rhetorical device in which the two halves of the portion under consideration are mirror-images of each other. If the lines are lettered consecutively in the first half, and in the reverse order (with an accent mark to distinguish them) in the second half then, if there are four lines in the portion, the chiastic structure is ab-b́á; if there are six lines, then the structure is abc-ćb́á; and so on. The second half is thus the reverse, in linguistic order, of the first half. An example[11] of the structure ab-b́á is provided by Matthew 7:6:

> (a) "Give not that which is holy unto the dogs,
> (b) Neither cast ye your pearls before swine,
> (b́) Lest they trample them under their feet,
> (á) And turn again and rend you."

The characteristic "cross" arrangement is seen if the lines are displayed as follows:

Lines (a) and (á) refer to dogs, while lines (b) and (b́) refer to swine.

---

[10] It is interesting to note that some studies have shown that the positive member of antonymous adjective-pairs is learned first (Clark, 1971, p. 271).

[11] Although many consider this a chiasmus, Lenski and Meyer do not.

When a larger section of material is cast in chiastic form, it does not seem to cause any serious problems of communication. But when it applies to a few adjacent clauses, such as the example quoted above, then it has been found to confuse the readers of the RL. If checking with native speakers shows that a chiastic arrangement is creating confusion as to the immediate constituents, then the translator may have to "unscramble" the chiasmus, and present it in a more straightforward manner. In this example of Matthew 7:6, the first and fourth lines are related. The intrusion of lines two and three between the first and fourth obscures the syntactic relation and may be translated as follows:

(a) Do not give dogs what is holy, (á) lest they turn and attack you, and

(b) do not throw your pearls before swine, (b́) lest they trample them underfoot.

Some other examples of chiasmus are given below:

Philemon 5

(a) "Hearing of thy love"   (b́) "which thou hast toward the Lord Jesus"

(b) "and faith"   (á) "and toward all saints"

Colossians 1:16 (part of the verse)

(a) "that are in heaven"   (b́) "visible"
(b) "and that are in earth"   (á) "and invisible"

Matthew 13:15

(a) "For this people's heart is waxed gross"   (ć) "lest at any time they should see with their eyes"

(b) "and their ears are dull of hearing"   (b́) "and hear with their ears"

(c) "and their eyes they have closed"   (á) "and should understand with their heart"

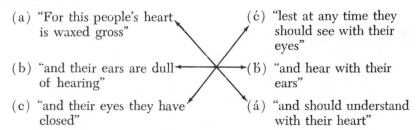

This last example is more complicated, so it is also presented in non-chiastic form:

(a) "For this people's heart is waxed gross" ⟶ (á) "lest they should understand with their heart"

(b) "and their ears are dull of hearing" ⟶ (b́) "lest they hear with their ears"

(c) "and their eyes they have closed" ⟶ (ć) "lest at any time they should see with their eyes"

Idiomatic preference in certain sequences

When certain sets of words occur together frequently, a language may develop a preference for one order of occurrence over another. In English, for example, we say "black and white," not "white and black"; but in Spanish "white and black" is the preferred order. Men are mentioned first in "men and women," but women are mentioned first in "ladies and gentlemen." "Four or five" is proper English, but some American Indian languages prefer "five or four."

In such cases, the translator should determine the preferred order in the RL and change the order of the original when appropriate. For example, in Auca (Ecuador) the most prominent member of a group is named last, not first, so that in the translation, "Peter, James, and John" had to be changed to "John, James, and Peter" to keep the same focus as the original.

CHAPTER 15

Rhetorical Questions

The question form is one of the constructions found in the Greek New Testament which is associated with more than one function. It is a relatively common construction, about 1,000 being found altogether. Questions can be divided into two groups — *real* questions and *rhetorical* questions.[1] The former are what are popularly thought of as questions — they are used to obtain information. They present no great problems to the translator, as they are found in all languages, and, indeed, are often the first forms learned by an outsider. Rhetorical questions, which constitute about 70 per cent of the questions found in the New Testament, are not so straightforward, however. Although they are cast in the form of a question, they are not used to obtain information. Rather, they are used to convey or call attention to information and to express the speaker's attitudes, opinions, etc.

As might be expected, real questions are found mostly in the historical books of the New Testament; all but five or six are found in the gospels and Acts, where they are mostly found in conversations. Rhetorical questions are found scattered throughout the New Testament, though they

[1] The content of this chapter is based on the material found in the article "Analyzing and Translating the Questions of the New Testament" by John Beekman, NOT 44, pp. 1-21. This issue of *Notes on Translation* is devoted to the study of rhetorical questions, not only those in the Greek New Testament, but also those used in a number of different languages. In this respect, it supplements the contents of this chapter, and should be consulted.

are particularly common in some of Paul's Epistles, such as Romans, with 83, and 1 Corinthians with at least 100 — more per page than any other book in the New Testament.

As in the other cases discussed in chapter 14, there is thus a lack of correspondence between the form of a rhetorical question and its purpose or meaning. This lack of correspondence is language-specific; no other language uses rhetorical questions in exactly the same way, and with the same frequency, as does the Greek of the New Testament. This means the translator must understand the function of the rhetorical questions he finds in the New Testament, and he must also understand the function of the rhetorical questions he finds in the RL. The two will not match, so a literal transfer of the rhetorical questions of the original into the RL is liable to give rise to lack of fidelity both exegetically and dynamically.

DISTINGUISHING REAL AND RHETORICAL QUESTIONS IN THE NEW TESTAMENT

As the translator studies the questions of the New Testament, he has basically two matters to resolve regarding each question:

(1) Is this a real or a rhetorical question?

(2) What is the purpose served by this question?

This section will discuss the criteria used to distinguish real and rhetorical questions, and the following one will discuss the various functions associated with both real and rhetorical questions.

In essence, it is the context which has to be studied to separate real and rhetorical questions — the immediately preceding context, and the following context.

The *preceding context* provides one straightforward piece of evidence: the three Greek words *erōtaō* and *eperōtaō* "to ask," and *punthanomai* "to inquire," are used only to introduce real questions, whether direct or indirect.[2] For example, Mark 8:5, "And he asked them, How many loaves have ye?" (Gk. *ērōta*), and Acts 4:7, "And when they had set them in the midst, they asked, By what power, or by what name, have ye done this?" (Gk. *epunthanonto*).[3] Other Greek words are also used to introduce questions, however, and they may introduce either real or rheto-

---

[2] There are, however, three instances in which *eperōtaō* is used to introduce questions which, on the basis of the context, may be analyzed as either real or rhetorical questions. They are Mark 7:5, "Then the Pharisees and scribes asked him, Why walk not thy disciples according to the tradition of the elders . . . ?"; Mark 15:4, "And Pilate asked him again, saying, Answerest thou nothing?"; and Acts 5:27, 28, "The high priest asked them saying, Did not we straitly command you that ye should not teach in this name?" An apparent exception involving *erōtaō* is found in John 18:21a, which reads, "Why askest (*erōtas*) thou me?" The question itself is a rhetorical question, equivalent in meaning to "Don't ask me," or "You should not ask me," but the "ask" refers back to v. 19, where it is used to introduce an indirect real question. Hence, it is not an exception to the use of *erōtaō*.

[3] *Erōtaō* appears to be used to introduce a real question (direct, indirect, or implied) in Matt. 16:13, 19:17 (RSV text), 21:24; Mark 4:10, 8:5; Luke 9:45, 19:31, 20:3, 22:68, 23:3; John 1:19, 21, 25, 5:12, 8:7 (Textus Receptus), 9:2, 15, 19, 21,

rical questions, so it is only these three words which give unambiguous help.

To appreciate the evidence provided by the *following context*, it is useful to remind ourselves of the basic difference in function between real and rhetorical questions. The real question is used to elicit information; the rhetorical question is used to convey or call attention to information. This being the case, it is reasonable to expect that when a real question is answered, it will be answered by someone other than the questioner. Conversely, it is reasonable to assume a rhetorical question will not be answered, but if it is answered, then it will be by the questioner himself, not by someone else.

Clearly then, the type of response, and the person who responds, are the sort of information that is sought in the context following the question. The above observations provide a good basic guideline for the majority of questions in the New Testament — if the question is answered by someone other than the questioner, it is a real question; if it remains unanswered or if the questioner answers it himself, then it is a rhetorical question. But to be able to analyze the data provided in the wide variety of contexts found in the New Testament, it is necessary to refine the above general statement with more specific statements, first for real questions, then for rhetorical questions.

Specific criteria characteristic of real questions

(1) A question which elicits information is a real question *even if the inquirer knows the answer*. Questions asked to see whether a student knows the answer, or in a polemic situation for the sake of argument, or to have someone commit himself to a particular view, are all real questions. An example is found in John 6:5, 6: "he saith unto Philip, Whence shall we buy bread, that these may eat? And this he said to prove him: for he himself knew what he would do." It is worth noting, however, that there are languages in which questions to which the inquirer already knows the answer are not used at all, or are used only in restricted contexts.

(2) A question is still analyzed as real *even if the characters are not historical persons*. This type of situation occurs in some of the parables. For example, in the Parable of the Tares (Matt. 13:24-30), the householder's servants ask him, "Wilt thou then that we go and gather them up?" (28b), and he answers their question in the following verse with, "Nay."

(3) Although an answer is to be expected to a real question, there are occasions when the answer is left implicit. *Even if the answer is*

12:21, 16:5, 19, 18:19, 21 (2x); Acts 1:6. *Eperōtaō* is used in Matt. 12:10, 17:10, 22:23, 35, 41, 46, 27:11; Mark 5:9, 7:17, 8:23, 27, 29, 9:11, 16, 21, 28, 32, 33, 10:2, 10, 17, 11:29, 12:18, 28, 34, 13:3, 14:60, 61, 15:2, 44; Luke 2:46, 3:10, 14, 6:9, 8:9, 30, 9:18, 17:20, 18:18, 40, 20:21, 27, 40, 21:7, 22:64, 23:6, 9; John 9:23, 18:7; Acts 23:34; Rom. 10:20; 1 Cor. 14:35. *Punthanomai* is used in Matt. 2:4; Luke 15:26, 18:36; John 4:52; Acts 4:7, 10:18, 29, 21:33, 23:19, 20.

implied, the question is still regarded as real. For example, in Luke 8:45, Jesus asks, "Who touched me?" This is followed by the comment, "When all denied," which implies that they all said, "Not me," or some equivalent. Similar examples are found in Mark 14:64; John 5:12, 18:16-27.

(4) A question is also regarded as real, *even if the person questioned evades the question or withholds or postpones an answer.* Thus, in Luke 10:25, Jesus is asked by a lawyer, "Master, what shall I do to inherit eternal life?" In the following verse, Jesus responds to this question by asking the lawyer, "What is written in the law?" and postpones a real answer to the lawyer's question until verse 28. On another occasion, Nicodemus asked Jesus, "How can these things be?" (John 3:9), and Jesus replied with a rhetorical question and some further explanation. Again, when Pilate asked the crowd, "Why, what evil hath he done?" (Matt. 27:23), the crowd avoided answering, but nonetheless acknowledged the question by responding with, "Let him be crucified." In the preceding chapter (Matt. 26:63), Matthew stated, "But Jesus held his peace." He refused to answer the question. Two other examples of deliberate silence are found in Mark 3:4 and Matthew 26:63 (in this case, it is not explicitly stated that Jesus did not reply, but it is clearly implied).

(5) Sometimes comments by the author indicate that, although the question was a real one, an *answer was unnecessary, inappropriate, impossible, or unknown.* As the three women approached the tomb, they said to each other, "Who shall roll us away the stone from the door of the sepulchre?" (Mark 16:3). The question has no need for an answer, for Mark comments in the following verse that they looked up and saw it had already been moved. Chapter 22 of Matthew closes with the question Jesus asked, "If David then call him Lord, how is he his son?" (Matt. 22:45), immediately followed by the comment, "And no man was able to answer him a word . . ." (22:46). There was no answer, because no one could provide one.

In some cases questions are referred to before they are asked or after they have been asked, so that an answer is impossible or unnecessary. For example, in Luke 7:19 John the Baptist sends two of his disciples to Jesus with instructions to ask him, "Art thou he that should come? or look we for another?" Naturally there is no answer, as the situation in which Jesus would be expected to answer had not yet arisen. Other examples of reference to future questions are found in Luke 19:31, 20:5, 22:11. John 4:27 (two questions), 16:5, and 21:12 are questions which his disciples did not dare to ask Jesus. A reference to a question already asked on an earlier occasion is found in John 21:20 where the disciple whom Jesus loved is further described as the one who had asked, "Lord, which is he that betrayeth thee?" Similar examples are found in Luke 8:45 (end of the verse) and John 21:17b. In John 7:11, when the Jews who were looking for Jesus at the feast asked, "Where is he?", no answer was given because no one knew where he was.

(6) Finally, there are a few examples where *two real questions function as one*, so that only one answer is given. The first question is generic, the second specific. For example, the end of Matthew 22:41, and 22:42 read as follows: "Jesus asked them, saying, What think ye of Christ? whose son is he? They say unto him, The son of David." "What think ye of Christ?" is generic, "whose son is he?" is specific, and the answer is a reply to the specific question, and hence, to the more generic question as well. The same interpretation could be applied to Matthew 21:28, 31, taking the question in v. 28 as generic, "But what think ye?", and that in v. 31 as specific, "Whether of them twain did the will of his father?"

Specific criteria characteristic of rhetorical questions

The above paragraphs have discussed in detail the information found in the context which indicates it is a real question. The same thing now needs to be done for rhetorical questions.

(1) Many of the rhetorical questions are found in the epistles, where there is no possibility of someone, other than the writer himself answering them, unless a written reply is made. The problems arise in connection with the historical books — the gospels and Acts — where there are live teaching situations in which the *listeners may respond to a rhetorical question*. This statement needs further clarification.

It may have been inferred from the above discussion that responses are only given to real questions, so if a response is indicated in the context, then the question is inevitably a real one. But this is an oversimplification of what is found. Rhetorical questions convey information, and since it is natural for a listener to respond to information, it is quite possible a rhetorical question may be met with a response. The question then arises: Was the response made to a real or to a rhetorical question? How are we to distinguish?

The matter is not straightforward, and the discussion of one or two examples is the best way to answer these questions. In Luke 13:7, 8 the owner of the vineyard says to his vinedresser, concerning the fruitless fig tree: "Why cumbereth it the ground?" The vinedresser responds with the statement, "Lord, let it alone this year also, till I shall dig about it, and dung it." This is not really an answer to the owner's question, as it stands. But if his question is interpreted as a rhetorical question equivalent to "Don't let this tree cumber the ground any more," then the vinedresser's request is a natural response to this negative command.

Another interesting example is found in John 7:51. The Pharisees were in discussion, and Nicodemus raises the question, "Doth our law judge any man, before it hear him, and know what he doeth?" This question seems obviously rhetorical — all the Pharisees knew very well that the law had to hear what the accused had to say, as did Nicodemus himself. Yet v. 52 reads: "They answered and said unto him, Art thou also of Galilee? Search, and look: for out of Galilee ariseth no prophet." The question then has to be asked — is this an answer to a real question, or a response to a rhetorical question? If Nicodemus' question was real, then the answer should have been, "No, our law does not judge a man before it hears him." However, if the Pharisees interpreted Nicodemus' question as saying, in effect, "We ought to give Jesus a fair trial," then their response makes sense. Jesus came from Galilee, and Nicodemus was taking his part — hence the sarcastic response, "Art thou also of Galilee?" The Pharisees were responding to the implications of a rhetorical question.

In principle, then, the responses from other than the questioner may be distinguished from each other. The answer to a real question provides the information sought for in the question; the response to a rhetorical question does not answer the question, as such, but responds to the implications lying behind the question form. It responds to the statement, or command, which is the meaning of the rhetorical question.

There are times, however, when the contextual evidence is such that the response can be interpreted in either way — as an answer to a real question, or as a response to the meaning of a rhetorical question. Acts 5:27-29 is an example of this, and reads as follows:

> "And the high priest asked them, saying, Did not we straitly command you that ye should not teach in this name? and, behold, ye have filled Jerusalem with your doctrine, and intend to bring this man's blood upon us. Then Peter and the other apostles answered and said, We ought to obey God rather than men."

Here we have a question, "Did not we straitly command you that ye should not teach in this name?" and an answer from those who were questioned, "We ought to obey God rather than men." This response could be regarded as an answer to the high priest's question, with the "Yes" implied, as is often the case. The full answer would be equivalent to, "Yes, you did. But we ought to obey God rather than men." Analyzed in this way, it is a real question, answered by those questioned. Alternatively, their statement could be regarded as a response to a rhetorical question, which is equivalent to, "We straitly commanded you that you should not teach in this name?" and an answer from those who were saying they disobeyed the high priest because they obeyed God.

In the occasional ambiguous situation of this sort, the translator's preference should be for a real question (with its answer), since the combination of a question plus an answer from the person (or persons) questioned is more typical of a real question than a rhetorical question. In this particular case, there is the further evidence that "asked" in v. 27 is the Greek word *epērōtēsen*, an aorist form of *eperōtaō*, which, as has been previously noted, is a verb used almost exclusively to introduce real questions.

(2) *A rhetorical question may be "self-directed" or "other-directed." A self-directed question is always considered rhetorical* since it it obvious in this case that an answer is not being sought from anyone except oneself. A self-directed question is similar to an other-directed rhetorical

question in that if the question is answered, it is answered by the speaker himself, not by others. In a sense, some self-directed questions seek for information, but since they look for the desired information in the speaker's own background, and since self-directed questions also express incertitude and evaluation, it seems best to classify all self-directed questions as a subclass of rhetorical questions. Luke 12:17 provides an example. The rich man "thought within himself, saying, What shall I do, because I have no room where to bestow my fruits?" He directs the question to himself, in his own thoughts, and also answers it himself in the following verse: "This will I do: I will pull down my barns . . . ." This type of evidence points unambiguously to a rhetorical question.[4]

With other-directed questions, however, the issue is not so simple — they may be rhetorical questions or real questions. One of the terms in Greek that signals other-directed questions is the reciprocal pronoun, usually in its accusative form (*allēlous*) or its genitive form (*allēlōn*). Thus, in Mark 4:41, we read, ". . . and they said one to another (Gk. *pros allēlous*), What manner of man is this, that even the wind and the sea obey him?" Similar examples are found in Luke 8:25; John 4:33, 11:56 (in this case, the Gk. is *met' allēlōn*). While these Greek forms signal that the questions are directed from one to another within a group, they leave unresolved the question of their being real or rhetorical.

The same applies to the reciprocal form *heautoi*. The sequence *pros heautous*, when used in connection with a question, indicates the question is reciprocal, asked of one another. See, for example, Mark 10:26 (following the generally accepted text), 16:3; Luke 22:23; John 7:35, 36, 12:19. However, when either the singular or plural form is preceded by *en* (*en heautō* and *en heautois*), then this indicates a self-directed question, which is therefore rhetorical. Examples are found in Luke 7:49, 12:17, and 16:3.

Not all questions discussed within groups are signaled by these particular Greek forms, so other clues have to be sought from the context. The questions found in Mark 2:7, "Why does this man thus speak blasphemies? who can forgive sins but God only?" are introduced with the statement in v. 6, "reasoning in their hearts." Clearly, then, these were reflexive, self-directed questions. In the parallel passage in Luke, the clue is given afterwards in 5:22, when it says "but when Jesus perceived their thoughts . . . ." Conversely, in Matthew 12:23 the crowd is reported as saying, "Is not this the son of David?" But the following verse reports that "the Pharisees heard it." Clearly, then, this question was other-directed. In John 16:18, a question is introduced simply with, "They said therefore." But when Jesus comments on their question (in the following verse), he uses the Greek forms *met' allēlōn* thus making it clear it was other-directed.

One of the contextual clues that points to a rhetorical question, there-

---

[4] So far as is known, self-directed rhetorical questions have not had to be recast into some other form in translations. This would perhaps confirm this analysis as a special subtype of rhetorical questions.

fore, is a self-directed question. This may be signaled by *en heautō/ heautois*, or it may be signaled by other clues such as "in their thoughts" or "in their hearts." Other-directed questions, however, may be either real or rhetorical, and different criteria have to be used to distinguish them.

If the answer to a question is common knowledge, already known by both the speaker and hearers, it is probably a rhetorical question. For example, when Jesus asks the Sadducees ". . . have ye not read that which was spoken unto you by God . . . ?" (Matt. 22:31), both he and they were already well aware of the fact they had read it. In this case, the implication is they were acting as though they had not read it.

The form of real and rhetorical questions

Up to this point, the discussion on distinguishing between real and rhetorical questions has focused attention on the *context* in which the question is found. But the question needs to be raised: "Does not the *form* of these questions provide any useful clues as to which type they belong to?" The answer is basically, no.

It may be that real and rhetorical questions were distinguished by intonation in Koiné Greek, but if so, we now have no evidence on this matter. Certainly, the internal form of real and rhetorical questions does not appear to differ. The same question words — what, when, where, who, why, how — are found in both real and rhetorical questions. Yes/no questions may use the negative particles *ou* and *mē* but these negative particles also are found in both real and rhetorical questions. For example, the following two questions are real, one using *mē*, the other *ou*.

John 6:67   *mē* — "Will ye also go away?"
John 18:26   *ouk* — "Did I not see thee in the garden with him?"

The next two questions are rhetorical, also using *mē* and *ou*.

Mark 2:19   *mē* — "Can the children of the bridechamber fast, while the bridegroom is with them?"
Mark 11:17   *ou* — "Is it not written, My house shall be called of all nations the house of prayer?"

Real and rhetorical questions are also formed without the use of either *ou* or *mē*.

Real question (with affirmative answer):
  Matt. 9:28   "Believe ye that I am able to do this?"

Real question (with negative answer):
  Matt. 13:28   "Wilt thou then that we go and gather them up?"

Rhetorical question (affirmation)
  Matt. 26:55   "Are ye come out as against a thief with swords and staves for to take me?"

Rhetorical question (negation):
  Luke 11:12   "Or if he shall ask an egg, will he offer him a scorpion?"

Such examples as the above could be multiplied to show that *ou* and *mē* are used in both types of question. Neither their presence, nor their absence, provides a basis for distinguishing real and rhetorical questions.[5] However, actual count shows there is a tendency to use *ou* and *mē* more frequently in rhetorical questions, and rather less frequently in real questions expecting a yes/no answer.

The resolution of ambiguities by means of parallel passages

Where there are parallel passages in the gospels, a question which is ambiguous as to being real or rhetorical may sometimes be resolved by reference to the parallel passage. Such an approach to these questions should be made with extreme caution, however, to be sure that passages which are genuinely different are not forced into conformity. Different authors report different details of an incident, selecting information and choosing a linguistic form to suit their particular purposes. Hence, it cannot be assumed that what is a rhetorical question in one account was also intended as a rhetorical question in a parallel account.

For example, in Matthew 21:40, 41 (at the end of the Parable of the Wicked Husbandmen) Jesus asks his audience, "When the Lord therefore of the vineyard cometh, what will he do to those husbandmen?" His audience replies, "He will miserably destroy those wicked men . . . ." Matthew, then, reports a real question, with a clear reply from those questioned. But in both Mark 12:9 and Luke 20:15, 16 an answer by Jesus himself is recorded, so that the question is clearly rhetorical. In this case, the evidence in the immediate context indicates conclusively that one of these three passages involves a real question and the other two rhetorical; there is no ambiguity. In such a case, it would be wrong to change the form of one passage to conform to that found in another just because they are reporting the same events.

In Mark 2:24, however, the question is ambiguous. The Pharisees, seeing Jesus' disciples pick and eat grain on the sabbath, ask him, "Behold, why do they on the sabbath day that which is not lawful?" Jesus then replies with a reference to David and his men which does not really answer the Pharisees' question. Jesus' reply can be regarded as a response to the meaning behind a rhetorical question which is in this case an accusation; or it can be regarded as postponing the answer to a real question, the answer itself finally being expressed in v. 28. In the case of an ambiguity such as this, reference to parallel passages is legitimate, and when the translator compares Matthew 12:2 he will note that in the report the Pharisees' challenge to Jesus is not a question at all, but a statement. (The corresponding passage in Luke 6:2 is similar to Mark.) The translator will thus be led to interpret Mark 2:24 as a rhetorical question equivalent in meaning to a statement. This interpretation is strengthened by the fact that several modern-speech English translations also render it as a statement or exclamation.

[5] The significance of the use of *ou* and *mē* in questions is discussed in Appendix C.

The Functions of Real and Rhetorical Questions

The purpose of the discussion so far has been to elucidate criteria by means of which real and rhetorical questions may be distinguished, even though there is a small residue of ambiguities. In this section, however, the distinction is assumed, and the question is asked: Granted this is a real question (or a rhetorical one), what function is it fulfilling in this context? The functions of real questions will be considered first, then those of rhetorical questions.

The functions of real questions

Real questions may be analyzed as serving two functions:

(1) to elicit unknown information by a learner or inquirer; and
(2) to elicit known information, generally by a teacher.

It seems likely that the first function represents the most frequent use of real questions in the New Testament. An example is found in Matthew 13:10, where the disciples ask Jesus why he spoke to the people in parables. They wanted to know because they did not understand why Jesus used this particular method of teaching. Examples of the second use are also common. John 6:5, 6 has already been mentioned as an example of this.

It has been suggested by some that a third function for real questions should be added. This function, they say, is to elicit an opinion (whether known or unknown to the questioner) for polemic reasons. But this can be analyzed as a specific purpose under either (1) or (2) above. To take one example: in Matthew 22:17, Jesus is asked, "Is it lawful to give tribute unto Caesar, or not?" Those who asked Jesus this did so deliberately, knowing that it was a controversial question, with both points of view being held strongly among the Jews. We do not know if they had any idea which view Jesus held, but whether they did or did not, the question served to elicit information. How the question may have served the inquirer is a specific matter which is separate from the two general functions of a real question.

Real questions, therefore, serve this one basic purpose — to elicit information from the person, or persons, to whom the question is addressed.

The functions of rhetorical questions

In contrast with real questions, rhetorical questions serve the purpose of *imparting* or *calling attention to* information, not eliciting it. They are thus semantically equivalent to statements, using this term in a broad sense to include commands. Four principal functions may be distinguished as follows:

1. a statement of certitude;
2. a statement of incertitude;
3. a statement of evaluation or obligation;
4. to highlight and introduce a new subject or a new aspect of the same subject.

1. *A statement of certitude*

Rhetorical questions which transform into statements of certitude do not carry any implications of evaluation or obligation. They simply express the fact that the speaker is sure of what he is saying, he speaks with certainty. If the information expressed is common knowledge to both the speaker and hearers, the speaker is calling the hearers' attention to it. (For examples of this, note Matt. 26:55, Luke 11:12, and 1 Cor. 12:17 in the three following paragraphs.) The statement into which a rhetorical question transforms may be an affirmation, a negation, or a combination of both.

Most of the *affirmations* contain either the particle *ou* or neither *ou* nor *mē*. For example, the question in Matthew 6:30 begins with *ou*: "... shall he not much more clothe you...?" This question is equivalent to the assertion, "he will certainly much more clothe you." An example of a rhetorical question without either *ou* or *mē*, which transforms into an affirmation, is found in Matthew 26:55. "Are ye come out as against a thief with swords and staves for to take me?"

Negations, or denials, contain *mē*, or neither *ou* nor *mē*. An example with *mē* is found in Mark 2:19, "Can the children of the bridechamber fast, while the bridegroom is with them?," for which the equivalent negation would be "The children of the bridechamber cannot fast while ...." An example with neither *ou* nor *mē* is taken from Luke 11:12, "Or if he shall ask an egg, will he offer him a scorpion?" In this case, the negation would be, "Or if he asks for an egg, he will not offer him a scorpion."

Examples of the use of such question-words as "who," "what," "where," and "how" in this type of rhetorical question are given below:

Mark 3:23 "How can Satan cast out Satan?" This asserts the same proposition as "Satan cannot cast out Satan."

Luke 9:25 "For what is a man advantaged, if he gain the whole world, and lose himself, or be cast away?" The question is equivalent in meaning to "A man is advantaged nothing, if ..."

Luke 16:11 "... who will commit to your trust the true riches?" This is equivalent to the negative statement, "No one will commit the true riches to your trust."

1 Cor. 12:17 "If the whole body were an eye, where were the hearing?" The last part of this question has the same meaning as the negative statement, "there would be no hearing."

Rhetorical questions which can be transformed into *both an affirmation and a negation* are often introduced by *ti* "which," and present two alternatives connected by "or." The choice thus presented is an obvious one, so that one part of the question can be transformed into an affirmative statement and the other into a negative one.

Mark 2:9 "Whether (*ti*) is it easier to say ..., Thy sins be forgiven thee; or to say, Arise, and take up thy bed, and walk?" It is, of course, easier to *say* the former, since the claim cannot be proved or disproved; in the second alternative, the proof or disproof will become immediately evident to all. The transform of this question could then read: "It is easy to say . . . Thy sins be forgiven thee; it is not easy to say, Take up thy bed and walk."

Gal. 3:2 "Received ye the Spirit by the works of the law, or by the hearing of faith?" This can be transformed into the two assertions, "You received the Spirit by the hearing of faith, not by the works of the law."

2. *A statement of incertitude*

Rhetorical questions are used not only to express certitude, but also to express incertitude in various forms, such as doubt, perplexity, and uncertainty; or contingency or deliberation. The first three represent a state of mind which may be entered after seeing evidence which does not lead to any firm conclusion. A contingency represents an event or state which is possible but not certain to occur or exist and which is the potential cause or reason for another event or state. Deliberation represents the process of thought by which the evidence is weighed and which will lead to some conclusion. Some examples of these different aspects of incertitude follow.

Doubt, or uncertainty, are expressed in Matthew 6:31, where Jesus focuses on such questions as "What shall we eat?", "What shall we drink?", and "Wherewithal shall we be clothed?" If such questions as these are raised in a family circle by one of the members, they would not represent real questions. Rather, in this context, they would communicate the idea of uncertainty, an uncertainty which very quickly passes into the worry which Jesus is forbidding in this passage. Such questions are equivalent to statements of the type, "We don't know what we will eat, or drink, or wear." A similar example is found in the second half of Matthew 13:56 where the people of Nazareth say concerning Jesus, "Whence then hath this man all these things?" This is a rhetorical question equivalent to "We do not know where he got all these things."

In 1 Corinthians 7:27, two questions are raised which transform into contingencies: "Art thou bound unto a wife? seek not to be loosed. Art thou loosed from a wife? seek not a wife." These questions are readily transformed into conditional statements: "If you are bound to a wife, do not seek to be loosed. If you are loosed from a wife, do not seek a wife."

A similar series of contingent questions is found in James 5:13, 14. "Is any among you afflicted? let him pray. Is any merry? let him sing psalms. Is any sick among you? let him call for the elders of the church . . . ." Again, these can be transformed in a straightforward manner into conditional statements. "If anyone among you is afflicted, let him pray. If anyone is merry, let him sing psalms. If anyone is sick among you, let him call . . . ."

Two examples from Luke's gospel will serve to illustrate deliberation. In Luke 12:17, the rich man asks himself, "What shall I do, because

I have no room where to bestow my fruits?" Similarly, in Luke 16:3, the unfaithful steward asks himself, "What shall I do?" Both were confronted with particular situations — a bumper crop in one case, the threat of dismissal in the other — and were thinking over what action they should take in the circumstances.

3. *A statement of evaluation or obligation*

Rhetorical questions are also used to make a statement of evaluation — whether of approval or disapproval. Judgments are made of the propriety, ethics, or value of an action, state, person, or thing, and such judgments are usually accompanied with emotional overtones and frequently imply an obligation on the part of the hearers to respond with appropriate action. It would seem that the question form is used as a more polite or less direct way to administer the rebuke or command.

It is worth noting that a wide range of emotional attitudes on the part of the speaker may accompany a rhetorical question of this type. These attitudes, however, are derived from the context of the question, and not from its actual form. However, many of the rhetorical questions which begin with "why" or "how say" reflect negatively upon the legitimacy of the purpose, reason for, or motive of another's actions or statements. Hence, they generally transform into statements using "ought" or "ought not," or the imperative forms "do" or "do not," and the negative statements are frequently referred to in commentaries as "prohibitions." Some examples of negative evaluation and obligation follow:

Matt. 7:3 "And why beholdest thou the mote that is in thy brother's eye, but considerest not the beam that is in thine own eye?" This is equivalent to a statement of the sort: "You ought not to behold . . . ." or "Do not behold . . . ."

Matt. 8:26 "Why are ye fearful?" With these words, Jesus was rebuking his disciples, so that the question means the same as "You shouldn't be afraid," or "Do not be afraid."

Mark 2:7a "Why doth this man thus speak blasphemies?" This is a self-directed question, and indicates a negative evaluation, rather than deliberation. They were definitely condemning what Jesus was saying. It is thus equivalent to: "This man ought not to speak blasphemies like this."

Mark 5:35 "Why troublest thou the Master any further?" This can be restated as "Don't trouble the Master any further," or, "It is not good for you to trouble the Master any further."

Mark 14:4 "Why was this waste of ointment made?" The preceding comment makes it clear that those who said this were angry, and were indignantly condemning the woman. Their rhetorical question is thus equivalent to: "This waste of the ointment ought not to have been made."

Luke 12:51 "Suppose ye that I am come to give peace on earth?" This could be transformed to "Don't think that I came to give peace on earth," or, "You are wrong if you suppose that I am come to give peace on earth." Two similar examples are found in the following chapter, Luke 13:2, 4, each using the Greek verb *dokeite* "do you suppose/think?"

John 18:21 "Why askest thou me?" This transforms to "Don't ask me," or "You shouldn't ask me." (Note that it is immediately followed by the corresponding affirmative command, "ask them which heard me . . . .")

1 Cor. 15:12 "Now if Christ be preached that he arose from the dead, how say some among you that there is no resurrection of the dead?" The "how say" in this verse is equivalent to the "why" of the previous examples, the whole being equivalent to "Since it is preached that Christ rose from the dead, those among you who say that there is no resurrection of the dead ought not to say that."

It should perhaps be emphasized again that these evaluative rhetorical questions differ from those which express certitude in that they express an opinion as to whether an action, or an attitude, is right or wrong, good or bad. Those questions which express certitude do not express judgment in any way — they simply make it clear the speaker is certain about his statement.

When the commentaries are studied with a view to getting help in interpreting rhetorical questions, it is usual to find that they focus on the emotional overtones carried by the question in its particular context. Such terms as "rebuke," "reprimand," "admonish," "scold," "upbraid," "rail," "berate," and "reprove" are used — but these all share the common component — negative evaluation. The finer overtones indicated by these terms are provided by the context.

Cases of positive evaluation are few. Some of these are punctuated as exclamations in texts and versions. For example, Luke 1:66 in the KJV is, "What manner of child shall this be!", but in the Greek texts of Nestle and the Bible Societies, it is punctuated as a question. Since the original was unpunctuated, the choice is a matter of interpretation. This exclamation or question of Luke 1:66 may be considered to be equivalent to, "This child will be very important."

The following are examples of positive commands often referred to as "entreaty," "exhortation," "obligation," or "necessity":

Mark 9:12 ". . . and how is it written of the Son of man, that he must suffer many things, and be set at nought?" This can be transformed into the positive command, "Consider, then, what is written . . . ," or "You should account for what is written . . . ."

Mark 12:35 "How say the scribes that Christ is the Son of David?" This can be transformed into a similar type of positive command, "Think further (or, "You should think further") about what the scribes say when they say that Christ is the Son of David."

In Matthew 17:25, a real question is introduced with the question, "What thinkest thou, Simon?" This introductory question may be interpreted as a generic real question followed by a specific real question, or as a rhetorical question, functioning as a command. If the latter view is taken, then it may be rendered by "Tell me your opinion, Simon." For two other parallel examples in Matthew's gospel, see 18:12 and 22:17.

4. *To introduce a new subject or a new aspect of a subject*

Rhetorical questions are also used to signal the start of a new subject, or some new aspect of the same subject — an inference, conclusion, explanation, or answer to a preceding discussion. If such questions have to be transformed into statements in the RL, then such statements will make use of such words as "to tell," "to consider," or "to conclude."

The following list gives examples where the verb "to tell" can be used in the transform:

Matt. 11:16 "But whereunto shall I liken this generation?" This can be recast in the form, "I will tell you what this generation is like." Cf. also Luke 7:31.

Matt. 12:48 "Who is my mother? and who are my brethren?" This can be rendered, "I will tell you who my mother is, . . ."

John 13:12 "Know ye what I have done to you?" Expressed as a statement, this becomes "I will tell you the meaning of what I have done to you."

Questions that can be transformed into statements using "to conclude" are such as those found frequently in the book of Romans. A number of times Paul asks the question, "What then?" (Gk. *ti oun*), or "What shall we say then?" (Gk. *ti oun eroumen*). These questions introduce conclusions, some of them Paul's own, some of them false conclusions, representing the view of those who distorted Paul's teaching. These latter are characteristically rejected with "God forbid." Paul's own conclusions can be expressed as statements of the sort, "We/I conclude, therefore , . . ." For example, the question in 8:31, "What shall we then say to these things?" can be restated as "We conclude, therefore, from these things that since God is for us . . . ." Or, again, in 9:30, "We conclude, then, that the Gentiles . . . ." A third example of this type is found in 11:7.

The conclusions that are rejected may be rendered as "We conclude, therefore, that . . . not . . . ." An example is found in Romans 6:1, which may be translated, "We conclude, therefore, that we are not to continue in sin that grace may abound." Other such examples are found in Romans 3:9, 6:15, 7:7, and 9:14.

Rhetorical questions introducing a new aspect of a subject are found in Romans 3:1. This chapter opens with the two questions, "What advantage then hath the Jew? or what profit is there of circumcision?" Chapter 2 discusses the question of the Jew from one angle — chapter 3 now discusses it from another, so these questions may be translated, "Let us consider whether the Jews have any advantage and whether there is any profit in circumcision."

These introductory questions lend themselves to several possible restatements, and the translator should choose that used in the RL in comparable contexts. For example, Matthew 11:16 contains the rhetorical question, "whereunto shall I liken this generation?" This question could be rendered in the form, "I will tell you what this generation is like," or "Let us consider what this generation is like."

Sometimes there is doubt as to whether such words as "to tell" are necessary, or whether a simple affirmation will do. For example, in Mark 13:2, Jesus asks, "Seest thou these great buildings?" This could be handled in the form, "I will tell you about these great buildings which you see," or more simply as, "Yes, look at those buildings!" using a form in the RL which is appropriate as an answer to the disciples' exclamation in v. 1. For similar uses of "to see" in questions, cf. Matthew 24:2 and Luke 7:44.

A similar type of choice is found in connection with Matthew 11:7. Jesus asks the crowds of people, "What went ye out into the wilderness to see?" This may be interpreted as equivalent to "I will tell you what you went into the wilderness to see," or as "You did not go into the wilderness to see a reed shaken by the wind."

The above discussion of the contrast between real and rhetorical questions, and the various functions they serve in the New Testament is summarized in chart 1.

CHART 1

QUESTIONS IN THE NEW TESTAMENT		
CLASSIFICATION		FUNCTION
R E A L	1	To elicit unknown information
	2	To elicit known information
R H E T O R I C A L	1	To express certitude — Negative / Affirmative / Both (obvious choice)
	2	To express incertitude, contingency, or deliberation
	3	To make an evaluation or a command — Affirmative or Negative
	4	To highlight and introduce a new subject or a new aspect of one

The connotative function of rhetorical questions

Rhetorical questions also have a connotative function that must be kept in mind by the translator. Although they convey basically the same information, the two English sentences, "While it remained, it was your own" and "While it remained, was it not your own?" are not fullly equivalent. The question form in itself has implications in English; it is more vivid, more focal, demands more attention. This is a regular feature of Greek and English rhetorical questions; whether they are conveying information, expressing doubt, or expressing an evaluation they also carry this component of vividness or focus.

As examples of rhetorical questions have been rephrased in nonquestion form in this chapter, it has generally been without reference to this feature of vividness, but it must be given consideration in translation.

THE TRANSLATION OF RHETORICAL QUESTIONS

When the rhetorical questions of the original are all rendered in the form of questions, wrong meaning is likely to be communicated. Two types of misinterpretations have been observed: (1) a rhetorical question is interpreted as a real one and (2) the meaning of a rhetorical question is misunderstood. These are illustrated below.

Rhetorical questions interpreted as real questions

When a rhetorical question is understood to be a real one, the reader often assumes that the speaker is seeking information which he does not know. When Jesus says in Mark 4:30, "Whereunto shall we liken the kingdom of God?" he uses a rhetorical question to introduce a new subject. The Cora Indian readers of Mexico understood this to mean that Jesus wanted the help of his hearers to decide what illustrations could best be used to teach what the kingdom of God is like. This same type of wrong meaning was also noted in the Trique language. The most puzzling problem for the language helper arose in translating 1 Corinthians 3:5. He remembered that Paul was the author of this letter and could not understand why he should pen the question: "Who then is Paul?" In Guarani of Brazil many rhetorical questions were also understood to be real. When Jesus asked his disciples, "Don't you understand?" it meant in this form, "I do not understand; tell me, do you?" instead of meaning "You ought to understand." In some languages, such as Chinantec of Mexico and Chuj of Guatemala, all questions using who, what, where, and when are understood only in an interrogative sense, i.e., as asking for information not known by the speaker unless he asks them in a classroom situation.

Rhetorical questions misunderstood

Even if a rhetorical question is correctly understood to be rhetorical, the reader may still be misled by the use of the question form. In Matthew 3:14 John the Baptist highlights the great importance of Jesus by using a question to indicate his reluctance to baptize Jesus. The question, "Do you come to me?", was understood to be an indication of exasperation on the part of John the Baptist who was busy baptizing many people; Jesus should have known how occupied he was and gone to someone else.

In one instance, the questions which Jesus used to show the importance of John the Baptist were answered wrongly. The questions are "What went ye out . . . to see? A reed shaken by the wind? . . . A man clothed in soft raiment?" In this context the emphasis that Jesus wants to communicate is definitely negative. However, the language helper, a mature Christian, answered both in the affirmative pointing out that John the Baptist had at one time doubted that Jesus was the Messiah and wore a garment of camel's hair, which must be quite rare and expensive.

Matthew 18:12 reads: "How think ye? if a man have an hundred sheep, and one of them be gone astray, doth he not leave the ninety and nine, and goeth into the mountains, and seeketh that which is gone astray?" The intention of this question is to indicate the reasonableness of leaving the ninety-nine to find the lost. When this verse was first translated into Chinantec of Mexico it was introduced as follows: "Do you think that if a man have a hundred sheep, etc." In this form the verse ridiculed the idea of leaving so many sheep to look for just one. Instead of leading one to an affirmative answer it led to a negative and wrong answer even though the question was recognized to be rhetorical.

Most languages have some questions which have been used so frequently in a rhetorical sense, that they become frozen forms which are used again and again in the identical form. In this form they no longer are interpreted as real questions. In English, for example, "Who do you think you are?" or "Just who do you think you are anyway?" may hardly be understood as asking for information. Sometimes these frozen question forms are used by the translator not realizing their special usage. "Do you know" is a frozen introduction to a full question which is used in some languages only to ridicule the person spoken to. When this form occurs in Scripture its meaning is: "You ought to know" or "Certainly you know" as in Romans 6:3, 16; 7:1; 1 Corinthians 6:19; 9:24. Thus a literal translation of the question will be understood to be a rhetorical question but the meaning communicated will be wrong.

Naturalness and the translation of rhetorical questions

If the rhetorical questions of the original are all rendered literally and even if they do not communicate wrong meaning, many of them will certainly be unnatural and probably introduce unnecessary ambiguities and obscurities. If rhetorical questions are to be rendered naturally in a translation of Scripture, it is important to know their frequency of usage in the RL, any restrictions as to discourse types, and the form which is not only correct but also generally used. Of course, from the previous discussion it is assumed that the basic communication functions of the rhetorical question of the RL will not be overlooked. These are not likely to be the same as the functions of the rhetorical questions used in the original.

Frequency of use of rhetorical questions is also important. When an RL uses rhetorical questions in one of the same functions as in the New Testament, the natural tendency in translation will be to translate all instances of that usage with a direct transfer of form, matching rhetorical questions in the original with RL rhetorical questions on a one-to-one basis. A thorough study of the RL, however, may indicate that, although rhetorical questions are used with the same function as in the original, they are not used with the same frequency.

The frequency with which a translator uses rhetorical questions in his translation will be affected by his ability to see contexts in which such questions would naturally be used even though a question may not occur at that point in the original. In one language, if rhetorical questions had been used only where they occur in the New Testament, their occurrence would have been much fewer in number. But since they were also used in other contexts, their number surpassed that of the New Testament and approximated the frequency found in native text materials. In Mark 2:19 the question is asked: "Can the children of the bridechamber fast, while the bridegroom is with them?" This question is followed by an answer. Then in v. 20 we are told when they will fast in the words: "and then shall they fast in those days." These words were framed in the form of a rhetorical question: "How thus can they eat and drink at that time?"

In a similar case, in Mark 15:29 the statement, "Ah, thou that destroyest the temple, and buildest it in three days" was rendered "You were going to tumble down the house of God said you? And you were going to build it again in three days said you?" Here, the questions indicate scorn and ridicule whereas statements would not have communicated this attitude. Thus, the question is not only more natural for this context but also more accurate.

In Matthew 13:54-56 a series of six rhetorical questions follow in close sequence. Such a series also occurs in other places in the New Testament, but in some languages it is never used and in others it is used only to indicate extreme anger. In the former it becomes necessary to change many of these questions to statements for stylistic reasons; in the latter to avoid ascribing a wrong attitude to those asking the questions.

The translator must also know whether rhetorical questions arise only in special contexts, since this may restrict their natural usage quite sharply. Among the Chols, the natural use of rhetorical questions has been largely confined to contexts of anger and grief. As Christianity has influenced the thinking of the people, they may have abandoned the use of rhetorical questions in contexts of grief. In past years, it was not uncommon to hear a grief-stricken wife following the bier of her husband crying out: "Why did you leave me? Why did you not harvest the corn? Why did you leave me with all our children? Why did you beat me?

Why did you not get firewood?" The translator needs to know the appropriate situations when rhetorical questions can be used.

In framing rhetorical questions the translator will probably be faced with what appears to be open choices. He may find that it is possible to use a question followed by an answer or a question without an answer or a direct statement. Given these possibilities he may choose to follow the form which occurs in the original so long as the correct sense is communicated, i.e., if a question is used, he uses a question and follows it with an answer only if one occurs in the original. This approach, while acceptable, does not give consideration to the natural form used in the RL. The choice of a natural form may be one of several possibilities depending on the function the rhetorical question fills, or it may be a single form characteristic of that particular language. For example, in one language rhetorical questions are changed to statements with a question following which seeks corroboration. Thus, "Was it not Moses who gave you the law?" (John 7:19) becomes: "It was Moses who gave you the law, was it not?" In other languages, such as Chontal of Oaxaca, it is typical to answer rhetorical questions, so most are rendered with an answer. Some examples from native texts include:

> "Like now, am I taken care of? We take care of ourselves.
> Is he generous? He certainly is selfish.
> How can you earn money like that? You can't."

The translator will also look for special linguistic signals that occur with RL rhetorical questions. These are important not only to assure that the form of the question is natural but also to communicate the right sense inasmuch as these special markers carry specific information.

While it is important to be aware of the use or non-use of rhetorical questions in the RL to ensure that the question form of the original is not carried over indiscriminately, it is equally important to be aware of the other discourse devices in the RL which correspond in function to the various uses of rhetorical questions in Greek. This is especially true of the effect of vividness, or focus, that the rhetorical question form brings out in Greek and English. The translator must be alert to use the corresponding devices in the RL for conveying the same effect.

In summary, the correct information and implication of both the real and rhetorical questions of Scripture must be communicated. When this is done, using the natural forms for each and with the same frequency for the latter, then the translator will be faithful to the original both in meaning and in dynamics.

CHAPTER 16

The Genitive Construction

PROBLEMS ASSOCIATED WITH THE GENITIVE CONSTRUCTION

The genitive case in Greek enters into a number of grammatical constructions, but the one that will be discussed here consists of two nominals, such as a noun and a noun, a noun and a pronoun, or a noun and an adjective, linked by the fact that one of the two nominals is in the genitive case. This is usually translated into English with a prepositional phrase using "of" (e.g., gospel of God, one of the days), or a possessive noun or pronoun (e.g., God's love, his mother). This construction, referred to by Blass-Debrunner as the "Adnominal Genitive" (1961, p. 89), has a wide variety of uses, and is very common. One Greek scholar says that the genitive is "immensely versatile and hard-worked" (Moule, 1960, p. 37). A count made on the four shortest books in the New Testament (Philemon, 2 John, 3 John, and Jude) and on four random chapters gave a total of some 150 examples of the genitive construction in 186 verses. While the frequency is probably lower in the historical books — although Frantz (1965, p. 209) suggests that genitives are particularly frequent in Luke's writings — a quick survey would indicate the frequency may well be higher than once per verse in Paul's Epistles. It seems reasonable to assume, therefore, that the translator is likely to encounter a genitive phrase of this type about twice in every three verses, if not more often.

Since each of the standard grammars provides its own analysis of the range of functions served by this particular construction, it might be thought the various senses borne by the genitive constitute a well-mapped territory, and this would be one of the areas where the translator could tread with relative confidence. To some extent this is so, but it is still possible for a translator to feel rather at sea when interpreting a genitive. There are a number of reasons contributing to this uncertainty.[1]

(1) The variety of meanings carried by the genitive construction together with the different analyses offered by grammarians, often using different classificatory labels, is confusing. Further, the commentaries give different interpretations of the same genitive. All of this tends to convey the impression that the genitive is a complicated construction semantically and may only really be understood by expert Greek scholars.

(2) One particular complication is the fact that the same genitive construction may have opposite meanings in different contexts. The phrase, "the love of God," to take the example usually quoted, can mean either "you love God" or "God loves you." Also, closely similar genitive constructions may have different senses. Consider the three examples, "the gospel of Jesus Christ" (Mark 1:1), "the gospel of God" (Rom. 1:1), and "the gospel of me"[2] (Rom. 2:16). The first means "the gospel *about* Jesus Christ," the second means "the gospel *which comes from* God," and the third means "the gospel *which* I *preach*." All have "gospel" for the first form, and the second form in each case refers to a living being, yet in each case the genitive construction signals a different semantic relationship between the pair of forms that are linked.

(3) Further, in spite of all the analysis of the genitive construction that has been undertaken, the translator may find, on looking in a grammar or commentary, that it simply says the two forms concerned are "associated" or "closely connected." He may also find some genitives not discussed at all. So the translator, who has to translate every verse, and handle every genitive construction, finds complex analysis on the one hand, and lack of analysis on the other.

(4) The fourth reason is one that does not seem to have been taken into serious consideration by studies of the genitive construction. Since in most cases two nouns are involved in this construction, it is not at all uncommon to find one or both of these nouns is an abstract noun.[3] This means the translator is facing a doubly complex problem — the function of the abstract noun(s), and the function of the genitival relationship. Also, a significant percentage of the genitive constructions found in the New Testament are associated with figures of speech — one of the nouns may be figurative, such as "light," or "bowels," or "way"; or one of the nouns may be involved in a figure in addition to its being

[1] See also the four reasons which "make it difficult for the student to clearly grasp and retain the significance of the genitive," given in Frantz (1965, pp. 202, 203).

[2] In quoting genitives, a literal translation of the Greek will be given, using "of" to signal the genitive case. The only adjustment that will be made is to use, or omit, the article so that it conforms to English usage. For example, Greek often uses the definite article with proper names and titles, such as "God" and "Jesus Christ," but it will not be translated by "the" in such contexts.

[3] See chapter 14 for a discussion of abstract nouns.

part of the genitive construction. An example of this is found in Acts 14:27, "he had opened the door of faith" in which "opened the door" is an idiom, but "door" is connected with "faith" (itself an abstract noun, in this case) by the genitive relationship. To ignore such factors could lead to peculiar analyses. In Colossians 1:18, Paul writes of Christ, "he is the head of the body." If the metaphorical use of both "head" and "body" is ignored, then the genitive would signal the relationship that the head is *part of* the body. But Christ is not part of the Church, so the metaphors have to be considered first, and then the significance of the genitive may be studied within the metaphorical setting.

A serious attempt, therefore, is made in this chapter to present an approach to the study of genitives which the translator can use for himself. Until a thorough and exhaustive study of the thousands of genitive constructions found in the New Testament is made available to the translator,[4] it is obviously essential that he have available to him some systematic method. Such a method would enable him to derive the sense of a given genitive for himself or to confirm the sense or choose from the senses given by commentators. The method presented in this chapter rests on the basic assumption that for the translator, the most useful way of identifying the actual sense of a given genitive is to restate its meaning by means of one or more propositions.[5] The purpose of propositions and propositional displays of books of the Bible is to do for a book what is proposed here for genitives — to state the meaning clearly and unambiguously using English, and matching semantic and grammatical classes.

The Genitive Construction Restated as a State Proposition

State propositions are defined in chapter 17 as propositions which communicate a relation rather than an event. Certain genitive constructions may be restated in the form of a State proposition. When this is the case, the two nominals usually represent Things, though there is a less common form in which an Abstraction and a Thing are represented.

The relations between two Things which can be signaled by the genitive construction are quite numerous. There is no claim that the relations identified in the following pages comprise an exhaustive list but they do give some indication of the range of meanings this particular type of genitive construction can signal.

For convenience in referring to the examples and for purposes of classification, the nominal which is not in the genitive case will be labeled A, and the one which is will be labeled B. The typical genitive construction is thus *A of B*, where "of" is used to represent the genitive

4 This, it would seem, would be an appropriate subject for a dissertation, which could then be popularized and made available to translators, rendering them an invaluable service.

5 A discussion of propositions and the relations between them is taken up in the next chapters.

case.[6] For each example, a translation in the form of A of B will be given by the authors. In addition, a restatement of the meaning of the genitive construction is given avoiding the use of "of" whenever possible so that the meaning is restated unambiguously.

1. POSSESSION *A is possessed by B*[7]

Matt. 26:51	"the sword of him"	his sword
Mark 10:50	"the garment of him"	his garment
Acts 8:28	"the chariot of him"	his chariot
Acts 21:8	"the house of Philip"	Philip's house

The label POSSESSION is applied only to the possession of things, such as "sword" and "house," but not to people, as in "a servant of God."

2. PART-WHOLE *A is part of B, the whole*

This classification includes three subtypes: (1) constituent-whole, (2) quantitative part-whole, and (3) attribute-whole.

Constituent-whole

In this subgroup, A represents a member part of B, the whole. B may be a house, with A some part, such as the roof or a door; or B can be the body, and A an arm or a leg, etc. In any case, A is one of the parts which goes to make up B.

Luke 13:19	"the branches of it [a tree]"	its branches
James 3:3	"the mouths of horses"	horses' mouths
James 3:6	"the members of us"	our (body) parts
Jude 9	"the body of Moses"	Moses' body
Jude 16	"the mouth of them"	their mouths
Rev. 12:14	"the two wings of the eagle"	the eagle's two wings

Quantitative part-whole

In this case, A is a part, measured quantitatively, of B, the whole. Note that the quantitative relationship may be definite, such as "a third" or indefinite, such as "some of," and that A is an Abstraction, not a Thing.

| Mark 6:23 | "half of the kingdom"[8] | no restatement |

[6] The usual order in Greek syntax is A *of* B, but occasionally the order *of* B, A is found. Where a genitive is cited which occurs in this nontypical order, this will be asterisked; but the English rendition will be given in the order A *of* B as this is easier to understand, and the syntactic variations do not affect the semantic relationship.

[7] This relation could be summarized as "A belongs to B," but "belongs to" is ambiguous in English, as it may indicate "possessed by," or "is a member of," depending on the context. In the latter case, examples would be "he belongs to the Republican party, or " 'dog' belongs to the class of animals."

[8] Sometimes genitives that are quoted are actually part of a concatenation of genitives, as in this case; the full construction is "half of the kingdom of me." Treating part of a concatenation of genitives has been done only when the relation being considered is unaffected. The matter of concatenation of genitives is discussed in Appendix D.

Luke 18:11	"the others/rest (Gk. *hoi loi-poi*) of men"	"	"
Luke 20:1	"one of the days"	"	"
Acts 21:26	"each one of them"	"	"
Rev. 8:7	"a third of the land"	"	"
	"a third of the trees"	"	"

Occasionally, part A is omitted, leaving only part B. An example of this is found in Acts 21:16 "There went with us also certain of the disciples." In the Greek, there is no word corresponding to "certain"; it is simply "of the disciples." This is equivalent to the indefinite quantity "some of."

Attribute-whole

Unlike the previous examples, either A or B may be the Abstraction. In either case, the Abstraction represents some characteristic or attribute of the whole, not an actual part. In the first group of examples, as with the previous ones, A is an Abstraction and B is the whole.

Rom. 2:4	"the goodness of God"	God is good
Rom. 3:5	"the unrighteousness of us"	we are unrighteous
Rev. 21:16	"the length and the breadth and the height of it (are equal)"	it is equally long and broad and high

In the second group of examples, B is the Abstraction, and A is the whole.

Luke 18:6	"a judge of unrighteousness"	an unrighteous judge
1 Pet. 5:4	"a crown of glory"	a glorious crown
2 Pet. 2:4	"pits of gloom"	gloomy pits

The difference between these two groups of examples can be described as "focus." Although there are occasional exceptions, normally the element A of the genitive construction is in focus, compared to the element B. Hence, in the first group of examples, it is the attribute that is being focused on rather than the possessor of the attribute. In the second group of examples, it is the person or thing that is highlighted. This possibility of having focus on either side of a relation does not apply to all the relations. In fact, attribute-whole is the first relation discussed so far exhibiting this feature; others will be noted later. It should be noted the unambiguous English rendition on the right is not always able to keep the focus because of restrictions on word order in English. Thus "God is good" above does not focus especially on the attribute.

3. DEGREE *A indicates the degree of B*

Two special genitive constructions, which are idiomatic, are similar to the Attribute-whole examples. However, here the whole is implied and B is an attribute which is intensified. These are the genitives "full of" and "riches of." Note that since A is either "full" or "riches," and B is the Abstraction, the person referred to is carried by the immediate context, not in the genitive construction itself.

Matt. 23:28	"full of hypocrisy and iniquity"	(you) are very hypocritical and wicked
Rom. 2:4	"the riches of the kindness . . . and the patience (of him)"	(he) is very kind . . . and patient
Rom. 15:14	"full of goodness"	(you) are very good

4. KINSHIP *A and B are related by kinship*

Matt. 20:30	"Son of David"	He is David's descendant[9]
Matt. 26:63	"the Son of God"	God's Son
Luke 3:2	"son of Zechariah"	Zechariah's son
Eph. 1:3	"Father of the Lord Jesus Christ"	the Lord Jesus Christ's Father
Jude 1	"brother of James"	James' brother

In some cases, however, the kinship term is omitted in the Greek, and two proper names are brought into a genitival relationship. In such cases, versions and commentaries will fill in the ellipsis. In the examples, the kinship term that has to be supplied is italicized.

Mark 15:47	"Mary of Joses"	Mary, Joses' *mother*
Luke 6:16	"Judas of James"	Judas, James' *son*
John 19:25	"Mary of Clopas"	Mary, Clopas' *wife*

5. ROLE *A and B are related by role*

In this relation, the two Things are nearly always people, who stand in some relationship to each other, apart from that of kinship.

Matt. 15:31	"God of Israel"	Israel's God
Matt. 26:51	"servant of the high priest"	the high priest's servant
Col. 1:3	"The Lord of us"	our Lord[10]

The role term may be omitted in Greek, in which case the context, along with versions and commentaries, may help to fill in the ellipsis. In the following examples, the term supplied is italicized.

1 Cor. 1:12	"I of Apollos"	I, Apollos' *follower*
Gal. 5:24	"they of Christ"	they, Christ's *disciples*

[9] This could perhaps be handled as figurative, since "son" here means not his actual son but a lineal descendant, but it seems better to regard "descendant" as a secondary rather than a figurative sense of "son." In either case, the genitive still has the meaning of a kinship relation.

[10] The relation of role could be treated as a type of Event proposition, with the Event implicit (see the appropriate section of this chapter for a fuller discussion). Words such as "God," "servant," and "Lord," when brought into a role relation with people, imply certain activities. Thus "God of Israel" could be restated as "the God whom Israel *worships*"; "servant of the high priest," as "one who *serves* the high priest"; and "the Lord of us," as "the One who *rules over* us." They are classed here under ROLE as it is felt that the primary focus of the genitive construction is the role relation, but this is not to deny the presence of implicit Events.

The prefix *sun-* in Greek frequently indicates a shared role. In this case, however, the other person with whom the role relationship is sustained, is not stated explicitly in the genitive construction itself. *Sun-* is translated "fellow-" in the examples which follow:

Eph. 2:19	"fellow citizens of the saints"	citizens together with the saints
Phm. 1	"fellow worker of us"	worker together with us
Phm. 23	"fellow prisoner of me"	prisoner together with me

In 1 Corinthians 10:20, Paul uses the genitive construction "partners of the demons." This may be interpreted as predicating a type of role relationship, one that could be described as a "mutual role." That is to say, there was a danger the Corinthian Christians and the demons would be in partnership, or fellowship, with one another. This, then, would be a particular type of role relation in which the parties have a mutual interaction.

6. LOCATION A *is located in B*

B is usually the name of an area, such as a province or region, while A is a location in that area.

Matt. 2:1	"Bethlehem of Judea"	Bethlehem *which is in* Judea
Matt. 3:1	"the wilderness of Judea"	the wilderness *which is in* Judea
Matt. 21:11	"Nazareth of Galilee"	Nazareth *which is in* Galilee
Luke 1:39	"a city of Judah"	a city *which is in* Judah
Acts 22:3	"Tarsus of Cilicia"	Tarsus *which is in* Cilicia

A special case of LOCATION occurs when A refers to a body of people, and B therefore identifies where they live.

Acts 8:9	"the nation of Samaria"	the people *who are in* Samaria

7. IDENTIFICATION A *is identified by B*

The relation of identification occurs in two forms. In one, the identification is simply by naming: A is a general term, and B gives a name to it. In the other, A is a location identified, not by name, but by the people who are found there.[11]

---

[11] There are a number of expressions in English translations which look as if they belong to this group. The most common of these is "Jesus of Nazareth" (as in Mark 1:24, 10:47, etc.), but there are others such as "Joseph of Arimathea" (Mark 15:43), and "Lucius of Cyrene" (Acts 13:1). However, these are not genitive constructions in the Greek. They are usually adjectival in form, as in Mark 1:24 "Jesus Nazarene." Occasionally, the preposition *apo* "from" is used, as in Mark 15:43 which is literally "Joseph the from Arimathea."

Type 1

Mark 1:28	"the region of Galilee"	the region *which is called* Galilee
Luke 24:49	"the city of Jerusalem"	the city *which is called* Jerusalem
John 12:3	"ointment of spikenard"	ointment *which is called* spikenard
Acts 21:38	"the four thousand men of the Assassins"	the four thousand men *who were called* Assassins

Type 2

Matt. 8:28	"the country of the Gadarenes"	the country *where* the Gadarenes *lived*
Matt. 10:5	"a city of Samaritans"	a city *where* Samaritans *lived*

8. CONTENTS *A contains B*

A is a container of some sort, and B specifies the contents.

Matt. 10:42	"a cup of cold water"	a cup *which contains* cold water
John 21:8	"a net of fishes"	a net *which contained* fish

9. MEASUREMENT *A measures B*

A is some type of measurement, and B is the substance that is measured.

Luke 13:21	"three measures (Gk. *sata*) of meal"	no restatement
Luke 16:7	"a hundred measures (Gk. *koroi*) of wheat"	no restatement
Rev. 6:6	"a measure (Gk. *choinix*) of wheat"	no restatement

10. REFERENCE *A is about B*

A is a type of message or communication, and B is a central topic of that communication.

Mark 1:1	"the gospel of Jesus Christ"	the gospel *which is about* Jesus Christ
Acts 13:44	"the word of God"	the message *which is about* God
Gal. 3:10	"the book of the law"	the book *which is about* the law
Col. 4:3	"the mystery of Christ"	the mystery *which is about* Christ

11. SUBSTANCE *A consists of B*

A is some Thing, and B describes what A consists of. B may give some of the constituents of A or all of them. This relation is thus similar to the PART-WHOLE relation, but it is in the reverse order and has a different significance.

Col. 1:22	"the body of the flesh"	physical body
Rev. 12:1	"a crown of twelve stars"	a crown consisting of twelve stars
Rev. 18:12	"merchandise of gold and of silver . . ."	merchandise consisting of gold, silver . . .[12]

THE GENITIVE CONSTRUCTION RESTATED AS AN EVENT PROPOSITION

Event propositions, represented by a genitive construction, consist of an Event linked by different relations to Things or Abstractions. Some of the relations between an Event and a Thing which have been distinguished are Agent (the participant who does the action), Experiencer (the participant who undergoes the action), Affected (the thing to which an action is done), Recipient (the participant who receives some thing), and Instrument (the thing by means of which the action is achieved).[12] In addition to these, there are the relations of Time, Place, Manner, and Degree.

Genitive constructions which can be restated in the form of an Event proposition can be considered in two groups. In the first of these, one of the nominals in the genitive construction is an abstract noun[13] representing an Event semantically. In this sense, there is an explicit Event signaled by the genitive construction. In the other group, there is no abstract noun representing an Event, so the Event is only carried implicitly and has to be supplied from the immediate context.

A restatement of the meaning of the genitive construction in the form of a proposition is provided with each example. Some of the genitives being considered are part of a concatenation of genitives and where the further genitives are relevant, they are given in parentheses with the literal translation of the genitive, and the information they provide is expressed in the propositional restatement.

The Event is explicit

In genitive constructions of this type, the nominal which does not represent the Event represents some Thing or Abstraction related to the

---

[12] For a discussion of relations of this type, see Fillmore (1968a). The list presented above is not intended to be exhaustive, nor are the definitions precise. The list is given here to provide a framework for the discussion of the meaning conveyed by certain types of genitive construction. Although the theory of the internal semantic structure of Event propositions is not yet fully developed, the use of the semantic relations between an Event and a Thing to provide a framework for this discussion is in line with the distinction drawn in the next chapter between semantic structure and grammatical structure.

[13] Abstract nouns are discussed in more detail in chapter 14.

Event by one of the relations discussed above. If it represents a Thing, then that Thing may function as Agent, Experiencer, etc. If it is an Abstraction, it may be related adverbially to the Event, or modify an implied Thing. The discussion which follows will be presented within the general framework of relations to the Event, taking up each relation in turn.

1. AGENT *B does A*

In the grammars of Greek, the term "Subjective" is used for this type of genitive construction, so it is used here for convenience, though it is really a grammatical rather than a semantic term. In the examples, B indicates the Agent of the Event symbolized by A.

Acts 1:22	"the baptism of John"	John baptized (people)
Acts 6:1	"a murmuring of the Hellenists"	the Hellenists murmured
Rom. 2:3	"the judgment of God"	God will judge (people)
1 Cor. 2:5	"the faith of you (pl.)"	you believe/trust
2 Cor. 8:5	"the will of God"	God willed/wished
Eph. 2:8	"the gift of God"	God gave (it to you)
Col. 1:13	"the kingdom of the Son"	the Son rules (people)
Phm. 4	"the prayers of me"	I pray
	"the obedience of you (sg.)"	you will obey
3 John 12	"the witness of us"	we bear witness
Jude 11	"the error of Balaam"	Balaam erred
	"the rebellion of Korah"	Korah rebelled

There are a number of genitives which show the same semantic relation as the above examples, but in which B represents the Event, and A the Agent or the Affected. It seems likely that in this less common order, the focus falls on the Agent; whereas in the examples discussed above it falls on the Event. However, there also seems to be some degree of emphasis or intensification of the Event. In these two examples, the subject is the Agent.

2 Cor. 13:11	"the God of love"	the God (who) loves (you)
2 Thess. 2:3	"the man of the sin"	the man (who) sins

One special form of this type of genitive occurs when the noun A is "son(s)." An example of this is found in Ephesians 2:2 and 5:6, where the expression "sons of disobedience" is used. This is equivalent to the restatement "they always disobey." (See the next section for further examples using this idiom, and carrying the component of certainty.)

2. EXPERIENCER *A happens to B*

Occasionally, B is not the Agent of the Event A, but rather the Affected or the Experiencer.

Matt. 1:18	"the birth of Jesus Christ"* (see footnote 6)	(Mary) gave birth to Jesus Christ[14]
John 11:13	"the death of him"	he died
Acts 2:38	"the gift of the Holy Spirit"	(God) will give the Holy Spirit (to you)
Acts 2:42	"the breaking of bread"	(they) broke bread
1 John 2:15	"the love of the Father"	(he) loves the Father
Jude 3	"the salvation of us"	(God) has saved us

Sometimes B is not an Agent, but a thing. In that case, the relationship is not one of an Experiencer but rather that of a thing that is affected. For example, in Matthew 7:27, "the fall of it," B is the Affected and A represents the Event.

The reverse form of the above occurs when B happens to A. A particular form of this reversal occurs in connection with the idiomatic expressions "sons of" and "children of." In such cases, "sons of" or "children of" indicates the persons to whom the action is done, and B indicates the Event. In addition, this idiomatic form often adds a component of certainty which is illustrated in the second and fourth examples.

Matt. 13:38	"the sons of the kingdom"	those who are ruled (by God)
John 17:12	"the son of destruction"	one who will surely be destroyed
Rom. 7:24	"the body of the death"	the body (which) will/must die
Eph. 2:3	"children of wrath"	those with whom (God) is surely angry

3. REGARD A *is done with regard to B*

The distinction between this relation and the preceding one is that, in this relation, B does not actually undergo the Event A. For example, John 7:13 states that the people feared their leaders. The leaders did not directly experience the fear; rather, it was directed toward them. It may have affected what they did, they may have been pleased by it, but they did not undergo it in a direct sense.

Matt. 12:31	"the blasphemy of the Spirit"*	(if you) blaspheme the Spirit
Luke 6:12	"the prayer of God"	(he) prayed to God
John 7:13	"the fear of the Jews"	(they) feared the Jews
Rom. 3:22	"faith of Jesus Christ"	(all who) believe in/trust Jesus Christ
Col. 1:10	"the knowledge of God"	(you may) know God

[14] The English reader will probably tend to think of "Jesus Christ" as the doer of A because of the more usual English form "Jesus Christ was born." But this is a passive form, and from the real-world standpoint, it is the mother who is the doer of the action, the baby being the one to whom the action is done.

In the Greek grammars, both of the above relations are covered by the general term, "Objective," and one of the issues that is always emphasized in connection with Subjective and Objective genitives is that there is formal ambiguity between them. That is to say, since the original form is the same — A of B, where A is an abstract noun representing an Event — ambiguity can arise as to whether a given genitive is to be understood as Subjective or Objective.

A good illustration of this possible double sense is provided by the genitive, "the love of God." This is used eleven times in the New Testament. Although there is hardly one reference among these eleven where versions and commentators are in complete agreement, yet there is a marked preponderance of opinion in each case. Five are regarded as Subjective, i.e., God's love to man; these are Romans 5:5, 8:39, 2 Corinthians 13:14; 1 John 4:9; and Jude 21. The other six are treated as Objective, i.e., man's love to God; these are Luke 11:42; John 5:42; 2 Thessalonians 3:5; 1 John 2:5, 3:17, 5:3. Hence, although it is true that genitives of this sort are potentially ambiguous, yet in many contexts, the ambiguity can be resolved.

4. CONTENT *B is the content of A*

Another form of the genitive, also often referred to as an "objective" genitive, occurs when B represents an Abstraction, rather than a Thing. In such cases, B is attributive, not to A, but to the implicit Thing, which is usually very generic, and the Thing plus its attribution constitute the content of A.

2 Thess. 2:10	"the love of the truth"	(they) love *that which is* true
Phm. 6	"knowledge of all the good"	(they/you) know all *that which is* good

5. TIME *One indicates the time of the other*

In this type of genitive construction, either A or B may indicate the time, and the other noun represents the Event which takes place at that time. In both cases, the noun signaling the time is "day" or "days." When A represents the Event, the Event is in focus; when B represents the Event, the time is brought to attention.

Examples where B represents the time:

Jude 6	"judgment of the great day"	(God) will judge (people) on that great day
Rev. 16:14	"battle of the great day"	(they will) fight on that great day

Examples where A represents the time:

Luke 21:22	"days of vengeance"	when (God) will avenge
Eph. 4:30	"day of redemption"	when (God) will redeem (you)

| 1 John 4:17 | "the day of the judgment" | when (God) will judge (men) |
| Rev. 11:6 | "the days of the prophesying (of them)" | while they are prophesying |

6. MANNER *One describes how the other took place*

| Luke 4:22 | "the words of the grace" | (he) spoke graciously |
| Jude 15 | "the deeds of ungodliness (of them)" | they had acted in an ungodly manner |

This relation can also occur with the reverse focus, that is, with the focus on the Abstraction rather than the Event.

| 1 Cor. 1:17 | "a wisdom of word" | (I) spoke cleverly |

7. DEGREE *A indicates the degree of B*

The relation of degree seems to be expressed only by certain idioms. In each case, B represents the Event and A is an idiomatic form which expresses the Abstraction of intensity of degree.

Acts 6:5	"full of faith"	(he) trusted/believed in (Jesus) very much
Acts 9:36	"full of good works"	(she) did very many good works
Rom. 15:29	"the fulness of the blessing (of Christ)"	Christ will bless (me) very much
2 Pet. 2:14	"(eyes) full of adultery"	(they want to) commit adultery very much

The Event is implicit

When the Event is signaled by neither A nor B, then this leaves both A and B free to stand in one of the possible relations to the Event. Deciding what these relations are, however, is more difficult when the Event to which they are related is only implicit. Nevertheless, it is possible to distinguish different types of this form of genitive construction. (In the examples, the implicit Event is italicized.)

1. GOAL *B does the implicit Event to A*

In these examples, B is the Agent, and A is the thing to which the implicit Event was done.

Luke 13:1	"the sacrifices of them"	the sacrifices which they *were offering* (to God)
Acts 13:39	"the law of Moses"	the law which Moses *wrote*
Gal. 3:15	"a will of man"	a will which a man *made*

2. MANNER *B does the implicit Event in the manner A*

A is an abstract noun representing an Abstraction which gives the manner in which B does the Event.

Matt. 15:6	"traditions of you"	you *act* traditionally (i.e., in a manner dictated by tradition)
Acts 21:35	"the violence of the crowd"	the crowd was *acting* violently
Rom. 6:4	"the glory of the Father"	the Father *acted* gloriously

3. MANNER *The implicit Event is done in the manner A with regard to B*

Rom. 10:2	"a zeal of God"	(they) *act* zealously toward God

4. TIME *B does the implicit Event at the time A*

A may also be the fixed expression "the days of . . ." in which case A gives the time at which B did the implicit Event. According to the sense of B, different implicit Events have to be supplied.

Matt. 2:1 (& Luke 1:5)	"in the days of Herod the king"	when Herod the king *was ruling*
Matt. 11:12	"from the days of John the Baptist"	since John the Baptist *was baptizing*
Matt. 23:30	"in the days of the fathers of us"	when our ancestors/ forefathers *lived*
Matt. 24:37	"the days of Noah"	when Noah *lived*
Luke 17:26	"the days of the Son of man"	when the Son of man *returns*
Acts 5:37	"in the days of the census"	when the census was *held/taken*

5. RECIPIENT *The implicit Event is done to the Thing A, and B is the recipient of A*

Matt. 15:26	"the bread of the children"	the bread which *is to be given* to the children
Matt. 16:9	"the five loaves of the five thousand"	the five loaves which *were given* to the five thousand
Mark 12:17	"the things of Caesar"	the things which *should be given* to Caesar
	"the things of God"	the things which *should be given* to God

6. AGENT *One causes the state represented by the other*

A rather special form of Event proposition is indicated by this description. In this type, one of the nominals refers to a being who brings about some state, such as peace or joy. Put more technically, there is an embedded State proposition in the Event proposition. In the first two examples, A is the causer of the state B; in the last one, the focus is reversed with attention drawn to the state.

Luke 13:11	"a spirit of infirmity"	a spirit who *causes* (people) *to be* sick
Phil. 4:9	"the God of peace"	God who *causes* (you) *to be* peaceful
Phil. 4:7	"the peace of God"	the peace(ful *state*) which God *causes*

THE GENITIVE CONSTRUCTION RESTATED AS TWO PROPOSITIONS

This section may be subdivided on the same general basis as the previous one. If a genitive construction consists of two abstract nouns, both of which represent Events, then each of these can be restated as an Event proposition, and the construction as a whole is restated in the form of two propositions. In this case, then the Events are explicit. There are other genitive constructions, however, where only one of the Events is explicit and the other implicit. These seem to be rather less common, as genitive constructions of this type may usually be restated in the form of a single proposition, rather than two. There also seem to be a few examples in which neither Event is explicit.[15]

Both Events are explicit

When two propositions are involved, it is not only necessary to elucidate the propositions themselves, but also the relation between them.[16] To do this is by no means simple since the genitive construction itself gives only one formal clue, and that is that the nominal A is normally the one in focus, so the relation to A of the proposition represented by B should be such that A is focal and B is not. However, it would seem that contextual considerations can occasionally override this general factor. The examples are grouped according to the relation posited between the two propositions, and the words in the restatement that signal the relation are italicized.

15 It will be noted that it is assumed that the two propositions are both Event propositions, either explicitly or implicitly. This is because no unambiguous examples involving State propositions have been found, as yet, but there is no *a priori* reason why such should not be found when a more exhaustive analysis of the genitive is undertaken.

16 A system of relations between propositions is discussed in detail in chapter 18, and the presentation at this point draws on that chapter.

1. Sequence

Event B follows Event A in time.

John 5:29	"a resurrection of life"	(people) will rise *and then* (they) will live
	"a resurrection of judgment"	(people) will rise *and then* (they) will be judged (by God)[17]
James 1:25	"a hearer of forgetfulness"	(he) hears *and then* (he) forgets

2. Result-Reason

Event B gives the reason why Event A takes place.

1 Thess. 1:3	"the work of faith"	(you) work *because* (you) believe (in God/Christ)
	"the labor of love"	(you) labor *because* (you) love (God/Christ)
	"the perseverance of hope"	(you) persevere *because* (you) hope (for glory)
1 Pet. 5:14	"a kiss of love"	(you) kiss each other *because* (you) love each other

3. Content

The proposition represented by the noun B is the content of the Event represented by A.

Acts 1:22	"a witness of the resurrection (of him)"	(he) will testify *that* he arose
Acts 2:38	"the forgiveness of sins (of you)"	(God) will forgive *that* you have sinned
Col. 1:9	"the knowledge of the will (of him)"	(you) may know *what* he wills/wants

A further example of the relation of Content is found in Galatians 3:2, "a hearing of faith." In this example, however, the content is signaled by A not by B. The normal focus of the genitive construction is considered to be reversed for two reasons. One is that in the immediate context, which is "Received ye the Spirit by the works of the law, or by the hearing of faith?", a sharp distinction is being drawn between "works"

---

[17] An alternative interpretation of the relation signaled by these two parallel genitives would be that of *purpose*: "(people) will rise *in order to* live" and "(people) will rise *in order to* be judged (by God)." In this case, the time sequence is out of focus and the cause-effect relation is in focus.

and "faith"; the other is that it would not be possible in Greek to give this genitive in the reverse order, i.e., "faith of hearing," which would have preserved the focus on "faith." A propositional restatement would be "(you) believed *what* (you) heard."

4. *Generic-Specific*

Event B is a more specific statement of Event A which is generic.

Rom. 4:11   "a sign of circumcision"   he was marked, *that is*, he was circumcised

5. *Circumstance*

B states the circumstances of the Event A.

Jude 9   "a judgment of reviling"   (he) judged (him) *and at the same time* (he) reviled (him)

Only one Event is explicit

Not too many examples of this type of genitive construction have been investigated as yet. One example, however, is provided by Galatians 2:16, "the works of the law." "Works" is an abstract noun representing the Event "to do" or "to obey." The "law" is an elliptic way of referring to what is written in the law, or what God commanded in the law, so a restatement might be in the form, "(you) did what was written in the law" or "(you) did what God commanded in the law" in which the implied Event "was written" or "commanded" has to be supplied. The relation is one of content, that is to say, B gives the content of Event A. A further example is found in Jude 7, "punishment of eternal fire." "Punishment" is an abstract noun representing the Event "to punish." "Eternal fire" might be considered simply a location, but it is much more likely there is an implicit Event "to place" or "to put" or "to assign" giving the propositional equivalent "(God) will punish (them) by assigning (them) to eternal fire." The relation would be one of result-means.

Second Peter 2:1, "heresies of destruction." "Heresies" is semantically equivalent to the Abstraction "falsely," requiring the implied Event "they teach." The relation would seem to be means-result, i.e., by means of teaching falsely, they destroy others.

No explicit Events

Again, not many examples of this type of genitive construction have been found as yet. One example which fits into this category is Acts 1:18, where it says that Judas bought a field with "a reward of wickedness." "Reward" is understood to be a Thing here, referring to the money he received, since he bought a field with it. "Wickedness" is an abstract noun representing the Abstraction "wickedly." Hence, it is necessary to supply two Events to give "he *received* a reward because he *acted* wickedly." The relation is a result-reason one.

CONCLUSION

It has already been pointed out that the genitive construction in Greek is difficult for the translator because, not only is it very frequent, but it can also signal many different meanings. Put in other words, the genitive is a grammatical construction which is markedly skewed relative to the semantic structure. This chapter has not attempted to present an exhaustive analysis of all the semantic structures and relations the genitive construction can signal, but it has attempted to give the translator some indication of the range of meaning signaled by this construction. It has also sought to convey some idea of how to work the meaning out when it is not explained in the grammars or commentaries, or when alternative meanings are given and a choice has to be made. Even when the meaning has been elucidated, the translator still has to find a way to express that meaning accurately and naturally in the RL. Since most languages have a grammatical construction considered equivalent to the genitive construction, it is particularly important that the translator be familiar with the range of meaning carried by the equivalent RL construction and so avoid the pitfall of assuming the original and the RL constructions match at every point. This is very unlikely, and other constructions will be needed to convey the full range of meanings signaled by the Greek genitive.

CHAPTER 17

Propositions and Semantic Structure

WHY AN ANALYSIS OF THE SEMANTIC STRUCTURE IS NEEDED

Throughout this book there has been a sustained emphasis on *meaning*. The first two chapters constantly reiterated that the translators task is to convey the meaning of the original in the RL. This should be done faithfully and naturally, using the RL lexical and grammatical resources to the full. The subsequent chapters have covered the same matter in more detail — the meaning of words, the meanings of figures, how to handle grammatical features of the original that have several possible meanings, have been discussed.

It has also been emphasized that the fullest possible use should be made of such technical works as commentaries, versions, grammars, and lexicons, which make available to the translator the fruit of Biblical scholarship and research into the meaning of the original. Without these aids, the translator's task would be much more difficult.

In spite of all that has been written explaining the meaning of the original, there still remains a "but," from the translator's standpoint. Invaluable and indispensable as these works are, with few exceptions, they are not designed to meet the special needs of a translator. In particular, there is one aspect of his work that sets the translator apart from other users of these aids. To translate accurately and faithfully he has to have a clear understanding of *every* part of *every* verse in *every* book. If the commentaries do not comment on some particular phrase, or, as is more often the case, if their comments do not answer the questions the translator (with his particular RL in mind) is asking, then he cannot simply leave that phrase out and pass on to whatever is next. Even though the commentator does not find it necessary to discuss everything in detail, this is just what the translator needs, because of the demands the translation process makes.

To put it in more technical terms, it may be said that what a translator needs is a detailed analysis of the *semantic structure* of the original text, presented in a way that makes the information readily available to him. Such an analysis is invaluable whether the translator is familiar with the original languages or not, for, even if the translator knows Greek and Hebrew, he still faces the task of deriving the meaning from the grammatical and lexical form of the original. An analysis of the semantic structure, however, gives him a much more direct access to that meaning.

One of the basic units in analyzing the semantic structure of a text is called a proposition. To analyze a text from a semantic standpoint, then, would involve identifying the propositions themselves; analyzing the semantic relations between the propositions; analyzing the propositions into smaller semantic units; and indicating how the propositions are grouped into larger semantic units. This chapter does not attempt to develop all of the theory implied by the above statements. It concentrates primarily on the proposition and its organization into larger semantic units. In particular, the relationships within a proposition are not taken up in detail, though a brief discussion of these may be seen in the chapter on the genitive construction; nor are the propositions analyzed into the smaller units of concepts and components. A system of relations between propositions is discussed in the next chapter.

This chapter, then, discusses the concept of semantic structure and also shows how the theory can be applied to the practical problem of analyzing a given text so as to arrive at its semantic structure.

SEMANTIC STRUCTURE AND SURFACE STRUCTURE

Consider the following two simple sentences in English:

1. My house is over there.
2. My daughter is over there.

The subject in each case consists of the same grammatical construction, a noun phrase consisting of a possessive pronoun and a noun. In the first example, however, "my house" expresses the idea that I live in the house and/or that I own the house. In the second example "my daughter" does not express either of these ideas, but the idea of kinship. Hence, it is both possible and useful to draw a distinction between the grammatical form in which ideas are expressed and the ideas themselves.

A further illustration of this distinction is given by Frantz in his article "Translation and Underlying Structure" (pp. 22, 23). He compares the three sentences:

1. I ate ice cream with my wife.
2. I ate ice cream with my pie.
3. I ate ice cream with my spoon.

These can now be rephrased to bring out the differences in meaning:

1. My wife and I ate ice cream together.
2. I ate ice cream and my pie together.
3. I used a spoon to eat my ice cream.

These examples show that a prepositional phrase using "with" in English may represent at least three different meanings, depending on the context in which it is used.

Further examples of the fact that one grammatical structure may be associated with several different meanings are found in some of the earlier chapters, particularly chapters 14, 15, and 16. In each of these chapters, some of the grammatical constructions found in the Greek of the New Testament are discussed because each signals more than one part of the semantic structure. This is particularly evident in the case of the genitive construction, which signals a great variety of different meanings.

The distinction between surface structure and semantic structure is not confined to the fact that a grammatical construction can represent several functions in the semantic structure; the converse is also true. A particular aspect of the semantic structure may be expressed in the grammatical structure in a variety of different ways.

Reason-result is one of the semantic relations we need to distinguish when analyzing the semantic structure of the Greek original. This relation can be signaled in Greek in a variety of ways. Consider the following examples:

Matt. 9:36 ". . . he was moved with compassion on them, because (Gk. *hoti*) they fainted, and were scattered abroad . . . ."

Luke 11:8 ". . . because (Gk. *dia* + accus.) of his importunity he will rise and give him . . . ."

Acts 12:23 "And immediately the angel of the Lord smote him, because (Gk. *anth' hōn*) he gave not God the glory."

1 Cor. 15:9 ". . . [I] am not meet to be called an apostle, because (Gk. *dioti*) I persecuted the church of God."

Heb. 11:11 ". . . and [Sarah] was delivered of a child when she was past age, because (Gk. *epei*) she judged him faithful who had promised."

This is by no means an exhaustive list of ways reason-result may be expressed in the Greek. Philemon 7 provides an example where a REASON proposition is signaled by *epi* plus the dative. Also, there may be no explicit marker of the relation at all, as in Col. 1:4 (kjv has "since") and Philemon 5 (kjv has no marker either; rsv has "because").

By the term "surface structure" is meant not only the grammatical structure, but also the lexical items used and their collocations. It also refers to the particular grammatical form used in the text — the use of a finite verb, rather than a participle; the use of an abstract noun to represent an Event; the arrangement of the material so that some information is in focus, other information is not; the use of syntactic shifts to indicate emphasis, etc. These and other grammatical and lexical features are embraced by the expression "surface structure," and an analysis of the semantic structure is an attempt to bring out the significance of all of the information carried by the surface structure.

This description of surface structure also implies that the reader or hearer of a communication makes use of all the surface structure clues in arriving at the meaning. For example, the reader may be pretty sure of the different meanings of the three sentences using "with" by observing the lexical items used in the prepositional phrases, and then relating them to the rest of the sentence. The grammar may be ambiguous; but, in this case, the lexical information resolves the ambiguities. Both, however, are integral parts of the surface structure.

The distinction between surface structure and meaning involves several points of difference. First, the surface structure of a language is specific to it; it is, in fact, unique. No two languages have identical surface structures, and experience with languages from all over the world has shown that they can differ markedly. This is well illustrated in Frantz's article, referred to earlier. In Blackfoot, a North American Indian language, the three sentences using "with" have to be expressed quite distinctly in the surface structure; the same structure for all three cannot be used as in English. In this particular respect, the surface structures of Blackfoot and English are quite different, and many other such examples could be produced.

In some real sense, however, the Blackfoot and English examples are saying the same thing. The meaning that is being expressed in such different ways in the two surface structures is basically the same although there may be different nuances of meaning. It may well prove, then, as further research is undertaken, that the structure of the meaning underlying a text in any particular language has some sort of universal validity. Certainly, some such assumption underlies all translation work. If the same meaning cannot be expressed in the complex variety of surface structures found around the world, then translation is impossible. An adequate theory of semantic structure is not yet available, but it is anticipated that when it is, it will have a universal significance that the analysis of the surface structure of a particular language does not.

A second difference between surface structure and semantic structure is the way in which they express the meaning. Surface structure is what may be termed "multifunctional." That is to say, a given grammatical construction may signal different meanings depending on the context; a lexical item may also have a number of senses. Further, and more significant, a given word or expression may be fulfilling several functions simultaneously. For example, when the apostle John addresses his readers as "beloved," he is using the vocative construction to call the attention of the readers to what is following, quite possibly a change of topic, or a new aspect of a topic. He is also giving expression to the relationship existing between himself and them, one of love. More than one semantic function is thus carried by a single grammatical construction or a lexical item in its grammatical form.

Semantic structure makes explicit the different facets of meaning carried by a single surface structure form. Also, it represents the meaning in a direct, one-to-one manner. It is, in principle, straightforward and unambiguous. An analysis of the surface structure with a view to arriving at the semantic structure, in other words, exegesis, may be considered to be the process of sorting out all of the multifunctional aspects of the surface structure and stating them as unambiguously as possible. What this involves is discussed in detail later in this chapter.

For such an analysis to be complete, every part of the semantic structure would have to be analyzed from the components of meaning to the largest semantic units. Such an analysis is not yet possible, but the analysis of part of the Epistle to Philemon presented in chapters 19 and 20 is a step in that direction. The analysis is presented through the medium of English, and this imposes limitations on how exact and complete the analysis of the semantic structure can be. It may be that a complete and exact analysis can be achieved only by means of a symbolic representation,[1] but for the practical purpose of providing a translator with an analysis of the semantic structure of the original, there are many advantages gained by using an actual language.

A third distinction is more in the realm of conjecture. If it is assumed, complex though the mental processes may be, that a speaker or writer starts from the meaning which he wishes to convey and then expresses that meaning in the surface forms of the language he is using, then the semantic structure is, in some sense, more fundamental. A good writer, for instance, knows what he wishes to say, but he may make many changes in the manuscript before it is published. The meaning has remained unchanged, but the surface structure has been modified until the writer feels that it most effectively expresses his meaning. Semantic structure would seem, therefore, to be more basic, prior in some way, and this may well be correlated with the likelihood of its proving to have a universal validity.

THE ORGANIZATION OF SEMANTIC STRUCTURE

The semantic units

In chapter 4, the term *component of meaning* was introduced and it was shown that the senses words carry may be analyzed into such

---

[1] Longacre (1972a), in the chapter "A Taxonomy of the Deep Structure of Propositions," uses a symbolic notation for the relations posited; see especially pages 87-90 for a discussion of the symbolic system.

components. A component of meaning is a semantic unit, that is to say, it is one of the units which is part of semantic structure. Further, such components of meaning are grouped into what may be termed *concepts*, with one of the components of meaning being nuclear. Concepts are also semantic units. A concept may be represented in the grammar of a language by a morpheme, word, or phrase. For this reason a word in one language may not always be translated by a single word into another language but may be translated either in the form of a phrase or of a morpheme. The concept remains unaltered in the translation process, but its formal expression in the grammatical structure may vary considerably.

It was also shown in chapter 4 that both components and concepts may be classified semantically as either Thing, Event, Abstraction, or Relation. In the case of concepts, the classification is that of the particular component which is generic and nuclear. Thus *island* was classed as a Thing since its generic or nuclear component is "land," island being defined as "land entirely surrounded by water."

Components may therefore be classed in two ways, (1) as to whether they function semantically (a) as the center or (b) as the support of a concept and (2) as to whether they function semantically to refer to a Thing, Event, Abstraction, or Relation.

Concepts may also be classed in two ways, (1) as to whether they refer to T, E, A, or R, depending on which component is central and (2) as to the semantic relation they fill within a proposition, i.e., as Agent, Instrument, Experiencer, etc.

A *proposition* is a grouping of concepts, again with one of the concepts central, that is, nuclear. It is a unit of communication, that is, it affirms, denies, questions, or commands something. Concepts and components of meaning do not do this; they might be termed "units of thought" but not units of communication in the sense that a proposition is.

However, a discourse is not just a long or short string of propositions —the writer, consciously or subconsciously, chooses a structure for his discourse appropriate to his theme. To achieve this end, the propositions are themselves grouped together. A grouping of propositions with one that is central or nuclear is called a *Statement* here. In a Statement one of the constituent propositions is nuclear or central and is called a *Main* proposition. The other propositions support the Main proposition in various ways. Statements are also combined into larger units — units which could be called *Semantic Paragraphs*. Such semantic paragraphs will have a *Theme* proposition that is central; the *Theme* proposition may be a Main proposition, or it may have to be abstracted from several Main propositions. Finally, it is posited that semantic paragraphs combine into *Sections* from which a central Theme proposition is stated or may be abstracted, and Sections combine into larger units until the total *Discourse* is reached. When the whole discourse has been thus analyzed, a final central proposition will represent the theme of the total discourse.

To help further distinguish semantic units from one another, it may be noted that units will relate to like units. Thus, propositions will relate to propositions, statements to statements, paragraphs to paragraphs, sections to sections, and larger units to larger units. This does not imply, however, that a single proposition can only relate to another proposition; it may relate to any higher semantic unit. When it does, it is then considered to be a proposition serving as a paragraph, or section, or whatever the semantic unit is to which it is related. The same principle applies to the other semantic units above a proposition. It becomes clear, then, that a larger semantic unit may consist of any one and only one of the smaller units. Semantic units are determined not only by their constituent parts (a section consists of paragraphs) but also by the unit to which they are directly related. Thus, a Statement (as a semantic unit) is not only a proposition or combination of propositions with one that is central, but the central proposition must be related to a central proposition of another Statement. Likewise, a paragraph not only consists of a Statement or a combination of Statements with a central proposition, but that central proposition must be related to the central proposition of another paragraph.

The interrelationship between grammar and semantics is of theoretical and practical interest. It has already been pointed out in an earlier chapter that there is nonmatching or skewing between grammatical and semantic units. Suffice it to say it would appear, from the present state of knowledge, that the larger the units involved, the less skewing there is between the two systems. Thus concepts may be expressed grammatically by either morphemes, words, or phrases, and Statements by either one or more clauses or sentences. It may be, however, that the boundaries of grammatical and semantic paragraphs nearly always coincide, although there is some evidence a grammatical paragraph may include several semantic paragraphs in Greek discourse.

More on the proposition as a semantic unit

Components of meaning and concepts have already been discussed in some detail in chapter 4. However, propositions need to be further clarified, since the following chapter introduces a system of relations between propositions, and the two subsequent chapters present a sample display of propositions from the letter to Philemon.

In defining a proposition, reference can be made to its communication function, and to its internal construction. A proposition could then be defined as follows: A proposition is the minimal semantic unit consisting of a concept or a combination of concepts which communicates an Event or Relation.[2]

---

[2] It is interesting to compare this definition with the following statement by Fillmore in "Some Problems for Case Grammar" (p. 37): "I see a transformational grammar with a case base as having in general the following properties. The propositional core of a simple sentence consists of a 'predicator' (verb, adjective, or noun) in construction with one or more entities, each of these related to the predicator in one of the semantic functions known as (deep structure) cases."

On the basis of this definition, two different classes of propositions may be distinguished: those which have an Event central are called Event propositions, and those which have a Relation central are called State propositions. These two classes of propositions will not be discussed in detail, but a few comments are given to try to make the distinction more explicit.

An Event proposition communicates an Event and consists of any other concepts related to that Event. The relations these other concepts have to the Event are what are often referred to as "case" relations or roles as developed by Fillmore in "The Case for Case" (1968 a), and usually have such labels as Agent, Experiencer/Patient, Instrument, etc.

A State proposition communicates a Relation, either between two concepts belonging to the same semantic class, or between an Abstraction and a Thing or Event. An example of the first type would be *that man is a doctor* where both "man" and "doctor" are Thing concepts and the Relation is that of role. Another example would be *red is a color* where both concepts are Abstractions and the Relation is one of classification. An example of the second type would be *this water is cold* where the Abstraction "cold" is in an Attributive relation to the Thing "water."[3]

Propositions may also be classified according to their function within the discourse. They may serve to develop or to support another semantic unit. There are thus Developmental propositions and Supporting propositions.

At the risk of sounding repetitious, it is emphasized again that concepts, propositions, statements, paragraphs, sections, and larger units as discussed above are *semantic* units. Although they are related to the more familiar grammatical units, nevertheless they are distinct. Thus, a noun in the grammar would become a proposition in the semantic structure if it represented an Event; on the other hand, a grammatical combination such as "making mention of you in my prayers" (Phm. 4)[4] could well be analyzed as communicating one Event "when I pray for you" even though the surface structure suggests that it communicates two. To analyze on a semantic basis is a distinct process from analyzing on a grammatical basis, using different units and criteria.

The interrelations between central propositions and communication units

As may be deduced from the previous pages, the semantic structure of a text or discourse is ultimately based on two semantic units, namely,

[3] Propositions of the types "Building houses is expensive" and "Building houses is an activity" present an apparent problem in terms of the above analysis. In each of these propositions, there appears to be two propositions, one centering on an Event ("building") and the other on a Relation (Attribution and Classification respectively). Are these propositions to be analyzed as Event propositions or as State propositions? To answer this question, the form chosen by the speaker or writer is taken into account and in both these examples the Relation is in focus, not the Event, for the proposition as a whole. Hence, they are analyzed as State propositions with an Event embedded within them.

[4] See chapter 19 for a detailed discussion of a semantic analysis of Philemon 4-7.

the concept (a unit of thought) and the proposition (a unit of communication).

The first basic semantic unit combines into propositions using a set of relations often referred to as case relations. As has been stated earlier, it is not the interest of these chapters to discuss the relations that exist between concepts within a proposition.

The other semantic unit which is basic to an analysis of semantic structure is the proposition. The set of relations which combine propositions to unfold a discourse are distinct (even though granting some overlap) from those which combine concepts into propositions. The specific relations are discussed in detail in the next chapter. Basically, however, all the specific relations between propositions may be subsumed under two types, namely, Addition and Association.

As propositions combine into larger semantic units, the same types of relations hold between these larger units as occur between the smallest unit of communication, the proposition. Thus, Statements are related to one another by some type of Addition or Association. Paragraphs and Sections are no exception. These two types of relations which may exist between propositions and the central propositions of larger units give two different ways in which propositions and larger units may function within a discourse. They may function to develop or to support another semantic unit. When developing a semantic unit, the relation between the propositions is by Addition; when supporting a semantic unit, the relation is by Association.

Let us first describe and illustrate a semantic Section where the larger units are Developmental and therefore related by Addition. A Theme proposition is central to a Section and develops a unit larger than a Section; a Theme proposition is also central to a Paragraph and develops a Section; a Main proposition is central to a Statement and develops a Paragraph. Propositions which are not central to any semantic unit may develop a Main proposition or a Support proposition. Main and Theme propositions move the discourse along and are thus Developmental; Support propositions clarify, orient, or argue for Developmental propositions. We may exemplify the above description in diagram 1 (see page 276).

Many Sections will contain semantic units related by Addition and others by Association. In the previous example, those propositions which are not further specified are in a support role and related by Association to some other proposition. Let us now describe and illustrate a hypothetical Section in which the larger units are related either by Addition or by Association. As in the previous illustration, Main propositions develop a Paragraph. However, in diagram 2, the relation of one Paragraph to the other is that of grounds to conclusion, an Associative relation. Without a written text before us, we shall assume that the writer has the conclusion in mind as more important in developing the Section. The Paragraph indicating the conclusion is thus set somewhat further to the left in comparison to the Paragraph stating the grounds (see page 277).

DIAGRAM 1

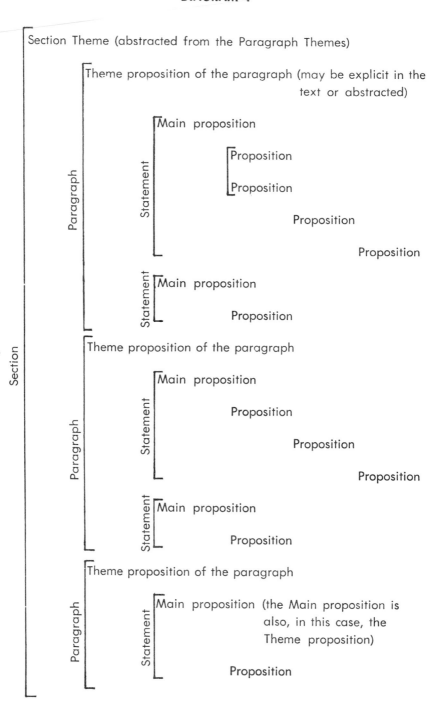

DIAGRAM 2

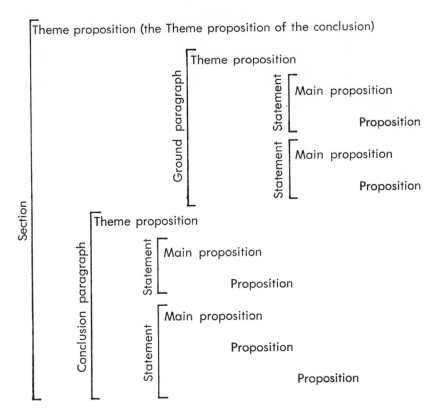

The interrelations between semantic units and central propositions may be summarized as follows:

Theme propositions of Sections develop a unit larger than a Section; a Theme proposition summarizes a Section; a Section generally consists of more than one Paragraph. Theme propositions of Paragraphs develop a Section; a Theme proposition summarizes a Paragraph; a Paragraph generally consists of more than one Statement. Main propositions develop a Paragraph; a Main proposition summarizes a Statement; a Statement generally consists of more than one Proposition.

The same may be said from a different perspective:

Theme propositions of Sections develop a unit larger than a Section; Theme propositions of paragraphs develop a Section; Main propositions develop a Paragraph.

A Section generally consists of more than one Paragraph; a Paragraph generally consists of more than one Statement; a Statement generally consists of more than one Proposition.

Analyzing the Larger Semantic Units of a Text

The larger units must be analyzed first

When the semantic units were discussed in the preceding section, the smaller units were mentioned first and the larger last. In analyzing a text or a discourse, however, the *reverse* order is followed. The discourse is first divided into sections, and then the sections into paragraphs, before more detailed work is done. For the translator of the Bible, the text is usually a book from the Old or New Testament, but the principles and criteria described below for analyzing the boundaries of the semantic units are, in principle, applicable to the analysis of any discourse.

In the following discussion, the criteria for the analysis of semantic structure will not be applied to units smaller than the proposition; that is to say, an analysis of propositions into concepts and components of meaning will not be discussed. To some extent, this level of analysis is presented in such detailed Greek-English lexicons as Arndt and Gingrich's (1957) and in the commentaries. The concern here is to undertake the analysis at the level of units of communication — propositions and upwards — rather than at the level of units of thought — concepts and components of meaning.

The discourse unit, in the case of the New Testament, is a book. Traditionally, such books, if long enough, are divided into chapters, but it should not be assumed that chapters always correspond to sections. Sometimes chapter boundaries are obviously in the wrong place. For example, it is clear that the instructions to masters in Colossians 4:1 is the last part of a series of instructions to different classes of people — to wives, husbands, children, parents (or fathers), slaves, masters. Hence Colossians 4:1 belongs to what precedes, rather than to what follows.

In other cases, the chapter is too small a unit. For example, it has long been recognized that Matthew, in his gospel, presents much of his didactic materials in five "blocks." The best known of these is the Sermon on the Mount, which comprises three chapters, namely, five through seven. Or again, in 1 Corinthians, Paul deals with a number of problems about which the Christians at Corinth had written to him. Chapters 12 to 14 deal with the only one of these, the question of spiritual gifts.

A further example is provided by the book of Acts. In Acts 1:8 Jesus tells the apostles they will receive the Holy Spirit and be witnesses for him, and then he indicates where: "in Jerusalem, and in all Judea, and in Samaria, and unto the uttermost part of the earth." This statement provides an interesting clue to the structure of the book of Acts. Chapters 1:1 to 6:7 describe the witness in Jerusalem; 6:8 to 9:31 describe how it spread throughout Judea and Samaria; and from 9:32 to the end of the book, its progress through the Roman Empire to Rome itself. The division of the book into these three major sections is further confirmed by the summary statements provided by Luke in 6:7, 9:31, and 28:30, 31.

It is essential, therefore, in any attempt to analyze the semantic structure of a total discourse, to delineate the boundaries of Sections and

Paragraphs first, and then to tackle the analysis of the Statements and propositions.

Criteria for delineating the larger units

In establishing Sections and Paragraphs, what criteria can the analyst use? The examples already given indicate some of the clues the text provides. The basic criterion is that a section, or a paragraph, deals with one theme. If the theme changes, then a new unit has started. There are many types of details, grammatical and semantic, to be drawn on to reach a decision, but what gives a section or paragraph its overall coherence as a semantic unit is the fact that one subject matter is being dealt with. Sometimes the theme is actually stated, as in 1 Corinthians 12:1, "Now concerning spiritual gifts, brethren, I would not have you ignorant." In other cases, it has to be deduced. Thus, no theme is spelled out for the Sermon on the Mount, nor is the theme for various sections of the book of Acts mentioned above. In this latter case, however, the summaries give some indication of the theme. Thus Acts 6:7 says ". . . and the number of disciples multiplied in Jerusalem greatly" giving the clue that it is the church in Jerusalem and its witness that has been described.

However, there is a considerable variety of supporting evidence that can be drawn on. For example, there are the formal grammatical clues such as the conjunctions, *oun, de, kai, tote, dio,* etc. In narrative materials, there are indications of change of time or location, giving the setting for a new series of events or a didactic discourse. Thus, the Sermon on the Mount is preceded by a statement indicating the location, "he went up into a mountain," and is also formally introduced by "he opened his mouth, and taught them, saying . . . ." Similarly, it is closed by the statement "And it came to pass, when Jesus had ended these sayings . . ." (Matt. 7:28). The end of each of the other four major teaching discourses in Matthew is signaled by a similar statement (Matt. 11:1, 13:53, 19:1, 26:1).

One of the functions of rhetorical questions is to introduce a new theme or topic (see chapter 15 for a detailed discussion). Thus Romans 6:1 says, "What shall we say then? Shall we continue in sin, that grace may abound?" The first question signals the switch to a new topic; the second question identifies it.

Another evidence of change of theme is the use of the vocative form of address. For example, after exposing the evil of the false teachers, Jude then proceeds to give instructions to his readers beginning with the words, "But you, beloved," (v. 17 RSV). The vocative may both distinguish paragraphs and tie a section together. A simple example, already mentioned, is found in Colossians 3:18 to 4:1, when different groups within the congregation are addressed directly. A more striking example is found in Matthew 23:13-36 in which Jesus repeatedly addresses the scribes and Pharisees directly with the words, "Woe unto you, scribes and Pharisees, hypocrites!"

An evidence of the unity of a passage is the repeated use of the same term, or synonymous terms, identifying the topic. One of the best known examples is 1 Corinthians 13 in which Paul uses the Greek word *agapē* "love" eight times in the thirteen verses. A more complicated example is found in Romans 5:12-21 which compares and contrasts Adam and Christ. Adam is associated with the three events — sin, judgment, death. Christ, on the other hand, is associated with grace, justification, and life. But these aspects of the comparison are not always represented by the same Greek word. Adam's sin is referred to by "sin" (*hamartia*), "transgression" (*parabasis*), and "trespass" (*paraptōma*); and "grace" (*charis*) and "free gift" (*charisma*) are interchanged on the other side of the comparison.[5]

Contrast may also indicate a basic unity. For example, Colossians 2:20 says, "If with Christ you died . . . ." (rsv) and Colossians 3:1 says, "If then you have been raised with Christ . . . ." (rsv). These parallel but contrasting statements indicate that the paragraphs of which they are the opening statements are part of a section including them both, and dealing with the ethical implications of these two statements.

Other details of the discourses, such as change of participant, or a change in the tense, mood, or aspect of a verb, may indicate that a new unit is starting. On the other hand, the repetition of a closely similar lexical item, or similar propositions may tie the beginning and end of a paragraph or section together. For example, Colossians 2:6, 7 introduces the first imperative in that epistle: "So walk ye in him." Colossians 3:17 is also an exhortation addressed to the congregation as a whole: "do all in the name of the Lord Jesus." It seems likely, therefore, that these two general commands signal the beginning and the end of a section dealing with Christian conduct relevant to the whole congregation. Colossians 3:18 then switches from instructions to the whole congregation to instructions to particular groups within it.

The criteria given above do not constitute an exhaustive list, but they do show that in the original text there are many clues to its semantic structure. The discussion does not imply the criteria are always so clear and unambiguous that the boundaries of these larger semantic units may be established without any problem cases at all. (Sometimes decisions reached concerning such boundaries are revised in the light of the analysis into propositions.) But it does imply, that, as these criteria are consciously applied and more skill is gained, it will rarely be impossible to decide with certainty on a boundary. But even before the techniques are developed to this point, it is vital the boundaries of these larger units be established before the details of the smaller units are worked out. Otherwise, there is the very real danger the translator will not be able "to see the forest for the trees" and so be unaware of the overall semantic structure or come to a somewhat distorted view of it. Since it is the meaning the translator is transferring into the rl, any ignorance of the

---

[5] For a detailed analysis of the structure of this passage, see "Discourse Analysis and the Greek New Testament" by Johannes P. Louw, 1973, (pp. 108-18).

overall semantic structure, or distortion of it, will have some adverse effect on the translation.

RESTATING THE CONTENT OF A TEXT IN THE FORM OF PROPOSITIONS

Deriving the propositions from the text

Having established the boundaries of the larger semantic units (such as sections and paragraphs), the next stage is to express the content of each of these units by means of propositions. It should perhaps be said that *statements*, that is, groups of propositions with one proposition as central, are not analyzed first and then propositions. Rather, the two are analyzed simultaneously, that is to say, as the propositions are worked out they can be seen to belong to groups smaller than the semantic paragraph, and these groups are what are termed statements.

When analyzing the text into propositions, the main task is to identify those items in the text which represent propositions and to construct the propositions themselves so they accurately represent the meaning. The skewing between the semantic structure and the surface structure means that propositions, although they may be characterized as having either an Event or a Relation as their nucleus, may be signaled by a considerable variety of grammatical constructions and lexical forms. Thus, constructing the propositions is not a straightforward task.

At this stage in the analysis, use is made of the distinction between Event and State propositions. The latter are usually much harder to identify in an initial study since a Relation is central. Therefore, the first step toward an analysis into propositions is to identify those terms in the text which are likely to represent Events since each Event proposition communicates an Event. This means identifying not only the verbs (which in Greek may be in the form of finite verbs, or participles, or infinitives) but also the abstract nouns which represent Events semantically. Thus, Colossians 1:4 reads in the Greek:

> *akousantes   tēn pistin   humōn   en Christō Iēsou*
> having-heard the faith   of-you   in   Christ Jesus

> *kai tēn agapēn   hēn   echete   eis pantas tous hagious*
> and the love   which you-have to   all   the saints

There are two verb forms *akousantes* "having-heard" and *echete* "you-have," so there would appear to be at least two Event propositions in this verse. But *pistin* "faith" and *agapēn* "love" are abstract nouns representing the Events "to believe (in)" and "to love." So this verse would initially be analyzed as having four Event propositions.

Not all Events are signaled explicitly in the Greek in this way. Many of the Events are only carried implicitly.[6] For example, the opening verses of Paul's letters carry no explicit verbs at all. When he is writing to Timothy, he does not say "I, Paul, am writing to you, Timothy" or "I,

---

[6] A detailed discussion of the principles underlying the use of implicit information will be found in chapter 3.

Paul, am greeting you, Timothy." He simply says "Paul . . . to Timothy." Also, as was pointed out in the preceding chapter, the genitive construction may imply an Event, even, occasionally, two; so may figures of speech, such as metaphor (see chapters 8 and 9); and so may the many prepositional phrases found in the Greek text.

Much of the material in a given paragraph will be accounted for by identifying the Events, but it is quite likely that there will be phrases still unaccounted for which represent State propositions, since they will be communicating Relations such as role, contents, etc.

Stating the propositions

Having thus identified the nuclei of the propositions, the propositions themselves now need to be stated. At this point, the analyst is conscious he is using English to represent semantic structure. In doing this he is guided by the following principles:

1. In the statement of the propositions, semantic and grammatical classes are matched. Thus, Events are represented by verbs, Things by nouns, etc. Also, as far as possible, words are used in nonfigurative ways and in nonextended senses, that is to say, in their primary sense (see chapter 5).

2. Implied information relating to participants is stated explicitly, but it is put in parentheses to indicate its implicit status.

3. Not only is the extended and figurative use of individual words avoided, if possible, but live figures of speech are also explained by giving the point of similarity, or the topic, as necessary.

The application of these principles in stating propositions often produces marked differences in form from a translation into English. Colossians 1:4 may be used again to illustrate this in a simple way.

An initial examination indicated there were four explicit Events in the semantic structure of this verse, which would be represented in the propositional statements by some appropriate form of the verbs "to hear," "to have," "to believe (in)," and "to love." A closer look, as the propositions are being formulated, reveals the situation is not this simple. In the Greek, the abstract noun "love" is linked to the verb "you-have" by the relative pronoun "which." Hence, "you-have" is not referring to some Event distinct from "to love," but to the same Event. That is to say, "you have love" is semantically equivalent to "you love."

The noun "faith" is followed by *humōn* "of you." This is a subjective genitive, that is to say, "you" is the Agent of the Event "to believe in." Stated in propositional form this becomes "you believe in."

At this point, please note that both of these verbs are transitive, i.e., you believe in something/someone and you love something/someone. In this verse, this information is supplied explicitly, so that the two propositions take the form:

> you believe in Christ Jesus
> you love all the saints

The Event "to hear" has not yet been put into an appropriate proposition. Who did the hearing? What did they hear? The answer to the first question is shown by the form of the participle, which is masculine plural, referring back to the main verb "we-thank." So "to hear" has the same subject as "to thank" whether "we" be understood as referring to both Paul and Timothy, or only Paul himself. The answer to the second question is shown in the accusative case of the two nouns *pistin* "faith" and *agapēn* "love" — this is what was heard or heard about. Hence, part of the proposition centering on "to hear" is:

(we) heard

and the other two propositions are preceded by "that" to show they state what was heard and complete the proposition.

Before discussing how these propositions may now be related to one another, the connection between focus and the form of a proposition needs to be mentioned. In the Greek of the New Testament, the passive voice of the verb is often used, and this way of referring to an Event takes attention away from the person actually doing the Event. For example, in the verse following the one discussed above, the word *apokeimenēn* is used. This is in the passive voice and could be translated, "is laid up," or "is stored up," or "is set aside." However, there is no mention of who actually did this Event, because the passive construction permits this omission. With passive verbs, therefore, the focus is on the Event itself or on those to whom it happened, and the doer of the Event is put into the background. This focus is reflected by using the passive in the statement of the proposition, but the implied Agent is supplied; in this case the implied Agent is "God," so that (by God) would be included in the proposition.

Relating the propositions to each other

To restate the content in propositional form is only one half of the task, however; the other half is to analyze the semantic relations that exist between the propositions. Each proposition is related in some way to another proposition or to the theme being developed. The semantic structure has not been adequately analyzed until these relations have been identified.

In analyzing the relations, as with stating the propositions themselves, full use is made of the overt clues in the Greek text, as well as the information provided by lexicons, grammars, commentaries, and versions. Sometimes there are words or particles in the Greek which signal relations, such as *kai, de, alla, gar, hoti,* and *hina.* But in most cases, a particular word or particle can signal several different relations, so that, while they narrow down the possibilities, further study of the content of the two propositions, and the context within the paragraph, needs to be made before a final decision may be reached. Often, however, there is no word or particle signaling the relations. Careful research is needed at this stage, just as much as in the previous one, to insure that the relations indicated do accurately represent the meaning of the original.

The following chapter discusses this topic in detail and defines and describes the system of relations between propositions posited in this volume. It is likely the list will be modified in various ways as more work is done in this area, both on Greek, and on different languages around the world. Even at the present stage of research, various finer distinctions could be introduced, but these, it is felt, would tend to reduce the usefulness of the list to the translator by making it complicated and cumbersome.

In identifying the relations, focus again plays a vital role. The distinction between some of the relations listed below depends on whether one of the two propositions is in focus and the other not, or whether they are equally in focus. By focus is meant their prominence as related to the theme or to other propositions. This division based upon focus is to be expected since the propositions are part of a paragraph which deals with one theme. Hence, certain propositions develop the theme, while others provide supplementary supporting information. The author, with his theme in mind, chooses what content is made prominent and what is not, and these choices affect the grammatical form and the relations that the propositions sustain to one another.

The following is the list of relations which will be discussed in the next chapter. They are set forth here under the headings of Addition and Association.

ADDITION RELATIONS

Sequence   Matched Support
Simultaneous
Alternative
Conversational Exchanges

ASSOCIATIVE RELATIONS

Manner   Condition-Consequence
Comparison   Concession-Contraexpectation
Contrast   Grounds-Conclusion
Equivalence   Time
Generic-Specific   Location
Amplification-Contraction/Summary   Circumstance
Reason-Result   Identification
Means-Result   Comment
Means-Purpose   Content

Three propositions were established for Colossians 1:4 as follows:

    we heard
    that you believe in Christ Jesus
    that you love all the saints

How are they related to each other? It has already been pointed out that the second and third propositions make clear what it was that was heard. This relation is referred to as CONTENT, and this applies equally to both of these statements. The relation can be indicated by a label at the right hand margin, thus:

we heard	
that you believe in Christ Jesus	CONTENT of heard
and that you love all the saints	CONTENT of heard

Note that the relation of ADDITION links the second and third propositions to each other and that this is signaled by the use of "and," just as "that" signals the CONTENT. This implies the third proposition has two relations, that of CONTENT with respect to the first proposition and that of ADDITION with respect to the second. This could be indicated as follows:

we heard	
that you believe in Christ Jesus	CONTENT of heard
and that you love all the saints	ADD. CONTENT of heard

But what about the first proposition? How is it related? It looks back to the first proposition in the paragraph, "We always thank God," and it states the reason why Paul thanked God, namely, he had heard a good report of the quality of the Colossians' Christian lives. Hence, it would carry the relation label REASON as follows:

we heard	REASON (for 1st proposition in paragraph)
that you believe in Christ Jesus	CONTENT of heard
and that you love all the saints	ADD. CONTENT of heard

By labeling the relations in this way, and using suitable connectors such as "and" and "that" wherever feasible, the relations linking propositions one to another may be made explicit, thus revealing the semantic structure of the text in a form a translator can readily understand.

Having worked out the analysis of the propositions in a paragraph, and labeled their relations, the analyst should then review his original decisions regarding the boundaries of the larger units in the light of the detailed analysis and modify those decisions if this seems necessary. Finally, from each paragraph and section the theme should be abstracted and stated at the head of the propositional analysis of that paragraph or section. Doing this is not only a help to the translator, but also to the analyst as a check on his analysis. Does his analysis of the propositions in fact tie in with the stated theme? If not, then some revision is necessary. Having established the boundaries, abstracted the themes, and worked out the propositions, the analyst is now in a position to prepare a display of the results for a translator to use.

DISPLAYING THE SEMANTIC STRUCTURE

The purpose of a careful analysis of the semantic structure of a New Testament book is to make the results available to translators. While every effort is made to insure that the analysis is accurate and faithful to the meaning on the one hand, and based on a sound theoretical approach on the other hand, nevertheless it ultimately has a practical aim in view — to help the translator make an idiomatic and accurate translation. To this end, it is necessary to display the results of the analysis in a form which a translator may use. The final chapter of this book is an example of how this is being done, using a system of indentation for the propositions; explicitly labeling each relation between propositions; and, for each semantic paragraph and section, stating the theme. In this way, the analysis of the units of communication may be made available to a translator.

However, to present just the results of a semantic analysis is not really sufficient. In the course of his analysis the analyst will have had to consider many different alternative ways of stating the propositions, of relating them, and of deciding on the boundaries of the larger units. The translator, or any one else, who sees only the final result may well wonder how such a result was reached. Together with the display, therefore, a discussion of the analysis underlying the display and, where necessary, alternative forms of display, are provided so the translator is fully aware of what lies behind the end product. It is anticipated, from preliminary work already undertaken, that new insights into the semantic structure of the original Greek will be attained. The discussion accompanying the display of propositions should serve to reassure the translator he has in front of him an accurate, reliable presentation of the meaning of the original.

Perhaps a final note of warning should be sounded at the end of this chapter. A display of the semantic structure is not meant to be translated literally, any more than is the original or a translation of it. Its purpose is to give the translator a more direct representation of the meaning than can be obtained in any other way. But that is all. Once the translator knows the meaning of the original he is in a position to consider how to express that meaning in a particular RL. However, all the principles spelled out in the previous chapters of this book are just as essential to a good translation whether the translator has a propositional display before him or not. The display is not to be translated directly into the RL as it stands, but it should provide an insight into the meaning of what is being translated in a way that other helps do not.

CHAPTER 18

Relations Between Propositions

THE SEMANTIC FUNCTIONS OF PROPOSITIONS

The interest of this chapter lies in establishing and describing a system of relations between propositions in the context of a discourse. In a discourse, the speaker or writer is constantly selecting and organizing his material, and this activity of selection gives rise to a complex set of relations. This complex set may be regarded as based on the relations which can be perceived in the real world. This is a smaller set than the set used in discourse and can be referred to as *perceptual relations*:

Sequence in time:	one Event follows another
Simultaneity in time:	two or more Events occur at the same time
Alternatives:	two or more Things or Events are perceived as alternatives
Differences:	two Events or Things or Abstractions are perceived as different
Similarities:	two Events or Things or Abstractions are perceived as the same or similar

These basic relations can be epitomized as follows:

A then B
A during B
A   or   B
A not B
A and B

This gives five basic relation formulae, four conjunctive ones — A then B, A during B, A and B, A not B — and one disjunctive, A or B.

The more complex set of relations used in speaking and writing may be referred to as *conceptual relations*, and it is these which will be discussed in detail later in the chapter. They derive from the fact that a writer or speaker is not content simply to state perceptions of the real world. Deductions are made from what is perceived; hypotheses are put forward to explain what is perceived; statements are repeated for emphasis; some of the information is made prominent, some of it is not; some of it develops a train of thought, some of it explains and clarifies the train of thought. In short, the speaker or writer selects the content of his communication, and also the function of that content, so as to achieve the purpose of his communication.

Developmental propositions

Propositions fulfill two distinct functions within a discourse. They may either develop some semantic unit of the discourse or support it. The semantic unit developed or supported may be a supported proposition within a paragraph, the theme of a paragraph, or the theme of a group of paragraphs. Propositions which develop a semantic unit are *developmental propositions* and are of equal rank semantically within the discourse.

The relation that exists between developmental propositions is that of ADDITION. Whenever two or more propositions sustain the same relation to another proposition, then they are related to each other by ADDITION. This applies for all types of semantic units. For example, if a conclusion proposition is supported by three grounds propositions, then the relation that exists between the grounds propositions is that of ADDITION. Similarly, if there are three paragraphs, each of whose topic proposition is in a grounds relation to a theme proposition, which is a conclusion, then the paragraphs are also related by ADDITION.

A theme that is developed is not necessarily stated explicitly in the discourse. It may be implicit and have to be abstracted. It may well be that this situation most commonly arises when the relation between the Theme proposition and its supporting units is one of the relations where there is an overlap in meaning between the two related units. (These relations are discussed in detail later in this chapter as subgroup 2 of relations between support propositions.) For example, a mother may tell someone about her children. She may mention various items of interest about Bill, and then go on to speak about her daughter Becky. Having said what she wished about Becky, she may then go on to describe her other children. The Theme propositions which summarize each paragraph are of equal rank and develop the implicit theme — "I will tell you about my children." This theme may be abstracted from the Theme propositions which summarize each of the paragraphs. The relation the Theme propositions have to this abstracted Theme proposition is that of specific to generic. The Theme proposition, "I will tell you about my children," is generic and each paragraph theme is in a specific relation to that Theme. This is one of the relations in which the related propositions share some meaning in common.

Development propositions are distinguished from support propositions in two ways. Firstly, developmental propositions have the same relation of ADDITION to one another, whether these are two or more supporting propositions within a paragraph, two or more Main propositions, or two or more Theme propositions. Secondly, since they all have the same relation, they are of equal rank semantically.

The type of ADDITION that occurs between developmental propositions is controlled to a considerable extent by the type of discourse in which they occur. In narrative material, many of the propositions are related by one of the two time relations, sequence or simultaneity. In a biography, the paragraphs may be united with developmental propositions[1] which add one location to another or one participant to another. In epistle material, one conclusion may be added to another or one reason to another.

Support propositions

Support propositions are always one of two propositions related by Association, such as means-purpose, or grounds-conclusion. In material that is arguing or proving a point, many of the paragraphs will be connected by an ASSOCIATIVE relation as, for example, when their Theme propositions are related by one of the cause-effect relations, such as grounds-conclusion or condition-consequence. Not all of the labels used to identify the relations between support propositions, however, are binary in form. But unitary labels, such as comparison, imply there are two parts. Thus comparison implies there is a topic and something compared with it to illustrate that topic.

Support propositions sustain associative relations to the proposition they support. In this respect they differ from developmental propositions which are linked together by sharing the same relation. Also, a support proposition is considered to be of unequal rank relative to the supported proposition. On the other hand, developmental propositions are of equal rank relative to one another.

Support propositions may be classified on the basis of their semantic function in a discourse. There are three functions, as follows:

1. The support proposition *clarifies* another proposition, by explaining or highlighting it.

---

[1] A somewhat more detailed discussion of discourse genres and the relations between their developmental propositions may be found in "Semantic Relations Between Whole Propositions in English" by Ronald L. Trail. See particularly pages 8-11. He also points out that "such relationships as cause-effect, antithetical, and alternative do not form the backbone of Narrative discourse, but are nevertheless used in Narrative as collateral material to give participant attitudes or accompanying description" (p. 10). The same observation applies, making the appropriate changes, to the other genres.

2. The support proposition *argues* for another proposition by giving its logical antecedent or consequent.
3. The support proposition *orients* another proposition by giving its setting relative to time or space or other Events.

The differences between these general functions will become clearer as the particular relations which are grouped under them are discussed in more detail.

Four subsets of support propositions are established on the basis of these semantics functions, those which clarify being divided into two subsets according to whether the meaning of the supporting proposition is distinct from or similar to that of the supported proposition.

1. Support by clarification (using a proposition with distinct information)

    MANNER
    COMPARISON
    CONTRAST

2. Support by clarification (using a proposition with similar infortion)

    EQUIVALENCE
    GENERIC-SPECIFIC
    AMPLIFICATION-CONTRACTION/SUMMARY

3. Support by argument

    REASON-RESULT
    MEANS-RESULT
    MEANS-PURPOSE
    CONDITION-CONSEQUENCE
    CONCESSION-CONTRAEXPECTATION
    GROUNDS-CONCLUSION

4. Support by orientation

    TIME
    LOCATION
    CIRCUMSTANCE

Conclusion

The relations between propositions within a discourse have been divided into two major groups — developmental propositions and support propositions. The former are of equal rank semantically in the discourse; the latter are not. The latter are then subdivided into four groups. However, this grouping applies only to those relations which obtain between full propositions. In addition, there are support propositions which are related to only part of another proposition. There are three relations between a whole proposition and part of another one:

    IDENTIFICATION
    COMMENT
    CONTENT

These relations which involve ADDITION and ASSOCIATION will be discussed in the rest of this chapter.[2]

SPECIFIC TYPES OF ADDITION RELATIONS

There are five particular forms of the relation of ADDITION which have been chosen for discussion. These are Chronological sequence, Simultaneity, Alternation, Conversational exchanges and Matched Support propositions. The first two are set in the general framework of time, and therefore tend to predominate in narrative type discourses. For the others, the time framework is in the background, and so they tend to be more common in discourse genres other than narrative. It is emphasized, however, that such statements are only generalizations. Any particular discourse being studied is likely to include examples of various relations. Within a discourse, any type of ADDITION relation may unite two or more settings, two or more generic statements, two or more reasons, etc.

1. *Chronological sequence*

The label of Chronological sequence identifies the type of ADDITION in which one proposition follows another in time in the referential world.[3]

The Events central to the propositions may occupy a short period of time, or a longer period of time. This type may connect any pair of Events, whether these are long or short in duration, and they may take place in the past or the future.[4]

Mark 1:31 "And he came and took her by the hand, and lifted her up . . . ." (sequence of events in the past)

Mark 4:28 ". . . first the blade, then the ear, after that the full corn in the ear." (generalized sequence of events)

1 Thess. 4:16, 17 "For the Lord himself shall descend from heaven . . . and the dead in Christ shall rise first: then we which are alive

---

[2] The set of relations outlined above owes much to the following earlier discussions of this subject: Fuller, 1967, NOT 28, 1-12; Frantz, 1968, NOT 30, 22-28; Bruce Hollenbach, 1969, NOT 31, 22-34; Deibler, 1969, NOT 31, 34-39; Beekman, 1970a, NOT 37, 6-23; Ballard, Conrad, and Longacre, 1971, 111-17; Longacre, 1972a, 51-92; Barbara E. Hollenbach, 1973b, 9-11.

Winterowd (1970, pp. 830-35), approaching this subject from a somewhat different standpoint, establishes 7 relations, or "transitions" as he calls them. He says (p. 831): "Analysis of thousands of transformational units in sequences reveals that there are seven relationships that prevail among T-units and, I would argue, in any stretch of discourse that is perceived as coherent. I have called these relations (1) coordinate, (2) obversative, (3) causative, (4) conclusive, (5) alternative, (6) inclusive, and (7) sequential." It can only be said that this seems too few to handle all the relations needed for discourse analysis, but it may be that Winterowd's seven are comparable to some form of broader grouping of the relations between propositions posited here.

[3] The expression "the referential world" is used, rather than the more obvious expression "the real world," because the speaker or writer may be referring to some type of world other than the real one — a world of fantasy, science fiction, etc.

[4] A more detailed treatment of this topic can be found in Hollenbach, Barbara (1973a, pp. 3-8).

and remain shall be caught up together with them . . . ." (sequence of events in the future).

2. *Simultaneity*

Two Events are regarded as simultaneous if they overlap with one another in time in the referential world of the discourse. Events in sequence do *not* overlap at all; simultaneous Events always overlap to some extent, either partially or completely.

As with Events in sequence, simultaneous Events may be of short or long duration and in the past, present, or future.

Matt. 24:29 ". . . [then] shall the sun be darkened, and the moon shall not give her light, and the stars shall fall from heaven, and the powers of the heavens shall be shaken:" (four simultaneous events in the future)

Mark 4: 37, 38 "And there arose a great storm of wind, and the waves beat into the ship . . . And he was . . . asleep on a pillow (two events, one continuous, take place during a continuous event in the past)

Rev. 3:20 "Behold, I stand at the door, and knock (two continuous events take place simultaneously in the present)

3. *Alternation*

Alternation may be either contrastive or supplementary. The contrastive form always occurs in pairs which are antonyms, such as *dead* or *alive*, or *present* or *absent*; or in pairs which are situational opposites such as *God* or *man, by air* or *by sea.* Supplementary alternatives occur with a series of two or more choices all of which stay within the same domain.

Matt. 6:31 ". . . What shall we eat? or, What shall we drink? or, wherewithal shall we be clothed?" (supplementary alternatives)

Matt. 11:3 ". . . Art thou he that should come, or do we look for another?" (situational alternatives: the two questions are equivalent to saying: "Are you the one or are you not?")

Rom. 14:21 ". . . anything whereby thy brother stumbleth, or is offended, or is made weak." (supplementary alternatives)

1 Cor. 11:4 "Every man praying or prophesying, having his head covered, dishonoureth his head." (supplementary alternatives)

James 2:3 ". . . and say to the poor, Stand thou there, or sit here under my footstool." (situational alternatives)

4. *Conversational exchanges*

At the present stage of analysis, the relation of ADDITION also describes the relation between the two halves of a conversation. One speaker "adds" to what the other speaker said, and so on.

5. *Matched support propositions*

The following examples exemplify ADDITION in its most usual form, that is, two or more propositions have the same relation to some other proposition which they support.

> Gal. 3:29 "And if ye be Christ's, then are ye Abraham's seed, and heirs according to the promise." (two conclusions)

> Col. 1:4 ". . . we heard of your faith in Christ Jesus, and of the love which ye have to all the saints . . . ." (two statements of the content of "heard")

> Jude 11 "Woe unto them! for they have gone in the way of Cain, and ran greedily after the error of Balaam for reward, and perished in the gainsaying of Korah." (three reasons for the pronouncement of judgment)

The two propositions may both be negated as in:

> Mark 8:26 "saying, Neither go into the town, nor tell it to any in the town" (two statement of the content of "saying")

> Luke 18:2 ". . . a judge, which feared not God, neither regarded man . . . ." (two descriptions of the judge)

In addition to these five types ADDITION is also the relation linking propositions together which have two points of difference and one of similarity. These look as if they are examples of the relation of CONTRAST, which is discussed later in this chapter, but they differ in that neither of the points of difference is a positive-negative opposition. Thus, the pair of propositions would be related by ADDITION.

> I worked with Mary at home,
> I worked with Helen at the office

SPECIFIC TYPES OF ASSOCIATIVE RELATIONS

Support propositions which are distinct in meaning and which clarify

In this group, the two propositions related to each other have distinct contents. This is not to say they have nothing in common semantically, but rather their meaning is not essentially similar, as is the case with the following group of relations. Their purpose in the discourse is to clarify another proposition either by describing how its Event took place, or by comparing or contrasting it, thus both adding new information to it and highlighting it.

1. MANNER

This relation links two propositions in such a way that the supporting proposition clarifies the Event in the supported proposition, by telling how it took place, in what way it happened. It answers the question: "*How* did this Event take place?" It is likely to be confused with three other relations, those of MEANS-RESULT, GENERIC-SPECIFIC, and CIRCUM-STANCE. In the first of these, the MEANS proposition also answers the question "how?" Propositions which are related by the MEANS-RESULT relation, however, are sequential in time, whereas MANNER is simultaneous with the Event which it clarifies.

The similarity to GENERIC-SPECIFIC is more subtle. Consider the following example: "He walked along the road, limping awkwardly because his right ankle was sprained." "Limping awkwardly" specifies how he was walking on this occasion, but it is not regarded as linked by the relation of MANNER to the principal Event because the two Events concerned, "walked" and "limping," are in a generic-specific relation to each other: limping is a particular form of walking. When this is the case, the relation is analyzed as that of GENERIC-SPECIFIC rather than MANNER. In other words, a MANNER proposition does not repeat any of the components of the Event being clarified, whereas a SPECIFIC proposition does. Thus, when MANNER, GENERIC-SPECIFIC, or even AMPLIFICATION-CONTRACTION seem to be appropriate labels, the relation will be classed as MANNER only if the proposition adds distinct information.

A CIRCUMSTANCE proposition answers a different question than that answered by a MANNER proposition. It answers the question, ''What else?" For example, if the above example were to be changed to "He walked along the road, whistling gaily as he went," the relation would now be one of CIRCUMSTANCE. "Whistling" does not describe how he was walking, but what else he was doing at the same time as he was walking.

2. COMPARISON

COMPARISON is a relation which is based upon some point of similarity between two Things, Events, or Abstractions. In addition to the point of similarity, both sides of the comparison must be positive, and there must also be a point of difference. Further, except for the case of metaphor, which is an implicit comparison, the comparison is signaled by some form in the surface structure such as "like" or "as" (Greek has terms such as *hōs* and *eoiken*, and occasionally a phrase such as *kath' homoiotēta*). These features distinguish it from the relation of CONTRAST (see below).

> Matt. 12:13 ". . . and it was restored whole, like as the other" (the point of similarity is the Abstraction "whole," the point of difference the two hands).
> Heb. 4:15 "but he was in all points tempted like as we are" (the point of similarity is the Abstraction "in all points," the point of difference, the participants involved).
> James 1:6 "For he that wavereth is like a wave of the sea driven with the wind and tossed" (the point of similarity is the Abstraction of instability, the point of difference the two Things involved; this comparison is actually a simile, with "wave" as the image).

Another form which COMPARISON may take is that of examples portraying some quality or characteristic. Consider 2 Timothy 2:3-6, which reads as follows in the RSV: "Take your share of suffering as a good soldier of Christ Jesus. No soldier on service gets entangled in civilian pursuits, since his aim is to satisfy the one who enlisted him. An athlete is not crowned unless he competes according to the rules. It is the hardworking farmer who ought to have the first share of the crops." The first sentence is a comparison between Timothy and a soldier, the point of similarity being that of having to suffer. However, the following three statements are also comparisons between Timothy (or Christians in general) and soldiers, athletes, and farmers, each with its own point of similarity, but they are implicit comparisons, that is, they are metaphors.

3. CONTRAST

The relation of CONTRAST occurs between two propositions if there are at least two points of difference between them, and if one of the points of difference is a positive-negative opposition. In addition, there is at least one point of similarity.

There are five different forms in which this relation can occur, depending on the particular way in which the negative-positive opposition is expressed. These are listed below, with two examples from English to illustrate each type, one using Event propositions, the other State propositions:

1. negation of the same predicate; e.g., He sings in his bath, but I don't (sing in my bath); he is clever, but I am not.
2. negation of synonyms; e.g., Bill came yesterday, but John didn't arrive; he is healthy, but I am not well.
3. negation implied by antonyms; e.g., He stayed, but I left; he is strong, but I am weak.
4. negation implied by difference of degree; e.g., He doesn't eat as quickly as I do; he isn't as heavy as I am.
5. negation of an alternative; e.g., He fell into the lake, not the river; he wasn't first in the race, he was second.

In each pair of examples, the negation is applied first to an Event and then to an Abstraction, except in type 4, where the negation is of an Abstraction in both examples, that is, of "quickly" and of "heavy."

The following examples from the gospel of Matthew are classified according to the above five types:

6:29 ". . . even Solomon in all his glory was not arrayed like one of these." (type 4: the degree of beauty of appearance of Solomon and the lilies is different)

10:28 "And fear not them . . . but rather fear him . . . ." (type 5: in the context there are two alternatives — fearing men, or fearing God; the former alternative is negated)

18:13 ". . . he rejoiceth more of that sheep, than of the ninety and nine . . . ." (type 4: the degree of rejoicing is contrasted)

19:26 "With men this is impossible; but with God all things are possible." (type 1: the Abstraction of "ability" is negated)

24:35 "Heaven and earth shall pass away, but my words shall not pass away." (type 1: the predicate "shall pass away" is negated in the second half)[5]

[5] While it is true that the formal negation follows the "but" in this example, the main proposition is the second one. This is because the Event "pass away" contains a negative component, and this negative component is negatived in the second proposition. The second proposition is therefore positive semantically, and is the main one.

24:40 ". . . the one shall be taken, and the other left." (type 3: "taken" and "left" are antonyms)

A special type of contrast is signaled by the use of the word "except." For example, Acts 8:1 says, ". . . they were all scattered abroad . . . except the apostles." This can be restated in the form of two propositions:

> They were all scattered abroad
> The apostles were not scattered abroad.

There are two points of difference: (1) the positive and negative of the predicates; and (2) the participants involved — "the apostles" and everyone else, which is what "they . . . all . . . except" indicates semantically. The point of similarity is the predicate "scattered abroad." The two propositions therefore fulfill the conditions for the relation of CONTRAST. Longacre (1972a, p. 56) suggests that this type be called CONTRAST by exception.

The relation of CONTRAST is sometimes difficult to distinguish from that of CONCESSION-CONTRAEXPECTATION. The latter is distinguished by the feature of reversal of expectancy, but it sometimes carries the components that indicate CONTRAST. Also, the reversal of expectancy is often implicit, and it is sometimes difficult to decide whether a CONTRAST relation has the implication that it was contrary to expectation. This problem seems to be connected particularly with the use of "rather than" (Gk. *mallon ē*) in an English translation.[6]

Consider, for example, John 3:19. This reads, ". . . men loved darkness rather than light . . . ." This may be restated as two propositions, as follows:

> men loved the darkness
> men did not love the light.

This is an example of CONTRAST, using a negated predicate. But if the "rather than" is understood to carry the implication of "oughtness," then they could be represented propositionally as:

> men ought to love the light
> men did not love the light
> men loved darkness instead.

Put in this form, there is a reversal of expectancy — they did not do what they should have done, but did something else instead. This analysis would indicate the relation of CONCESSION-CONTRAEXPECTATION. This would seem to be a difficult area of interpretation, so each example of "rather than" would have to be considered carefully in its context before it could be decided whether there was an implicit reversal of expectancy.

---

[6] "Rather" (Gk. *mallon*) without "than" is also used in CONTRAST; see the example above from Matt. 10:28. In such cases, however, there seems to be no evidence for an implicit expectancy reversal.

Support propositions which are similar in meaning and which clarify

This group of relations is distinguished in that there is an "overlap" in content between the two related propositions, and this "overlap" is an essential part of the relation. The overlap may involve Things, Events, or Abstractions, or any combination of them. However, the overlap is not necessarily one of grammatical or lexical form; the overlap may be different in form, but the same in meaning. Trail (1973, pp. 21, 22) puts it this way: ". . . a conjunctive relationship in which one proposition repeats or restates, either verbally or conceptually, part or all of another and modifies it in some way." This last part of Trail's statement corresponds to our statement that this particular group of propositions has the semantic function of clarifying the supported proposition, by adding further explanatory information and/or by highlighting it within the discourse. More details concerning the overlap in meaning are given in the discussion of each particular relation.

1. EQUIVALENCE

Two propositions which convey the same meaning are linked by the relation of EQUIVALENCE. This relation occurs in two forms. In the one, the same content is expressed by means of words or expressions which are synonymous in the particular context; this is given the label of synonymous expression. In the other, the content of the supporting proposition is in the form of a *negated antonym*, and this is used as a label to identify this type of EQUIVALENCE.

Some examples of EQUIVALENCE by synonymous expression are given below. Many would fall into the classification of doublets, either of the synonymous or near-synonymous type.[7] This form of EQUIVALENCE would appear to emphasize by semantic repetition.

Matt. 5:12 "Rejoice and be glad" (RSV)
Matt. 6:24 ". . . for either he will hate the one and love the other; or else he will hold to the one, and despise the other."
Rom. 9:2 "I have great sorrow and unceasing anguish . . . ." (RSV)
Rom. 12:19 "Vengeance is mine; I will repay, saith the Lord"
Gal. 4:14 "you did not scorn or despise me" (RSV)
Phm. 18, 19 ". . . put that on my account . . . I will repay it . . . ."

Probably translations of statements made in Aramaic should be included here. For example, Mark 5:41 says, ". . . Talitha cumi: which is, being interpreted, Damsel . . . , arise." The statements in the two languages are semantically equivalent.

EQUIVALENCE in the form of a negated antonym could be confused with CONTRAST, since one form of that relation also uses antonyms. However, the relations may be distinguished by two criteria. One is that CONTRAST is saying something different, while EQUIVALENCE is saying the same thing (a good test is to put "that is" between the two equivalent propositions and see if the meaning is unaffected). The other is that in

---

[7] A detailed discussion of "doublets" is provided by Bruce Moore in NOT 43, 1972.

EQUIVALENCE the antonym is negated, whereas in CONTRAST it is not. This type of EQUIVALENCE highlights the positive proposition.

> Matt. 5:17 "I am not come to destroy, but to fulfill." ("not destroy" is equivalent to "fulfill" in this context; this is a negated antonym in which the subject of the verb is unchanged)
> Matt. 21:21 "If ye have faith, and doubt not . . . ."
> Acts 18:9 ". . . speak, and hold not thy peace"
> Rom. 9:1 "I say the truth in Christ, I lie not."

2. GENERIC-SPECIFIC

In this relation, what is stated generically in one proposition is restated in the other using specific terms covered by the generic term(s) of the other.

> Mark 6:48 "he cometh unto them, walking upon the sea" ("come" is generic, "walk" is specific)
> Col. 1:9 "we have not ceased to pray for you, asking . . . ." (RSV) ("pray" is generic, "ask" is specific)
> Phm. 20 "Yes, brother, I want some benefit from you in the Lord. Refresh my heart in Christ" (RSV) ("benefit" is generic, "refresh my heart" is specific)

This is a relation that readily extends to groups of propositions. Consider, for example, Colossians 1:10-12: "That ye might walk worthy of the Lord . . . being fruitful in every good work, and increasing in the knowledge of God; strengthened with all might . . . giving thanks unto the Father . . . ." Paul's prayer starts with a generic statement, "walk worthy of the Lord," and this is then followed by four specific statements, giving a whole group of propositions with an overall GENERIC-SPECIFIC relation. Dealing with larger semantic units, Matt. 6:1-18 may be analyzed in this way, with verse 1 a generic command and a reason, "Beware of practicing your piety before men in order to be seen by them; for then you will have no reward from your Father who is in heaven" (RSV). Then verses 2-4 deal with almsgiving, 5-15 with prayer, and 16-18 with fasting, all specific examples of the "piety" referred to in verse 1.

3. AMPLIFICATION-CONTRACTION/SUMMARY

In this relation, more information is provided in one of the propositions than in the other. This means that one of the two propositions is expressed with less detail. For example, only the Event is stated, or the Event together with an Agent or Patient, or the two parts of a State proposition. The amplified proposition then adds such extra information as the location or time or manner of the Event, or another participant, or descriptive material relating to participants already mentioned. Longacre (1972a, p. 60) gives the following statement: "Often, what is added . . . is . . . a further participant or a phrase referring to a place, time, or manner." Trail (1973, p. 22) focuses on what is repeated: ". . . requiring that at least the Actor or Undergoer and the Predicate of one proposition be repeated by the second proposition."

There are three forms of this relation which seem to be used in the New Testament.

The first of these is the use of a summary. A summary is a particular form of CONTRACTION in which the focal content of a group of propositions is stated. For example, Acts 6:7 could be considered a case of three statements combining to summarize the contents of the book up to that point: "And the word of God increased; and the number of the disciples multiplied in Jerusalem greatly; and a great company of priests were obedient to the faith." Acts 9:31 could also be analyzed in the same way.

The second is what is often referred to as a "leading question," that is, a real question in which the speaker indicates what he expects the answer to be. In English, these usually occur in the form of "tag questions" such as, "You are going to come, aren't you?" where the speaker shows he is expecting the answer, "Yes, I am."

In Appendix C, the use of *ou* and *mē* in questions is discussed. It shows that real questions using *ou* anticipated the answer "yes," whereas real questions using *mē* anticipated the answer "no." The speaker included in his question a particle which indicated the type of answer he expected to get. This means the speaker is really using both a question and an answer — an expected answer. Take for example Matthew 17:24, which is translated in the KJV as, "Doth not your master pay tribute?" In the Greek, the particle *ou* is used, showing those who were collecting the temple tax expected the answer, "Yes, he does." The question could thus be better expressed in English by some such translation as "Your master pays tribute, doesn't he?" If the "tag" at the end is spelled out in full, then there is a parallel question and statement:

> Does your master pay tribute?
> I expect that he does (pay tribute).

Put in this way, the overlap in meaning between the two propositions becomes much clearer. This type of question further adds the mood of expectancy and is analyzed as a particular form of the relation of AMPLIFICATION-CONTRACTION.

In the following examples, the Greek questions have been translated into English by tag questions so as to bring out the significance of the use of *ou* and *mē* more clearly.

Matt. 26:25 ". . . Master, It isn't I, is it?" (*mē* used)
Luke 22:35 ". . . you didn't lack anything, did you?" (*mē* used)
John 8:48 ". . . When we say you are a Samaritan and have a demon, what we say is right, is it not?" (*ou* used)
John 9:40 ". . . We aren't blind also, are we?" (*mē* used)
Acts 21:38 "Then you are that Egyptian . . . , aren't you?" (*ou* used)

The third special form is that of a rhetorical question together with an answer to it. Consider, for example, Romans 6:1, 2: "Shall we continue in sin, that grace may abound? God forbid." The "God forbid" is equivalent to the statement, "We shall not continue in sin, that grace may abound." This negates the content of the question, so it may be considered as a particular form of amplification, adding the component of negation. Here again, to the interrogative mood is added another, this time the indicative.

Support propositions which argue

Each pair of propositions in this group is associated by the general relation of cause and effect. That is to say, one of the two propositions represents a cause, and the other the consequent effect. It is in this sense that one argues for the other by giving its causal antecedent or subsequent.

Under this general heading, there are six different relations, each of which treats the cause-effect relation from a particular point of view, emphasizing some aspect or other involved in it. Before taking up the details of these relations, chart number 1 is presented as a guide to this section, stating the contrasts in a summary manner.

CHART 1

THE CAUSE-EFFECT RELATIONS CONTRASTED

RELATION		CONTRASTS	
Cause	Effect	Cause	Effect
REASON	RESULT	Answers the question: "**Why** this result?"	stated as **definite**
MEANS	RESULT	Answers the question: "**How** did this result come about?"	stated as **definite**
MEANS	PURPOSE	Answers the question: "**What** action was undertaken to achieve the desired result?"	implied as **desired**
CONDI-TION	CONSE-QUENCE	Answers the question: "**What** supposed or hypothetical condition could cause the consequence to become actual?"	stated as **definite**
CON-CESSION	CONTRA-EXPECTA-TION	Answers the question: "**Why** is the actual result unexpected?"	stated as **definite**, but is **not** the **expected** result
GROUNDS	CON-CLUSION	Answers the question: "**What** fact(s) is this conclusion based on?"	given the grounds, the speaker **deduces a conclusion**

1. REASON-RESULT

This relation is probably most familiar to speakers of English when presented in the surface structure in the reverse order, with the result first, and then the reason, the latter usually being introduced by "because." In either order, the reason states why the particular result came about, whether by the action of a rational agent, or otherwise. This particular relation is common in the New Testament.

Matt. 8:24 ". . . there arose a great tempest in the sea, insomuch that the ship was covered with waves . . . ."

Matt. 18:25, 26 ". . . his lord commanded him to be sold . . . . The servant therefore fell down and worshipped him, saying , . . ."

Mark 6:6 "And he marvelled because of their unbelief." (result first)

Acts 15:25, 27 "It seemed good to us . . . to send chosen men unto you . . . . We have sent therefore Judas and Silas . . . ."

Phm. 1 "a prisoner of Jesus Christ" (RSV: "for") (result first)

James 4:2 ". . . ye have not, because ye ask not." (result first)

The example from Philemon needs a little more explanation. This genitive construction (the Greek is *desmios Christou Iēsou*) represents two propositions, *I am a prisoner* and *I (follow/preach) Christ Jesus*, and the two may be connected by "because." The reason for Paul's imprisonment was his relation to Christ, or his preaching about him. It is therefore an example of a result followed by the reason for it.

It is also worth adding that not only may this relation be signaled by different forms (e.g., "therefore," "insomuch that," "because," etc.), or by none at all, and not only may it occur in the temporal and reverse temporal orders, but it may also occur in a "multiple" form. That is to say, a given result may arise from a number of reasons, or a reason may be related to several results, or both may be multiple. In the following example for Acts, a generic reason is followed by two specific reasons, and then the result.

Acts 17:11, 12	"These were more noble than those in Thessalonica	(generic reason)
	in that they received the word with all readiness of mind	(specific reason)
	and searched the scriptures daily, whether those things were so.	(specific reason)
	Therefore many of them believed . . . ."	(result)

2. MEANS-RESULT

This relation is closely similar to the previous one, and in practice it is not always easy to decide whether a given pair of propositions stands in a REASON-RESULT relation, or a MEANS-RESULT relation. As the summary chart which appears earlier in this section indicates, the difference between them is in the "cause" proposition; in the former relation this gives the reason "why," whereas in the present relation it gives the means "how."

The relation of "means" is also to be distinguished from that of "instrument." An "instrument" is usually an inanimate object used to do something, as in "He smashed the window with a hammer," or "He fished it out of the river with a long stick." The term "means" is applied, however, when an Event is involved, by means of which the stated result takes place. It should be noted that, in many of the examples of MEANS-RESULT found in the Scriptures, the Event in the means proposition is implied, rather than stated. In some cases, what appears to be an "instrument" is really a "means" stated figuratively. In all but one (Rom. 15:4) of these examples from the New Testament, the logical order is reversed, the result being stated first and then the means used to achieve it.

> Acts 21:19 ". . . what things God had wrought among the Gentiles by his ministry . . . ."
>
> Rom. 15:4 "we through patience and comfort of the scriptures might have hope"
>
> Col. 1:20 "having made peace through the blood of his cross"
>
> Col. 1:21, 22 "And you . . . hath he reconciled in the body of his flesh through death . . . ."
>
> Titus 3:5 ". . . he [God] saved us, by the washing of regeneration, and renewing of the Holy Ghost" (two means are stated)
>
> 1 Pet. 1:18, 19 ". . . ye were ransomed . . . not with perishable things such as silver or gold, but with the precious blood of Christ . . . ." (RSV) (note the contrast with "instrument")

As you read through these examples, it may appear possible to use the relation RESULT-REASON to connect them. This only emphasizes the close connection between this relation and the previous one, and it may be that "means" presupposes "reason," but it is the "means" rather than the "reason" that is in focus in the actual form of the statement. A test which can be used to distinguish MEANS-RESULT from REASON-RESULT is to restate the propositions changing the result into a purpose. Only if the relation is MEANS-RESULT will the shift to purpose make sense. For example, Titus 3:5 "he saved us by . . . washing . . . , and renewing . . . ." can be changed into a MEANS-PURPOSE relation by turning it around to read as follows: "he washed us and renewed us in order to save us." If, however, Mark 6:6 (see previous section), "And he marvelled because of their unbelief" is reversed like this to give, "They did not believe so that he would marvel," it no longer makes sense.

3. MEANS-PURPOSE

Both this relation and the previous one have MEANS as the label for the "cause" side of the relation. This is because they both state the action that was taken to achieve the result. However, in the MEANS-RESULT relation, the result takes place; in MEANS-PURPOSE the result is desired, but it is not stated whether it took place or not. The emphasis is on intention rather than achievement. There is, therefore, an implicit volitional element in this relation, and if this volitional factor is made explicit, then the purpose becomes the motivating cause and the means becomes the result or effect.

Consider the following example from Mark 3:10, "they pressed upon him for to touch him . . . ." Clearly, the *purpose* of the people was to touch Jesus, and the action they took to achieve their purpose was that of thronging Jesus, of pressing close to him; this was the *means*. Making the desire of the people explicit, the part of the verse under consideration would then read: "they wanted to touch him, therefore they pressed upon him." This gives a clear REASON-RESULT relation: the reason for their thronging him was their desire to touch him. However, the reason is complex in form, as it consists of a verb expressing desire, and the desired result, "to touch him." Also, "they pressed upon him" serves a double role. Not only is it the result of the desire, but even though not in focus, it is simultaneously the means for fulfilling that desire. When the desiderative element is dropped from focus, then the means and the desired result are brought into prominence.

MEANS-PURPOSE may be restated as REASON-RESULT. In the one, the volitional factor is implicit in the statement of the purpose; in the other the volitional factor is made explicit so that purpose becomes part of the reason. However, since the form in which this relation occurs most frequently in the New Testament is MEANS-PURPOSE, this label is retained. Some examples follow:

Mark 7:9 "Full well ye reject the commandment of God, that ye keep your own tradition."

Col. 4:8 "Whom I have sent unto you for the same purpose, that he might know your estate, and comfort your hearts." (double purpose)

John 9:39 "For judgment I am come into this world, that they which see not might see; and that they which see might be made blind." (This is a more complicated example with a generic purpose stated before the means, and two specific purposes stated after it.)

The use of the word "lest" signals negative purpose. For example, Mark 14:38 begins: "Watch ye and pray, lest ye enter into temptation."

This is just another way of saying: "Watch and pray, in order that you do not enter into temptation." This, too, is a means-purpose relation, but the purpose is a negative one, one not to be achieved.

4. CONDITION-CONSEQUENCE

In this relation, the cause-effect sequence is clearly maintained, but the speaker presents the cause-effect relation in the light of his own contrafactual assumptions, or his own uncertainty concerning the cause.[8] He may assume as certain that the cause did not happen or he may assume as uncertain whether the cause will happen or when it will happen. A division into two semantic subtypes is therefore made. In the first, the speaker assumes the condition stated is false to reality as he conceives of it; in the second he is uncertain — he just does not know whether the cause is in accord with what will happen or not.

The first of these subtypes is the easiest to identify, and is usually referred to as the *contrary-to-fact* (or *contrafactual*) type. In this type, the speaker indicates the event referred to in the conditional proposition never actually took place, or the facts stated are not true in his opinion; realization is precluded, so far as the speaker is concerned. (Whether, in fact, the event took place or not, or whether the facts are true or not, has to be determined from the context.) The consequence proposition states what the speaker supposes would have happened or would be true, given the occurrence of the condition.

> Matt. 23:30 ". . . If we had been in the days of our fathers, we would not have been partakers with them in the blood of the prophets."

> Mark 14:21 ". . . good were it for that man if he had never been born." (reverse order)

> Luke 7:39 "This man, if he were a prophet, would have known who and what manner of woman this is . . . ." (note that this is the *opinion* of the speaker regarding Jesus, but that it was, in fact, false)

> John 8:19 "Ye neither know me, nor my Father: if ye had known me, ye should have known my Father also."

> John 8:42 "If God were your father, you would love me." (Jesus is stating *his* opinion, as opposed to *their* opinion, made clear in the previous verse: "We have one Father, even God.")

In the second type the facts referred to in the condition proposition are open to realization. If the condition is true or is realized, then the consequence will follow. Within this second type, it is possible to make a distinction between the particular and the general. In many of the general conditions, the speaker assumes as certain that the condition will happen sometime but as uncertain as to when, how often, or with whom.

---

[8] In the grammars, the conditional clause is referred to as the "protasis" and the consequence clause as the "apodosis." When it is assumed by the speaker that the protasis has happened or is a fact, the grammars class such clauses as conditions also. While it is true that such clauses begin with "if," they are neither contrary to fact nor are they assumed to be uncertain. Semantically there is no uncertainty. Perhaps a condition form is used to allow the hearer himself to supply certainty to the protasis so that he will be ready for the conclusion. This hypothesis is strengthened when we note that this usage occurs frequently in a sentence designed to convince or to persuade. See the comments under number 6 of this section on GROUNDS-CONCLUSION.

This type of condition is often introduced with *when, whenever,* or *he who,* rather than with *if.* Some examples of the general type follow:

Matt. 15:14 "And if the blind lead the blind, both shall fall into the ditch."

Matt. 22:24 ". . . If a man die, having no children, his brother shall marry his wife . . . ."

1 Cor. 7:28 ". . . if a virgin marry, she hath not sinned."

It is perhaps worth pointing out that the general condition may be negative, in which case it is often signaled in an English translation by such introducers as "unless" and "except." For example:

John 3:3 "Except a man be born again (If a man is not born again), he cannot see the kingdom of God."

2 Tim. 2:5 ". . . he is not crowned, except he strive lawfully (if he does not strive lawfully)" (reverse order)

The particular types does not state general suppositions, but gives a particular supposition relating to a particular situation.

Matt. 8:2 "Lord, if thou wilt, thou canst make me clean."

Mark 9:22 ". . . but if thou canst do anything, have compassion on us . . . ."

Acts 9:2 ". . . that if he found any of this way . . . , he might bring them bound unto Jerusalem."[9]

5. CONCESSION-CONTRAEXPECTATION

In this relation, the effect takes the form of an unexpected result. The result is definite, as with REASON-RESULT and MEANS-RESULT, but the concessive proposition carries the implication that this is not the expected result, but a different one. It is this component of *expectancy*, and its reversal, that characterizes this type of CAUSE-EFFECT relation.

As was noted in the discussion of CONTRAST, exegetically it can be difficult to decide whether there is a reversal of expectancy or not, as

---

[9] Those familiar with the discussion of Greek conditional clauses in the grammars will notice that nothing is said in this section on the CONDITION-CONSEQUENCE relation about the use of *ei* or *ean,* nor about the mood or tense of the verbs used in the protasis and apodosis. This is deliberate. Although there is a fairly close connection between the grammar of conditional constructions and their semantic analysis, it is not completely one-to-one. The contrary-to-fact type is in one-to-one correspondence with the grammar, with *ei* in the protasis, *ean* in the apodosis, the indicative mood in both, and the tenses restricted to the imperfect, pluperfect, and aorist. The subtype expressing uncertainty is, however, more complicated, with various combinations of *ei, ean* and the moods and tenses. The general statements always seem to have *ean* and the subjunctive in the protasis, and the indicative in the apodosis. So it would appear that the differing combinations are found in the particular statements. The grammars have done extensive work in this area, but they are not in full agreement with one another, nor is it completely clear how the various grammatical distinctions correlate with the semantic ones. More exhaustive research is still needed before the interplay of grammar and meaning can be spelled out in detail.

the expectancy is often culturally bound. For example, Philemon 11 is expressed in the form of a contrast: "which in time past was to thee unprofitable, but now profitable to thee and to me." The two points of difference are present — "time past" versus "now" and "unprofitable" versus "profitable." But there may also be the expectancy that a runaway slave could never be of any use again. He might never be found, or even if he were, and was not punished with imprisonment or death, he could not be trusted again. Hence this statement of Paul's could be an example of this relation of CONCESSION-CONTRAEXPECTATION, if there is a reversal of expectancy carried implicitly.

Another example is provided by Romans 5:10: "For if, when we were enemies, we were reconciled to God by the death of his Son, much more, being reconciled, we shall be saved by his life." The material under consideration is "when we were enemies, we were reconciled to God." This might simply be analyzed as TIME, the first clause giving the time of the second. But the general teaching of Scripture is that there were no grounds for *expecting* God to take steps to reconcile evil men to himself. Indeed, it is constantly urged as a reason for profound praise and gratitude that he ever did so. Hence, "when we were enemies, we were reconciled to God" is analyzed as CONCESSION-CONTRAEXPECTATION.

Occasionally, the unexpected result may be coordinated with a further amplificatory statement, as in Mark 5:26, "and [she] had spent all that she had, and was nothing bettered, but rather grew worse." The expected result is that she would get better; this is negated, and then further amplified by stating she was actually worse.

This particular relation readily enters into complex forms of the CAUSE-EFFECT relations; see the discussion which follows GROUNDS-CONCLUSION.

6. GROUNDS-CONCLUSION

This relation states an observation or known fact and a conclusion deduced from that observation or fact. The observation or fact represents the ground; the deduction represents the conclusion. The "result," therefore, is not actual or desired, but concluded. Consider the following example from English:

She is looking very pale today, so she must be feeling ill. The grounds is followed by the conclusion and typical of this relation is the possibility of inserting some words indicating that the conclusion has been deduced as:

She is looking very pale today, so, *I conclude*, she must be feeling ill.

(This conclusion assumes a prior connection has been established between a pale appearance and feeling ill. Such assumptions may be culturally oriented rather than universal.)

This type of relation seems to be used in two major contexts in the New Testament. The first is in arguments, when a conclusion is drawn from known facts, and stated as such. The second is when the conclusion drawn is not presented as a statement, but as a command: given this, or these, particular facts, then . . . you, or we, should undertake some appropriate action. This is a common pattern in the New Testament, where many different facts are adduced as grounds for exhortations to Christian conduct.

The first, the argument type, is exemplified below:

Rom. 5:9 ". . . being now justified . . . , we shall be saved . . . ."

Rom. 9:15, 16 "For he said to Moses, I will have mercy on whom I will have mercy, and I will have compassion on whom I will have compassion. So then it is not of him that willeth, nor of him that runneth, but of God that sheweth mercy." (Note the double grounds and the conclusion expressed both negatively and positively.)

1 Cor. 6:2 ". . . and if the world shall be judged by you, are ye unworthy to judge the smallest matters?"

Notice that this type of argument, in Greek, may be marked by the occurrence of "if" in the grounds from which the conclusion is drawn, and that the conclusion is quite readily presented in the form of a rhetorical question. However, sometimes the speaker does not state the conclusion himself, but asks someone else to provide it, as in Mark 12:23, where the Sadducees, having told the story of the woman married successively to seven brothers, then say, "In the resurrection therefore, when they shall rise, whose wife shall she be of them?" In other words, as the "therefore" indicates, they were asking, "Given these facts, what conclusion is to be drawn from them?"

The second type puts the conclusion in the imperative form — on the basis of the grounds stated, the readers are told to do or not to do something. For example:

Matt. 5:36 "Neither shalt thou swear by thy head, because thou canst not make one hair black or white."

Matt. 9:37, 38 ". . . The harvest truly is plenteous, but the labourers are few; pray ye therefore the Lord of the harvest, that he will send forth labourers into his harvest."

Heb. 4:14 "Seeing that we have a great high priest . . . let us hold fast our profession . . . ."

1 Pet. 4:7 "But the end of all things is at hand; be ye therefore sober . . . ."

1 Pet. 5:8 "Be sober, be watchful. Your adversary the devil prowls around like a roaring lion, seeking someone to devour" (rsv).

The conclusion in the example of Matthew 9:37, 38 is not as direct as in the other examples. The command focuses on the means of accomplishing the implied conclusion, namely, the need for laborers. Therefore, it seems best to analyze this as a type of GROUNDS-CONCLUSION relation which may need to be expanded in some languages to make an explicit reference to the conclusion.

Complex forms of the CAUSE-EFFECT group of relations

This particular group of relations occurs in complex forms, of which one or two are illustrated below. This area of relations between propositions is not fully investigated yet, so all that is intended here is to alert the translator to the possibility of such complexities.

Sometimes the relations of GROUNDS-CONCLUSION or CONDITION-CONSEQUENCE occur together with the CONCESSION-CONTRAEXPECTATION relation.[10] That is to say, a cause is stated as uncertain, and then it is stated the expected result arising from that cause will not take place, but some other result; or the expected conclusion from some grounds is replaced by an unexpected conclusion.

> Matt. 26:35 "Even if I must die with you, I will not deny you" (RSV). (Here CONDITION-CONSEQUENCE is combined with CONCESSION-CONTRAEXPECTATION.)

One complex form of CONCESSION-CONTRAEXPECTATION uses "but." For example, the statement, "I was going to go to the store, but it rained," is best understood as concessive. This statement may be analyzed as follows. There is an implied negated expected result "I did not (go)," which is also the result of the reason "it rained." In other words, expressed more fully it would be: "I was going to go to the store, but I did not because it rained." There is a fusion of the two pairs of propositions, "Even though I was going to go to the store, I did not," and "I did not go to the store, because it rained." A possible example from the New Testament of this type of CONCESSION-CONTRAEXPECTATION could be 1 Thessalonians 2:18, "Wherefore we would have come unto you . . . but Satan hindered us." The implicit statement would be, "We did not come to you," or "We have not yet come to you." Expressed more directly as concessive, it would read, "Although we wanted to come to you, Satan hindered us."

Another type of complexity occurs when the two propositions in a CAUSE-EFFECT relation are also stated to be in proportion to one another, either directly or inversely. This type of complex relation is signaled in English by "the more . . . the more," "the more . . . the less," etc.

> Mark 7:36 ". . . the more he charged them to tell no one, the more zealously they proclaimed it" (RSV). (Seen in context, this is basically a CONCESSION-CONTRAEXPECTATION relation: "Although he charged them to tell no one, they proclaimed it zealously." In addition, the two propositions are set in proportion to one another, so an increase in his charging was matched with an increase in their proclaiming.)
>
> 2 Cor. 12:15 "If I love you the more, am I to be loved the less?" (RSV). (This appears to be essentially a GROUNDS-CONCLUSION relation:

---

[10] Trail (1973, p. 13) discusses which relation has priority when two relationships are encoded in a single sentence. He suggests the "first is primary," but in private correspondence suggests that "the relationship which dominates the other is primary."

"I love you, therefore I conclude that I ought to be loved." In addition, the two propositions are in inverse proportion so an increase in his love for them is matched by a decrease in their love for him. The whole is put in the form of a rhetorical question.)

Support propositions which orient

This group of propositions provides what can be termed background information, or the setting for another proposition. They give its orientation with respect to time, or place, or some other accompanying Event. Because the members of this group have this particular semantic function, they are often related to groups of propositions, such as paragraphs, by providing the orientation for the whole group, especially in narrative material. As was mentioned in chapter 17, a change of setting often serves to mark the beginning of a new semantic unit. This distinguishes them as a group from MANNER, which is not used in this way.

1. TIME

This relation gives the time at which the main proposition took place; in other words, it answers the question, "When?" The TIME proposition may precede or follow the supported one in time, or it may be simultaneous with it. In either case, the proposition looks like the relations of CHRONOLOGICAL SEQUENCE or SIMULTANEITY, but they differ in that CHRONOLOGICAL SEQUENCE and SIMULTANEITY hold between propositions of equal rank, developing a theme, whereas TIME is a support proposition, of unequal rank, and simply provides background information.

Matt. 13:25 "But while men slept, his enemy came and sowed tares . . . ." (simultaneous in time, the main Event occurring at an indefinite point during the setting).

Mark 1:32 ". . . when the sun did set, they brought unto him . . . ." (the main Event takes place after the Event stated in the setting, i.e., there is sequence in time).

Mark 14:30 ". . . this day, even in this night, before the cock crow twice, thou shalt deny me thrice" (the main Event takes place before the Event stated in the setting, so this is a case of reversed sequence in time).

Luke 8:5 ". . . and as he sowed, some [seed] fell by the way side . . . ." (simultaneous Events covering the same period, but the sowing is continuous, the falling by the way side intermittent).

Luke 17:29 "But the same day that Lot went out of Sodom it rained fire and brimstone from heaven" (simultaneous Events taking place on the same day which is itself identified by an Event).

John 17:12 "While I was with them in the world, I kept them . . . ." (coterminous simultaneous Events).

2. LOCATION

This relation provides the background information concerning the place where the main Event happened; it answers the question, "Where?"

It often seems to be combined with TIME, and since LOCATION is one of the relations communicated by a State proposition, it can occur in that form.

> Mark 1:39 "And he went throughout all Galilee, preaching in their synagogues and casting out demons" (RSV). (The main Events of "preaching" and "casting out demons" are located throughout the whole of Galilee by the first proposition.)
>
> Rom. 15:20 "Yea, so have I strived to preach the gospel, not where Christ was named . . . ." (a negative definition of the places where Paul preached)

If a proposition indicating location clarifies a Thing word, rather than a proposition, then it is not an example of the relation of LOCATION, but of IDENTIFICATION or COMMENT. For example, the italicized clause in Luke 22:10, ". . . follow him into the house *where he entereth in*," identifies which particular house.

In the following examples, the LOCATION proposition is in the form of a State proposition and also serves the purpose of introducing a new participant or new participants.

> Luke 2:8 "And there were in the same country shepherds . . . ." (Location is mentioned and a new group of participants is introduced)
>
> Luke 2:25 "And, behold, there was a man in Jerusalem, whose name was Simeon . . . ." (Location and a new participant are given.)

3. CIRCUMSTANCE

This relation answers the question, "What else?" The support proposition centers on an Event which is simultaneous with the main one, and which also has the same subject. The background information does not relate the main proposition to time or location, but to another simultaneous Event.

Under discussion of the relation of MANNER, the distinction between MANNER and CIRCUMSTANCE was indicated. The distinction may be summarized as follows: the Event in a MANNER proposition answers the question "How did the Event take place?"; the Event in the CIRCUMSTANCE proposition answers the question, "What else took place at the same time as this Event?"

> John 19:5 "Then came Jesus forth, wearing the crown of thorns, and the purple robe."

Although no participant or thing setting has been posited here, it is quite possible that these may be used in the course of a discourse to introduce the presence (physically or conceptually) of a person or thing that will be described. For example, in Luke 2:36, Anna is introduced as a prophetess apart from any reference to time or location. Perhaps these can be included under the relation of CIRCUMSTANCE, at least for the present.

Support propositions which are related to part of a proposition

In accounting for the relations of all the propositions in a paragraph, it is sometimes necessary to make use of the relations which link a whole proposition with only part of another proposition. Two of the relations relate to a noun, which usually represents a Thing, but ocasionally an Event, the third relates back to a particular type of verb.

1. IDENTIFICATION

A proposition which has this relation serves to identify a Thing, in contrast with other Things; it singles it out semantically. It is the semantic equivalent of a restrictive relative clause, and often occurs in that form, but not necessarily so. It may occur singly, in the general flow of the discourse, or it may occur in a series of identificational propositions, in connection with the introduction of a new participant into the discourse. This latter type is often a State proposition.

John 6:50 "This is the bread which cometh down from heaven" (The relative clause singles this bread out from all other sorts of bread.)

2. COMMENT

An identifying proposition picked one Thing out from other similar Things so as to distinguish it; a comment proposition does not do this, but simply gives information about some Thing. It is thus the semantic equivalent of a nonrestrictive relative clause, though it does not necessarily occur in that form. As Burton puts it (1966, p. 166), "[it] may be used to describe a person or thing already known or identified." Both IDENTIFICATION and COMMENT, however, are signaled by the same grammatical forms in Greek, so each instance has to be studied in its context to determine whether it is IDENTIFICATION or COMMENT.

Gal. 1:15 ". . . God, who separated me from my mother's womb and called me by his grace" (two comments on God).

Col. 1:5, 6 "For the hope which is laid up for you in heaven, whereof ye heard before in the word of the truth of the gospel; which is come unto you . . . ." (two comments on the hope, and one on the gospel).

Rev. 12:9 "And the great dragon was cast out . . . which deceiveth the whole world" (The dragon was introduced in verse 3, and this is a further comment on him.)

3. CONTENT

There are certain clauses that are often, though by no means always, followed by "that" and one or more further clauses. Such clauses contain verbs like *know, understand, think, see, tell, said,* that is to say, verbs of perception, cognition, speech, emotion, desire, etc. Such verbs are common in the Scriptures, and the semantic information that follows such verbs is analyzed as being in the relation of CONTENT to the particular verb. Any proposition which completes the predicate of another proposition by answering the question "What?" is analyzed as a CONTENT proposition.[11]

> Matt. 5:21 "Ye have heard that it was said by them of old time . . . ."
> Luke 8:47 "And when the woman saw that she was not hid . . . ."
> John 17:25 ". . . these have known that thou hast sent me . . . ."
> 1 Cor. 14:23 ". . . will they not say that ye are mad?"

[11] It is anticipated that, when a detailed semantic grouping of Events has been undertaken, the relation of CONTENT will be further refined. At this state, however, the above definition will serve.

CHAPTER 19

Analyzing and Displaying the Larger Semantic Units

THE FORM OF A DISPLAY

There is a saying that "the proof of the pudding is in the eating." The two preceding chapters have discussed how the semantic structure of a text may be analyzed and how propositions may be related to each other. This chapter and the next put these theories into practice in a partial analysis of the semantic structure of the epistle to Philemon. This particular book of the New Testament has been selected simply because it is short and may therefore be discussed within the compass of two chapters.

Before getting down to the details of Philemon, however, it is necessary to explain in somewhat more detail the conventions that underlie the form of a display.

A display may be considered to be doing the following four things:

1. indicating the paragraph and section structure of the discourse, with the theme of each stated;
2. displaying the internal semantic structure of the paragraphs by means of indenting propositions in relation to one another;
3. specifying the relations between propositions by labeling them;
4. giving the results of specifying the propositions so that the grammatical classes match the semantic classes.

The last of these has already been discussed in chapter 17, and will be further exemplified in the detailed discussion of Philemon 4-7 that is in the next chapter. The first of these will also be illustrated from a discussion of the structure of Philemon. But there are some general comments that need to be made about the two middle statements.

Rank and indentation

A semantic paragraph may have different structures semantically. The writer may (1) start with a Main proposition (which may also represent the Theme proposition), and then go on to support it; or he may (2) gradually work down to a Main proposition; or he may (3) give it somewhere in the body of the paragraph; or he may (4) have a series of Main propositions which develop an implicit Theme proposition. In a display, the Main proposition or propositions would be farthest to the left, so the above types of semantic structure would have the following general shapes respectively:

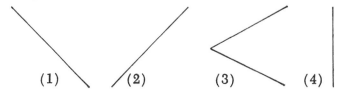

Propositions, however, when stated in a specific language are lineal in form and are better represented by horizontal lines. If, for the sake of simplicity, it is assumed that in each of these examples there are four propositions, then a more accurate representation of these displays would be as follows:

The first three examples represent a combination of propositions with one that is central or Main, i.e., a Statement. The Main proposition of each Statement is placed farthest to the left, with the supporting propositions indented to the right. With three such Statements, one following the other, a typical display would look something like the following:

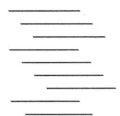

This last diagram brings more sharply to the foreground the question of the ranking of propositions, and how this is shown in a display. The previous chapter, on relations between propositions, distinguished three types of relations; those of unequal rank between a full proposition and part of a proposition; those between full propositions of equal rank; those between full propositions of unequal rank. In a display, propositions of equal rank are equally indented; those of unequal rank are unequally indented. Thus, if a conclusion is stated and then this is supported by three grounds, the display would have the following shape:

As illustrated above, when propositions of unequal rank are related, the support propositions are moved one indentation unit to the right in relation to the proposition which they support. Thus, in the above diagram, it is assumed the grounds are the support propositions so they are each placed one indentation unit farther to the right than the conclusion.

The three relations that connect a proposition to part of a proposition, namely, IDENTIFICATION, COMMENT, and CONTENT, are special cases. There is a sense in which IDENTIFICATION and COMMENT are of lower rank than any of the other relations, since they are generally related to a Thing. This being so, these two relations are *doubly* indented to the right if there are other propositions related to the same proposition. Hence, if in the above example it is supposed there is a COMMENT proposition related to some Thing in the conclusion proposition, then the display would take the following form,

with the COMMENT proposition the one doubly indented. Occasionally, however, a Main proposition will be supported by either of these two types of propositions with no other support proposition following, such as when a new character is introduced. For instance, this type of situation is found in the opening verses of many of the epistles, where the writer identifies himself and the recipients of the letter in various ways. Epaphras is similarly described in Colossians 1:7b, 8. In such cases, the double indentation for these two relations is not necessary, and they are only singly indented.

The other relation between a proposition and part of a proposition is that of CONTENT. In general, the CONTENT proposition is singly indented relative to the proposition containing the Event to which the CONTENT is related, but there probably will arise occasions when the overall theme of the paragraph will give the CONTENT more or equal significance with that part of the proposition which introduced it.

Before leaving the question of the indentation system used in these displays, it is important to draw attention to the *order* in which the propositions are presented in the display. The basic assumption underlying these displays is that the order chosen by the original writer to express what he was saying should be reflected in the display. More light will be thrown on this question when discourse analyses of the Greek have been undertaken, but it is currently assumed that preservation of the original order best maintains the focus of the writer. Hence, the propositions are presented in the order of the original unless to do so obviously distorts the focus of the original, in which case a shift in the order would be permissible.

Specifying the relations

One of the main purposes of a display is to make clear the semantic relations linking the propositions one with another. This is done by labeling the relation at the end of the line on which the proposition itself is stated. The relation may refer forward to another proposition or backward. In the example that has been used before, the relations refer backward and if the propositions are numbered 1 through 5, then the labels would be as follows:

1	——————————	
2	——————————	COMMENT on some Thing in 1
3	————————	GROUNDS of 1
4	————————	GROUNDS of 1
5	————————	GROUNDS of 1

This simple example highlights certain of the conventions of the labeling system. Along with the name of the relation there is also a phrase which specifies the particular proposition with which the relation is sustained. In general, the relation is with the preceding proposition which is indented one degree to the left, but since this may be several propositions away in the display, it makes it simpler for the user to have the proposition identified by specific reference.

Two other points need emphasizing. One is that equally ranked propositions, sustaining the same relation to another one, are labeled in the same way. In the above example, proposition 4 could be labeled GROUNDS of 1 and ADDITION to 3, but this second relation is carried implicitly by the equal indentation and identity of labeling. The other is that the proposition farthest to the left carries no label. In a display, the propositions which are not indented at all, that is, the Main or Theme propositions, are unlabeled, since they develop the discourse. The lack of a label in this particular example, therefore, signals two facts: one is that this is a Main or Theme proposition; the other is that it is in a CONCLUSION relation to the three GROUNDS. In other words, when a relation is directed backwards through the display — which is not always the case — then only the second of the two propositions carries a label. The first member of the pair will be either a Main or Theme proposition, and so will not be labeled, or it will carry its own label relating it to some preceding proposition.

The labeling also serves the minor purpose of clarifying a potential ambiguity in the indentation system. Normally, two propositions of equal indentation are in the same relation to some other proposition, as in the above example where there are three grounds stated. Occasionally, however, two propositions are equally indented, not because they sustain the same relation to another proposition, but because they are both related to it, but with different relations. Consider the following example from Colossians 1:21, 22:

1	(Christ) has now reconciled you (to God)	
2	by means of dying physically	MEANS of 1
3	in order that you will be holy	PURPOSE of 1

Propositions 2 and 3 are both independently related to 1, the first as MEANS, the second as PURPOSE. Note that this implies that not only is proposition 1 a Main proposition (hence unlabeled), but it is also the PURPOSE of proposition 2 and the MEANS of proposition 3. The relations are quite unambiguous, but the downward linear system of labeling carries its own implicit features. This example from Colossians also underscores the principle of maintaining the order of the original, even when perhaps some other order might have been thought preferable, such as 2, 1, 3.

THE LARGER SEMANTIC UNITS IN THE EPISTLE TO PHILEMON

It was emphasized in chapter 17 that the analysis of the semantic structure of a text needs to proceed "downwards," from the larger semantic units to the smaller ones. This is a relative statement, however, for in practice the analyst works both up and down until the analysis at every level of semantic structure is an integrated whole. Nevertheless, while judgments as to the boundaries of the larger units are subject to revision as the details of the propositions are worked out, they are logically prior.

Chart number 1 (page 318) shows the division of Philemon into paragraphs by ten different versions, chosen at random. The horizontal lines indicate the paragraph breaks, double lines being used in those cases where the version distinguishes between major breaks and single lines for minor breaks.

One thing stands out clearly on the chart — some divisions are widely agreed upon, others are not. Thus, all the versions have a paragraph break at the end of verse 3, and the majority do, also, at the end of verses 7, 20, 22, and 24. But between verses 7 and 20, only one paragraph division commands the support of even half of the versions, and all the others less than half. It seems likely this situation arises because at certain points in Philemon, the various types of evidence converge — the grammar, the lexical form, the semantic thrust — whereas at other points this is not the case, especially in the body of the letter itself. The following discussion is an attempt to draw on evidence available in the text to establish the boundaries of the larger units throughout the letter, but especially in verses 8-20 which constitute the major part of the body of the letter.

Some basic assumptions

In Greek, the finite verb carries more significant information than the other two verbal forms, the participle and the infinitive, since it is the

CHART 1

Phm.	A	B	C	D	E	F	G	H	J	K[1]
1						[2]				
2										
3										
4										
5										
6										
7										
8										
9										
10										
11										
12										
13										
14										
15										
16										
17										
18										
19										
20										
21										
22										
23										
24										
25										

[1] The versions represented on the chart are the following: A — J. B. Phillips, *The New Testament in Modern English*; B — *Revised Standard Version*; C — H. B. Montgomery, *The New Testament in Modern English*; D — C. K. Williams, *The New Testament: A New Translation in Plain English*; E — *Good News for Modern Man*; F — *The New English Bible*; G — G. H. Ledyard, *The New Life Testament*; H — R. F. Weymouth, *New Testament in Modern Speech*; J — C. B. Williams, *The New Testament: A Translation in the Language of the People*; K — *New American Standard Bible*.

[2] This division does not coincide with the end of verse 1, but is actually part way through it.

only form which signals the categories of person and mood. It therefore serves to introduce these two categories and to signal changes in one or the other or both. Further, since the other two verbal forms are dependent on finite verbs for these categories, it is quite general to find that the finite forms of the verb develop the theme.

Since the principal feature of a paragraph is the theme which gives it unity, the initial step in the task of delimiting the larger units is to study the finite verbs in the text, since the theme will generally be carried forward by them. However, not all finite verbs serve to carry the theme forward. Thus, for each verb, a decision has to be reached concerning its semantic function in the discourse — is it developing a theme, or is it in a supporting role, clarifying, arguing, or orienting? To reach a decision, other evidence has to be taken into account, specifically the connectives, the choices of lexical form made by the author (synonyms, antonyms, repetitions, words in the same semantic domain, etc.), and the order in which the information is presented.

The analysis of the larger semantic units of Philemon will follow the above procedure. Each finite verb will be considered in turn, and evidence presented to support a decision as to its role, and hence as to where the boundaries of the larger units lie. For clarity of presentation the discussion is divided into subsections, each subsection discussing the evidence for one of the paragraphs that are proposed in the analysis.

An analysis of the larger semantic units of Philemon

Verses 1-3

This is the most clearly marked section of the letter, as the total agreement among the versions indicates. No decisions based on finite verbs can be made, however, since there are none in these three verses, and the start of the next section is indicated by the occurrence of the first finite verb. This introduction to the letter has many parallels in the other letters in the New Testament, which fact confirms its analysis as a unit.

This introductory section has two paragraphs. The first consists of verses 1 and 2, in which the writer of the letter identifies himself and those to whom he is writing, the distinctions being carried by the case system, since there is no finite verb. The nominative case indicates the writer and his associates, the dative case the recipients. The first word in each of these two cases identifies the writer, Paul, and the principal recipient, Philemon. The second paragraph consists of verse 3, which is a benediction (very similar in form to verse 25) on the recipients of the letter.

Verses 4-7

There are five finite verbs in this paragraph, *eucharistō* "I-thank," *echeis* "you-have," *genētai* "it-may-become," *eschon* "I-had," and *anapepautai* "they-have-been-refreshed." The first and fourth have Paul as their subject; the second has Philemon as subject, the third *koinōnia* "fellowship"; and the grammatical subject of the last verb is *ta splanchna* "the insides."

Of these five finite verbs, only the first is unambiguously a Main proposition, i.e., it is neither subordinate grammatically nor semantically. The fourth finite verb appearing in verse 7, *eschon* "I-had," is introduced with the connective *gar* "for" which as explained in the next chapter is interpreted here to be a paratactic connector rather than a hypotactic subordinator. Following this interpretation, there are two Main propositions giving Paul's reactions to the news he received about Philemon; one in verse 4 and the other in verse 7.

The boundaries of the paragraph are thus tentatively established by this parallelism of two Main propositions which mark the beginning and end points. The parallelism emerges more clearly by observing further that the first finite verb "I-thank" is followed with the reason for that thanks and the fourth "I-had (joy and encouragement)" is followed with the reason for that joy and encouragement.

There are thus two parallel parts of this paragraph, both giving Paul's reaction to the news of Philemon's love *agapē* for his fellow Christians (*hagioi* "saints"). In verse 8, however, there is a change of relation to the news about Philemon. It is not Paul's reaction that is being given, but a conclusion that he draws from this news. This shift is signaled by the use of the inferential particle, *dio*, as well as the fact that the Event signaled by the next finite verb, *parakalō* "I appeal," is now directed to Philemon, whereas the Events in verses 4-7 are not.

In deciding on the theme, however, further considerations need to be discussed. Verse 4 mentions Paul's prayers for Philemon, and verse 6 gives the content of those prayers. The Event of praying in verse 4 is, however, subsidiary to "I thank." It is represented in the surface structure by a participle and two abstract nouns, and when *hopōs* is used in verse 6 to introduce the contents of the prayer, no finite verb is used. Hence, although 'I pray' is a reaction to the news about Philemon, just as "I thank" is, it is analyzed as relevant to the specific request Paul is contemplating but not the main emphasis of this paragraph. On the basis of grammatical evidence and the content of the next paragraph it is, therefore, considered to be subthematic.

In verse 5 Philemon's love and faith are both mentioned as reasons for Paul's thanks. However, in stating the theme of this paragraph, love is chosen as the most significant of the two. This decision is made on the basis that love is again mentioned in verse 7 and, although external to this paragraph, it is again mentioned in verse 9. Although faith is also repeated from verse 5 as part of the content of the prayer in verse 6, it is not the topic of the prayer but rather serves merely to characterize fellowship. Some see thematic significance in that love is mentioned first in verse 5. On the basis of these considerations, the focus is primarily on love, not faith. The theme, therefore, will not only include a generic representation of the three reactions Paul had to the news, namely, "I thank," "I rejoice," and "I am encouraged" but also the main reason for these reactions. The theme may thus be stated as: "I have been moved because you, Philemon, love all the saints."[3]

Verses 8-11

This paragraph opens with *dio*, "therefore," indicating that the theme of this paragraph is a conclusion based on the evidence of the preceding one. This factor, then, has to be taken into account when deciding what the theme is.

There are only three finite verbs in this paragraph, and two of these are the same, as Paul repeats them for emphasis. The verbs are *parakalō* "I-appeal," and *egennēsa* "I-begot." The second of these occurs in a relative clause referring back to the noun *teknou* "child" in the main proposition. It does serve, however, to introduce an important piece of information, the name of his spiritual child, Onesimus. Again, the paragraph boundaries may be determined by the finite verbs which are clearly developmental, in that they are not grammatically subordinate and represent two Main propositions to which the rest of verses 8-11 are support. And again, the paragraph has a parallel structure. The first finite verb is followed by an aside, describing Paul, who is making the appeal; the second one is followed by the name of Onesimus with a play on words based on the meaning of Onesimus. Both asides have two parts, and the second part of each is introduced by *nuni de* "but now."

The theme, then, of this paragraph is straightforward: "I appeal to you on behalf of Onesimus." Since it was introduced by *dio*, it is a conclusion based on the grounds of Philemon's love for the saints. This is further confirmed by Paul's reference to a choice which faced him — to command or to appeal. He concluded that the latter was preferable *dia tēn agapēn* "because of love." The two themes may thus be related as follows: "You, Philemon, love the saints. Therefore, I am appealing to you on behalf of Onesimus."

Verses 12-16

Of the different paragraphs in this Epistle, this is the most interesting from the point of view of its semantic structure. The chart of the para-

---

[3] Here the theme of the paragraph is stated not in the form of a Proposition but a Statement. This may arise from factors that have not been discussed. The emotional or cognitive orientation of the speaker or writer to the data is sometimes introduced along with equally or more focal information. Here, the former is encoded with finite verbs and the latter in some other form. It may prove to be the case that performatives (I say, I thank, I hear, etc.) always rank lower semantically than the information which they introduce, but this is not certain.

Another factor relates to some propositions which generally represent information carried by Concepts rather than by a separate proposition such as manner or time. When these occur in the form of a proposition and are part of the focal information of the Theme, a Statement form will result.

A final factor may explain vv. 4-7 of Philemon. In a letter, such as Philemon, it is not surprising to find a paragraph with a dual focus — one on the writer, the other on the addressee. It may be, then, that we have a paragraph with a double theme, namely, *I have been moved* and *you love all the saints.* Both are important. However, the first theme relates only to the paragraph unit while the second relates to the succeeding paragraphs and thus to the main argument of the book.

graphing in the versions shows that paragraph breaks have been made after verses 12 and 14, as well as after 16. What, then, are the criteria that indicate that verses 12-16 form a single semantic unit?

The first question arises with the first finite verb, *anepempsa* "I-am-sending-back." This is preceded by *hon* "whom." Grammatically, it is parallel with the hon *egennēsa* "whom I-begot" of verse 11, and the *hon egō eboulomēn* "whom I would-have-liked" of verse 13. Although these three constructions are parallel, verse 12 (beginning with *hon anepempsa*) is considered as initial in this paragraph. Why is this?

There are several reasons. In discussing the previous paragraph it was stated that *hon egennēsa* "whom I-begot" referred back to the noun *teknou* "child" which occurs in the Main proposition of that paragraph. It is functioning as a comment on part of that proposition, and so is in a supporting role. However, *hon anepempsa* "whom I-am-sending-back," looks forward and is linked through a number of lexical ties with the following verses. In the next verse Paul says he would have liked to keep Onesimus, and he uses the infinitive *katechein*, a near antonym of "send back," and a near synonym with *apechēs* "you might keep" of verse 15 (Arndt and Gingrich, 1957, p. 84). Then the infinitive "do nothing" of verse 14 is a generic opposite to the specific desires which Paul entertained to keep Onesimus. As such, we have another near synonym to "send back." In verse 15, Paul uses the verb "he departed" which is also clearly related semantically to "keep" and "send back." Thus in this span of verses we draw heavily upon the lexical choices to establish the boundaries of the paragraph. Verses 12 to 15 use verbs from the same semantic domain and verse 16 is dependent grammatically and semantically on verse 15. Moreover, verse 17 introduces a shift to the imperative mood, thus, in this case, signaling a paragraph break.

It is concluded, therefore, that verse 12 initiates and verse 16 closes a paragraph which has to do with the return of Onesimus. But just what is the theme more exactly, and how are the finite verbs to be assessed as to their function within the paragraph?

The next finite verb after *anepempsa* is *estin* "is." This is part of a clause, however, referring back to *auton* "him," i.e., Onesimus, so it is a comment related to the emphatic pronoun, and has a supporting role, not a developmental one. It also serves to pave the way for the following clause about Paul's desire to keep Onesimus with him.

The next finite verb is *eboulomēn*, "I-would-have-liked." This is the first verb in a unit with two parallel halves, in which a finite verb of desiring is followed by an infinitive expressing the content of the desire, and then the purpose of the content is introduced by *hina*. The two halves are linked together by *de* indicating some type of contrast between the two halves. There are also lexical ties, such as the near synonyms *eboulomēn* "I-would-have-liked" and *ēthelēsa* "I-wished"; the infinitive *poiēsai* "to do" is a generic substitute for the first infinitive *katechein* "to keep back"; and the emphatic *egō* "I" is contrasted with *sēs* "your." This whole unit serves to clarify the opening statement, "I am sending him back to you," by stating why he was doing so and commenting that it was no easy decision for him — he would have preferred to keep Onesimus with him. Hence, it does not develop the theme, but points to "I am sending him back to you" as the theme proposition.

The finite verb which follows this unit is *echōristhē* "he-went-away." It is preceded in the sentence by *tacha* "perhaps" and the connective *gar* "for" and *dia touto* "because of this." It is not at all easy to elucidate the semantic function of the connectives *gar* and *dia touto*. The initial *tacha* "perhaps" indicates that Paul is stating something tentative, about which he was not prepared to speak with certainty. Arndt and Gingrich (1957) point out, under *dia* BII2 (p. 180), that *dia touto* followed by *hina* (as is the case here) has the sense "for this reason, (namely) that," and they refer to this verse as one example. Following this approach makes good sense. Paul is suggesting what the purpose of divine providence might have been in Onesimus' running away, namely, that Philemon might have him back forever. This *dia touto* gives the reason (tentatively) for *echōristhē* "he-departed," and gives it in the form of a purpose *hina aiōnion auton apechēs* "that you might keep him for ever."

But what about *gar*? What is its function here? It normally functions to introduce a reason or explanation for something that has already been stated. Since the Theme proposition is "I am sending him back," it seems best to consider the *gar* as introducing a reason why he was doing so. The reason is simply that which has just been discussed, namely the purpose of divine providence. If, as Paul is tentatively suggesting, God's purpose was that Philemon might welcome Onesimus back forever, then for Paul to retain him would be going counter to the divine purpose.

The finite verb, *echōristhē* "he-departed," is therefore linked by these connectives to the Theme proposition and has a supporting role in relation to it.

The last verse of this paragraph has not yet been commented on. It consists of two contrasts. The first is, "no longer as a slave, but more than a slave"; and the other is, "especially to me, but how much more to you." Standing in apposition to the highlighted positive phrase "more than a slave" are the two words *adelphon agapēton* "a beloved brother." This type of construction, together with the lexical contrast "slave" and "brother," serves to highlight the phrase "a beloved brother." It may be that this highlighted phrase in the accusative refers back not only to *auton* "him" in verse 15 but also to *auton* "him" in verse 12. At any rate, Paul sent Onesimus back to Philemon that he might keep him as a beloved brother.

Verses 17-20

Verse 17 is introduced by *ei oun* "if, therefore," and the following consequence is in the form of a command. Paul often introduces commands with *oun*, and if they are based on some expressed assumption, then the assumption is introduced with *ei oun*. For example, compare Philippians 2:1; Colossians 3:1, 5, 12. Paul has now stated the considerations which he feels are relevant to the situation, and on the basis of these, and the further consideration introduced by *ei*, he uses a command. These factors distinguish verse 17, and what follows, from the preceding paragraphs, where the moods of the finite verbs are indicative and subjunctive, not imperative.

But how far does the paragraph extend? Verse 18 also contains a command to Philemon, and so do verses 20 and 22. However, the command in verses 18 and 20 are related semantically to the opening command as they also deal with the question of receiving Onesimus back. The command in verse 22, however, is a request on Paul's own behalf, not on behalf of Onesimus, so it is analyzed as not being part of the same paragraph introduced by the command in verse 17.

The paragraph is therefore considered to extend from verse 17 to verse 20. But what is its theme, and how do the finite verbs relate to it? And do more detailed considerations support the above analysis?

The command in 17 is to receive Onesimus back as if he were Paul himself. Before looking in detail at the finite verbs in verses 18 and 19, it is worth noting that five of them are taken from the same semantic domain, business, and, in particular, that of debts and repayments. The second verb mentioned is *opheilein* "to owe (something)," and the last verb mentioned is *prosopheilein*, a compound form of the same verb with a synonymous or nearly synonymous meaning, so that the beginning and end of verses 18 and 19 are linked together lexically.

The first two verbs in verse 18 are introduced by *ei* "if," thus subordinating them to the following verb which is a command, *elloga*, "charge it to (my) account." This command is reinforced by a double use of the emphatic pronoun *egō* in the next two clauses, and the verb *apotisō* "I-will-repay." The last two finite verbs in verse 19 are part of the clause introduced by *hina me*, which is not attached immediately to a particular clause but is more in the nature of an aside, or a further comment. The sense of the first five words *hina mē legō soi hoti* may be expressed in English by "—not to mention that."

Although these two verses form a close-knit unit, the question still remains: What is their relation to the theme? In his opening command, Paul said that Philemon is to receive Onesimus as if he were Paul himself. The next two verses focus on a particular problem — what about any debts Onesimus might owe to Philemon? In these verses Paul is saying, in effect, "Receive him as if he had no debts, just as you would me." They are thus supporting the main statement by clarifying certain details implied by it.

Verse 20 has two finite verbs, the second of which is an imperative, but it is preceded by one of the few cases of the optative mood in the New Testament. This is similar to a command semantically. *Mē genoito*, translated in the KJV by "God forbid," is also in the optative mood and shows the same similarity to a command semantically. The optative and the imperative of verse 20 are both directed to Philemon, as is the command in verse 17. Verse 21 shifts to the indicative mood which gives another reason to close the paragraph with verse 20. The emphatic pronoun *egō* "I" is used with the optative, and there may be some emphasis implied by the fact that *mou* "of-me" precedes the noun phrase to which it is attached. This emphasis shows that the optative and the imperative support the opening command in verse 17 by indicating how much Philemon's obedience would mean to Paul.

The theme, therefore, is stated in verse 17b: "Receive him as you would receive me." This command specifies the content of the appeal to which Paul only alludes in verse 9, and the intervening verses have prepared the way for it. In other words, this command is the theme of the whole letter.

Verses 21-25

These verses are considered together, although they are not considered to constitute one paragraph. But they do form a section, a concluding section to the letter. The purpose of the letter has now been fulfilled, and Paul's request has been made to Philemon. Paul now closes the letter with some miscellaneous remarks.

Verse 21 has three finite verbs, *egrapsa* "I-have-written," *legō* "I-say," and *poiēseis* "you-will-do." In some ways, it is like an echo of verses 4-7. Paul is expressing his confidence in Philemon that he will do what Paul has asked him to. In that sense, it is a concluding comment on the contents of the letter, which is probably why a few versions treat it as part of the preceding paragraph. But as a concluding comment it stands on its own as a paragraph expressing Paul's confidence in Philemon and part of the formal conclusion of the letter. Moreover, verse 22 is linked with verse 21 by the three opening words *hama de kai. Hama* means "at the same time," and introduces a further request from Paul for a guest room to be prepared for him. There are two other finite verbs in this verse beside the command, but they are introduced by *gar* "for" and support the command by giving a reason why he would need a room.

Verses 23 and 24 constitute the third paragraph in this closing section. There is just the one finite verb, *aspazetai* "he-greets," followed by a list of those who were sending greetings to Philemon.

Verse 25 is the final benediction, and has no verb at all, the relation being handled by the cases of the various nominals. With variations, it has parallels in the other Pauline letters except where there is a final doxology. Close parallels to verse 25 are found in Galatians 6:18 and Philippians 4:23.

A formal display of the larger semantic units of Philemon

The results of the preceding discussion may be displayed in a formal manner in the same way the results of an analysis into propositions can be displayed. Each paragraph is represented by a proposition stating its theme, and these propositions may then be indented relative to one another in the same way that support propositions can.

The particular discourse being analyzed is a letter, which may be divided into three parts. These parts are basically distinct from each other in the sense that the paragraphs within any one part cannot be related to those in another part. There may be lexical or other links, but no overall relating of paragraphs is possible.

The first section of the letter consists of verses 1-3 and has two paragraphs, whose Theme propositions are the following:

1, 2   I, Paul, greet you, Philemon.
   3   May God bless you (pl.).

The last section consists of verses 21-25, and has four paragraphs, with the following themes:

21   You (sg.) will do more than I have requested.
22   Prepare a room for me.
23, 24 My fellow-workers here greet you (sg.)
25   May the Lord Jesus Christ favor you (pl.)

The main body of the letter therefore consists of verses 4-20. It has four paragraphs, whose themes can be related to one another in the following way:

  4-7 I am moved because you (sg.) GROUNDS of 8-11
  love all the saints.

8-11   Therefore, I am appealing to you (sg.) on behalf of Onesimus.

  12-16 I am sending him back to you as GROUNDS of 17-20
  a brother.

17-20   Therefore, welcome him back as you (sg.) would welcome me.

It may be seen from this display of verses 4-20 that there are two themes which serve to support two other themes. Each pair forms a section, and these sections have Theme propositions which can be related as follows:

4-11   I appeal to you (sg.)
  12-20   that you welcome Onesimus back. CONTENT of 4-11

The theme of the whole letter can be abstracted from 4-20. The Theme proposition would be:

   Welcome Onesimus back.

CHAPTER 20

Analyzing and Displaying the Propositions Within a Paragraph

AN ANALYSIS OF PHILEMON 4-7 INTO PROPOSITIONS
  Identifying the Event words in the paragraph
  Constructing the propositions based on explicit Events
  Constructing any other necessary propositions
  Relating the propositions to one another
A PROPOSITIONAL DISPLAY OF PHILEMON 4-7

AN ANALYSIS OF PHILEMON 4-7 INTO PROPOSITIONS

So far, the semantic analysis of Philemon has been confined to identifying the larger semantic units. One of these larger units has now been selected to demonstrate a further stage in the analysis. This is presented in detail for one paragraph only, as it is not possible to go into the necessary detailed discussion for all of Philemon within the scope of one chapter. However, a display of all of Philemon is given in Appendix E even though it has not been possible to include the reasons for each decision. The paragraph consisting of verses 4-7 has been selected to exemplify what is involved in analyzing a paragraph into propositions.

Although the analyst, in practice, tackles all aspects of the analysis simultaneously, the analytical procedures involved may be separated out and presented in a logical order. This is what is done throughout the rest of this section.

Identifying the Event words in the paragraph

In connection with the definition of a proposition (see chapter 18) it was stated there are two types of propositions, Event propositions and State propositions. Having identified a paragraph, the next step is to go through it carefully identifying all the words or phrases which represent Events. This means not only the verbs (finite, participial, and infinitive forms), but also the abstract nominals which represent Events. To enable the reader to follow what is being done, the following transcription of the Greek text of Philemon 4-7, with a word by word translation, is provided. Words representing Events are numbered sequentially, by means of final superscripts; verse numbers are given on the line in parentheses.

(4) *eucharistō*[1] *tō   theō   mou   pantote mneian*[2] *sou   poioumenos*[3]
    I-thank   the God   of-me   always mention   of-you   making

epi tōn proseuchōn[4] *mou,*   (5) *akouōn*[5] *sou   tēn agapēn*[6] *kai*
at the   prayers   of-me   hearing of-you   the   love   and

tēn pistin[7] *hēn   echeis*[8] *pros   ton kurion Iēsoun kai eis pantas*
the faith   which   you-have   toward   the   Lord   Jesus and to   all

tous hagious,   (6) *hopōs hē   koinōnia*[9] *tēs   pisteōs*[10] *sou*
the   saints   that the   fellowship   of-the   faith   of-you

energēs   genētai[11] *en epignōsei*[12] *pantos agathou   tou   en*
effective may-become in knowledge   of-all   good   of-the   in

hēmin eis Christon.   (7) *charan*[13] *gar pollēn eschon*[14] *kai*
us   to   Christ   joy   for   much   I-had   and

paraklēsin[15] *epi tē   agapē*[16] *sou   hoti   ta splanchna   tōn*
encouragement   at the   love   of-you because the   insides   of-the

hagiōn   anapepautai[17] *dia   sou, adelphe.*
saints   has-been-refreshed through   you   brother

This paragraph yields 17 Event words, but closer inspection reveals that some of them are best considered "dummy" verbs in the sense they combine with an abstract nominal to represent a *single Event* only. These are as follows:

mneian[2] . . . *poioumenos*[3] = "mentioning"
mention   making

agapēn[6] . . . *pistin*[7] . . . *echeis*[8] = "you love" and "you believe/trust"
  love   faith   you-have

charan[13] . . . *eschon*[14] . . . *paraklēsin*[15] = "I rejoiced" and "I was
  joy   I-had   encouragement   encouraged"
    encouraged"

There are thus 14 Events referred to explicitly in this paragraph. Each of these will be the center or nucleus of an Event proposition, so there are at least 14 Event propositions.

Constructing the propositions based on explicit Events

The next step is to state the proposition associated with each Event. This means the participants connected with the Event have to be specified; it also means that other modifications of the Event, such as its time, place, manner, etc., are stated. At this stage, the fullest possible use is made of the explicit information of the Greek, together with commentaries, grammars, versions, and lexicons, to insure the meaning conveyed by the propositions really is the meaning expressed by the original. If there are differences of interpretation, these are noted, together with the reasons for preferring one over the other (wherever possible), so that the translator, making use of the propositional analysis, will be fully aware of the choices facing him.

Each Event word is taken in turn, and is numbered as in the text above. The words associated with it in the Greek text are considered at the same time. This Greek material is then discussed, first with a view to ascertaining its meaning, and then with a view to seeing how that meaning may be suitably expressed in propositional form, as discussed in the previous chapter.

1 *eucharistō tō theō mou* "I-thank the God of-me." No detailed comments are needed. For the moment "my God" suffices to express the meaning of the Greek genitive construction "the God of-me," but it will be discussed in more detail later. The corresponding proposition would be "I thank my God."

2-3 *mneian sou poioumenos* "mention of-you making." The participle *poioumenos* is in the nominative case thus indicating it has the same subject, "I," as the main verb "I-thank." The abstract noun *mneian* is the grammatical object of the participle, giving the sense "making mention." Since this is a semantic display, and only one Event is represented, the display will use some form of the verb "to mention." *Mneian* is followed by *sou* "of-you," a genitive construction which is Objective in meaning, so that "you" is the grammatical object of the verb "to mention." This yields the basic propositional form "I mention you." Like the main verb, the participle is in the present tense and may express habitual or repeated action.

There is one detail that can best be dealt with at this point. *Pantote* "always" is found between "I thank my God" and "I mention you" in the Greek, leaving it ambiguous grammatically as to which clause it is attached. Two arguments may be presented in connection with this question: (1) When there is such a choice, most grammarians and commentators prefer to attach *pantote* to the main verb "I-thank," rather than to the participle. (2) Semantically, it seems more natural to say, "When I mention you, I always thank God (for you)" rather than "When I thank God, I always mention you." In other words, when Paul mentioned Philemon in prayer, he always thanked God for him. Reasons for these thanks follow, as is usual in Paul's letters. Hence the first proposition becomes "I always thank my God." (It would also be possible to add "(for you)" as implied, to give "I always thank my God (for you).")

4 *epi tōn proseuchōn mou* "at the prayers of-me." *Proseuchōn* is an abstract noun, representing the Event "to pray." Grammatically it is part of a prepositional phrase consisting of *epi* followed by the genitive case. In this grammatical construction, *epi* may have a number of meanings, but the most natural here is to indicate the time of an Event (Arndt and Gingrich, *epi*, I.2). *Proseuchōn* is followed by *mou* "of-me." This gives a genitive construction with a Subjective meaning, "I pray." However, since *epi* conveys the time, the proposition is given the form "when I pray."

There is an interesting alternative to the analysis of Events 2-4 presented above. Burton, in his volume *Syntax of the Moods and Tenses in New Testament Greek* (p. 88) says "such phrases as *kamptō ta gonata* (Eph. 3:14), and *mneian poioumai epi tōn proseuchōn* (Eph. 1:16; Phm. 4; cf. Col. 4:12) . . . are paraphrases for *proseuchomai*." Put in propositional terms, Burton is saying that Events 2-4 are simply a paraphrastic way of saying in Greek "I pray for you." There are two considerations which lend support to this viewpoint. One is that the collocation of *mneian* with the verb *poieō* is always followed by the phrase *epi tōn proseuchōn*. When *mneia* is found elsewhere, it is not collocated with either *poieō* or *epi tōn proseuchōn*, and it means "remembrance" (cf. Arndt and Gingrich, *mneia*, 1). The other is that it is not uncommon in Greek to find an abstract noun like *mneia* collocated with *poieō*. But the abstract noun, "prayers," used here, is not found in this type of collocation; *proseuchas poioumai* is never found in the Greek New Testament. This evidence would indicate, therefore, that Burton is right and that the whole expression is equivalent to "I pray for you." This is the view taken in this analysis.

5 *akouōn* "hearing." This present participle is also in the nominative case, indicating the person hearing is "I" in agreement with "I-thank." This gives the proposition "I hear." The tense being present, however, it could mean "I keep on hearing" if a number of reports had come to Paul's ears, as is quite possible.

6-8 *sou tēn agapēn kai tēn pistin hēn echeis* "of-you the love and the faith which you-have." "Love" and "faith" are abstract nouns representing the Events "to love' 'and "to believe/trust." The subject of the finite verb "you" and the *sou* "of-you," which precedes *tēn agapēn*, make it clear that "you" is the Agent of these two Events yielding the propositions "you love" and "you believe/trust."

These are both transitive verbs, however, so the question of who is loved and who is believed/trusted needs to be resolved from the context. In the Greek this information is supplied by two prepositional phrases following the verb *echeis*; these are *pros ton kurion Iēsoun* "toward the Lord Jesus" and *eis pantas tous hagious* "to all the saints." Since there are two verbs and two objects associated with them, it has to be decided which verb is to be connected with which object. There are two possible answers: (1) both with both, that is, both "love" and "faith" are shown toward 'the Lord Jesus" and "all the saints"; (2) "faith" is connected with "the Lord Jesus" and "love" with "all the saints." (The view that connects faith and love with the Lord Jesus and love only with all the saints, while true to the rest of Scripture, is rejected as arbitrary in this context as it violates the symmetry of the Greek construction.) While both of these alternatives are grammatically possible and have their advocates among the commentators and the versions, there are three arguments which, in our opinion, favor the second view.

1. There is no example in the New Testament writings of *agapē* collocated with *pros*, as is presupposed by the first of these two views. An interpretation which falls within established collocational ranges is to

be preferred to one which necessitates postulating a unique collocation.

2. The expression "faith towards all the saints" does not seem to be a Scriptural one, which is probably why some commentators link both faith and love with the Lord Jesus, but only love with all the saints.

3. It is generally agreed that Philemon was written about the same time as Ephesians and Colossians, especially the latter. In Ephesians 1:15 and Colossians 1:4 Paul states he had heard of the addressees' faith in (*en*) the Lord Jesus and their love toward (*eis*) all the saints. In these two epistles the Greek constructions used are unambiguous and give parallel statements to the second view here.

It should be pointed out that the second view here assumes the occurrence of the figure of speech called chiasmus[1], occasionally used by Paul elsewhere. This is a figure in which the first and last members of a set of four expressions are connected together, and the second and third. In this case, "love" would be linked with "all the saints" and "faith" with "the Lord Jesus."

In the light of these arguments the two propositions represented by the Greek would be "you love all the saints" and "you believe/trust the Lord Jesus."[2]

9-10 *hē koinōnia tēs pisteōs sou*, "the fellowship of-the faith of-you." This is the opening phrase of verse 6, which is widely recognized by the commentators as the most difficult verse in Philemon. One commentator says it is "notoriously the most obscure verse in this letter." The difficulties in interpretation arise because there is a concatenation of constructions which are difficult for the interpreter — three abstract nouns, a genitive construction, and three prepositional phrases. Further, there are only two explicit references to participants in the whole verse, so it is not at all easy to decide who does the Events and to whom they are done.

Again, within a somewhat limited compass, it is not possible to consider individually, and in detail, all the interpretations suggested for this verse. The approach here will be to present the arguments for the interpretation reflected in the propositional analysis but these, by implication, will give reasons why other interpretations are not considered satisfactory.

To be considered valid, any interpretation of this verse must take into account the following two contextual factors:

[1] See chapter 12 for a discussion of this figure. Blass-Debrunner (p. 151, section 477[2]) quote this verse as an example under their discussion of chiasmus.

[2] This interpretation assumes that, in this context, no distinction is to be drawn between the two prepositions *pros* and *eis*. That Paul does vary his use of prepositions for style is exemplified by Rom. 3:30 where he says, "and he will justify the circumcised on the ground of their faith (*ek pisteōs*) and the uncircumcised through their faith (*dia tēs pisteōs*)" (RSV). Since he is emphasizing in this passage that God is one and justifies both Jews and Gentiles in the same way, by faith, no distinction can be intended in this context between *ek* and *dia*. Moule, *An Idiom-Book of New Testament Greek* (p. 68), says "Phm. 5 . . . looks like a purely stylistic variation of prepositions." Lange and Lightfoot both link the variation in preposition with the chiastic structure.

1. Although the letter is addressed to Apphia, Archippus and the believers who met in Philemon's house, as well as to Philemon himself, verses 4-7 are addressed solely to Philemon. Paul uses *sou* "of-you (sg.)" five times in these verses, as well as the verb *echeis* "you (sg.)-have." Therefore, any interpretation of this verse must have Philemon clearly in focus. In particular, understanding this verse (with the great majority of commentators) to be Paul's prayer, it must be prayer for Philemon. This contextual consideration materially affects decisions concerning participants in the Events.

2. Verses 4-7 are not an end in themselves — they pave the way for the difficult request Paul is going to make of Philemon. Hence, any explanation of the content of this prayer must be directly relatable to the overall purpose of the epistle — the request that Philemon would welcome Onesimus back again. This fact may also help to explain in part why this verse is difficult; what Paul is saying is kept general because he is not yet ready to present his specific request to Philemon.

This opening phrase contains two abstract nouns linked together in a genitive construction; one is *koinōnia* "fellowship," and the other is *pistis* "faith." These are understood to refer to the Events "to have fellowship with" and "to believe/trust." The collocation *tēs pisteōs sou* "of-the faith of-you" is an echo of the similar phrase in the preceding verse, and is a Subjective genitive, equivalent to the statement "you believe/trust," as in the preceding propositions. Implied is the same object of that faith as was mentioned previously, "the Lord Jesus." Thus, the full form of the proposition would be "you believe/trust (the Lord Jesus)."

Koinōnia is not directly linked in the grammar with any participants, though there are parallel constructions, such as *humōn tou ergou tēs pisteōs*, "of-you the work of-the faith" in 1 Thessalonians 1:3, where the "you" identifies the Agent of *both* Events. *Koinōnia* is a word that refers to a mutual sharing; fellowship is a two-way activity, not a one-way one. Thus Kittel, on *koinōnia*, says, "It expresses a two-sided relation . . . . Paul uses *koinōnia* for the religious fellowship (participation) of the believers in Christ and Christian blessings, and for the mutual fellowship of believers" (1972, III, p. 798).

But who has fellowship, and with whom? These questions are answered from the context. Paul is praying for Philemon, so it is Philemon who is having fellowship — and the parallel genitive construction quoted above shows that the *sou* can signal the Agent of both Events. Further, the immediately preceding context has just spoken of Philemon's love for "all the saints," the people of God with whom he was having fellowship.

Paul, therefore, is praying for Philemon's fellowship with his fellow-Christians. Faith is immediately linked with fellowship because this is the basis of the fellowship. Paul is not thinking of a fellowship based on social factors, or intellectual interests, or racial identity. He is referring to the fellowship which arises from a common faith in the Lord Jesus. The relevance of such a prayer to what he is going to ask of Philemon is clear — he is praying that Philemon, as a believer, will be able to have fellowship with his former slave, even though he ran away, and perhaps stole from him. As Lenski says, commenting on verse 5, "Philemon's faith puts him into fellowship with all the saints" — including, therefore, Onesimus.

This genitive construction is thus analyzed as representing two propositions: "(you) have fellowship (with others/with the saints)" and "you believe/trust (the Lord Jesus)." The form these take in the display, however, may have to be modified since this genitive construction is the grammatical subject of the verb *genētai*, and to express this as a proposition may require some adaptations in the basic form of the propositions.

An alternative view that is preferred by commentators such as Lightfoot, Hendriksen, and Barclay (1973, 1965, and 1960 respectively) is that *koinōnia* represents the Event "to share (one's goods)." It is clear from the letter itself that Philemon was a generous Christian. Two reasons would seem to argue against this view, however: (1) the fact that Paul himself offers to meet any financial loss incurred by Philemon, so it would be strange if he were praying for an increase in Philemon's generosity; and (2) it was a loving welcome to a Christian brother that Paul was asking Philemon to show, and "fellowship" is the meaning most relevant to such a request.

11 *energēs genētai*, "effective may-become." *Genētai* is one of the forms of the verb *ginomai*. One of the senses of this verb is a change of state. Arndt and Gingrich, 1957 (*ginomai* 4, p. 158) put it this way: "of pers. and things which change their nature, to indicate their entering a new condition: *become something*." The "something" is expressed by the adjective *energēs*, which is given various renderings into English such as "effective," "powerful," etc. The grammatical subject of the verb, however, is not a Thing, but *koinōnia*, an Event. So Paul is praying that an Event, already taking place, will "become effective." The natural way to express this in English is to use the collocation "become more (and more)." Also, a suitable collocation is needed to express the idea of *energēs* when applied to the Event of having fellowship. Possibilities are such expressions as "richer," "fuller," "more extensive," etc. Lange (n.d., p. 14, 15) puts it like this: "the Apostle prays that his friend's participation in the blessings of Christian fellowship . . . may become more and more perfect." Koch (1963, p. 186) says: "The deep and intense prayer of Paul interceded for Philemon to the intent that his fellowship would be equal to the demand laid upon him. Prayer for the strengthening and empowering of the active progress of the fellowship of faith . . . ." Jones (1949, p. 460) suggests that "the object of Paul's prayer is that the *koinōnia* may become active and productive."

Again, the propositional form will depend on how the preceding propositions are expressed. At this stage, however, it may be left in the general form "may become more and more effective."

12 *en epignōsei*, "in knowledge." "Knowledge" is the third abstract noun in this verse. It represents the Event "to know," although different renderings such as, "to acknowledge," "to recognize," and "to understand"

are also suggested. For a propositional analysis, it is necessary to answer the questions: "Who knows?" and "What do they know?"

The former question is answered by reference to the context again. Paul is praying for a development of Philemon's fellowship with his fellow-believers, and as is usual in his letters, knowledge lies behind all growth. If the Christian does not know what God requires of him, then he is hardly in a position to put it into practice. So Philemon is the one who is to know. Lightfoot (1973, p. 336) comments: "In all the epistles of the Roman captivity St. Paul's prayer for his correspondents culminates in this word *epignōsis*. . . . The *epignōsis* therefore which the Apostle contemplates is Philemon's own." Vincent (1897, p. 180) supports this: "The larger his knowledge of such good things, the more he will be moved to deal kindly and Christianly. He will recognise through this knowledge the rightness of Paul's request . . . ." Hendriksen reaches the same conclusion: "The more thoroughly Philemon recognizes how greatly he himself has benefited, the more inclined will he be to extend mercy and pardon to others, specifically to Onesimus."

The matter of what is known is referred to explicitly in the Greek by the following phrase *pantos agathou* "of all good." This, in turn, is linked by the article *tou* to the prepositional phrase *en hēmin*[3] "in/by us." *Agathos* is an adjective, but there is no noun expressed — Paul does not say what he is describing as "good." However, it is not uncommon to find an adjective used as a noun in Greek. For example, the word *hagioi*, translated "saints" in many versions, is the plural of the adjective "holy" and the generic term "ones" has to be supplied. So also here, a generic term "things" can be supplied.

The question then arises: How does the *en hēmin* relate to the "good things"? There are two possible answers — either we do the good things, or we receive them, they are "in us." The Greek preposition *en* has both senses when collocated with terms referring to human beings. Further, either view makes good sense in the context. If Philemon comes to a fuller understanding of all the good that we, as Christians, can do, then that would include welcoming Onesimus as a brother in the Lord. On the other hand, if he comes to a fuller understanding of all the good things God has done for Christians, forgiving us, welcoming us as sons, reconciling us when we were enemies, then that, too, provides a strong reason for Philemon's behaving equally graciously toward Onesimus.

Two considerations would seem to point to the former view, however. One is that Paul is leading up to a request to Philemon to undertake a particular action. The other is that in verse 14 Paul uses the expression *to agathon sou* "the good of-you," and there the reference is clearly to a good deed he is asking Philemon to do.

---

[3] Following the generally preferred reading, rather than *humin* "you (pl)." The difference in meaning is not substantial, but it seems more likely that Paul is identifying himself with Philemon and other believers at this point. The ensuing discussion will make this clearer. See also the comments in Bruce M. Metzger's *A Textual Commentary on the Greek New Testament* on the choice of readings here.

The Greek phrases *en epignōsei pantos agathou tou en hēmin* can thus be considered to represent the propositions "(you) know all the good (things)" and "which we (can do)," where "which" refers to "all the good things."

13-15 *charan . . . pollēn eschon kai paraklēsin*, "joy great I-had and comfort/encouragement." As noted earlier, "I had joy" and "I had comfort/encouragement" are equivalent to the Events "I rejoiced" and "I was comforted/encouraged." There are two minor matters for consideration: (1) Does the adjective *pollēn* "much" go with *charan* only or with both *charan* and *paraklēsin*? All seem agreed that it modifies both nouns. (2) *Eschon* is the first person singular aorist form of *echein* "to have." In terms of a display in English, what tense does it represent? The commentators agree that it refers back to the time of the "hearing" mentioned in verse 5, so that the sense of the aorist is best represented in English by the simple past tense. The propositions then take the form "I rejoiced greatly" and "I was much comforted/encouraged." It is hardly possible to choose between "comforted" and "encouraged" as *paraklēsis* covers both senses, there really being no fully adequate English equivalent to this Greek word. Since Paul refers several times in this letter to his "bonds," "encouraged" should perhaps be given the preference.

16 *epi tē agapē sou*, "at the love of-you." *Epi* is a preposition that has many senses. Here it is followed by the dative case, and Arndt and Gingrich (1957) cite this example under section II 1b (p. 287) as illustrating the general sense "of that upon which a state of being, an action, or a result is based." In other words, Philemon's love is the basis for Paul's joy and encouragement.

The *sou* indicates the one who is performing the Event, thus giving, "you love." But who does Philemon love? If the *eschon* is to be linked with the earlier *akouōn*, then it is the love Philemon keeps showing to "the saints." Also, "the saints" are again mentioned in the next statement. This proposition can therefore be restated in the form "you love (the saints)."

17 *ta splanchna tōn hagiōn anapepautai dia sou, adelphe*, "the insides of-the saints have-been-refreshed through you, brother." Although none of the usual problems associated with abstract nouns, genitive constructions, etc., arises here, there are one or two matters of interest from the point of view of a propositional display.

1. The Greek verb is in the passive voice — "have been refreshed." The question arises of how a passive verb should be represented in a propositional display. There are somewhat conflicting considerations here. On the one hand, it seems very likely that the passive construction is often used to take the focus off the Agent and place it on the Patient. The focus of the original can be retained in an English representation of the proposition by using the passive. On the other hand, many languages for which translations are being made either have no category of passive, or can only use it in restricted contexts, such as when the Agent is unknown, or deliberately concealed. Recasting the proposition

in an active form would be of considerable help to translators in such languages. Faced with this type of choice, it is felt that the primary purpose of a display is to state the meaning of the original.

In this particular example, however, there is a further consideration. It seems likely that the passive form was chosen to name the recipients of the love mentioned in the previous phrase and to introduce a parallelism in form by placing the Agent last in both "the love of you" and "have been refreshed by you." The position of *dia sou*, "through you," at the end of the sentence, immediately before the final vocative, is probably emphatic (cf. the NEB translation, which places it in initial position). It is, however, not very natural English to emphasize an Agent by means of a prepositional construction. The emphasis is better expressed by making "you" the subject, and saying, "you are the one who . . . ," followed by an active form of the verb. Hence, in this particular context, an active form is chosen as best representing the meaning of the original, even though passives in the Greek are usually represented by passives in the display.

2. The expression "the insides of the saints" is a literal translation of a Greek idiom, and this form is not natural in English. Most translations replace "insides" by "hearts" as a more natural English equivalent, but "hearts have been refreshed," although understandable, is not normal English. Further, the commentators seem unsure whether there is a synecdoche here, in which "the insides" of the saints is put for the saints themselves, or whether Paul is saying that they were refreshed inwardly, rather than outwardly, that is, spiritually rather than physically. Probably the clearest way to express this in English is to say "refreshed in spirit." In that case, the proposition takes the form "you are the one who has refreshed the saints in spirit." However, the interpretation as a synecdoche seems a reasonable alternative. This would give the proposition "you are the one who has refreshed the saints, brother."

Constructing any other necessary propositions

The propositions based on the explicit Event words have accounted for most of the propositions necessary to express the semantic structure of this paragraph in Philemon. However, there is some information not yet dealt with, which will be considered now.

tō theō mou, "the God of-me." This genitive construction was left in proposition 1 in the form "my God." However, this is not wholly adequate for a semantic analysis for it leaves quite unspecified what the relation between "me," that is, Paul, and God is. This genitive construction represents a State proposition predicating the relation of ROLE between God and Paul. As was stated in chapter 16, the ROLE relation often implies an Event, and the relation would be made clearer here if such an Event were stated. The most natural Event would seem to be "to worship," although there are a number of other alternatives. "The God of-me" would therefore be expressed in the form "the God whom I(worship).'" This form of the proposition keeps "God" in focus as it is in the Greek.

eis Christon, "to Christ." This phrase is found at the end of verse 6, and has not been discussed yet. Although a number of versions translate this phrase as if it were equivalent to "in Christ," there is widespread agreement among the commentators that it is an elliptic way of saying "to the honor/glory of Christ." This is what Paul has ultimately in mind as he prays for Philemon — that Christ would be glorified. Expressed in propositional form, it is necessary to supply an implicit Event such as "to honor," "to praise," or "to glorify." Also, since Christ is in focus, it will be expressed in the passive, in some such form as "so that Christ (will be honored)." Who will honor Christ? Since Paul, tactfully, has switched to "us" for "you (sing.)" in the immediately preceding phrase, it seems most appropriate to the context here to supply the implicit Agent "by us," even though it is a particular act of Philemon's that is prominent in the letter as a whole.

Relating the propositions to one another

As stated in chapter 17, the semantic investigation is incomplete without an analysis of how the propositions are related to one another semantically. Sometimes there are specific relator words in the Greek, and sometimes the relation has to be deduced from the content of the propositions themselves, and the form of the lexical choices. In either case, commentaries, lexicons, and grammars are consulted to insure that as the propositions are related to one another no distortion of the meaning is inadvertently introduced.

For convenience of reference, the propositions are listed below in their preliminary form and in the order of the Greek. Also, they are now numbered as they would be in an actual display, that is, by verse number and lower case letter of the alphabet.

4a I always thank God
 b whom I (worship)
 c I pray for you
5a I hear
 b you love all the saints
 c you believe/trust the Lord Jesus
6a (you) have fellowship (with others/with the saints)
 b you believe/trust (the Lord Jesus)
 c (6a) may become more and more effective
 d (you) know all the good (things)
 e which we (can do)
 f so that Christ (will be honored by us)
7a I rejoiced greatly
 b I was much comforted/encouraged
 c you love (the saints)
 d you are the one who refreshed the saints in spirit, brother

Proposition 4b is in the COMMENT relation to "God" in 4a. Proposition 4c relates back to 4a in that both are simultaneous Events, as is shown by the present tense particple *poioumenos*.[4] The question here is: Is Paul simply saying he thanks God for Philemon and he prays to God for Philemon, without relating the ideas any more closely, or is he saying he thanks God *when* he prays for Philemon? Although it is not easy to choose between these, the theme of this paragraph would not seem to be his prayer to God. He does give the content of his prayer in verse 6, but in relation to the whole letter this paragraph is saying how grateful he is to God that Philemon is the sort of Christian to whom he could, with confidence (cf. verse 21) make such a difficult appeal. It accords more with this theme to treat the reference to his praying as subsidiary, giving the time setting of his thanks. Thus, 4c would be introduced by "when" and labeled TIME.

Verse 5 is interpreted by most commentators as giving the reason why Paul was moved to thank God, namely, the good report that had been brought to him concerning Philemon. That is to say, 5a would be introduced by "because," and labeled REASON for 4a. There is no overt marker of this relation in the Greek, but it is an established function of the participle.[5]

It seems useful, at the present stage of theory and analysis, to distinguish two types of REASON. One is the reason which gives objective information leading to the stated result. In this case, the objective information was the report Paul heard concerning Philemon. This type of reason will be labeled REASON (objective). The other is the reason which gives subjective information. By "subjective" is meant the reactions, feelings, emotions of the person involved. An example of this is found later in this same paragraph when Paul refers to his own joy and encouragement which some interpret as reasons for thanking God. REASON (subjective) will be used as a label in such cases.

Propositions 5b and 5c give the content of what Paul had heard as is shown by the accusative case of the two nouns, *agapēn* and *pistin*. To show this, they are preceded by "that" and are labeled CONTENT of "hear" in 5a.

Verse 6 is introduced by *hopōs*, and again, it is widely agreed that *hopōs* introduces the content of the prayer mentioned in 4c. From a propositional standpoint, this means introducing in 6a "(I pray)" as an implied proposition, and this is simply labeled as implied from 4c.

Within verse 6, the relations are more complicated. The essence of his prayer is "I pray that you may fellowship with others more and more effectively." The proposition 6d is the means by which this fellowship becomes increasingly effective, so that 6d would have to be restated in the form "by means of (your) coming to know all the good (things)" and would be labeled MEANS of 6c. The phrase "coming to know" reflects

---

[4] "The Present Participle most frequently denotes an action in progress, simultaneous with the action of the principal verb." (Burton, 1966, p. 54).

[5] See, for instance, p. 170 in Burton, 1966.

better the aorist form of the verb to which the prepositional phrase is attached. Proposition 6e is simply a COMMENT on "(things)." Proposition 6f illustrates a common problem in deciding on the relation where the preposition *eis* introduces a phrase: Is it the RESULT of what precedes, or is the PURPOSE of it? In this particular case there is also the question of whether it is related to the increasingly effective fellowship or to the good that we do. Since Paul is looking ahead, as he is praying, to what Philemon has yet to do, it seems more appropriate to analyze it as PURPOSE and to attach it to "we do."

This analysis still leaves the proposition 6b (above) unrelated. Undoubtedly, faith is the basis of the fellowship; it is only those who believe who are involved. However, if the supporting proposition "because you believe in (the Lord Jesus)" is attached to the main proposition directly, it gives the impression the increase in effectiveness is because of Philemon's faith, which distorts the meaning. Since the fellowship is characterized by faith, the best solution may well be to describe the "others" referred to in the main proposition as those "who believe/trust (the Lord Jesus)." In addition, Philemon himself has faith, so the proposition is expanded by adding "also" and "with you" to include him. The propositional analysis of verse 6 would then be as follows:

6a	(I pray)	Implied from 4c
b	that (you may) fellowship more and more effectively (with others)	CONTENT of "pray" in 6a
c	who also believe/trust (the Lord Jesus) with you	IDENTIFICATION of "those" in 6b
d	by means of (your) coming to know all the good (things)	MEANS of 6b
e	which we (can do)	ATTRIBUTIVE to "things" in 6d
f	in order that Christ (may be honored by us)	PURPOSE of 6e

The Greek nouns corresponding to propositions 7a and 7b are joined by *kai* "and" so they have a relation of ADDITION to each other. Proposition 7c, "you love (the saints)," is derived from a prepositional phrase consisting of *epi* followed by the dative case, and as was mentioned earlier, this use of *epi* indicates the grounds or basis for something else. Expressed in terms of the system of relations described in the preceding chapter, 7c would be labeled REASON (objective) for 7a and b, and introduced by "because."

The Greek from which the final proposition is derived is introduced by *hoti*. This conjunction, in terms of semantic relations, serves either to introduce the CONTENT of some Event, or the REASON for one. There is no Event in this verse that would take a CONTENT proposition, so it is analyzed as introducing the objective reason for Paul's joy and comfort. The previous proposition, however, did the same thing — how, then, are these two objective reasons related to each other? "You love (the saints)" is a general statement; "you are the one who refreshed the saints in spirit" is more specific. These two reasons, then, are considered to stand in a GENERIC-SPECIFIC relation to each other.

Two questions remain to be considered. Verse 7 contains the conjunction *gar* "for," so it has yet to be decided what relation *gar* signals, and what it relates back to.

In the discussion of the paragraphs and sections, it was stated this paragraph under discussion could be analyzed as consisting of two parallel halves. Each part has a performative Event (I thank and I had joy and encouragement), in the form of a finite verb, given as resulting from the news of Philemon's love, and the *gar* connects these halves together.

There is, therefore, a choice open to the analyst since *gar* has two functions either of which would be acceptable here. The first, and certainly the commonest in the New Testament, is to give a reason or explanation for some previous statement. This would mean that *gar* introduced further reasons for Paul's thanksgiving, in this case, subjective reasons. He thanked God because of the joy and encouragement the news about Philemon had brought him.

The second use is for "expressing continuation or connection" (Arndt and Gingrich, 1957, *gar*, 4, p. 151). This use would lend itself to the view that Paul is adding other reactions he had to this good news. His first stated reaction was to thank God. Having dealt in some detail with that reaction, and the subsidiary one of prayer, he then goes on to refer to his own joy and encouragement at the news.

At the moment, there seems little in the way of evidence to choose one or the other view. In the accompanying display, the latter view is represented, and the former is footnoted as an alternative view.

A PROPOSITIONAL DISPLAY OF PHILEMON 4-7

The analysis is now completed, but if it is to be of value to a translator it needs to be presented or displayed so that the translator can benefit from it. Some of the features of a display have been mentioned in this and the two preceding chapters, but they are brought together here for convenience.

1. Each section and paragraph is introduced by a statement, in propositional form, of the theme of that particular semantic unit.

2. Each proposition is numbered alphabetically within the verse.

3. Each proposition is labeled with a relation label at the right hand side. This label is in upper case, and it also states with which proposition(s) the relation is sustained. In addition, the proposition is introduced by a connecting word or phrase which signals that relation in English.

4. The propositions are indented relative to one another. Main or Theme propositions are on the extreme left, and propositions supporting these, or others, are indented to the right.

5. Occasionally, within a paragraph, a subtheme is developed by an embedded Main propositions. In such cases, the subtheme may be moved toward the left in the indentation system, and the particular term, such as "gospel" or "mystery," which relates the subtheme to the main theme, is placed within a box and the two occurrences are linked with a line. In Philemon 4-7, the subtheme of prayer is given the same indentation as 4c.

6. When the analyst feels that there are valid interpretational alternatives to the display, either in terms of the propositions themselves, or their relations, these are footnoted at the bottom of each page and identified by the proposition number. In such cases, the reasons why the analyst considers there is insufficient evidence to make a choice one way or the other will be presented in the comments on the display.

7. Certain words and expressions are followed by an asterisk if they are considered to be technical Christian terms. The meaning of such terms will be explained in a glossary attached to the displays.

8. Lexical alternatives which represent the same interpretation are separated by a slash when either (a) there are equally good alternatives in English for the Greek term used, or (b) no English term is fully adequate, so another term or expression is needed to convey the sense of the Greek.

PROPOSITIONAL DISPLAY OF PHILEMON 4-7

Philemon 4-7   I was moved because you love all the saints*.

4a	I always thank God	
b	whom I (worship)	COMMENT about God in 4a
c	when I pray for you	TIME of 4a
5a	because I hear	5a-c give the REASON (objective) for 4a
b	that you love all the saints*	CONTENT of hear in 5a
c	and that you believe/trust the Lord Jesus	CONTENT of hear in 5a
6a	(I pray)	implied from 4c
b	that (you may) fellowship more and more fully (with those)	6b-f give the CONTENT of pray in 6a
c	who also believe/trust (the Lord Jesus) with you	IDENTIFICATION of those in 6b
d	by means of (your) coming to know all the good (things)	MEANS of 6b
e	which we (incl.) (can do)	COMMENT about things in 6d
f	in order that Christ (may be honored by us (incl.).	PURPOSE of 6e
7a	Moreover, I rejoiced greatly	
b	and I was greatly encouraged/ comforted	
c	because you love (the saints*)	REASON (objective) for 7a, b
d	specifically, because you are the one who refreshed the saints* in spirit, brother.*	SPECIFIC restatement of 7c

6a	The display of verse 6 reflects the interpretation preferred by the authors. For a detailed discussion, see the comments.
6e	Or, that we (have received).
6f	Or, PURPOSE of 6b.
7a, b	These propositions could be labeled REASON (subjective) of 4a and indented one unit to the right, along with their support propositions.
7d	Or, omit "in spirit."

APPENDIXES

APPENDIX A

Some Further Considerations Relating to Idiomatic Translations

The idiomatic approach to translation is sometimes criticized. Four of the objections which have been raised to this approach are (1) an idiomatic translation is not consonant with the doctrine of inspiration; (2) it is the work of the Holy Spirit to make the meaning of the Scriptures clear, not the work of the translator; (3) it makes the ministry of the teacher of Scripture irrelevant; and (4) when published in a diglot version, it invites unfavorable comments when compared with the national version. These are discussed with each objection restated in a positive form.

An idiomatic translation is consonant with the doctrine of inspiration

The distinction between form and meaning, discussed in the earlier sections of chapter 1, is often made in works on the inspiration of Scripture. Thus Preus in his work *The Inspiration of Scripture* (pp. 15, 16) says, ". . . as in every writing brought about by an intelligent and rational agent, so also in the prophetic and apostolic Scripture two things should be borne in mind, first the letters, syllables and words are written and which are outer symbols indicating and expressing the ideas of the mind: second the thoughts themselves, which are the things signified, expressed with the symbols of letters, syllables, and words. Accordingly, in the term Scripture we include both of these, but especially the latter."

This view, that both the form and meaning of the Scriptures are inspired, has long been held. Preus, (1957, p. 45) summarizes the view of the seventeenth century Lutheran theologians as follows: "Content cannot be expressed without words: the very purpose of words is to convey thoughts or content. In the case of something already written, meaning cannot be known except from the words which express the meaning. Consequently, unless we can say the words of Scripture are given by God, we cannot say that Scripture is inspired, for Scripture consists of words . . . ." In the volume edited by Carl F. H. Henry, *Revelation and the Bible*, Finlayson makes essentially the same point as did the theologians of three centuries earlier (pp. 221-234): "Words, in all literature, must be accepted as the vehicles of thought, and the arrangement of words that gives adequate expression to the thought is correct to the exclusion of any other arrangement that fails to do this. Only if the thought is verbally correct is the communication what it is intended to be. If the content of revelation is of God, its communication in writing obviously must ensure that it is given as God would have us receive it. In this case, writing communicates the content of revelation, and inspiration guarantees its veracity."

In short, these writers show that *both* the linguistic form *and* the meaning of the Scripture are inspired. Not unnaturally, therefore, the question arises whether or not the doctrine of inspiration requires that the translator of the Word of God should faithfully preserve both the linguistic form and the meaning since both are inspired. The answer to this question has two aspects, one doctrinal and the other linguistic.

The first has reference to the purpose of inspiration. If as Finlayson says, the purpose of inspiration is to ensure the veracity of revelation, then, once the content of that revelation has been written, the primary purpose of inspiration has then been fulfilled. The grammatical and lexical structures used in the original then become the basis for a proper understanding of the content of Scripture. To assume further that the purpose of inspiration is also to give the grammatical and lexical form to be followed for all translations finds no support in theology or linguistics.

The second answer to this question is basically a *linguistic* one, not a doctrinal one. The linguistic arguments which support the view that an idiomatic approach to translation is fully compatible with the doctrine of the inspiration of the Scriptures are basically three: (1) the linguistic form of the original conformed to the idiomatic usage of the native speakers of the time; (2) linguistic form is subservient to the meaning communicated; and (3) the differences between languages preclude the transfer of this original form to any particular RL.

(1) It cannot be too strongly stressed that the original authors wrote in a form natural and idiomatic at the time of their writing. The extensive discovery of papyri, during the last century and this, has made it clear that the New Testament writers wrote in the Koiné Greek of their time, expressing themselves naturally and idiomatically in it. Warfield, in his work *The Inspiration and Authority of the Bible* (p. 438) expressed this forcibly: "And the Holy Ghost in using human speech, used it as He found it. It cannot be argued then that the Holy Spirit could not speak of the sun setting, or call the Roman world 'the whole world.' The current sense of a phrase is alone to be considered, and if men so spoke and were understood correctly in so speaking, the Holy Ghost, speaking their speech would also so speak." Since the Holy Spirit chose to honor and to employ the then current and natural usage of the original languages, it seems only reasonable translators should do the same and use the forms which are current and natural to the people for whom they are translating.

(2) The subservience of form to meaning has already been stressed in chapter 1. The illustration of a "vehicle" served to exemplify this point. The linguistic forms of a given language are simply the means by which the meaning is conveyed. Every language in the world has a unique system of grammatical and lexical forms, and these are quite adequate

to convey the same message as is conveyed by the forms of the original. But these forms are quite different from those in the original, so that the latter do not provide a suitable vehicle for communicating the message in any other language. The following quotation from Hulst, discussing the translation of the Old Testament into Dutch, further emphasizes this (1963, pp. 79-82): "Instead of separating the content of the Hebrew sentence from its form and transferring this into a Dutch mould, both the form and the content of the source language are sometimes rendered into words of the receptor language without the full recognition of the fact that the original Hebrew form frequently does not coincide with the form required in Dutch. As a result the 'translation' is disfigured by numerous Hebraisms. Of course, one can contend that he has made as literal a translation as possible and can insist that the unity of form and content may not be destroyed, but the result is not a translation in the true sense of the word."

(3) The original form was natural and idiomatic and was the appropriate means used by the Spirit to convey the divine message — but that form is different from the form used in every other language. From the linguistic standpoint, the differences between the grammatical and lexical structures of any two languages may hardly be overemphasized. It is true, there are always some similarities, but, apart from very close dialects, these are few and coincidental, whereas the differences are extensive, both in number and kind. Differences in pronunciation are obvious enough to anyone who has tried seriously to talk another language. And even within the study of related European languages, such as French, Italian, and Spanish, differences in grammar soon become apparent. It is often incorrectly assumed, however, that such differences do not extend to the lexicon — to the meanings words have, and the contexts in which they are used. Here, it is often held, languages are closely similar. While it is recognized there are some differences — Eskimo, for instance, has many more words for snow than English — these are felt to be peripheral.

Perhaps three examples from the Greek New Testament will serve to underline that lexical differences between languages are also significantly different. The verb *parakaleō* is used almost 100 times in the New Testament, and the related nouns *paraklēsis* and *paraklētos* more than 30 times altogether. In the KJV, the following English verbs are used to translate *parakaleō*: beseech, call, comfort, desire, exhort, entreat, and pray; *paraklēsis* is translated by comfort, consolation, exhortation, and entreaty; and *paraklētos* by Comforter and advocate. The variety of English renderings arises from the fact there is no single English root corresponding to this Greek root in meaning. In fact, because of the difficulty of translating the term *paraklētos* into English, in commentaries and scholarly works it is now often simply transliterated as "Paraclete."

The second example is provided by the verb *katargeō*, a favorite Pauline verb, which occurs 27 times in the New Testament (only two occurrences are outside the Pauline epistles). This verb corresponds to such a wide variety of English meanings that even the American Standard

Version (the American counterpart of the Revised Version), perhaps the most literal of English versions,[1] uses no less than nine different ways of translating this verb.[2]

A final example comes from part of Acts 10:44, "the Holy Ghost fell on all of them." In one language this was translated literally using the normal verb for "to fall" in the physical sense. Because of the use of this word, the language helper could only conclude the Holy Spirit was walking about in heaven, tripped and fell down upon the people. It was clear from the story in Acts that no one was hurt, so he also concluded the Spirit was light in weight so that even though he fell all the way from heaven, he did not hurt those on whom he fell. Greek could use "fall" in an extended sense in this context; the particular language could not.

Inspiration guarantees the form and message of the original — this is not the issue being questioned. But if that inspired message is to be faithfully transmitted to others in their own language, it will be in the appropriate forms of that language, not those of Greek, or English, or some other language.

Before taking up another objection to idiomatic translations, it is necessary to correct at this point a possible false impression. The constant emphasis on *meaning* as over against *linguistic form* may have given the idea that the translator who translates idiomatically ignores the form of the original entirely. But this is not so. In the translation process, the linguistic form of the original is of primary and basic importance. Only from a careful study of the grammar and the lexicon of the original can a translator arrive at the meaning which he is to communicate in the RL version. This involves the process of exegesis which calls into use commentaries, grammars, lexicons, and other exegetical tools. Once the precise meaning of the original has been determined from the linguistic forms of the text, then the translator is ready to look at the grammar and lexicon of the RL to choose a form which will convey the same meaning. The form is likely to be different, but basic to the form chosen in the RL is the meaning of the original which, in turn, is derived from the form of the original. The linguistic form of the original thus lies at the heart of all translation work.

It is compatible with the illuminating work of the Holy Spirit

Another question sometimes raised when a translation is obviously not being understood by the readers is whether or not it is the work of the Holy Spirit to clarify and to give understanding rather than that of the

---

[1] Cf. the comments of F. F. Bruce (1963, p. 233): "If he [the reader] wants an accurate and severely literal representation of the original, calculated to serve the requirements of the careful student, he will prefer the Revised. One obvious advantage of the Revised Version from this point of view is the Revisors' policy of rendering a single word of the original by a single English word where the sense permits."

[2] It is of some interest to note that of these nine, only two are one-word equivalents; the others involve up to four words. At this point, even English is unable to match the Greek by a single word.

translator. This question usually derives from the statement in Scripture which says, "the natural man receiveth not the things of the Spirit of God . . . neither can he know them, because they are spiritually discerned" (1 Cor. 2:14).

Some quotations from other writers should help to clarify this issue. Preus (1957, pp. 156-58) says, "Unless Scripture is clear, it cannot be said to be sufficient. How can we be saved through faith in a message of Scripture if that message is not clear? . . . Even an unbeliever is able to comprehend the literal and historical meaning of Scripture . . . . But a true spiritual understanding . . . of Scripture is attained only by the regenerate and only by means of illumination which the Holy Spirit bestows through Scripture . . . . There are many impenetrable mysteries in Scripture which are unclear in that they cannot be grasped by human intellect, but these mysteries have not been recorded in Scripture in obscure or ambiguous language." Bromiley (1958, p. 212) quotes Whitaker as saying, "We say that the Holy Spirit is the supreme interpreter of Scripture, because we must be illuminated by the Spirit to be certainly persuaded of the true sense of Scripture . . . . For no saving truth can be known without the Holy Ghost." In the same work, Ramm says (p. 257), "Man blinded by sin, needs a special illumination in his heart enabling him to grasp the truth of God as truth . . . . The sense of divine truth, and the religious certitude over divine truth which the Christian possesses, stem from the inner operation of the Holy Spirit upon the human heart."

In other words, the Scripture is clear and straightforward, and is intended to be understood by anyone who reads or hears it. But the message of the Word of God will not be believed, or acted upon, unless the Spirit of God opens the understanding and brings that same message home to the heart. But if, because of a poor translation, the message is obscure, or even wrong, what then? Is it the Spirit's task to correct it? Surely it is we who are to blame for putting in his hands a blunt sword instead of a sharp two-edged one.

It is compatible with the office of the Christian teacher

An idiomatic translation makes it easier for the teacher to expound the Scriptures on the basis of the text before him. He may still need to provide the necessary background information to "fill out the picture" for his hearers, since such information was known and left implicit for the hearers of the original but is not known by the readers of the translation.

There is a very real danger if the teacher is constantly having to correct the translation. If every other reference to the Scripture is prefaced with remarks such as, "I know that is what it *says*, but actually it *means* something else," or "It isn't clear from the way the verse has been translated, but in the original it means this," then the believers will tend to assume that *only* those who have the gifts of training of a teacher can understand the Word of God. They will gradually abandon their privilege of doing as the "noble" Bereans did, who "searched the scriptures daily, whether those things were so" (Acts 17:11). But the conclusion to depend on the teacher to make the Word understandable defeats the very purpose of translation which is that everyone should have direct access to God's Word in his own language.

It helps bilinguals to understand the national version

National language versions have usually been translated from a modified literal approach. This is not always a serious disadvantage in a national version since the translation has to serve a culture of considerable diversity. Further, the Church already has a well-established teaching ministry, the proportion of literates is relatively high, and there are usually aids of various sorts available to the readers. However, it is sometimes objected that when a diglot is produced, that is to say, the RL and national language versions are bound together in one volume, bilinguals will compare the two to the disadvantage of the idiomatic translation, since, naturally enough, the national language version has more prestige. At the same time, it is argued that if the minority language version had been translated more literally, then any comparison would not have given occasion to raise questions concerning differences in form.

Offsetting this objection is the fact that since the national language may not be completely understood, and since translations in such languages have been more literal than idiomatic, the reader from a minority group generally has considerable difficulty in understanding correctly a translation in a national language.

Knowledge of the national language (apart from a few who are well educated or where a minority group is actually abandoning its own language) is confined to such practical matters as trade, or contacts with officials, covering a limited area of the national language vocabulary. Even schooling, although it broadens the knowledge of the national languages, does not basically affect this situation. The national language is not the language of the heart and is no substitute for it. In fact, experience shows that *religious* terminology is the last to be acquired with any degree of understanding. So the need for an idiomatic translation, even where bilingualism is entering, is just as pressing as it is for a group who know nothing, or almost nothing, of the national language. An idiomatic translation will communicate the gospel message clearly and naturally, and serves to give meaning to the technical terminology encountered in the national version.

Any critical comparisons made between the versions will soon reveal to those who make them that while the form of the two translations is different, the meaning intended to be communicated by each is the same. Generally speaking, where such comparisons have been made, the reader has often verbalized his appreciation for the translation in his own language since it serves to give meaning to many words of the national language which were previously unknown to him. Change of form does not perturb him; from his knowledge of the two languages he is already aware that this is the case, even in such a simple matter as greetings. However, if the meaning between the versions is to be the same, the translator who is going to publish in diglot form will normally choose to follow the text underlying the national version, and also, where possible, he will follow the interpretational choices made in the national version.

It is easier to read, especially for new readers

The previous subsections have dealt with various objections rai..d concerning idiomatic translations; this subsection mentions one of the distinct advantages of an idiomatic translation.

New readers tend to take a casual look at the phonetic shape of a word and guess what the word is. In an idiomatic translation, these guesses are often correct since not only the subject matter limits the range of words which might be expected but also the immediate context leading up to the word generally restricts the choice to the correct one. However, when a translation is not idiomatic, the combination of words used falls outside the range of normal usage. The context in which words are found is strange and makes it necessary to read every syllable of each word. Such a necessity placed on new readers slows them down so that more attention is paid to the mechanics of reading and less to the information to be comprehended. Reading then becomes a chore rather than a pleasure with the result that only the most highly motivated readers struggle on in their effort to understand God's Word. An idiomatic translation is conducive to a widely read book.

APPENDIX B

An Experiment on the Use of Primary Senses by Native Speakers

A list of 200 words was given to three separate adult native speakers. The first of these was told only to write sentences using each word given in the 200-word list. She produced 138 nonoriginal sentences as a result, yet, even so, 68 percent of the words were used in their primary sense. When she was told that all sentences were to be original, her use of primary senses rose to 89 percent.

The second subject was told to use no quotations, and on her first run she scored 94.5 percent. She was then told the purpose of the test, and raised her score slightly to 95 percent.

The third was told that all the sentences were to be original to her, but was given no other instructions. Her score was 88.5 percent. When she was told that each word was to be used in its primary sense, her score rose to 98 percent.

No attempt was made to explain to the three subjects what "primary sense" meant, and in scoring their work, a use was accepted as a primary sense only if this was so for society in general, and not for a small segment of society. It seems likely that, at certain points, their choice of a primary sense was influenced by their particular profession, and that, if they had been warned about this, their scores would have been even higher.

Naturally, no sweeping general statements may be based on a test where there were so few subjects, and testing procedures were not identical for all. Nonetheless, it seems reasonable to deduce that, asked to put a word into a sentence, the adult native speaker will use it in its primary meaning about nine times out of ten. Hence, a translator, or a consultant, seeking to check on the primary sense of a term, is justified in isolating it and asking a native speaker to give an illustration of its use. Repeating with several such speakers will help to discover the 10 percent or so of cases where a nonprimary sense has been given.

APPENDIX C

The Use and Significance of OU and MĒ in Questions

In chapter 15 it was noted that the negative particles *ou* and *mē* do not serve to distinguish real from rhetorical questions, but occur in parallel ways in both types of questions. However, this does not mean these particles are of no relevance to the translator. The following discussion will show there is good evidence that the use of these particles may guide the translator in his choice of the form used in the RL when translating real and rhetorical questions.

The use of ou and mē as defined by Greek grammars

Marshall, in his volume, *The Interlinear Greek-English New Testament*, discusses the significance of *ou* and *mē* in his Introduction (p. xiii).

> Incidentally, though of importance, these two negative particles, or their compounds, when introducing questions, expect different answers. *Ou* appeals to the fact, anticipating "Yes, it is so"; *e.g.*, John *ch.* 11, *v.* 9, "Are there not twelve hours of the day?" The answer would be "Yes, there are." *Mē* on the contrary, denies the suggestion and expects the reply "No, it is not so"; or, if not so explicit as that, doubts whether it is so; *e.g.*, John *ch.* 18, *v.* 35. The form of the question in the Authorized Version and the Revised Version indicates that Pilate was asking for information, whereas he was rejecting the idea with scorn and contempt — "I am not a Jew [am I]?" The answer, if any would be — "No, certainly not." This distinction is largely overlooked in the English versions.

This statement by Marshall is typical of those found in the grammars. Burton, in his *Syntax of the Moods and Tenses of New Testament Greek* (pp. 178, 179), states: "What is said respecting the simple negatives *ou* and *mē* applies in general also to their respective compounds when standing alone . . . . In questions that can be answered affirmatively or negatively, *ou* is used with the Indicative to imply that an affirmative answer is expected; *mē* to imply that a negative answer is expected." Goetchius (1965, pp. 229, 230) agrees: "*Mē*, when used with the *indicative* mood, introduced a question to which a *negative* answer is expected . . . . *Ou* (*ouk, ouch*) and *ouchi* sometimes introduce questions to which an *affirmative* answer is expected . . . ." Other grammars, such as Blass-Debrunner, Dana and Mantey, Robertson and Davis, and Turner, say essentially the same thing in other words.

But, good as these statements are, they fail to represent the full range of data in two respects. One is they do not take account of the distinction between real and rhetorical questions, and, in particular, the fact that rhetorical questions do not expect an answer at all, affirmative or negative, but serve a different purpose. The other is that there are questions — rhetorical questions — using *ou*, which if transformed into an affirmative statement, would not convey the correct meaning, and those using *mē*, which if transformed into a negative sentence would not be correct. It would seem, then, that a more specific statement of the function of *ou* and *mē* needs to be made, and that one important aspect of this more specific statement is to take into account the difference between real and rhetorical questions.

Ou and mē in real questions

The writers of the Greek New Testament had a choice open to them when framing a real question whose answer was yes or no. They could state the question without using either *ou* or *mē*, or they could use *ou* or *mē*. In the former case, the question revealed nothing of the writer's attitude concerning the answer — it was neutral and uncommitted. In the latter case, the use of *ou* or *mē* indicated what he considered the answer to be — resulting in what would be called in English a "leading question." Since the writer in Koiné Greek had this choice, it seems logical to conclude it was a significant one, and that therefore it should be reflected in the translation, if this is at all possible. (The quotation from Marshall suggests how this may be done in rendering the question, "Am I a Jew?") The following examples illustrate how this difference can be reflected in English for real questions using either *ou* or *mē*, or neither.

Matt. 9:28 "Believe ye that I am able to do this?" This question uses neither *ou* or *mē*, so no anticipated answer is indicated. In more modern English the question would start, "Do you believe that . . . ?"

John 9:8 "Is not this he that sat and begged?" This is a question asked by the neighbors of the blind man, who had known him before he was healed. This question starts with *ouch* in the Greek, and shows that the neighbors considered the answer to be yes. An alternative way of expressing this in English would be, "This is he that sat and begged, isn't it?"

John 4:33 "Hath any man brought him ought to eat?" This is a question the disciples asked, and in framing it they used *mē*, showing that they did not think anyone had brought him anything. An alternate form of this is, "No one brought him anything to eat, did they?"

These three examples conform to the statements made in the grammars — *ou* anticipates the answer yes, *mē* anticipates the answer no, and the omission of both leaves the answer open; it may be either yes or no.

Some further examples using *ou* are found in Matthew 17:24, 27:13; John 8:48, 18:26; and Acts 21:38. Note that although the answer the questioner himself considered to be true was *yes* in each case, in fact, only in the first reference was that answer actually given. In Matthew 27:13, Jesus does not answer at all, and in each of the last three cases the answer given by the person addressed was *no*. The speaker may indicate his opinion in favor of a particular answer, but, for various reasons, he may not get the answer he expects. This does not affect the analysis, however.

Further examples of real questions using *mē* are found in Matthew 26:25; Mark 14:19; Luke 22:35; John 6:67, 9:40, 18:17, 25, 21:5. Of these questions, in which the speaker's opinion favored a negative answer, an affirmative answer was given in Matthew 26:25 and John 9:41.

Ou and mē in rhetorical questions

When a rhetorical question is used, an answer is not really expected, but this form is used to convey information. This general statement regarding rhetorical questions applies also to those which use *ou* or *mē* in them. Since no answer is expected the statements found in the grammars might better be recast as follows: When *ou* is used in a rhetorical question, the speaker is communicating an *affirmative* statement. It is most often a statement of certitude, in which he conveys information or calls the attention of his hearers to something which they already know or, in certain contexts it may express an evaluation, pointing out something which his hearers should have done but in fact have not done. Two examples of each type follow (an equivalent in non-question form is included in parenthesis):

Matt. 22:31 ". . . have you not read that which was spoken unto you . . . ?" (You have all read that which was spoken unto you . . . .)

Acts 5:4 "Whiles it remained was it not thine own?" (While it remained it was your own.)

Matt. 26:40 "What, could ye not watch with me one hour?" (You should have been able to watch with me one hour.)

Mark 7:18b "Do ye not perceive, that whatsoever thing from without entereth into the man, it cannot defile him . . . ?" (You should have perceived that . . . .)

Although grammars generally connect *mē* with questions expecting negative answers, they do recognize that the negative attitude conveyed may be tempered to correspond more with incredulity, doubt, or uncertainty. Thus, for example, Turner (1963, p. 283) says: "In some passages the strength of *mē* is somewhat modified: John 4:29 *mēti houtos estin ho Christos he must be* (or *perhaps he is*) *the Messiah*; hardly *num* a negative answer here; it is more like *ou*; the distinction is sometimes difficult to draw for much depends on the tone of the speaker; it is here rather hesitant, as in 4:33." Arndt and Gingrich (1957, p. 522), under *mēti* say, "interrog. particle in questions that expect a negative answer . . . . Also in questions in which the questioner is in doubt concerning the answer *perhaps* Matthew 12:23; John 4:29; . . . ."

We may summarize this by saying that *mē* in a rhetorical question usually indicates a negative statement of certitude, but may in some contexts indicate a statement of incertitude. Following are two examples of each, together with an equivalent in non-question form (Greek questions with mē are usually translated into English by questions with no negative particle.):

Matt. 7:9 "Will he give him a stone?" (He will not give him a stone.)

Rom. 3:3 "Shall their unbelief make the faith of God without effect?" (Their unbelief will not make . . . .)

John 4:29 ". . . is not this the Christ?" (Arndt and Gingrich translate this as "Perhaps this man is the Messiah.")

Acts 7:28 "Wilt thou kill me . . . ?" (Perhaps you want to kill me . . . .)

In some contexts *mē* can be translated as, "you speak as if." For example, in John 7:51 Nicodemus points out to his fellow-Pharisees that the law did not judge anyone until it had heard what he had to say in his defense. To this comment, they reply with the rhetorical question, "Art thou also of Galilee?" The question begins with *mē*, and the Pharisees knew well enough that Nicodemus was not a Galilean. But they interpret Nicodemus' statement as if he were coming to the defense of a fellow-Galilean, so that their rhetorical question may be rendered, "You speak as if you were a Galilean."

Questions with the compound *ouchi* are almost always rhetorical, usually indicating statements of certitude. *Mēpote*, when it occurs in a rhetorical question, always has the sense of "perhaps." For example, John 7:26 may be translated, "Perhaps the rulers really know that this man is the Christ."

One device English speakers may use to keep in mind the functions of *ou* and *mē* questions is to equate them roughly with two English sentence patterns, exemplified by, "This is true, is it *not?*" and, "This is *not* true, is it?" Both of these English question patterns involve a negative morpheme, and yet one anticipates a positive answer and the other a negative answer; and in this they are similar to Greek questions with *ou* and *mē*. In the illustrations that follow, some of the examples cited above are restated in this form:

Matt. 22:31 You have read that which was spoken unto you . . . , haven't you?

Matt. 26:40 You could have watched with me one hour, couldn't you?

Matt. 7:9 He won't give him a stone, will he?

John 4:29 This isn't the Christ, is it? (With the implication that he just might be).

The significance of the double negative, mē ou and ou mē

Burton (1966, p. 179) says: "In Rom. 10:18, 19; I Cor. 9:4, 5, 11:22, *mē ou* is used in rhetorical questions equivalent to affirmative statements. Each negative has, however, its own proper force, *ou* making the verb negative, and *mē* implying that a negative answer is expected to the question thus made negative." Turner (1963, p. 283) says the same: "Where *mē* negatived the whole sentence the verb alone may already be negatived by *ou* (Paul, as class.), and so *mē* . . . *ou* stands with a sentence which expects a positive answer: Romans 10:18ff . . . I Corinthians 9:4ff . . . 11:22 , . . ." One of the examples cited by these grammarians will suffice to illustrate this type. 1 Corinthians 11:22 reads, "What? have ye not houses to eat and to drink in?" This question begins with *mē* and *ouk* precedes the verb *echete* "you have." The question is obviously equivalent to a strong affirmiation, "you most certainly have houses in which to eat and drink."

Ou mē with the aorist subjunctive in a question can denote a stronger affirmation than *mē* alone. An example is found in Luke 18:7, 8, which reads, "And shall not God avenge his own elect . . . ? I tell you that he will avenge them speedily." Jesus' own comment makes it clear that the rhetorical question is equivalent to an affirmation, "God will certainly avenge . . . ." Other examples are John 18:11 and Revelation 15:4.[1]

CONCLUSION

In summary, it may be said that *ou* in a real question indicates that the speaker thinks a *yes* answer is in order, and in rhetorical questions it corresponds to either an affirmative statement or an evaluation; and that *mē* in a real question indicates the speaker thinks a *no* answer is in order, and in a rhetorical question it corresponds to either a negative statement or a statement of incertitude.

---

[1] John 11:56b appears to be an exception to the use of *ou mē* in rhetorical questions. It reads, in the KJV, "What think ye, that he will not (*ou mē*) come to the feast?" Most texts and versions punctuate as two questions, as in the KJV, but it is interesting to note that the NEB translates it as "Perhaps he is not coming to the festival." However, if it is taken to mean "He certainly will come, won't he?" this also fits the context well, while retaining the emphatic affirmative sense of *ou mē*.

APPENDIX D

A Discussion of Some Complicated Genitives

Two types of complicated genitives are discussed in this appendix. One is referred to in the grammars of Greek as a "concatenation of genitives," that is, there is more than one nominal in the genitive case linked to the nominal A. The other is the case, mentioned in chapter 16, where the genitive construction involves the use of figurative terms.

Concatenation of genitives

The study of the genitive construction in chapter 16 was confined to genitives of the form A of B, in which only two nominals were involved. Occasionally, in some of the examples, however, a third nominal, often a pronoun, was added in parentheses. There are, in fact, a number of genitive constructions in which three nominals are linked together as in a chain which can be represented by the formula A of B of C, and occasionally as many as four are found, i.e., A of B of C of D.

As might be expected from the earlier discussion, there is no one-to-one correspondence between the number of nominals involved in the genitive construction and the number of propositions represented by it. It has already been shown that the simple form A of B may represent one or two propositions. The same observation applies to chains of genitives. The presence of three or four nominals does not imply that three or four propositions are represented; each genitive construction has to be considered individually in its context to see how it can be restated. The following three examples from Colossians, chapter 1, serve to illustrate this.

In Colossians 1:9 the genitive construction "knowledge of the will of him" occurs. Since "knowledge" and "will" are both abstract nouns representing Events, at least two Event propositions are represented. The addition of "of him" supplies the Agent for the Event "to will." That is to say, "the will of him" is a Subjective genitive, equivalent to "he wills" and this proposition is the content of the Event "to know." In this case, therefore, the addition of "of him" added a participant to one of the Events already signaled, and this is commonly the case with pronouns at the end of a genitive construction.

A more complicated construction is found in Colossians 1:13. This is "the kingdom of the Son of the love of him" with four nominals, two being abstract nouns representing Events and two representing Things.

"The love of him" is a Subjective genitive, equivalent to "he loves." "The kingdom of the Son" is also a Subjective genitive, representing the proposition "the Son rules (us)." The two are connected together by the fact that the Son is the Experiencer of the love, so that the whole genitive construction may be restated in the form, "He loves his Son who rules (us)." To maintain the focus on A, however, this can then be restated in the form, "(we) are ruled by his Son whom he loves," which consists of two propositions, the second being attributive to "Son." In this case, then, although there are four nominals, there are only two propositions. However, it will be noted that this is the only example so far in which the Agent and the Experiencer of the same Event are given in the same genitive, so that such chained genitives do introduce new combinations not seen in the shorter constructions.

The third example is found in Colossians 1:22. Here the genitive construction is "the body of the flesh of him." As was mentioned in the section on State propositions, "the body of the flesh" is a State proposition predicating the relation of SUBSTANCE, that is, "the body consisting (partly) of flesh." But how does "of him" relate to this? It adds a further State proposition, "the body of him," which is a PART-WHOLE relation, "he" being the whole person, his "body" being part of him. Hence, there are two State propositions, one predicating the relation of SUBSTANCE, and the other PART-WHOLE. In general, it seems to be the case that when State propositions are involved, each nominal introduces a further State proposition predicating a further relation. These two State propositions could then be restated in English in the form "his physical body."

Some further examples of chained genitives which represent two State propositions are given below:

Acts 23:16	"the son of the sister of Paul"	KINSHIP-KINSHIP
Acts 24:5	"a ringleader of the sect of the Nazarenes"	ROLE-IDENTIFICATION
Rev. 12:4	"the third of the stars of heaven"	QUANTITY-LOCATION
Rev. 12:17	"the others of the seed of her"	QUANTITY-KINSHIP

One final example will be discussed which is more complicated than those previously discussed. In this example, found in Romans 2:5, it seems simplest to proceed backwards along the genitive construction working out each relation in turn, and this may well be a procedure that can be used to elucidate this type of complex chained genitive. The full Greek form is: *in a day of wrath and revelation of righteous-judgment of God.* There are really two genitive constructions "in a day of wrath of God" and "in a day of revelation of righteous-judgment of God" fused into a single complex expression since it is all one "day" that is being referred to. It is the second of these genitives that will be discussed here.

Labeling it as indicated above gives:

a day of revelation of righteous-judgment of God
  A   B   C   D

"Revelation" represents an Event, equivalent to some form of the verb "to reveal." "Righteous-judgment" (Gk. *dikaiokrisia*) is a compound abstract noun, representing both the Abstraction "righteous" and the Event "to judge."

Taking the genitives in the reverse order, the genitive C-D, "the righteous-judgment of God," may be restated as *God judges (people) righteously*, basically a Subjective relation (God is the Agent). It is this fact that will be revealed (B), so a further restatement could read *it will be revealed that God judges (people) righteously*. This is a case of the CONTENT relation. Finally, B, C, and D are related to A as time, so the whole may be expressed as: *a day when it will be revealed that God judges (people) righteously*. In this restatement, the focus has been maintained, though it will be noticed the passive form, "it is revealed," has been used in the restatement.

Genitives used in figures of speech

Figures of speech such as metonymy, synecdoche, metaphor, and euphemism are used throughout the New Testament, and, as might be expected, some of these figures involve the genitive construction. It is necessary, therefore, when seeking to understand the significance of the genitive construction in such contexts, to take into full account the figure of speech with which the particular genitive is connected. If the figure is live, the image is kept if possible; if dead, the image is not kept. In the latter case, a proposition similar to those discussed earlier is chosen to represent the relation signaled by the genitive. The following brief discussion exemplifies the principles discussed in more detail in chapter 17.

Genitives used in live figures

In almost all cases in which live figures are involved in genitive constructions, either (1) A is figurative and B is nonfigurative, or (2) both A and B are figurative. In either case, the restatement takes the form of a comparison.

When only A is figurative, it may be the image of a metaphor with B expressing the topic. In the examples, only one restatement will be presented for figurative genitive constructions; in most cases there would be others which would be equally valid depending on the requirement of the RL.

1 Cor. 5:8	"(keep the feast . . . with) the unleavened bread of sincerity and truth"	just as (the feast must be kept with) unleavened bread, so (our lives must be) sincere and true
2 Cor. 5:5	"(hath given unto us) the earnest of the Spirit"	(has given us) the Spirit who is like a guarantee/pledge
Eph. 6:16	"(taking) the shield of faith"	believing, because that will be like having a shield

| Eph. 6:17 | "the sword of the Spirit, (which is the word of God)" | the word of God, which is like a sword given (to you) by the Spirit |

In the following examples both parts of the genitive construction are involved in a live figure:

| 2 Cor. 5:1 | "the earthly house of the tabernacle of us" | our earthly body, which is like a temporary house |

Although "tabernacle" belongs to the Thing class semantically, it is used in a synecdoche for the Abstraction "temporary" "transitory."

| Phil. 4:18 | "(the things which were sent . . . ,) an odour of a sweet smell, (. . . well pleasing to God)" | (the things which were sent . . . ,) which were pleasing to God like a sweet fragrance is pleasing to us |

This genitive construction is a form of doublet, "odour" and "sweet smell" being virtual synonyms in this context.

| Col. 1:20 | "(having made peace through) the blood of the cross (of him)" | (having made peace by) shedding his blood when he died on the cross |

Similes involving the entire genitive construction are also found. Since similes do not usually present problems in translation, one example only is given here (the point of similarity, "brightness," is made explicit in the restatement of the simile).

| Rev. 19:12 | "(His eyes were as) a flame of fire" | (His eyes were as) bright as a burning flame. |

In a few cases, A indicates neither topic, image, nor point of similarity, but the abstract fact of comparison.

| Rom. 5:14 | "(them that had not sinned after) the likeness of the transgression of Adam" | (those who had not sinned) like Adam sinned |

Genitives used in dead figures

When dead figures are involved in genitive constructions, it may be either A or B or the whole construction which is figurative. The figures most commonly encountered are metaphor, synecdoche, and metonymy, although others are occasionally found.

1. A is figurative

| Luke 16:15 | "(abomination in) the sight of God" | God considers (it an abomination) |
| Acts 11:30 | "(sent it . . . by) the hands of Barnabas and Saul" | (sent it . . .) with Barnabas and Saul |

| 2 Cor. 5:10 | "(appear before) the judgment seat of Christ" | (appear before) Christ, for him to judge[1] |
| 2 Tim. 4:17 | "(I was delivered out of) the mouth of the lion" | (I was delivered from) great danger |

The preceding examples are of metonymy; following are one of metaphor and one of simile.

| 1 Cor. 11:3 | "the head of every man (is Christ)" | (Christ) is every man's ruler |
| Heb. 6:19 | "(which hope we have as) an anchor of the soul" | (which hope we have to) keep our soul firm |

2. *B is figurative*

| Gal. 2:7 | "the gospel of the uncircumcision" | the good news (preached to) the non-Jews |

3. *A and B are both figurative*

| Mark 10:5 | "(for) the hardness of your heart (he wrote you this precept)" | (he wrote you this precept because) you are obstinate |

---

[1] This takes the view that "judgment seat" is a metonymy for what takes place there, i.e., judgment itself.

APPENDIX E

A Propositional Display of Philemon

THEME: Welcome Onesimus back.

Section vv. 1-3: I greet you and may God bless you.

Theme vv. 1-2: I, Paul, greet you, Philemon.

1a	(I,) Paul, and Timothy (greet) (you,) Philemon	
b	I am a prisoner	COMMENT on Paul
c	because (I serve) Christ Jesus	REASON of b
d	He is our (incl.) brother,	COMMENT on Timothy
e	We (excl.) love you	COMMENT on Philemon
f	You work with us	COMMENT on Philemon
2a	(We also greet) Apphia, Archippus, and the believers/church	
b	She is our (incl.) sister	COMMENT on Apphia
c	He is like a soldier along with us	COMMENT on Archippus
d	who meet in your (Philemon's) house	COMMENT on believers

Theme v. 3: May God and Jesus Christ bless you.

3a	May God our Father and the Lord Jesus Christ give you grace/favor you	
b	May God and the Lord Jesus Christ give you peace	

Section vv. 4-20: Welcome Onesimus back as you would me.

Theme vv. 4-7: I was moved because you love all the saints.

4a	I thank God	
b	whom I (worship)	COMMENT about God in 4a
c	when I pray for you	TIME of 4a
5a	because I hear	5a-c give the REASON (objective) for 4a
b	that you love all the saints	CONTENT of hear in 5a
c	and that you believe/trust the Lord Jesus	CONTENT of hear in 5a
6a	(I pray)	implied from 4c

b	that (you may) fellowship more and more fully (with those)	6b-f give the CONTENT of pray in 6a
c	who also believe/trust (the Lord Jesus) with you	IDENTIFICATION of those in 6b
d	by means of (your) coming to know all the good (things)	MEANS of 6b
e	which we (incl.) (can do)	COMMENT about things in 6d
f	in order that Christ (may be honored by us (incl.).	PURPOSE of 6e
7a	Moreover, I rejoiced greatly	
b	and I was greatly encouraged/comforted	
c	because you love (the saints)	REASON (objective) for 7a, b
d	specifically, because you are the one who refreshed the saints in spirit, brother.	SPECIFIC restatement of 7c

Theme vv. 8-11: Therefore, I want to request something of you for Onesimus.

8a	Therefore, (I appeal to you)	CONCLUSION of 4-7
b	Although I might be very bold	CONCESSION of 9a
c	because I belong to Christ	REASON of b
d	so that I command	RESULT of b
e	that you do what is right/ what you should	CONTENT of d
9a	I appeal to (you)	CONCLUSION of 8b, c, d, e
b	instead of commanding you	CONTRAST to a
c	because (you) love (the saints)	REASON of a, b
d	Although I am Paul, an ambassador	CONCESSION of 10a and 9a
e	And although I am now a prisoner	CONCESSION of 10a and 9a
f	because (I serve) Jesus Christ	REASON of e
10a	I appeal to you on behalf of Onesimus	CONCLUSION of 9d, e, f, and AMPLIFICATION of 9a
b	(He is like a) son to me/(He is) my convert	COMMENT on Onesimus and (with 10c-11b) REASON for 10a
c	(I became like) his father/I led him to believe	COMMENT on Onesimus CONTRAST to b
d	while I am here in prison	TIME and LOCATION of c
11a	Before he was useless to you	COMMENT on Onesimus
b	Now he is of use to you and to me	

Theme vv. 12-16: I am sending Onesimus back to you as a brother.

12a	I am sending him (back to you)	
b	I love him very much	COMMENT on him
13a	Even though I thought	CONCESSION of 14a
b	that I would keep him (here) with me	CONTENT of thought
c	in order that he might serve me on your behalf	PURPOSE of b
d	while I am here in prison	TIME and LOCATION of c
e	because (I preached) the gospel	REASON for d
14a	I decided not to do anything/not to keep him	CONCLUSION of 13, and 13, 14 are REASON of 12a
b	without your consent/(unless first) you decided	CONDITION of a
c	in order that you would not be compelled	CONTRAST to e
d	that you do good (to me)	CONTENT of c
e	but in order (that you do good) voluntarily/because you chose to (do that good)	PURPOSE of a
15a	Because, perhaps he left you for awhile	a, b are REASON of 12a
b	in order that you might keep him forever	PURPOSE of a
16a	(He is) no longer (just) a slave	CONTRAST to b
b	(He is) more than/better than (just) a slave	COMMENT on him
c	He is a brother	SPECIFIC of b and COMMENT on him of 12a
d	whom (we incl.) love	COMMENT on brother
e	I love him very much (as a brother)	e-h is AMPLIFICATION of d
f	You will love him even more	CONTRAST to e
g	because he is your slave	REASON of f
h	and because he (believes) our Lord	REASON of f

Theme vv. 17-20: Therefore, receive him back as you would me.

17a	Therefore (in view of what I have said) (in 12-16)	GROUNDS of d
b	and since you consider	b, c are GROUNDS of d
c	that I am your partner	CONTENT of b

d	receive him	CONCLUSION of a, b, c
e	like you would receive me	COMPARISON
18a	If he has wronged you in some respect	CONDITION of c
b	that is, if he owes you	SPECIFIC of a
c	charge that to me	CONSEQUENCE of a, b and SPECIFIC of 17d, e
19a	I, Paul, write this with my own hand.	19 is SPECIFIC of 17d, e
b	I will pay you	CONTENT of a
c	what he owes you	CONTENT of b
d	I will not tell you	d, e are COMMENT on b, c
e	that you are indebted to me	CONTENT of d and CONTRAST to c
f	because I converted you	REASON of e
20a	Yes, brother, I want	20 is a REASON for 17d, e
b	that you help/benefit me	CONTENT of a
c	since we are in the Lord/ believers	REASON of b
d	you refresh/encourage me	SPECIFIC of b
e	since we are in Christ/ believers	REASON of d

Section vv. 21-25: I express confidence, make a request, and send greetings and blessings.

Theme v. 21: I am sure that you will do more than I ask.

21a	I wrote/am writing to you	
b	because I am confident	REASON of a
c	that you will obey	CONTENT of b
d	because I know	REASON of a
e	that you will do more than I ask	CONTENT of d and AMPLIFICATION of c

Theme v. 22: Prepare a room for me.

22a	At the same time (that you receive Onesimus)	TIME of b
b	Prepare a room for me	
c	because I hope/expect	REASON of b
d	that I will see you	CONTENT of c
e	because you pray	REASON of d

Theme vv. 23, 24: Many greet you.

23a	Epaphras greets you	
b	He is in prison with me	COMMENT on a
c	because he believes Christ Jesus	REASON of b

24a   Mark, Aristarchus, Demas, and
      Luke also (greet you)

  b   They work with me.   COMMENT on a

Theme v. 25: May our Lord give you grace.

25a   May our Lord Jesus Christ favor
      you (pl.)/give you grace.

A propositional display chooses to analyze a text very explicitly. It is not to be assumed, however, that any particular language will require all the information in explicit form that is shown in this or any other propositional display. Since the patterns of implicit and explicit information differ from one language to another, one translator's needs will differ from those of another. To be of greatest help to the translator, therefore, the propositions are stated in explicit form including as well the information that may be needed to resolve some ambiguities which otherwise would be left obscure. The translator is cautioned not to assume that whatever is explicit in a propositional display may legitimately be made explicit in his translation (see chapter 3 for guidelines).

It will also be noted that unlike the presentation of Philemon 4-7 in chapter 20, no discussion of reasons underlying the analysis has been made. At a later date, a complete presentation will be made available which will include comments for each verse of this letter.

BIBLIOGRAPHY

Included in this bibliography are the books and articles cited in the text of *Translating the Word of God*, vol. 1. The reader will also find listed many source materials which contributed to the background knowledge of the authors during their years of research.

Bible Texts and Versions

Greek New Testament. Novum Testamentum Graece Cum Apparatu Critico Curavit. 1960. Eberhard Nestle. Novis Curis Elaboraverunt Erwin Nestle et Kurt Aland. For the American Bible Society New York. 1st pr. 1898. rev. 1927. Stuttgart: Privileg. Württ. Bibelanstalt.

Greek New Testament, The. 1966. Edited by Kurt Aland, Matthew Black, Bruce M. Metzger, and Allen Wikgren. London: United Bible Societies.

Holy Bible, The: American Standard Version. 1901.

Interlinear Greek-English New Testament, The: the Nestle Greek Text with a Literal English Translation. 1964. Tr. by Alfred Marshall. London: Samuel Bagster and Sons Ltd.

New American Standard Bible. 1960. Text Edition. La Habra, Calif.: Foundation Press Publications.

New Life Testament, The. 1969. Tr. by G. H. Ledyard. Canby, Ore.: Christian Literature Foundation.

New Testament, The: A New Translation in Plain English. 1952. Tr. by Charles Kingsley Williams. London: S.P.C.K and Longmans, Green and Co.

New Testament, The: A Translation in the Language of the People. 1950. Tr. by C. B. Williams. Chicago: Moody Press.

New Testament in Greek and English. 1968. "Preface to the English Translation," v-vii. As printed by Robert Aitken. American Bible Society. New York: Arno Press.

New Testament in Modern English, The. 1924. Tr. by H. B. Montgomery. Philadelphia: The Judson Press.

New Testament in Modern English, The. 1958. Tr. by J. B. Phillips. New York: The Macmillan Co.

New Testament in Modern Speech, The: An Idiomatic Translation into Everyday English from the Text of the Resultant Greek Testament. 1912. Tr. by Richard Francis Weymouth. 3rd ed. London: James Clarke and Co.

New Testament of Our Lord and Savior Jesus Christ, The: According to the Received Greek Text, Together with the English Authorised Version. 1968. London: The British and Foreign Bible Society.

New Translation of the Bible, A: Containing the Old and New Testaments. 1935. Tr. by James Moffatt. New York and London: Harper and Brothers Publishers.

Revised or English Revised Version. 1881. *The New Testament*.

Revised or English Revised Version. 1884. *The Old Testament*.

The following translations are frequently referred to by an abbreviation:

KJV   *Authorized or King James Version*. 1611.

NEB   *The New English Bible: New Testament*. 1961. Printed in the United States of America: Oxford University Press and Cambridge University Press.

RSV   *The Holy Bible: Revised Standard Version Containing the Old and New Testaments*. tr. 1611. rev. 1881-1885 and 1901. rev. 1952. New York: Thomas Nelson and Sons.

TEV   *Good News for Modern Man: The New Tetsament in Today's English Version*. 1966. 3rd ed. New York: American Bible Society.

Bibliography

Since they appear so often in the bibliography, two journals have been abbreviated as follows:

Key

NOT   *Notes on Translation*. Published quarterly by Wycliffe Bible Translators, Inc.

TBT   *The Bible Translator*. Published quarterly by the United Bible Societies.

Anatal, László. 1963. *Questions of Meaning*. The Hague: Mouton and Co.

————. 1964. *Content, Meaning, and Understanding*. The Hague: Mouton and Co.

Andrews, Henrietta. 1972. "Rhetorical Questions in Otomi of the State of Mexico." NOT 44:25-28.

Arndt, William F., and Gingrich, F. Wilbur. 1957. *A Greek-English Lexicon of the New Testament and Other Early Christian Literature*. A translation and adaptation of Walter Bauer's Griechisch-Deutsches Wörterbuch zu den Schriften des Neuen Testaments und der übrigen urchristlichen Literatur, 4th rev. and aug. ed. 1952. 5th impression

1960. Chicago, Ill.: The University of Chicago Press.

Aulie, Wilbur. 1957. "Figures of Speech in the Chol New Testament." TBT 8:109-13.

Ballard, D. Lee. 1968. "Studying the Receptor Language Lexicon." NOT 29:11-15.

———. 1973. "On the Translation of Greek Relationals." NOT 47:18-21.

———. 1974. "Telling It Like It Was Said." Parts 1 and 2. NOT 51: 23-31.

Ballard, D. Lee, and Pallesen, Kemp. 1974. "Being Less Than Explicit." NOT 51:31-35.

Ballard, D. Lee; Conrad, Robert J.; and Longacre, Robert E. 1971. "The Deep and Surface Grammar of Interclausal Relations." *Foundations of Languages* 7:70-118.

Barclay, William. 1954. *The Letters to the Corinthians*. Edinburgh: The Saint Andrew Press.

———. 1960. *The Letters to Timothy, Titus and Philemon*. Philadelphia: The Westminster Press.

———. 1968. *The Gospels and the Acts of the Apostles*. The New Testament: A New Translation, vol. 1. London and New York: Collins.

Beekman, John, ed. 1965a. *Notes on Translation with Drills*. Santa Ana, Calif.: Summer Institute of Linguistics.

———. 1965b. "Lexical Equivalence Involving Consideration of Form and Function." In Beekman, ed. pp. 83-123.

———. 1965c. "Son of Man." In Beekman, ed. pp. 177-93.

———. 1965d. "Ambiguity or Obscurity of Pronominal Reference." NOT 16:7-12.

———. 1965e. "Idiomatic versus Literal Translations." NOT 18:1-15.

———. 1965f. "Extended Usage of Number and Person." NOT 19:1-10.

———. 1966. "'Literalism' a Hindrance to Understanding." TBT 17: 178-89.

———. 1967a. "Introduction to Skewing of the Lexical and Grammatical Hierarchies." NOT 23:1.

———. 1967b. "Metonymy and Synecdoche." NOT 23:12-25.

———. 1968a. "Eliciting Vocabulary, Meaning and Collocations." NOT 29:1-11.

———. 1968b. "Implicit Information and Translation." NOT 30:3-13.

———. 1969. "Metaphor and Simile." NOT 31:1-22.

———. 1970a. "Propositions and their Relations within a Discourse." NOT 37:6-23.

———. 1970b. "A Structural Display of Propositions in Jude." NOT 37: 27-31.

———. 1972. "Analyzing and Translating the Questions of the New Testament." NOT 44:3-21.

Bendix, Edward Herman. 1966. "Componential Analysis of General Vocabulary: The Semantic Structure of Verbs in English, Hindi, and Japanese." Part 2. *International Journal of American Linguistics* 32: 2:1-190.

Berkhof, Louis. 1950. *Principles of Biblical Interpretation.* Grand Rapids, Mich.: Baker Book House.

Betts, LaVera. 1971. "The Parintintín World View." NOT 41:16, 17.

Blass, F., and Debrunner, A. 1961. *A Greek Grammar of the New Testament and Other Early Christian Literature.* Tr. by Robert W. Funk. Revision of the 9th-10th German edition incorporating supplementary notes of A. Debrunner. Chicago: University of Chicago Press.

Blight, Richard C. 1970. "An Alternate Display of Jude." NOT 37:32-36.

––––. 1972. "Translation Problems from A to Z." NOT 46:13-24.

Bratcher, Robert G. 1958. "The Art of Translation." TBT 9:84-89.

Bratcher, Robert G., and Nida, Eugene A. 1961. *A Translator's Handbook on the Gospel of Mark.* Leiden, Netherlands: E. J. Brill.

Bromiley, Geoffrey W. 1958. "Church Doctrine of Inspiration." In Henry, ed. pp. 205-17.

Brooke-Rose, Christine. 1958. *A Grammar of Metaphor.* London: Secker and Warburg.

Brower, Reuben A., ed. 1959. *On Translation.* Cambridge, Mass.: Harvard University Press.

Brown, Stephen J. 1955. *Image and Truth.* Rome: Catholic Book Agency.

Bruce, F. F. 1957. *Commentary on the Epistle to the Colossians.* Grand Rapids, Mich.: Wm. B. Eerdmans Publishing Co.

––––. 1963. *The Books and the Parchments.* London: Pickering and Inglis.

––––. 1965. *The Letters of Paul — An Expanded Paraphrase.* Grand Rapids, Mich.: Wm. B. Eerdmans Publishing Co.

Bullinger, E. W. 1898. *Figures of Speech Used in the Bible.* London: Eyre and Spottiswoode.

Burton, Ernest De Witt. 1956. *A Critical and Exegetical Commentary on the Epistle to the Galatians.* Edinburg: T. and T. Clark.

––––. 1966. *Syntax of the Moods and Tenses in New Testament Greek.* From 1898 ed. Edinburgh: T. and T. Clark.

Butler, Inez M. 1965. "Implicit Exclusiveness in Villa Alta Zapotec." NOT 16:4, 5.

––––. 1967. "Use of Third Person for First Person in the Gospel of John." NOT 26:10-14.

Buttrick, George A., editor-in-chief. 1962. *The Interpreter's Dictionary of the Bible.* New York: Abingdon Press.

Callow, Kathleen. 1970. "More on Propositions and their Relations within a Discourse." NOT 37:23-27.

Campbell, Caroline. 1955. "Bambara People and Language." TBT 6:63-68.

Campbell, George. 1963. *The Philosophy of Rhetoric.* 1776. Reprint. Ed. by Lloyd F. Bitzer. Carbondale, Ill.: Southern Illinois Univeristy.

Casagrande, Joseph B., and Hale, Kenneth L. 1967. "Semantic Relationships in Papago Folk Definitions." *Studies in Southwestern Ethnolinguistics.* The Hague: Mouton and Co.

Catford, J. C. 1965. *A Linguistic Theory of Translation.* London: Oxford University Press.

Chafe, Wallace L. 1970. *Meaning and the Structure of Language.* Chicago: University of Chicago Press.

Chomsky, Noam. 1965. *Aspects of the Theory of Syntax.* Cambridge, Mass.: Massachusetts Institute of Technology Press.

Clark, Eve V. 1971. "On the Acquisition of Meaning of BEFORE and AFTER." *Journal of Verbal Learning and Verbal Behavior* 10:266-75.

Coleman, Edward. 1961. "Responses to transformations: remembering and understanding." Paper Annual Meeting Linguistic Society of America, Chicago.

Conklin, Harold C. 1955. "Hanunoo Color Categories." *Southwestern Journal of Anthropology* 11:339-44.

Cook, Walter A. 1971. "Case Grammar as a Deep Structure in Tagmemic Analysis." *Languages and Linguistics Working Papers Number 2.* Washington, D. C.: Georgetown University.

Cowan, Marion M. 1960. "The Translation of Questions into Huixteco." TBT 11:123-25.

Crouch, Marjorie. 1972. "Rhetorical Questions in Vagla of Ghana." NOT 44:32-36.

Dana, H. E., and Mantey, Julius R. 1949. *A Manual Grammar of the Greek New Testament.* New York: The Macmillan Co.

Darmesteter, A. 1962. "*The Talmud,* 7." In 'The Talmud and Midrash, I Talmud." *The New Bible Dictionary.* p. 1237. Grand Rapids, Mich.: Wm. B. Eerdmans Publishing Co.

Deibler, Ellis W. 1966. "Comparative Constructions in Translation." NOT 22:4-10.

————. 1968. "Translating from Basic Structure." TBT 19:14-16.

————. 1969. "Basic Structure of I Corinthians." NOT 31:34-39.

————. 1971. "Semantics and Translation." NOT 39:12-16.

Dodd, C. H. 1962. "Some Problems of New Testament Translation." TBT 13:145-57.

Doublas, James Dixon, ed. 1962. *The New Bible Dictionary.* Grand Rapids, Mich.: Wm. B. Eerdmans Publishing Co.

Elkins, Richard E. 1971a. "Reducing Decoding Error in Translations." NOT 40:23, 24.

————. 1971b. "The Structure of Some Semantic Sets of W[estern]B[ukidnon] Manobo." NOT 41:10-15.

————. 1972. "Supposition Rules for Rhetorical Questions in English and Western Bukidnon Manobo." NOT 44:21-24.

Fillmore, Charles J. 1968a. "The Case for Case." In *Universals in Linguistic Theory.* Edited by Emmon Bach and Robert T. Harms. New York: Holt, Rinehart and Winston, Inc.

————. 1968b. "Lexical Entries for Verbs." *Foundations of Language* 4:373-93.

————. 1969a. "Types of Lexical Information." In *Studies in Syntax and Semantics.* Edited by Ferenc Kiefer. Dordrecht, Netherlands: D. Reidel.

————. 1969b. "Review Article" on "Componential Analysis of General Vocabulary: The Semantic Structure of a Set of Verbs in English, Hindi, and Japanese" by Edward Herman Bendix. *General Linguistics* 9:1:41-65.

———. 1971. "Some Problems for Case Grammar." Paper presented at the 1971 Georgetown Roundtable on Linguistics, at Georgetown University on March 11, 1971.

Fillmore, C. J., and Lehiste, Ilse. 1968. *Working Papers in Linguistics, No. 2.* Technical Report No. 68-3 On Work Performed Under Grant No. GN-534, National Science Foundation. Columbus, Ohio: The Ohio State University.

Finlayson, R. A. 1958. "Contemporary Ideas of Inspiration." In Henry, ed. pp. 221-34.

Fleming, Ilah. 1971. "Logical Relationships." In "Instructions for the preparation of data relevant for the analysis of semological constructions and their grammatical realizations." Mimeographed. Seattle, Wash.: Summer Institute of Linguistics.

Flesch, Rudolph. 1949. *The Art of Readable Writing.* New York: Harper and Brothers Publishers.

Forester, Leonard. 1958. "Translation: An Introduction." In Smith, preface. pp. 1-28

Frake, Charles O. 1961. "The Diagnosis of Disease Among the Subanen of Mindanao." *American Anthropologist* 63:113-32.

France, R. T. 1972. "The Exegesis of Greek Tenses in the New Testament." NOT 46:3-12.

Frantz, Chester I. 1965. "Genitives." In Beekman, ed. pp. 200-14.

Frantz, Donald G. 1968. "Translation and Underlying Structure I: Relations." NOT 30:22-28.

————. 1970. "Translation and Underlying Structure II: Pronominalization and Reference." NOT 38:3-10.

Fuller, Daniel P. 1967. "Delimiting and Interpreting the Larger Literary Units." NOT 28:1-12.

————. 1973. "Analysis of Romans 11:11-32." NOT 48:2-4.

Gale, Herbert M. 1964. *The Use of Analogy in the Letters of Paul.* Philadelphia: The Westminster Press.

Garvin, Paul L.; Brewer, Jocelyn; and Mathiot, Madeleine. 1967. "Predication-Typing: A Pilot Study in Semantic Analysis." *Language* 43:2: Part 2. Language Monograph No. 27.

Glover, Mr. and Mrs. Maurice. 1972. "Upon the Green Grass." NOT 46:26, 27.

Goddard, Burton L. 1967. "Concerns in Bible Translation: Introduction." *Bulletin of the Evangelical Theological Society* 10:2:85-87.

Goetchius, Eugene Van Ness. 1965. *The Language of the New Testament.* New York: Charles Scribner's Sons.

Gove, Philip Babcock, ed. 1966. *Webster's Third New International Dictionary of the English Language.* Springfield, Mass.: G. and C. Merriam Co., Publishers.

Greenlee, J. Harold. 1950. "The Genitive Case in the New Testament." TBT 1:68-70.

————. 1969. "The importance of syntax for the proper understanding of the sacred text of the New Testament." Heidemann Lectures. Concordia Theological Seminary. Springfield, Ill.

Grether, Herbert G. 1968. "Questions for Bible Translators (and those who help them)." TBT 19:166-71.

Grimes, Joseph E. 1963. "Measuring 'Naturalness' in Translation." TBT 14:49-62.

————. 1968. "Fidelity in Translation." TBT 19:164, 65.

————. 1972a. *The Thread of Discourse.* Technical Report No. 1, National Science Foundation Grant GS-3180. Ithaca: Cornell University.

————. 1972b. "Outlines and Overlays." *Language* 48:513-24.

Gudschinsky, Sarah C. 1967. "Frequency Counts, Naturalness, and Style." NOT 28:13, 14.

Gutt, Ernst-August. 1973. "Structural Phenomena in Acts 22:6-11." NOT 48:11-23.

Ham, Pat. 1965. "Figures of Speech in Apinaye." NOT 16:2.

————. 1971. "Shifts from Linguistic Order." NOT 39:16-21.

Harbeck, Warren A. 1970. "Mark's Use of GAR in Narration." NOT 38:10-15.

Headland, Thomas N. 1971. "Spirit Beings." NOT 41:17-21.

————. 1973. "A Method for Recording Formal Elicitation." NOT 50:22-27.

Healey, Alan. 1968. "English Idioms." *Kivung, Journal of the Linguistic Society of the University of Papua and New Guinea* 1:71-108.

Hendriksen, William. 1964. *Exposition of Colossians and Philemon.* Grand Rapids, Mich.: Baker Book House.

————. 1965. *Exposition of the Pastoral Epistles.* Grand Rapids, Mich: Baker Book House.

Henry, Carl F. H., ed. 1958. *Revelation and the Bible.* Grand Rapids, Mich.: Baker Book House.

Hershberger, Ruth. 1943. "The Structure of Metaphor." *Kenyon Review* 5:433-43.

Hill, Archibald A. 1958. "Principles Covering Semantic Parallels," Ditto printed as "A Program for the Definition of Literature." University of Texas *Studies in English 37.* pp. 46-52.

Hollander, John. 1959. "Versions, Interpretations and Performances." In Brower, ed. pp. 205-31.

Hollenbach, Barbara E. 1970. "Some Limitations of the Question Technique." NOT 36:26-28.

————. 1973a. "A Preliminary Semantic Classification of Temporal Concepts." NOT 47:3-8.

————. 1973b. "Some Further Thoughts on Relations Between Propositions." NOT 47:9-11.

Hollenbach, Bruce. 1969. "A Method for Displaying Semantic Structure."
NOT 31:22-34.

Howley, G. C. D.; Bruce, F. F.; and Ellison, H. L. 1969. *A New Testament Commentary*. London: Pickering and Inglis, Ltd.

Hughes, Philip E. 1962. *The New International Commentary on the
the Second Epistle to the Corinthians*. Grand Rapids, Mich.: Wm. B.
Eerdmans Publishing Co.

Hulst, A. R. 1963. "Bible Translating into Dutch." *Babel* 9:1-2:79-82.

Hymes, Dell H., and Bittle, William, eds. 1967. *Studies in Southwestern
Ethnolinguistics*. The Hague: Mouton and Co.

Jamieson, Carole. 1970. "The Relationals of Modern Mathematical
Logic. NOT 37:3-5.

Jones, J. Estill. 1949. "The Letter to Philemon — An Illustration of
Koinonia." *Review and Expositor* 46:454-66.

Joos, Martin. 1958. "Semology: A Linguistic Theory of Meaning."
Studies in Linguistics 13:3-4:53-70.

Jordan, Clarence L. 1966. *A Letter to the Christians in Atlanta or First
Corinthians in the Koinonia "Cotton Patch" Version*. Americus, Ga.:
Koinonia Publications.

Kalland, Earl S. 1967. "Considerations of Verbal and Idea Rendition."
Bulletin of the Evangelical Theological Society 10:2:88-92.

Keach, Benjamin. 1856. *Tropologia, A Key to Open Scripture Metaphors*.
London: William Hill Collingridge.

Kelly, J. N. D. 1963. *A Commentary on the Pastoral Epistles*. London:
Adam and Charles Black.

Kilham, Christine. 1971. "Bilingual Dictionaries." *Kivung, Journal of
the Linguistic Society of Papua and New Guinea* 4:1.

Kirk, John R., and Talbot, George D. 1966. "The Distortion of Information." In Smith, ed. pp. 308-16.

Kirkpatrick, Lilla. 1972. "Rhetorical Questions in Korku of Central
India." NOT 44:28-32.

Kittel, Gerhard, ed. 1972. *Theological Dictionary of the New Testament*.
Tr. and Ed. by Geoffrey W. Bromiley. Grand Rapids, Mich.: Wm. B.
Eerdmans Publishing Co.

Koch, Eldon W. 1963. "A Cameo of Koinonia: The Letter to Philemon."
Interpretations 17:183-87.

Lange, John Peter. n.d. *The Commentary on the Holy Scriptures; Critical, Doctrinal and Homiletical*. vol. 23. Tr. by Philip Schaff. Grand
Rapids, Mich.: Zondervan Publishing House.

Langer, Susanne K. 1942. *Philosophy in a New Key*. New York: The
New American Library of World Literature, Inc.

————. 1953. *An Introduction to Symbolic Logic*. New York: Dover
Publications.

Larson, Mildred L. 1965. "A Method for Checking Discourse Structure in Bible Translation." NOT 17:1-25.

————. 1967. "The Relationship of Frequency Counts and Function." NOT 28:14-16.

————. 1969. "Making Explicit Information Implicit in Translation." NOT 33:15-20.

Lauriault, James. 1957. "Some Problems in Translating Paragraphs Idiomatically." TBT 8:166-69.

Lenski, R. C. H. 1942. *The Interpretation of Saint John's Gospel.* Columbus, Ohio: Lutheran Book Concern.

————. 1943. *The Interpretation of St. Matthew's Gospel.* Columbus, Ohio: Wartburg Press.

————. 1946a. *Interpretation of I and II Corinthians.* Columbus, Ohio: Wartburg Press.

————. 1946b. *The Interpretation of St. Paul's Epistles to the Colossians, to the Thessalonians, to Timothy, to Titus and to Philemon.* Columbus, Ohio: Wartburg Press.

————. 1951. *The Interpretation of St. Paul's Epistle to the Romans.* Columbus, Ohio: Wartburg Press.

Levinsohn, Stephen. 1972. "Questions in Inga of Colombia and Their Use in Mark's Gospel." NOT 44:36-39.

Lightfoot, J. B. 1973. *St. Paul's Epistles to the Colossians and Philemon.* 1956. Reprint. Grand Rapids, Mich.: Zondervan Publishing House.

Lightfoot, J. B.; Trench, Richard Chenevix; and Ellicott, C. J. 1873. *The Revision of the English Version of the New Testament.* New York: Harper and Brothers, Publishers.

Lithgow, David. 1967. "Exclusiveness of Muyuw Pronouns." NOT 26:14.

————. 1971a. "Change of Subject in Muyuw." NOT 41:17-21.

————. 1971b. "What to Ask in Translation Checking." NOT 42:21-23.

————. 1973. "New Testament Usage of the Function Words GAR and EI." NOT 47:16-18.

Lloyd-Jones, D. Martyn. 1970. *Romans (Exposition of Chapters 3:20-4:25).* London: Banner of Truth Trust.

Lofthouse, W. F. 1955. " 'I' and 'We' in the Pauline Letters." Reprinted from *The Expository Times,* May 1953. TBT 6:72-80.

Longacre, Robert E. 1958. "Items in Context Their Bearing on Translation Theory." *Language* 34:482-91.

————. 1968. *Discourse, Paragraph and Sentence Structure in Selected Philippine Languages,* vols. 1, 2, and 3. U. S. Department of Health, Education, and Welfare, Office of Education, Institute of International Studies. Santa Ana, Calif.: The Summer Institute of Linguistics.

————. 1970. "Sentence Structure as a Statement Calculus." *Language.* 46:783-815.

————. 1971a. "The Relevance of Sentence Structure Analysis to Bible Translation." NOT 40:16-23.

————. 1971b. "Translation: A Cable of Many Strands." NOT 42:3-9.

————. 1972a. *Hierarchy and Universality of Discourse Constituents in New Guinea Languages: Discussion.* Washington, D. C.: Georgetown University Press.

————. 1972b. "Rhetorical Questions in Trique." NOT 44:39, 40.

————. 1972c. "Some Implications of Deep and Surface Structure Analysis for Translation." NOT 45:2-10.

Lord, John B. 1964. *The Paragraph, Structure and Style.* New York: Holt, Rinehart and Winston.

Loriot, James, and Hollenbach, Barbara. 1970. "Shipibo Paragraph Structure." *Foundations of Language* 6:43-66.

Lounsbury, Floyd G. 1956. "A Semantic Analysis of the Pawnee Kinship Usage." *Language.* 32:158-94.

Louw, Johannes P. 1973. "Discourse Analysis and the Greek New Testament." TBT 24:108-18.

Lund, Nils Wilhelm. 1942. *Chiasmus in the New Testament.* Durham, N. C.: University of North Carolina Press.

Mansen, Richard. 1971. "Understanding the World of the Supernatural." NOT 39:3-12.

Mascall, E. L. 1963. *Theology and Images.* London: A. R. Mowbray and Co. Ltd.

McIntosh, Angus. 1961. "Patterns and Ranges." *Language* 37:325-27.

Metzger, Bruce M. 1971. *A Textual Commentary on the Greek New Testament: A Companion Volume to the United Bible Societies' Greek New Testament.* 3rd ed. London and New York: United Bible Societies.

Meyer, Heinrich A. W. 1884. *Critical and Exegetical Hand-book to the Gospel of Matthew.* New York and London: Funk and Wagnalls.

Mickelson, A. Berkeley. 1963. *Interpreting the Bible.* Grand Rapids, Mich.; Wm. B. Eerdmans Publishing Co.

Milligan, George. 1953. *St. Paul's Epistles to the Thessalonians: The Greek Text with Introduction and Notes.* Grand Rapids, Mich.: Wm. B. Eerdmans Publishing Co.

Minear, Paul S. 1960. *Images of the Church in the New Testament.* Philadelphia: The Westminster Press.

Moore, Bruce R. 1964. "Second Thoughts on Measuring 'Naturalness.'" TBT 15:83-87.

————. 1972. "Doublets." NOT 43:3-34.

————. 1973. "Symbolic Action and Synecdoche." NOT 49:14, 15.

Morgan, G. Campbell. 1943. *The Parables and Metaphors of Our Lord.* London: Marshall, Morgan and Scott Ltd.

Morris, Charles. 1955. *Signs, Language, and Behavior.* New York: George Braziller, Inc.

Morris, Leon. 1969. *Studies in the Fourth Gospel.* Grand Rapids, Mich.: Wm. B. Eerdmans Publishing Co.

Moule, C. F. D. 1960. *An Idiom Book of New Testament Greek.* 2nd ed. Cambridge: Cambridge University Press.

Moulton, W. F., and Geden, A. S. 1963. *A Concordance to the Greek Testament*. Edinburgh: T. and T. Clark.

Murray, John. 1965. *The Epistle of Paul to the Romans*. vols. 1 and 2. The New International Commentary on the New Testament, F. F. Bruce, General Editor. Grand Rapids, Mich.: Wm. B. Eerdmans Publishing Co.

Nida, Eugene A. 1947. *Bible Translating*. London: United Bible Societies.

————. 1950. "Translation or Paraphrase." TBT 1:97-106.

————. 1952. "A New Methodology in Biblical Exegesis." TBT 3:97-111.

————. 1955. "Problems in Translating the Scriptures into Shilluk, Anuak and Nuer." TBT 6:55-63

————. 1959. "Principles of Translation as Exemplified by Bible Translating." TBT 10:148-64.

————. 1960a. *Message and Mission*. New York: Harper and Brothers.

————. 1960b. "The Bible Translator's Use of Receptor-Language Texts." TBT 11:82-86

————. 1961. "New Help for Translators." TBT 12:49-55.

————. 1964. *Toward a Science of Translating*. Leiden, Netherlands: E. J. Brill.

Nida, Eugene A., and Taber, Charles R. 1969. *The Theory and Practice of Translation*. Leiden, Netherlands: E. J. Brill for the United Bible Societies.

Nolan, Rita. 1970. *Foundations for an Adequate Criterion of Paraphrase*. The Hague: Mouton and Co.

Oettinger, Anthony G. 1959. "Automatic (Transference, Translation, Remittance, Shunting)." In Brower, ed. pp. 240-67.

Ogden, C. K., and Richards, I. A. 1952. *The Meaning of Meaning: A Study of the Influence of Language upon Thought and of the Science of Symbolism*. 10th ed. New York: Harcourt, Brace.

Olson, Donald, 1972. "Those Pesky Loan Words." NOT 46:28-31.

Pallesen, Kemp. 1970. "More on Elicitation." NOT 36:20-26.

Pike, Eunice V. 1966. "Nonfocus of Person and Focus of Role." NOT 20:17, 18.

————. 1967. "Skewing of the Lexical and Grammatical Hierarchy as it Affects Translation." NOT 23:1-3.

Pike, Kenneth L. 1966. "Tagmemic and Matrix Linguistics Applied to Selected African Languages." Final Report Contract No. OE-5-14-065 U. S. Department of Health, Education, and Welfare, Office of Education, Bureau of Research. Ann Arbor, Mich.: University of Michigan.

————. 1967. *Language in Relation to a Unified Theory of the Structure of Human Behavior*. The Hague: Mouton and Co.

Plummer, Alfred. 1956. *A Critical and Exegetical Commentary on the Second Epistle of St. Paul to the Corinthians*. Edinburgh: T. and T. Clark.

Preus, Robert. 1957. *The Inspiration of Scripture.* Edinburgh and London: Oliver and Boyd.

Rabin, C. 1958. "The Linguistics of Translation." In Smith, preface. pp. 123-45.

Ramm, Bernard. 1956. *Protestant Biblical Interpretation.* Boston, Mass.: W. A. Wilde Co.

————. 1958. "The Evidence of Prophecy and Miracle." In Henry, ed. pp. 253-63.

————. 1961. *Special Revelation and the Word of God.* Grand Rapids, Mich.: Wm. B. Eerdmans Publishing Co.

Rich, Rolland and Furne. 1970. "Believe." NOT 36:31.

Richert, Ernest. 1965. "Multiple Meanings and Concordance." NOT 16:3.

Ridderbos, Herman N. 1953. *The Epistle of Paul to the Church of Galatia.* Grand Rapids, Mich.: Wm. B. Eerdmans Publishing Co.

Robertson, A. T. 1934. *A Grammar of the Greek New Testament in the Light of Historical Research.* Nashville, Tenn.: Broadman Press.

Robertson, A. T., and Davis, W. Hersey. 1933. *A New Short Grammar of the Greek Testament.* New York and London: Harper and Brothers Publishers.

Robinson, Dow F. 1963. "Native Texts and Frequency Counts as Aids to the Translator." TBT 14:63-71.

Rubinstein, S. Leonard, and Weaver, Robert G. 1966. *Frameworks of Exposition.* New York: Holt, Rinehart and Winston.

Ruegsegger, Manis. 1966. "Reduplication and Redundancy." NOT 22:1-4.

Russell, Robert L. 1968. "Discourse Analysis and Bible Translation — A Few Suggestions." NOT 31:40-43.

Sanday, William, and Headlam, Arthur C. 1955. *A Critical and Exegetical Commentary on the Epistle to the Romans.* 1902. 5th ed. Reprint. Edinburgh: T. and T. Clark.

Sapir, Edward. 1944. "Grading, a Study in Semantics." *Philosophy of Science* 11:93-116.

Sayce, Archibald Henry. 1880. *Introduction to the Science of Language.* London: C. Kegan Paul and Co.

Schramm, Wilbur. 1966. "Information Theory and Mass Communication." In Smith, ed. pp. 520-34.

Schwarz, W. 1955. *Principles and Problems of Biblical Translation.* London: Cambridge University Press.

Sheffler, Margaret. 1969. "Results of Network Diagramming: as Applied to the Revision of Munduruкú Mark." NOT 32:2-32.

————. 1970. Prepublication draft, "Munduruкú Discourse."

Slocum, Marianna C. 1971. "A Positive Use for the Negative." NOT 42:17-19.

Smith, A. H., preface. 1958. *Aspects of Translation: Studies in Communication 2.* London: Secker and Warburg, Ltd.

Smith, Alfred G., ed. 1966. *Communication and Culture.* New York: Holt, Rinehart, and Winston.

Spratt, David and Nancy. 1973. "Limited Use of Metonymy." NOT 47:22.

Stauffer, Ethelbert. 1964. Article 'EGO' in *Theological Dictionary of the New Testament,* vol. 2. Edited by Gerhard Kittel. Grand Rapids, Mich.: Wm. B. Eerdmans Publishing Co.

Stern, Gustaf. 1931. *Meaning and Change of Meaning.* Göteborg: Elanders Boktryckeri, Aktiebolog.

Stott, J. R. W. 1964. *The Epistles of John.* Grand Rapids, Mich.: Wm. B. Eerdmans Publishing Co.

Sturtevant, E. H. 1917. *Linguistic Change, An Introduction to the Historical Study of Language.* Chicago: The University of Chicago Press.

Swete, Henry Barclay. 1968. *An Introduction to The Old Testament in Greek.* Rev. by Richard Rusden Ottley. New York: KTAV Publishing House, Inc.

Taber, Charles R. 1966. "The Structure of Sango Narrative." *Hartford Studies in Linguistics* No. 17, Parts I and II. Hartford, Conn.: The Hartford Seminary Foundation.

————. 1970. "Explicit and Implicit Information in Translation." TBT 21:1-9.

Tancock, L. W. 1958. "Some Problems of Style in Translation from French." In Smith, preface. pp. 29-51.

Taylor, John M. 1965. "Notes on the Greek Genitive." In Beekman, ed. pp. 194-200.

Terry, Milton S. 1964. *Biblical Hermeneutics.* 1890. Reprint. Grand Rapids, Mich.: Zondervan Publishing House.

Thomas, David. 1972. "Comments on Sentences, Propositions, and Notes on Translation 37." NOT 45:11-14.

Toussaint, Stanley D. 1966. "A Proper Approach to Exegesis." NOT 20:1-6.

————. 1967. "A Methodology of Overview." NOT 26:3-6.

Toy, Crawford Howell. 1884. *Quotations in the New Testament.* New York: Charles Scribner's Sons.

Trail, Ronald L. 1973. "Patterns in Clause, Sentence, and Discourse in Selected Languages of India and Nepal. Part I, Sentence and Discourse." Final Report Contract No. OEC-0-9-97721-2778 (014) Institute of International Studies, U. S. Department of Health, Education, and Welfare. Norman, Okla.: Summer Institute of Linguistics of the University of Oklahoma.

Turner, Nigel. 1963. *Syntax.* A Grammar of New Testament Greek, vol. 3. Series by James Hope Moulton. Edinburgh; T. and T. Clark.

Ullman, Stephen. 1962. *Semantics, An Introduction to the Science of Meaning.* Oxford: Basil Blackwell.

————. 1963. "Semantic Universals." In *Universals of Language*. Edited by Joseph H. Greenberg. Cambridge: Massachusetts Institute of Technology Press.

Urban, Wilbur. 1939. *Language and Reality: The Philosophy of Language and the Principles of Symbolism*. New York: Macmillan.

Vincent, Marvin R. 1946. *The Epistles of Paul*. Word Studies in the New Testament, vol. 3. Reprint of 1890. Chicago: Moody Press.

————. 1955. *The International Critical Commentary, A Critical and Exegetical Commentary on the Epistles to the Philippians and to Philemon*. Reprint of 1897. Edinburgh: T. and T. Clark.

Wallis, Ethel E. 1971a. "Contrastive Plot Structures of the Four Gospels." NOT 40:3-16.

————. 1971b. "Discourse Focus in Mezquital Otomi." NOT 42:19-21.

————. 1973. "The Rhetorical Organization of Luke's Discourse." NOT 48:5-10.

Walpole, Hugh R. 1941. *Semantics — The Nature of Words and Their Meanings*. New York: W. W. Norton and Co.

Walvoord, John F., ed. 1957. *Inspiration and Interpretation*. Grand Rapids, Mich.: Wm. B. Eerdmans Publishing Co.

Warfield, Benjamin B. 1927. *The Inspiration and Authority of the Bible*. 1948 republication. Edited by Samuel G. Craig. Philadelphia: The Presbyterian and Reformed Publishing Co.

Winterowd, W. Ross. 1970. "The Grammar of Coherence." *College English*. 31:828-35.

Wise, Mary Ruth. 1968. "Identification of Participants in Discourse: A Study of Aspects of Form and Meaning in Nomatsiguenga." Ph.D. dissertation, The University of Michigan.

Wonderly, William L. 1961. "Some Factors of Meaningfulness in Reading Matter for Inexperienced Readers." In *A William Cameron Townsend en el XXV Aniversario del Instituto Lingüístico de Verano*. Prologue by Manuel Gamio and Raul Noriega. Cuernavaco, Mexico: Tipografica Indigena.

————. 1968. *Bible Translations for Popular Use*. London: United Bible Societies.

GENERAL INDEX

BIBLICAL INDEX

6:23	123
6:38	154n, 214n, 215, 215n
6:41, 42	109
6:43, 44	135
6:44	206
7:6	100
7:19	232
7:31	243
7:35	221
7:39	304
7:42, 43	50
7:44	244
7:49	235
8:5	309
8:9	231n
8:16	186
8:18	214
8:25	235
8:29	36
8:30	231n
8:35-38	63
8:45	232
8:47	312
9:5	123
9:13	52
9:18	231n
9:25	239
9:45	230n
9:62	203
10:3	204
10:13	122
10:22	114
10:25	232
10:28	232
10:32	200
10:34	27
11:3	99
11:8	269
11:9	214
11:10	214
11:12	236, 239
11:42	260
11:51	181
12:1	127, 130
12:3	207
12:10	214
12:13	58
12:17	240
12:17, 18	235
12:20	215, 215n
12:24	203
12:31	214
12:48	215, 215n
12:49	126
12:50	140n
12:51	241
12:54, 55	57
13:1	261
13:2	242
13:4	242
13:7, 8	233
13:9	52
13:11	263
13:19	252
13:21	256
13:29	120
13:32	128, 138, 149
14:11	215
14:14	215
14:26	119
15:8-10	61
15:16	187
15:18	103
15:24	119
15:26	231n
15:32	119
16:3	235, 241
16:7	256
16:9	215, 215n
16:11	239
16:15	361
16:31	105
17:2	205
17:20	231n
17:26	262
17:29	309
18:2	293
18:6	253
18:7, 8	357
18:11	253
18:13	122
18:14	215
18:18	231n
18:36	231n
18:40	231n
19:9	26, 221
19:31	230n, 232
19:46	181n
20:1	253
20:3	230n
20:4	98
20:5	232
20:9	54
20:15, 16	237
20:21	231n
20:24	180
20:27	231n
20:40	231n
20:41	115
21:7	231n
21:15	213
21:22	260
22:7	48
22:10	310
22:11	232
22:23	235
22:35	299, 355
22:64	231n
22:68	230n
23:3	230n
23:6	231n
23:9	231n
23:31	135, 139
23:39-43	112
24:26	115
24:46	115
24:49	256

JOHN	158n
1:15	53
1:17	221
1:19	117, 230n
1:21	230n
1:25	230n
1:29	166
2:13	196
2:16, 17	181n
2:19-21	144
3	225
3:3	305
3:9	232
3:16	98, 160
3:16-18	114n
3:19	296
3:28	200
4:1-3	28
4:10	115
4:27	232
4:29	355, 356
4:33	235, 354, 356
4:37	202
4:52	231n
5:8-12	63
5:12	230n, 232
5:19-23	114
5:24	110
5:25	114
5:29	264
5:42	260
6:5, 6	231, 238
6:27-30	113n
6:33	187
6:35	187
6:37	183
6:38	226
6:40	114
6:50	311
6:53-56	113n
6:58	115
6:67	236, 355
7:11	232
7:13	259
7:19	248

7:21	50	17:25	312	5:4	355
7:23	50	18:7	231n	5:27, 28	230n
7:26	356	18:11	357	5:27-29	234
7:35, 36	235	18:16-27	232	5:37	262
7:48	116	18:17	355	6:1	258
7:51	233, 356	18:19	230n, 231n	6:5	261
7:52	233	18:21	230n, 231n, 242	6:7	278, 279, 299
8:2	117	18:25	355	6:8-9:31	278, 279
8:7	230n	18:26	236, 355	7:9	30
8:12	43	18:28	216	7:24	119
8:17	56	18:35	353	7:28	356
8:19	304	19:5	310	7:40	166
8:35, 36	114	19:11	120	7:44	195, 197
8:42	304	19:25	254	7:47	181n
8:48	299, 355	19:26	115	7:48	100
8:52	30	19:27	115	7:60	120n
8:56	98	19:29	186, 197	8:1	296
9:2	230n	19:39	225	8:1, 2	224
9:8	354	20:2	115	8:9	255
9:15	230n	20:3-10	115	8:20	161
9:19	230n	21:5	355	8:28	195, 252
9:21	230n	21:7	115	8:32	128
9:23	231n	21:8	256	9:2	305
9:35	114	21:12	232	9:5	130
9:37	115	21:17	126, 232	9:15	126
9:39	303	21:20	116, 232	9:31	278, 299
9:40	299, 355	21:20-24	115	9:32-28:31	278, 279
9:41	355	21:24	116	9:36	261
10:8	117			10:11	186
10:12	195	**ACTS**	39, 278	10:18	231n
10:36	115	1:1-6, 7	278, 279	10:29	231n
11:4	114	1:6	231n	10:44	348
11:9	353	1:8	167, 278	11:30	361
11:11	120n	1:12	57	12:3	196
11:13	259	1:13	46	12:6, 7	36
11:35	28	1:18	265	12:23	269
11:44, 45	54	1:22	258, 264	13:1	255n
11:56	235, 357n	1:25	105, 213	13:11	99
12:3	256	1:26	196	13:17	189
12:19	118, 235	2:4	154	13:29	195
12:21	231n	2:9-11	116	13:35, 36	52
12:24	138	2:11	154	13:36	120n
12:46	149	2:15	47	13:39	261
13:5	160	2:16	56	13:44	256
13:12	243	2:20	121, 147	13:51	123
13:23	115, 161	2:27	116	14:14	123
13:24, 25	115n	2:38	259, 264	14:17	213
14:13	115	2:39	120	14:19, 20	54
15:1	133	2:41	100	14:23	31
15:2-8	135	2:42	259	14:27	135, 189, 251
15:4	51	3:6	101	15	98
15:24, 25	51	3:10	31	15:1	197
16:5	231n, 232	3:16	101	15:10	148, 189
16:18, 19	235	4:7	230, 231n	15:21	98
16:19	231n	4:10	101	15:25, 27	301
17:1	115	4:12	220	16:3	31
17:3	115	4:29	116	16:24	197
17:12	259, 309	4:31	48	16:27	59